Catch
and

A Paperback Original
First published 1989 by
Poolbeg Press Ltd.
Knocksedan House,
Swords, Co. Dublin, Ireland.

ISBN 1 85371 063 6

Cover design by Steven Hope
Cover Photographs by Ray McManus
Typeset by Print-Forme,
62 Santry Close, Dublin 9.
Printed by The Guernsey Press Ltd.,
Vale, Guernsey, Channel Islands.

Catch and Kick

Eoghan Corry

POOLBEG

Acknowledgements

Many thanks to Ray McManus, Jim Connolly,
Colman Doyle and the *Irish Press* for photographs.
to Penny and the staff of Maynooth College library
to the staff of the National Library
to all who gave interviews and answered queries
to Anne for coffee
to Jo O'Donoghue who put me on the right track
to Ida

And the Answers
(to the questions on the back cover)
1. 1911
2. Michael Hamilton in 1937
3. Monaghan in 1920
4. John Joe Sheehy
5. Five Moving Quarrymen in 1900 played for both Kilkenny
   and Tipperary

Dedicated to the next Kildare team to win an All-Ireland

Foreword

THROW-IN

The story of the story of Gaelic football, like the game itself, has survived despite a few major mishaps. In October 1985 I had most of the research completed for a history of the GAA championship. All of my notes had been carefully gathered together for a meeting, and placed securely in a briefcase in the boot of my blue Datsun Sunny, while I was at work. When I returned to the car the boot had been forced. In horror, I looked at the place where my briefcase used to be. Four years of research, results, scores, annotations, interview notes with players (some of which were dead even by then) were lost.

A small group of people helped me get over this. Among them was the staff of Maynooth College Library. Long mornings in the Russell Library with Penny helped me get over the grief as I tackled my task anew.

Maybe the theft was a good thing. *Catch and Kick*, mark 2, differs from its more statistical predecessor. I wanted to assemble the details of who scored what and when in all the major games over the past 105 years. I wanted to offer some commentary on what was happening politically within the GAA and why. I wanted to capture the humorous and the bizarre, and to depict the spirit in which the game is played. To record some of the jokes that were shared after the 2,000 or so matches I recall.

Above all, it was great to learn that so many of these matches are still being replayed. The goals that shouldn't have been allowed are still being disputed. The blind referees, the curses, the illegal players, the crowd invasions, are all being argued over into the second century of catching and kicking, handpassing and fielding and scoring and cheering. Long may it remain so.

Contents

Chapter One

Fathers of Invention

PORK FUTURES

They dragged the first pig in screaming and snorting from the forest about 11,000 years ago, and marvelled at the wonder of an animal which would clear the debris around the settlements and which was so bountiful that any part of it could be eaten. When they had finished picking the last spare rib, they examined the bladder. The bladder, filled with air or straw, could be turned into a plaything, for youngsters to kick and roll from one place to the other.

Ireland has never attempted to join the half dozen or so parts of the world which each claim to have invented football. Football seems to have been a natural development in several parts of the world simultaneously when man first came across the pig's bladder. Almost all of the ancient civilisations had a football-type game. In China, where the hog became the common domestic animal, "Tsu-chin" was played in the third and fourth centuries BC. It disallowed the use of arms and served to keep the players' feet warm, a practical consideration in North China where the game was played. The ancient Greeks played "Episkyros" and the Romans "Harpastrum." A football game called "Kamari" was played in the sixth century AD in Japan.

In days when Celtic purity was in vogue, it was noticed that each of the Celtic countries has a distinctive but related football game. "La Soule" was played in Brittany, "Knappan" in Wales, while a Cornish rough-and-tumble football game was known as "hurling."

In ancient Ireland football was referred to as "Iomáin" as

against "Iomáin le camán," or our hurling. For this reason it is often difficult to distinguish between the two, but it has been contended that some type of football was played in Ireland from ancient times.

Football is first mentioned in Ireland by the Statutes of Galway (1527) which allowed football to be played, while banning hurling and handball on pain of a fine of 8d:

> At no tyme to use ne occupye ye hurlinge of ye litill balle with the hookie stickies or staves, nor use no hand balle to play without the walls, but only the great foote balle.

When Scotsman Hugh Montgomery set up a school in Newcastle, Co Down, in 1620 he allowed the scholars "a green for recreation at golf, football, and archery."

Eccentric London bookseller, traveller and political satirist, John Dunton (1659-1733), came in search of the real Ireland in 1698-9. In his *Conversation in Ireland* Dunton left an important description of hurling but referred to football only very briefly when he said:

> They do not play often at football, only in a small territory called Fingal near Dublin where the people use it much, and trip and shoulder very handsomely.

Eighty years later another traveller, Coquebert de Montbret from France, found football only in Leinster.

In contrast to hurling, references to football in Irish prose or verse are sparse. Six poems refer to football matches.

Seamus Dall MacCuarta's *Imirt na Boinne* describes a match at Fennor, on Slane Castle estate on the banks of the Boyne in 1712, on a confined field with predetermined goals.

Matt Concannon describes a six-a-side game between Lusk and Swords at Oxmantown Green in Fingal in 1720, with a piper to lead the teams on to the field, marked-out goals, catching, kicking, carrying, wrestling, tripping, and even a half-time, for which the prize was "six Holland caps" and "Besides, our Squire, the Conquerors' hearts to cheer/ Will treat them with with a cask of humming beer."

Redmond Murphy describes a match in Omeath in 1740,

which was either eight or sixteen a side, in which one of the players was seriously injured and died afterwards.

Fragments of a poem describe a game between Louth and Fermanagh at Inniskeen, Co Monaghan, in 1806, with 12 players a side, plus the captains, and bouts of wrestling to match.

Another song about a mid-19th-century match in Annagassan, near Drogheda, Co Louth, was published in 1915. Edward Lysaght described a match at College Green in Dublin in 1780.

Dudley Bradstreet leaves an account of a match in Aughamore in 1737 between Longford and Westmeath where he himself played the role of a Eugene McGee for the Longford team:

> I divided my troops into small parties, placing the strongest bodied men to resist the first shock, the nimble near at hand, and the *corps de résistance* to attend to myself. The enemy seeing the day lost at football attempted to retrieve their honour by strokes, which were altogether as fruitless for our discipline availed us as much at them as it had done at the ball.

Newspaper notices and reports survive from the 18th century. Money and drink were the main excuses for chasing the bladder. Kildare played Meath for "a piece of plate" in the 18th century and Meath played Louth for "a piece of plate and fifty sovereigns."

In Dangan, Co Meath, in 1731 and in Birr in 1746 the local bachelors played the married men. When the Liffey froze over in 1741 the citizens of Dublin played a football match on the ice.

In 1754 a party of soldiers and constables was called to break up a football match in Baggot Street. The sheriff surprised a group of footballers on Oxmantown Green later in 1754.

The bakers played the brewers of Dublin in a football match on Royal Hospital lands in Kilmainham in April 1765 and another match took place in Milltown the same month.

Discipline at these matches was marginal at the best of

times. Contemporary newspapers objected to the "profanity" of players who disregarded the Establishment's strongly held views on how the Sabbath should be observed. Their indignant pronouncements were usually accompanied (in what must be admitted was an extremely hostile press) by reports of how the matches degenerated into drunken faction-fights. A riot resulted from a match near Finglas bridge in 1759. A "desperate quarrel" ensued from a match at Three Rock mountain above Rathfarnham in 1779. Soldiers quelled a riotous mob made up of men who assembled weekly to play football in Drumcondra in 1774, and eventually in 1792 in Timolin, Co Kildare:

> A match at football between the villages in this neighbourhood has been attended with effects particularly distressing. The lads met on the green at Ballitore, from whence, when the sport was over, they, with many of the spectators, adjourned to this place in perfect good humour; but the demon of discord, whiskey, soon introduced a battle, in which all were engaged and almost all suffered.

Wogan Browne of Clongowes Wood was a magistrate for three counties when, in 1797, in the words of his friend Lord Cloncurry:

> He was some Friday riding past a field where the country people were about to hold a football match. The whole assembly of course recognised and paid their respect. He got off his horse and opened the sports by giving the ball the first kick—a sort of friendly sanction of the amusements of their neighbours which was then not unusual among the gentry in Ireland. The custom, however, was not approved of by the Government and the Lord Chancellor Clare, on being informed of what Wogan Browne had done, at once superseded him from the Commission of the Peace.

With the collapse of the economy after the Acts of Union and an end to 18th-century prosperity, there was a decline in the reports of football activity during the 19th century. Kildare and Meath teams met at Maynooth in 1845 and the game was banned for clerical students in Maynooth College in 1836.

FINDING A PEDIGREE

While hurling had a fine historical tradition, with frequent references in legends, poetry and ancient laws, trying to prove that football was equally ancient and equally Irish was more difficult.

Football historians like Morris Marples were able to claim, from the absence of football outside the settlement towns of Galway and the Pale area, that football was introduced to Ireland from abroad.

Folklore Commission researchers found that football existed in many parts of the country in a diluted version of faction-fighting. Most of the football lore was found in Antrim, Donegal, and Kerry.

Caid was the Irish for the ball used in ancient Kerry, from a pig's bladder or bull's scrotum. The versions of the game written about with nostalgia in the 1940s were highly noble, civilised affairs. P D Mehigan wrote in his *History of Gaelic Football:*

> Old and young took part in this fine communal game which, we are assured, was played very fair and with good humour. This is in marked contrast with England, which was so rough and combative that it called down successive prohibitive decrees making football a criminal practice because of the associated assaults and disturbances, often amounting to riotous behaviour, with grievous threat to life and limb. Christmas time in particular and Winter generally, when the crops were cleared off the land, was the football season. Feats of individual players have been brought down from father to son and told at firesides today: tradition dies hard.

> Father Ferris, who was an authority on *caid*, revived the fine old form of the game very successfully in the Christmas period of 1926 and 1927, when tournaments on the Cork-Kerry border roused local enthusiasm. Carrying the ball and wrestling, in the form of tackling and holding,

were permitted. Fleet runners, specially placed on the outskirts of the crush, often gained considerable ground, or took the ball home for victory. The full manhood strength of each parish was marshalled for the fray, which often lasted the run of a Winter's day from Mass-time to dusk.

Mehigan relied for his information on a history of *caid* written by Father Liam Ferris of Glenflesk, Killarney and later Ballylongford. Father Ferris got firsthand information from an 80-year-old Irish speaker in Ballyferriter, who played both field *caid* and cross-country *caid* in the days of his youth. Father Ferris claimed as late as 1969 that *caid* was a carrying game, played with a not very spherical ball, closer to modern rugby than to the Gaelic code that developed with an emphasis on propelling the ball. In truth, propelling the ball must have been impossible in the heyday of *caid*. It would be hard to imagine anyone propelling with any strength or accuracy a pig's bladder dressed in leather and filled with hay.

Whereas there was plenty of evidence that hurling was played in Kerry, there seemed to have been no more football played than in the less "traditional" regions.

Kerry emigrants to New York in the 1890s seemed to prefer to play hurling, to point out that Kerry was occupied hurling territory, not the original Irish football county.

Pat Begley of Killorglin described pre-GAA football in less eulogistic terms:

> At that time there was no game in the country but rough and tumble. That was the biggest curse that ever came on the country. Two parishes organised a match, the day and the place appointed, usually on some boggy commonage as there were no shoes worn but every man got out in a white shirt and flannel underpants. The ball was set in motion and before ten minutes every two in the pitch were at each other's necks with friends on both sides giving and taking heavy blows. This was renewed on market day and repeated the fair day.

The pneumatic bladder was invented in the 1860s and suddenly players found they had a lighter ball to chase. The wealthy public school boys of England were the first to benefit, and both soccer, where the ball was propelled, and rugby, where the ball was carried, had codes of rules developed in the upper-class schools. The balls were soon widely available, and by the time the GAA was founded in 1884, several clubs in rural Ireland were already playing by rules drawn up by the highly popular but unionist Rugby Football Union. This included Kerry, home of *caid*; there is much evidence that most of the football played here was of a dreaded foreign variety, played with an oval ball, introduced through the influence of immigrants working on Valentia Island telegraphy station, opened in 1768.

According to Pat Begley, later GAA champion captain J P O'Sullivan started a rugby club in Killorglin after one rough-and-tumble match "between Ballymac and Ballyvourney."

He was not alone. Kerry had its share of rugby clubs in the 1870s. In Dingle (Seán Ó Dubhda recalls a match played there in 1884 as being "between rugby and Gaelic," and remembers that young people called the form of rugby they played in the 1870s "the scrummage"), in Killarney, Valentia, Ballyhar, Firies and Killorglin where, according to Pat Begley's reminiscences, J P O'Sullivan captained the rugby team and "rugby was installed, with soccer on the way coming."

Five matches played in Killarney in April and May 1874 and again in March 1875 were recorded by the *Cork Examiner*. They were almost certainly of the rugby type, within a confined area. But the scorelines suggest some local improvisation. On April 26th 1874 a match was reported: "The townspeople scored eight cooles, the Poulnamuck men scored seven." Another result was recorded as "ten cooles against seven."

PEASANT GAMES

While the rugby and soccer codes emanated from the public schools of England, the GAA was later to claim that their sport descended directly from the popular game of the people. The first rules give little clue as to whether the sport involved carrying or propelling the ball. It is highly likely that Gaelic players preferred to carry the ball in the first decade of the game's development, as they would have in pig's bladder days, and then settled on a catch-and-kick propulsion game in 1895.

If the reaction to rugby is anything to go by, rural people reacted favourably to the carrying game that the upper classes had pioneered. In 1854 a football club was founded in Trinity College. Among its earliest officials was an old Rugbeian Robert Henry Scott. Clubs followed in North of Ireland (1868), Wanderers (1869), Lansdowne Irish Champion and Athletic Club (1872), Dungannon (1873), Carlow (1873) University College Cork (1874), and Ballinasloe (1875). Clongowes Wood College had its own type of football, the Jesuit Rules, until 1890. On December 12th 1874 the Irish (Rugby) Football Union was founded in Dublin. Even though the peasantry was not involved in these early class-conscious clubs, many of the middle classes were. There are claims from the time that rugby was "suitable for Irishmen."

Irishmen agreed. The game of rugby and the older game of cricket, which was organised in Leinster and the south of Ireland from 1830 on, had attracted the interest of many rural Irish sportsmen. Early clubs included Kilruane Cricket and Football Club (1876), the Carrick-on-Suir Athletic, Cricket and Football Club (1879), and Killean Cricket and Football Club (1879). An abundance of clubs could be found along the west, all calling themselves "Cricket and Football Clubs." Future GAA president Maurice Davin was an officer of Carrick-on-Suir Cricket and Football Club. Another founder, Belfastman John McKay, had played both soccer and rugby. "Cricket had all but supplanted hurley, handball was succeeded by lawn tennis, football was being played à la rugby or Oxford," the *Irish World* complained in 1885.

In contrast, soccer was slower to arrive and failed to catch the imagination to the same extent. In 1878 Scotsman John McAlery organised a demonstration of soccer between Queen's Park and the Caledonians at the Ulster Cricket Club. Cliftonville was the first club in 1879, the Irish Football Association was founded in November 1880, and a club,

Dublin Association, was formed in Dublin in 1883. There were 31 soccer clubs in Ireland in 1885 and one, Wicklow Town, switched to Gaelic football when the GAA was founded.

As late as 1907, the *Irish Packet* claimed: "It was the narrow-minded views of Orange Rugby Ireland which forced Ireland to invent her grand national football game."

Sunday play was undoubtedly an issue. When the religion of the aristocracy did not permit play on Sundays, the labourers who worked six days a week cannot have been impressed. All matches were held on Saturdays, even though a Munster club, Kincora FC, sought a ruling from the Irish Rugby Football Union in 1887 on the playing of matches on Sundays, and were told that there was nothing in the laws of the Union which prohibited Sunday play.

Among the rugby players of the Lansdowne Irish Champion and Athletic Club was one Michael Cusack. In 1880 Cusack's academy had a rugby 15. In 1882 he stopped playing rugby and hurling, the precursor to hockey. The following year he had founded a club "to revive the grand national game of hurling," and had also founded an athletics club which rejected Amateur Athletics Association rules. There was, as yet, no mention of football.

But Cusack wrote in *United Ireland* on October 13th 1884:

> Irish football is a great game and worth going a long way to see, when played on a fairly laid out ground under proper rules. Many old people say that hurling exceeded it as a trial for men. I would not like to see either game now as the rules stand at present. I may say there are no rules, and therefore these games are often dangerous. I am anxious to see both games revived under proper rules.

Legend has it that Michael Cusack wished to model the new Gaelic football more on the traditional rush-and-tumble precursor of football codes everywhere, not the much-vaunted *caid*. Father Ferris firmly believed that:

> Cusack introduced the kicking game we call Gaelic football. It merely modified the soccer rules of 1867

slightly by allowing the use of the hands. Cusack, by the stroke of a pen, killed the thousand-year-old game of *caid*.

HOWLING GAELS

Football was to be used in the intellectual warfare between two cultures. Froude was arguing in his *History of the English in Ireland* (1872) that the Gaels were totally incapable of establishing any social organisation because of their inherent passion and instability; and "like the Asiatics" they needed the strongly ordered English to govern them, by force if necessary (and according to Froude it was almost always necessary).

Irish historians rushed to pick up cudgels on opposite sides of the argument, challenging the purity and superiority of the Anglo-Saxon race, with its many Nordic, Celtic, Roman, and Germanic influences. An impure race could not aspire to classical civilisation in the way the Irish could, they argued. Cusack could be found in the coffee-houses of Dublin arguing along these lines.

Irish ethnocentrists argued that not only was Ireland not inferior to the "strongly ordered English," but it was in fact purer than and superior to England. Historians like John Mitchel presented Irish history as a pure and uninterrupted struggle for independence by the harassed Irish against the unethical and scheming English.

This sort of argument was new, vibrant and a source of great excitement in the new nationalist intellectual circles in the mid-19th century. In 1892 Douglas Hyde's lecture, "The necessity of de-Anglicising Ireland," captured the nationalist mood of the time, when "being Irish" meant learning the language, reading the Fenian and Táin Bó Cuailgne legends, and playing the "ancient" Irish games of football and hurling. Ironically, the GAA was to expel Hyde 40 years later for making an unbearable concession to the Gall by attending a soccer match in his capacity as president of Ireland.

That sport should eventually get embroiled in all of this was not surprising. Sport was remarkably chauvinistic until well into the 20th century.

At the time the GAA was founded, sport had helped Germany emerge from disunity to world power. Its vigorous sports educational programme, the Turnbewegung was renowned.

Sweden had revived its morale after the disasters of the Napoleonic Wars with its remarkable *gymnastika*. These suppressed competition between individuals and emphasised the duty to support those who are less naturally gifted.

Elsewhere, a consciously Jewish gymnastics movement was emerging. On the other side of the Atlantic, Walter Camp was changing American college football from the English public school rules to a distinctive American game. The football reported in a Melbourne newspaper as being played by Irish miners on the gold-fields of Ballarat and Bendigo in 1850, "a combination of many things, including football, wrestling and rough house," was converted into a distinctive Australian code by Tom Wills and Henry Harrison in 1856. By 1866 the definitive rules were in force, and the oval ball replaced the round ball in 1867. Originally the first team to score two goals would win; this was changed to fixed-length matches in 1869. Umpires and oval pitches were introduced in 1872, the Victorian Football Association was founded in 1877 and point-posts followed in 1897.

Newly independent Greece had held "restored" Olympic games in 1859, 1870, 1875 and 1888. These were political celebrations, all designed to lend legitimacy to the notion of a central Greek nation. In between these festivals, an aroused Greece won back Thessaly, Epiros, Macedonia, and much of the Aegean Islands from Turkey, with Crete to follow in the flush of victory after the real Olympic revival in 1896.

Trim-born Arthur Wellesley, the Duke of Wellington, had made physical education famous with the claim that: "The Battle of Waterloo was won on the playing fields of Eton." Cricket, tennis, croquet, rugby football, were largely confined to Britain and its empire, as was association football until the second decade of this century. British sporting superiority was expressed in racial and even religious terms by British statesmen and journalists.

So when the GAA was born in the middle of a passionate

confrontation between Irish nationalists and unionists, it was natural that a body of Irish sports thinkers would want to opt out of the British sporting "empire."

The GAA was later to become part of a movement to get Mitchel's and Hyde's ethnocentricity established as the dominant form of Irish historiography in the 20th century. The GAA, with its own school of writers such as P J Devlin and Paddy Mehigan, was spurring them on. Devlin wrote of the GAA's foundation:

> It was a national effort to recall a national inheritance; to emancipate a people from an alien, social thraldom; to save them from brooding, melancholy and physical degeneration; to discipline them in the practice of their traditional amusements, in the atmosphere of active nationalism and for the ultimate achievement of national independence.

That was written 60 years later, when the Irish ethnocentrists had won the day. P W Joyce wrote the schoolbooks, and De Valera formulated a vision of Ireland that was rural and uncluttered by material evils from the outside world. Until the 1960s GAA rule-books were introduced with a passage stating:

> The GAA was founded to check a grave racial menace in the deterioration of the pastimes of the people through want of organised control, and to combat the influence of other games and customs which threatened to destroy the surviving cultural inheritances of the Gael.

That view was illegal and subversive in the 1880s, but may not be far off the mark in explaining why the GAA apparently "invented" a football code of their own. On becoming a patron of the GAA, Archbishop Thomas W Croke wrote:

> One of the most painful and frequently recurring reflections that, as an Irishman, I am compelled to make in connection with the present aspect of things in this country is derived from the ugly and irritating fact that we are daily importing from England, not only her manufactured goods, but her fashions, her accents, her vicious literature, her

music, her dances and her manifold mannerisms, her games also, and her pastimes, to the utter discredit of our own grand national sports and the sore humiliation, as I believe, of every genuine son and daughter of the old land.

Not surprisingly, the newspapers of the time refused to publish the letter.

One final event inspired the seven men who gathered to found the GAA at Thurles to show Britain that Ireland, too, could compete at manly games, "racy of the soil" (a phrase Archbishop Croke used in that letter of acceptance on becoming patron of the GAA), and of benefit to the young Gaels of Ireland. The GAA men saw the success of the Caledonian Games at the Royal Dublin Society early in 1884. Here was a display of Scottish muscle to impress the world. The Scots were Gaels too, were they not?

The dust had been cleared off the centuries of Irish manuscripts by scholars John O'Donovan and Eoghan Ó Comhraidhe earlier that century. The two had popularised the chronologies of ancient Ireland, and athletics was part of that chronology.

The Tailteann Games had previously been dated to the death of Queen Tailte in 2500 BC, when boxers, athletes, charioteers, hammer-throwers, swimmers and spear-throwers had gathered to compete. More scientific methods than Micheál Ó Cléirigh's transcripts had been used to trace the origin of the games to 1829 BC, making it still the oldest sports festival on record.

Similar sports festivals had been held on the Curragh of Kildare, where horses raced on the open plains that still stage Ireland's racing Derby, and in Wexford. Even in the 18th century local agents had their work cut out to quell the locals' habit of gathering on the Tailteann site at Teltown, Co Meath, because of "the drunkenness and faction-fighting it generated." The last games had in fact been held in 1179.

The GAA men were impressed. Here was a legacy to continue; the Scots had done something similar, so why not a Tailteann festival with the Scots and the Irish, the Manx, Cornish, Welsh and Bretons, to show that the Celts were the legitimate heirs to the Olympic tradition? A few eccentric ethnocentrists even claimed that the Greeks had got the idea of the Olympics from the Tailteann Games.

When the GAA men talked about reviving the games the *Daily Telegraph* in London thundered abuse at the audacity of such a notion: an auspicious amount of publicity for an as yet unproven organisation.

The Tailteann Games did not get going in 1886 because of lack of funds. Ten years later Baron de Cobertin revived the Olympic games in Athens. It was another 10 years before the GAA, having bankrupted itself preparing for the Tailteann project and then been torn apart by political intrusions, was put back on a sound financial footing.

THIRTEEN AT THE TABLE

The Gaelic Athletic Association was founded on November 1st 1884 at a meeting in a billiards room at Hayes' Hotel, Thurles. Seven people definitely attended the meeting. Cusack claimed 22 years later that nine had been there. As many as 13 could have attended. The sensitivity of naming known IRB men at the gathering might have influenced Cusack's initial reports.

Michael Cusack was born in 1876 in Carron, Co Clare, of Irish-speaking parents, Cusack became a schoolteacher. He first came in contact with handball and rugby football when he came to teach in Blackrock "French" College in 1874. In 1877 he set up his own academy. Cusack promoted sport there and played on the academy rugby team himself. He proposed a new body to control Irish athletics in three letters to the *Irish Sportsman* in 1881. In 1882 he founded the Dublin Athletics Club and the Dublin Hurling Club and became involved in the language revival movement by joining the Gaelic Union for the Preservation and Cultivation of the Irish Language. In 1883 he attended athletics meetings in Munster on what he called his "Gaelic mission." Finally, he was impressed by the response to an article he wrote in the *United Irishman* of October 11th 1884, "A word about Irish athletics." He was the author of the circular which called the delegates to the meeting.

The first GAA president also played rugby. Maurice Davin was a member of the Carrick-on-Suir Athletics Cricket and Football Club. He was world hammer-throw record holder in 1884, and a long-standing campaigner that Irish athletics should be controlled by an Irish organisation. Davin wrote the original code of ten rules for football, but it is unlikely that there is a lot of truth in the story told by Canon Philip Fogarty that it was done after a 32-a-side match in Hurley's field in Glinn, near Carrick-on-Suir, between Kilcash (from south Tipperary) and Waterford. According to Fogarty, the Davin brothers were returning home when Maurice said to Pat: "For heaven's sake, draft rules for football," and Pat replied, "I'll do so for hurling and you do it for football."

John McKay was also well-versed in football matters. A Belfast-born football player and a journalist with the *Cork Examiner* at the time of the meeting, he was to be instrumental in dramatically revising the rules of Gaelic football in its first year.

John Wyse-Power was there for political reasons. He was a Fenian, an IRB member, an athletics enthusiast, and at the time editor of the *Leinster Leader* in Naas. His widow, Jenny, became a member of the new Irish Senate in 1922.

John K Bracken, also a nationalist and IRB member, was a building contractor in Templemore. His son became Minister for Information in Churchill's British War Cabinet. Joseph Ryan was a young solicitor with offices in Callan and Thurles who was a moderating influence in the stormy early years of the GAA. George St John McCarthy, later District Inspector, was a rugby international, an athlete and an officer of the Royal Irish Constabulary based at the Templemore training centre. Policemen were excluded from athletics as run by the English Athletics Association at the time because they were not "amateurs." He was not subsequently involved in the GAA and, unknown to the Association, he was the only founder to attend the jubilee hurling final in Croke Park in 1934, a paying spectator on Hill 16.

Other names associated with the foundation of the GAA were William Foley of Carrick-on-Suir, John Butler of nearby Ballyhuddy, Thurles residents Dwyer C Culhane, William Delahunty and Michael Cantwell. Illness prevented IRB member John Sweeney of Loughrea from attending.

Most of the discussion at the first meeting was about athletics. Cusack outlined his idea of a national athletics body, similar to the Amateur Athletics Association in England, that would be controlled by Irish people. He mentioned a scheme for a Celtic athletics festival and advocated a meeting comparable to the Caledonian Games which had been held in Ballsbridge the previous spring. This festival could raise funds for the infant association. Hurling and football were scarcely mentioned at this meeting.

Official GAA historian, Marcus de Burca, concludes that there was no political motivation for the foundation meeting. He accepts Cusack's argument that the GAA's opposition to English organisations and English games was to help democratise the new body, but that was as far as nationalism went. Before founding the movement, Cusack had consulted with nationalist politicians William O'Brien, Justin McCarthy and Tim Harrington, but also with moderate nationalist Hyde and a prominent unionist, the Reverend Maxwell Close.

Others such as Pádraig Puirseal and William Mandle say that this was not an "innocent nationalist" gathering but an Irish Republican Brotherhood plot. Three IRB members were there: Wyse-Power, Bracken and F R Moloney. Moloney may have been so deeply involved that Cusack did not make his presence at the meeting public. According to Thomas Markham, writing in 1934, the IRB Supreme Council had drawn up plans for a nationalist athletics body at a meeting in Cork in 1883.

With three patrons identified, Archbishop Croke, Charles Stewart Parnell, and Michael Davitt, this first meeting was adjourned to December 17th 1884.

On December 15th 1884, Clara from County Offaly became the first club to join Cusack's Metropolitan Hurling Club in the new association.

On January 17th 1885 the GAA drew up rules for football and hurling. That same day Killimor defeated Ballinakill by two goals to nil in the first hurling match, played before 6,000 spectators at Tynagh, Co Galway. It was held while the rules for hurling were being drawn up at a meeting in Cork, probably under Killimor rules that had first been published by Pat Larkin in 1869. Gort from County Galway and Killanan from County Clare also claim to have played the first hurling match under the rules of the GAA, at Gort. On February 8th a hurling match was played in Belfast.

Footballers were slower out of the dressing-rooms. On February 15th 1885, a month after the rules were drawn up, three football matches were played under the new GAA rules. At Callan, Kilkenny Commercials played Callan. At St Canice's Park in Kilkenny town, two town clubs St Patrick's and St Canice's met. And in Naas, Co Kildare, Naas played Sallins. All three were scoreless draws.

The first convention of the GAA drew representatives from 300 clubs in November 1885. It is claimed that the GAA had 1,000 clubs at the end of its first year. Cusack later described the early growth of the Association as being "like a prairie fire."

Most early GAA meetings, by July too numerous to list in the newspapers, were in athletics. Although it was reported that every county in Leinster had a football club by the end of 1885, few football games were recorded. Nobody was sure how the skeletal new rules should apply. Local customs on exactly how the ball should be shifted from place to place prevailed.

UNRAVELLING THE DAVIN RULES

According to Cusack, "On the 17th January 1885 a sub-committee met at Thurles to consider rules for football, hurling, athletics, etc., which Mr Davin had drafted." The rules that were adopted in January 1885 and published in *United Ireland* on February 7th 1885 would have been virtually unrecognisable even five years later. They give no idea of how the game should be played. A soccer goal is used. Even the number of players on a team is indeterminate. Whether the ball should be carried, as in rugby, or propelled, as in soccer, is not specified:

1. There shall be not less than fifteen or more than twenty-one players a side.

2. There shall be two umpires and a referee. Where the umpires disagree the referee's decision shall be final.

3. The ground shall be at least 120 yards long, 80 yards in breadth, and properly marked by boundary lines. Boundary lines must be at least five yards from fences.

4. The goal posts shall stand at each end in centre of goal line. They shall be 15 feet apart, with a cross-bar eight feet from the ground.

5. The captains of each team shall toss for choice of sides before commencing play, and the players shall stand in two ranks opposite each other until the ball is thrown up, each man holding the hand of one of the other side.

6. Pushing or tripping from behind, holding from behind or butting with the head, shall be deemed foul, and the player so offending shall be ordered to stand aside, and may not afterwards take part in the match, nor can his side substitute another man.

7. The time of actual play shall be one hour. Sides to be changed only at half-time.

8. The match shall be decided by the greater number of goals, if no goal be kicked the match shall be deemed a draw. A goal is when the ball is kicked through the goal posts under the cross-bar.

9. When the ball is kicked over the side-line it shall be thrown back by a player of the opposite side to him who kicked it over. If kicked over the goal-line by a player whose goal-line it is, it shall be thrown back in any direction by a player of the other side. If kicked over the goal-line by a player of the other side, the goal-keeper whose line it crosses shall have a free kick, no player of the opposite side to approach nearer than 25 yards of him till the ball is kicked.

10. The umpires and the referee shall have, during the match, full power to disqualify any player, or order him to stand aside and

discontinue play, for any act which they may consider unfair, as set out in rule 6.

There is no mention of offside, nor do the rules mention how long a player could handle the ball. The rules for hurling, which closely parallel those for football, say the ball may not be lifted off the ground with the hand. Only rule 6 gives any clue of what was likely to happen when two teams tried to play under these rules. What was not mentioned there was presumably permissible!

The soccer-style goals survived for just a year, when point-posts were added on either side and thus the scoring area remained until 1910. The throw-in from the sideline survived until 1946. All players were required to stand in the middle of the field for the throw-in until 1910. After that, the backs and goalkeeper were allowed to stay in position. Until 1965 the eight forwards and midfielders lined up for the throw-in. Teams were reduced to 17 a side in 1892 and 15 a side in 1913.

MURPHY'S LAWS

Getting football into the GAA rule-books was the easy part. Playing it, when the founding fathers weren't quite sure how it was supposed to be played, was a trifle more difficult.

Even Cusack was making no extravagant claims for the pedigree of his new game, which looked like adapted soccer to many. In one newspaper article he referred to the "national game of hurling" and then added "as well as football according to Gaelic rules."

In Cork there were suspicions that some rugby clubs had changed their allegiance but not their playing rules. In April 1885, Cusack declared that, under Gaelic rules, "the ball must not be carried." The rules that were in use in Cork city were branded as "rugby undisguised" at a GAA meeting in October 1885.

On February 26th 1886, the new rules had been in use for a year without any further clarification and the first serious signs of dissatisfaction with them were emerging.

J H Murphy of Cork was removed from vice-presidency of the Association because he had "framed the so-called National Football Rules in opposition to the GAA." Murphy's laws had a big following in Cork. On March 7th 1886 a meeting in the Foresters' Hall in Cork formed the Munster National Football Association, elected Murphy president and managed to get the allegiance of Lees, John McKay's club. Secretary of the new MNFA, Jim Forrest, declared:

> Gaelic rules might do very well for country clubs. But they are not suitable for clubs in the city. If a young man behind the counter received a black eye or scratch playing football under GAA rules it would be of more consequence to them than a player not employed in the city. He would be sent playing football for the other six days of the week.

Almost certainly at Cusack's behest, another Cork group from Blarney, Riverstown and Little Island met to disagree. Cusack attended and was not in conciliatory mood. These clubs wanted J F Murphy to talk to the GAA about the differences in the rules. The MNFA resolved not to play under rugby rules, although it was claimed by GAA personnel that "opponents of the GAA were present at the meeting in the Foresters' Hall." Maurice Davin advised the Cork footballers that they could play under the Munster rules and still be recognised by the GAA as athletes.

Cusack resisted. In a February 1886 issue of *United Ireland* he vilified Murphy and "the English League" he was running, playing "the garrison game of rugby, characterised by collaring and carrying." The GAA continued to claim at their special convention in Thurles in May that "several clubs in the south are playing football under rugby rules." Cusack defended his code, saying:

> This was intended to bring out the working man at such times as they were at liberty to go, and leave more respectable people to his colleagues.

There were other problems with Davin's rules apart from

black eyes. Scoreless draws abounded. The highlight of 1885 was a Gaelic festival in Thurles in April. Six matches produced just one goal between them. In May, Dunleary scored a rare goal against Grocers' Assistants, and on June 14th in Dublin Maurice Davin, the author of the rules, was present at another scoreless hurling match. He suggested that Nenagh should be declared winners against Athenry because they "had hit the ball over the crossbar, Galway having gained no point."

There the phrase originated. Scores were soon being counted unofficially as "overs," and a July 4th meeting suggested that "going over the end line five times should count as a point."

In August, Wexford County Board arranged a county championship with the most remarkable scorelines in Gaelic history. Rosslare beat Lady's Island by two tries to nil, Ballymore by three tries to one, and Crossabeg by three tries to two after extra time, to win a championship which was not acknowledged in subsequent record books. Wexford's "tries" were probably the same as the previous month's "overs," scored by going over the end-line.

On July 4th an amendment to the rules abolished wrestling and handigrips. "Handigrips have always been much abused," *Sport*, a weekly newspaper, declared. Dan Fraher spoke at a meeting in Waterford four days later complaining that the move was "subversive to Gaelic rules," and that "to abolish catching the man below the knee would be more suitable." Cusack too was dissatisfied, suggesting that they might as well ban the handpass as well and "then we have the Association game." Kilkenny officials objected too, but conformed.

Gaelic football was evolving into a game in its own right, 17 months after rules were first drawn up. Some of the distinctive features of the 1886 game survived: the ball could not be lifted off the ground with the hands, but could be knocked on with the hand or arm, and could not be carried or thrown but could be caught. A free kick had to be taken from the ground, not dropped from the hands (this appears to have been a major issue in Cork). All games were shortened from the occasional 80-minute match to a uniform hour long.

The differences between the GAA and Munster rules were brought down to a minimum. Founder member John McKay was still in an invidious position. In August, McKay resigned as Cork secretary, and in September he resigned from the vice-presidency of the Association. But by November Lees had re-embraced GAA rules.

On October 10th the concept of a point was defined further when a rule was made that point-posts be erected 21 yards on each side of the goal-posts. A trial period until November 1st met with great enthusiasm and the rules were altered for the third time in a six-month period. The days of the scoreless draw were over, and Gaelic football had got through a traumatic first two years.

The game was still cumbersome. Close rushed ground play with a phalanx of forwards trying to rush the ball in the opposite direction was still the sole tactic. The ball was heavy and not yet quite of spherical shape.

Local variations persisted, like the Australian-sounding game on the Ring of Kerry recalled by *Sceilg* in the 1940s:

> When one player fielded the ball, he stood back; and no member of the opposing team was permitted to approach beyond the mark thus made until the man in possession had kicked off. One was not allowed to catch from a hop, nor was lifting with the toe allowed, except when it was done without bending the body. When a goal was scored, the teams changed sides.

These rules remained in force until the arrival of school-teachers from Drumcondra, where Erin's Hope team were one of the leading exponents of the newly evolved Gaelic rules in Dublin.

Even as Gaelic rules began to stabilise, the political climate around the Association was frothing. The defeat of Gladstone's Home Rule Bill in June 1886 meant that Parnell had failed to deliver the promise of Home Rule and constitutional nationalism was demoralised. Fenian armed rebellion looked inviting to the Irish populace once again, and the IRB, who had such a big hand in the foundation of the

GAA, began to make its move to take over the organisation.

GAA members marched in their togs through the streets of Ennis in November to commemorate the Manchester Martyrs, who had died in the Fenian cause just 20 years earlier. Among the many speakers who attacked Parnell's parliamentarianism at a meeting afterwards was a proposed GAA patron, John O'Leary, and a future GAA president, Edward Bennett.

Other sections of the GAA were strongly identified with constitutional nationalism. Another GAA political demonstration a few days earlier was of lasting significance to the future of the games. Wicklow and Wexford County Boards got together to hold an inter-county contest, matching six clubs against six clubs in half-hour games. Parnell himself was in London but his mother, his brother John, and sister Emily attended. Mrs Parnell graciously supplied reporters with enlightened comments such as: "How they do run."

The pride of both counties was at stake, and spectators warmed to the idea. "The future of the Association lies in inter-county competition," Wexfordman P P Sutton suggested in *Sport*. He recalled that:

> Previous to the union county contests in hurling were a regular occurrence, even inter-provincial ones occasionally.

The GAA was growing confident enough to organise a championship. It was about to enshrine the county system, introduced by the Normans and regularised by King John in 1210. Saxon borders would prevail.

The irony did not go unnoticed and a short-lived newspaper, *The Gaelic Athlete,* called in 1912 for the abolition of the county system, formed as it was by the hated British "in varied sizes and most irregular and absurd shapes." But the GAA was not going to throw out what had by then become a winning formula.

Chapter Two

The 21-a-side Days

COMPETITION AT LAST

Nobody had, as yet, objected to the Saxon connection in 1886. So when the GAA decided to organise a championship for its 635 clubs, it was on a county basis. The games were not organised on the county committee structure as yet. More than anything else, the long-term success of the All-Ireland championship was guaranteed by that accident of the 1880s Gaelic Athletic Association.

The entry fee for the new championship was 2/6. It was arranged that clubs in a county would play out their ties first, and that the winner of the final would be entitled to represent the county. It was scheduled that the county championships would be run off between February 1st and March 17th, and that the All-Ireland final would take place in the last week in April or the first week in May.

Twelve counties entered the first All-Ireland football championships. The draws resulted in a new time-scale, which was also too ambitious:

> Wicklow v Clare, Athlone, Tuesday July 19th
> Louth v Waterford, Dublin, Thursday July 21st
> Kilkenny v Cork, Dungarvan, Sunday July 24th
> Galway v Wexford, Dublin, Sunday July 24th
> Meath v Limerick, Maryboro, Monday July 25th
> Tipperary v Dublin, Mountrath, Saturday July 30th

Within weeks there were objections. Wicklow pulled out because:

> While Galway, Waterford, Louth, Meath, Wexford and Limerick are accorded the privilege of playing at Elm Park Merrion...we must decline to ask any team to go to Athlone at this season for a match.

Dublin champions, teacher-training team Erin's Hope, asked for a postponement because many of their players were on holidays. It also emerged that Galway were interested in fielding in the hurling championships only. Galway's football champions Kilbaceanty protested but Galway County Board scarcely acknowledged them.

That left nine counties to try conclusions. But the championship was slow to get going. It was April 1888 before the 1887 championship was completed. Even then, it was a bit of a miracle that the final took place at all.

At the start of 1887 the GAA had two official journals and an impending crisis between clergy-led and IRB-inspired officials. They also had a highly politicised central committee, all of whom were entitled to attend any county committee meeting. That meant that the GAA's rambling Executive, IRB-men all, could overrule any local decisions with which they disagreed for the price of a few train tickets.

In June and September 1887 athletics meetings held by Grocers' Assistants and *Freeman's Journal* clubs were proscribed by the Executive in a row over the handicapper for their sports (but really related to the IRB question). November's convention in Thurles featured a one-hour pitched battle between Fenians and Parnellites, with fists flying, catcalls, and tables being overturned before eventually the clerical delegation walked out.

Croke intervened and in January 1888 a reconstruction convention put priests and Parnellites back into office.

When attention eventually turned to the playing-fields, it was the well-trained urban teams that dominated the first championships. The town teams that Jim Forrest talked about were grouping in the work-place and starting clubs, often with the blessing of employers. They were able to work out an approach to the new rules, and parkland such as the Mardyke, Market's Field, or Phoenix Park was easily accessible around large towns. And whereas rural clubs were strongest in athletics and hurling, urban clubs gained an early foothold in the football power struggle. Compared with Tipperary, who had 130 clubs in 1887, Dublin had just 40, less than Louth. In Cork and Limerick, it was the urban clubs who quickly controlled the local championships.

Limerick Commercials' sudden rise from obscurity was one of the success stories of the early GAA. The club was founded for the drapers in the town in 1885 by Dan H Ryan of Thurles, a Shannon Rowing Club oarsman who was one of the prime movers against the Munster Association rules on the grounds that they were "too like rugby," along with Maurice Fitzgibbon, John McNamara (non-playing captain in the All-Ireland final), Tom O'Connor and Pat Treacy.

Limerick Market's Field was an outstanding sporting venue and, unlike Phoenix Park, admission could be charged to the field. In 1886 a monster athletics sports organised by Commercials went on for three successive Sundays and raised £310.

Before the championship began Commercials built up a fine record in challenge matches against Munster teams. But in 1887 Dan H Ryan was transferred to Dublin (where he set to work organising the Dublin drapery houses in the Kickhams club). Pat Treacy, although not a player, took over the captaincy. As the political split tore Limerick in two, Commercials stood by the old IRB board, chaired by Paddy "Twenty" O'Brien, against Father Sheehy's board. A massive crowd turned out when the rival county champions played off, Commercials versus St Michael's at Croom, and for the first time a special train was organised for a Gaelic football match. Commercials lost the final only to win a walk-over when opponents St Michael's found that five rugby-playing members were barred from the replay by the new "foreign games" ban.

The Commercials star was Malachy O'Brien, not yet 17, man of the match as Limerick beat Dowdstown of Meath by 3-2 to 0-2, Kilmacow of Kilkenny by 1-3 to 0-5 in a replay,

Templemore of Tipperary by 1-8 to 0-4 in another replay and Dundalk Young Irelands of Louth by 1-4 to 0-3 in the final.

When O'Brien kicked the winning goal, allegedly from midfield, against Dowdstown of Meath he was invited to tea by Lord de French, who hosted the game. The Victuallers' Band turned out when the team returned home and they were carried in triumph through Georges Street: and that was only the first round!

There were rows and eruptions along the way. Commercials were aggrieved that Central Council ordered their match against Kilmacow to be replayed. They claimed they won the original semi-final by two points. Then the Central Council changed the replay venue at the last minute from Clonmel, which had been agreed by the teams, to Bansha.

In the final, Louth, having won the toss, played with the wind in the first half and led 0-3 to 0-1 at half-time but went down by 1-4 to 0-3 in the end.

It was William J Spain, later to win a hurling medal with Dublin, who scored the winning goal 11 minutes into the second half. It came after a long dribbling run almost from his own 21-yard line by McNamara, and a three-man handpassing movement. Then they saved what looked like an inevitable goal for Louth.

After the match the Commercials dispersed. When their medals were eventually presented 25 years later many were dead or had emigrated. Some stayed in the drapery trade when they moved to places such as Dublin. Michael Slattery left for Australia, James Purcell went on to the Philippines, W J Spain, Timothy Fitzgibbon, Richard O'Brien, Ned Casey and Denis Corbett all went to the United States. In 1897 a new Commercials team captured another smash-and-grab All-Ireland football title but until 1978, when a similarly "mercenary" Thomond College team won an All-Ireland club title, Limerick football has been in the doldrums since.

Referee John Cullinane, later an MP, was just out of jail for his activity in the Land War. Dundalk Young Irelands had already developed a form of the handpass: "hand-play punting of Dundalk was a credit to the side" the *Freeman's*

Journal reported, while "fast, determined charging won the match for the Garryowen team."

The techniques of the early game included "dandling" the ball with one hand, hopping it, and striking the ball with the forearm. According to the GAA's first historian, Thomas F O'Sullivan, "it was not unusual to see players sending the ball a distance of almost fifty yards by this fashion."

The handpass also penetrated Ulster. Dundalk Young Irelands were an important influence on early football in Monaghan and Cavan. They supplied coaches, referees, and opposition for matches. One member of the Young Irelands, James Campbell from Lurgan, was uncle to future GAA president Alf Murray.

Ulster's oldest club, Ballyconnell, had played as early as 1885 when the RIC arrived to stop their match under ancient Sunday Observance Acts. The "First Ulsters," as they called themselves, were beaten by Maghera McFinns in the final of the inaugural 13-club Cavan championship. Cavan had 38 clubs in 1888, Monaghan had 32, Armagh 17, Fermanagh 15, Derry 3, Down 3, Antrim 2 and Tyrone 1. Only one other county held a county championship; Inniskeen Grattans beat Clones Red Hands in the Monaghan final.

Problems were still arising under the vague Gaelic rules when teams from different localities arranged to meet. When adjoining Monaghan and Cavan teams played off for the Ulster title they differed even on the size of teams. Inniskeen Grattans had only 15 players when Cavan arrived to play them with 21, so Cavan shed their six extra players. When the match was drawn 0-2 each, Inniskeen refused to play extra time.

When the replay was played three weeks later with 21 a side Inniskeen had improved considerably in skills such as handpassing and won by three points to one. According to the *Anglo-Celt* Maghera McFinns were having a meal when the Inniskeen team arrived late, and were none too pleased about being called out to play a game of football. A bereavement prevented the three Mulvaney brothers, including team captain William, from playing with Maghera.

HUMBLE INVADERS

In May 1888 the notion of reviving the ancient Tailteann festival was revived. The GAA Executive decided they would need to raise £5,000 for the project, and in a climate where individual clubs were able to raise £310 in a single month, they felt that was feasible. But the solution to the problem was daft, even by the standards of the poorly organised body that was the GAA of 1888. An Association that was already £500 in debt decided on a trip to the America that would cost £1,000. They called it the "Invasion."

The only thing that was successfully invaded in 1888 was the All-Ireland championship, abandoned at the height of its interest, despite the fact that no players on the football teams left in the championship were involved in the United States tour. The Leinster final was not even played until a week after the "invaders" had left.

The tour was a disaster in every way. The grandiose venture was ignored by the newspapers. Instead it was swamped by a remarkable American presidential election in which Republican candidate Benjamin Harrison received 100,000 fewer votes than Democrat Grover Cleveland but almost 50 more electoral college seats. An early winter snowed off some of the American meetings and caused the cancellation of the Canadian leg of the tour. Most importantly, the invaders got caught up in a bitter battle for control of American athletics. The National Amateur Athletics Association (NAAA) and the American Amateur Athletics Union (AAAU) were locked in combat, boycotting each other's meetings. The GAA sided with the NAAA, whom they had entertained (as the New York Athletics Club) in Dublin in 1887. But the "Nationals" lost the athletics war: the GAA found themselves unwelcome in most athletic centres.

This contributed to the financial failure of the GAA's much-heralded "invasion." At one stage the party was locked in their hotel, unable to pay bills until they were rescued by wealthy New York newspaper-owner Patrick Ford. GAA patron Michael Davitt had unwisely guaranteed £400 from his own pocket. He was never repaid, even when he faced bankruptcy proceedings four years later.

The failure was a major blow to the morale of the infant Association. Of the 48 who travelled, 17 never came home, including the flower of GAA athletics, world hammer-throw champion James Mitchell, who became sports editor of the New York *Sun*. Earlier in the same year, the GAA's top track athlete, Tommy Conneff from Kildare, had emigrated to New York because he opposed the IRB take-over of the Association. In America he set a world mile record that survived for 16 years.

As a result of all this, a scheme for a grand Celtic festival of athletics, to be held in Dublin in 1889, was shelved. There were several more false starts before the Tailteann Games were eventually revived in 1924. The invasion almost bankrupted the organisation, which remained in debt until 1905.

An appeal for £1 per club (there were now 1,700 clubs) to pay off the GAA's £850 debt met with no response at all. President Maurice Davin, who had come back to heal the split of 1887, walked out of the 1889 convention in a row over the Association's rocky finances.

Completing the championship might have helped, but there was no attempt to do this. That the championship of 1888 ground to a premature halt was a pity, as the attendances at Leinster championship matches were showing just how popular the new Gaelic football code could become, with its intricate combination of parochial and territorial rivalries.

Special trains brought several thousand people up from Kildare for the first Leinster championship match, played between Fiach McHughs, a team chosen from the "French" College, Blackrock, representing Dublin, and Clane of Kildare. Both sides wore green and black which was described as "very disagreeable for the spectators, who found it very difficult to distinguish the players." Three of the best Clane players had emigrated since the Kildare championships, and Dublin won by 1-6 to 0-1.

Wicklow champions Annacurra tested the notion of selected county teams five years before it was legal to do so when they picked two players from Avoca and one each from Brittas and Aughrim to help them against Wexford. Their opponents, the Blues and Whites from Wexford town, objected but the match had to be replayed anyway when local supporters stormed the field to join in a fracas.

"The Wexford lads were tidy, hardy active kind of fellows, the kind of lads to be found around a town," Wexford native P P Sutton recorded in *Sport*, adding that the match became "rough—vicious" and an Annacurra player, Kirwan, had to leave his clothes behind as he escaped the mob by climbing over a wall.

Handpassing techniques were failing in the face of sheer old-fashioned muscle. A crowd of 5,000 attended the Leinster semi-finals at Clonskeagh where the phalanx of brawny men from Kilmacow, Co Kilkenny, beat Dundalk Young Irelands and Wexford's hardy townies, the Blues and Whites, beat Blackrock College. The crowd was even bigger for the Leinster final at New Ross, the last match of the 1888 championship to be played. Kilkenny and Wexford were level for most of the match, were tied at 0-1 each at half-time and at 0-2 each with five minutes to go before Kilmacow scored a lucky breakthrough goal and followed up with two insurance points to win by 1-4 to 0-2.

Wexford objected that some of the Kilkenny players had been chosen from outside Kilmacow parish but were unable to prove their case. According to the *Freeman's Journal* the Kilmacow men were "brawny countrymen, magnificent kickers who possess a good turn of speed."

They never got a chance to prove their prowess at All-Ireland level, however, and win what could have been Kilkenny's only football championship. The lack of any administration meant the championship fell through, leaving Leinster champions Kilmacow and Ulster champions Inniskeen in limbo.

There was nobody to sort out the mess in Munster where Limerick Commercials, Newmarket-on-Fergus of Clare, and Bohercrowe were all claiming the provincial title.

Bohercrowe were one of five separate football teams based in Tipperary town, and were scarcely a year in existence when they became the first Munster football champions. They had been somewhat surprise champions in Tipperary, winning the county semi-final against Grangemockler on objection after losing on the field of play, and surprising undefeated Fethard, for whom Dick Cummins was possibly the finest footballer in the country at the time, by four points to one in the county final. They defeated John McKay's highly rated Cork champions, Lees, in the Munster semi-final and were declared champions when Limerick Commercials failed to turn up on a weekday for the final. Limerick Commercials got a reprieve to qualify for that Munster final. Newmarket-on-Fergus, who beat defending All-Ireland champions Commercials in the first round, had been disqualified for the increasingly familiar complaint that they had fielded players from outside clubs.

TIPPING THE TOP

Bohercrowe had the chance to go all the way in 1889. Their star was the young Willie Ryan, outstanding player of several championships in the 1890s. They beat Midleton of Cork by 1-2 to 0-3 in a hectic 1889 Munster final, having earlier beaten Waterford champions Aglish-Ballinameela and got a walk-over from Kildysart of Clare. Midleton defeated Laune Rangers from Kerry on the same day as the final.

Bohercrowe had an easy task in the All-Ireland final against Maryboro from Queen's County, in an era before both changed their names to Portlaoise and Laois respectively. Bohercrowe kicked an early goal, led 1-5 to nil at half-time, and eventually won a tempestuous game by 3-6 to nil. A fourth Tipperary goal was "rightly disallowed" as the ball had crossed the line and there were "one or two scenes" as the "match was characterised by entirely too much roughness." Every altercation was accompanied by a crowd invasion.

Another gripe was that semi-finals involving Ulster and Connacht champions were advertised without the slightest chance of the matches coming off. In fact the Bohercrowe—Maryboro match was really a semi-final, as Connacht and Ulster had been drawn in the other semi-final, and Tipperary technically got a walk-over in the All-Ireland final! As there wasn't a single entry from the two weaker provinces for the championship, this was rather academic.

Bohercrowe had played 36 matches up to the 1889 All-Ireland final, with the best known a fund-raising match for the Oblate Fathers' new church in Inchicore. Bohercrowe won a tournament in aid of that church. Joe Ryan, club president, was of the IRB wing of the Association. The team trained on his land and Jack Frewen also gave fields for GAA purposes. The Land War saw many club members involved in the New Tipperary fight in 1891 and Willie Ryan was imprisoned. The Parnell split, in which Joe Ryan was fervently involved on the pro-Parnell side, eventually caused the club to break up in disarray in 1892. Many club members returned to play with Arravale Rovers in 1893.

Maryboro was a different type of club. Winning a Leinster title in 1889 should not have been difficult, considering that only Louth, Dublin and Queen's County were affiliated at the time. Bray Emmetts, later to win an All-Ireland title representing Dublin, turned out as Wicklow champions because they were the only Wicklow club which recognised the Central Council at the time, despite the fact that Annacurra and Valleyknockan were advertised to play in the Wicklow final a few weeks later!

When Bray beat Newtown Blues of Drogheda by 1-7 to 1-4 on September 15th they claimed that they had won the "final of Leinster" because Queen's County and Kilkenny had not shown up for semi-finals and a final that were to be played on the same day. Kilkenny club Kells said they failed to show for their semi-final against Louth because they were fixed to play in the local county final on the following weekend and wanted to train for that match.

Nobody seemed to be in control of affairs at the venue to decide whether Louth and Wicklow were entitled to walk-overs. Messengers were dispatched to seek out Central Council members while the teams played their "Leinster final" anyway.

It took just four days for the result to be quashed and Bray to stop their celebrations, and Maryboro found themselves facing a new semi-final and final on October 13th. Despite having to beat Wicklow by 0-9 to 0-4 while Drogheda had beaten Dublin six weeks earlier, Maryboro were, if anything, fresher in the second match. Kildare opted out because a Maynoothman, Thomas Cullen, had died as a result of injuries sustained playing against eventual county champions, Mountrice club Wilfred Scawen Blunts.

St Patrick's Field near the Oblate church on Inchicore Road was the venue for the All-Ireland final. The Oblate church had been largely funded on the proceeds of GAA matches on the ground. The present Tyrconnell Park housing estate was built on the site of the field.

In the final Maryboro (for whom five Cushions were playing) beat Bohercrowe (with five Ryans on the team) in a "wildly exciting game" by three points to two. It was played on an appalling day. The pitch was speckled with pools of water. *Sport* mourned "it must be designated the roughest match yet played at Inchicore," with "too much tripping, catching and general fouling." That complaint was to continue to punctuate GAA coverage for over a decade. Among the 3,000 spectators at the game were several police spies, who gleefully reported on every incident of violence.

The police were not the only ones to notice that IRB members were taking back the positions they had lost at the 1888 reconstruction convention. The clergy was actively campaigning against the GAA in many areas and the Association in parts of Ulster, especially in Fermanagh and Monaghan, was practically wiped out. Priests in Newry, Enniskillen, and Clones, and bishops in Clogher and Dromore condemned the GAA from the pulpit.

In Laois one priest made shopkeepers take down a notice advertising a GAA game and then stood at a crossroads turning back people who would have attended the match.

AT LOW EBB

The 1890 championship got off to a hectic start with a first-round match between Kilkenny and Wexford that was full of incident. Shortly before the match was due to begin, the referee Dan Fraher discovered he had no football. Nor had anyone else in the grounds. Someone was sent downtown to get one and it was seven o'clock before the game started, which meant most of the Wexford supporters missed the steamer back to New Ross.

The pitch was reduced in size to no more than 50 yards wide by advancing spectators, and crowds of spectators stood in front of the goal-posts during the game. Due to a transport difficulty Ballyhale from Kilkenny started with 19 men, instead of 21 a side, when the original fixture was replayed in Dublin two months later, and withdrew complaining about roughness early in the game.

Wexford went on to beat Drogheda Davitts from Louth by 0-3 to 0-2, and in the final against Dublin Isles of the Sea took a 1-3 to nil half-time lead and held out by the skin of their teeth to win by 1-3 to 1-2 when the final whistle was blown, four minutes early according to the captain of Isles of the Sea. The final was originally fixed for Avondale, where noted exhibition matches had been held in front of Charles Stewart Parnell's house in 1886. But the game was refixed at a late stage for the more accessible Clonturk Park before a small crowd, consisting mainly of about 400 supporters who came by special train from Wexford.

Clonturk was first used as the venue for the 1890 athletics championship and went on to replace Inchicore and become the major GAA venue of the early 1890s. The venue for four football and four hurling All-Ireland finals, it was comfortable and accessible, situated as it was in a natural hollow on the banks of the Tolka, opposite where St Patrick's College is today, but soon it proved impossible to control access to the ground and gate receipts suffered. The housing estate built on the site is called Clonturk Park.

Captained by Jim Power, a member of the noted athletic family from Ballywalter in North Cork, Midleton beat Waterford club Kinsalebeg. Power was a noted sprinter, and later joined Lees in Cork city when he set up a drapery shop there. As well as Power, Midleton had a flying winger with fine ball control, Ted "Tit" Downey.

Midleton then beat Killorglin of Kerry in an unusual

replay. Midleton were not as well-built as J P O'Sullivan's Laune Rangers, but the final ended prematurely when the ball burst three minutes from the end and a replacement could not be found, the Killorglin men having neglected to bring a ball. Killorglin missed Jer Hayes from the replay; he was hobbling along the sideline in crutches "with his racing cards" after having his "knee cap kicked off" in the drawn game.

Midleton won the replay convincingly with team captain Jim Power scoring a spectacular drop-kick point "with his hands still on his hips." Kilkennyman John Langford had kicked the ball out from the 10-yard line, a slight wind made the ball veer to where Power was standing "in a white uniform with a white handkerchief around his neck," Power prepared to catch but changed his mind when a Killorglin man got ahead of him, stepped back a pace or two, put each hand on a hip and met the ball with a drop-kick as it hit the ground to send it back to drop under the crossbar.

The All-Ireland final has been fixed, rather hastily, for Clonturk Park at a special meeting of the Central Council the previous Monday at Limerick Junction. A vague notice arrived in Dublin about the events, two football semi-finals and both hurling and football finals set for Sunday, with an addendum that the four provinces would be sending teams. But rumours persisted that neither Connacht nor Ulster would show.

Ulster's first semi-finalists showed up all right. Armagh Harps emerged as one of the foremost clubs in Ulster during tournament matches in 1889, and there was not much surprise when they defeated Antrim by 3-7 to 0-1 and Cookstown Owen Roe O'Neills by 2-8 to 1-2 on the same day to win the provincial championship. Armagh Harps arrived at Amiens St at 11.30 on Sunday morning with the William O'Brien fife and drum band and 250 supporters. Armagh did not manage to get past the half-way line, trailed 0-7 to nil at half-time, and lost by 1-14 to nil as two Corkmen helped force the game's only goal entering the last quarter.

Midleton eventually beat Blues and Whites by 2-4 to 0-1. Wexford were short four of their team, and missed a great goal chance as they fell 1-3 to 0-1 behind at half-time. Then came a stop-start second half: 13 minutes of play, eight minutes seeking a substitute for an injured player, three minutes more play, seven minutes of delay as a Corkman was injured near the sidelines, three minutes later the first Wexford goal then a second goal immediately afterwards.

Connacht didn't turn up, probably due to the incredibly inefficient organisation, roundly blamed on Mr Clery by the press, who declared that "Sunday was more or less a failure" and described the scenes as "confusion worse compounded."

Wexford appealed against the result and a replay was ordered for March 13th 1892 but was cancelled because of a fair in Midleton that day. Another replay was set for June 26th. Midleton were not enthusiastic to put their honour at stake again and the decision proved wise.

YOUNG IRELANDS

"Confusion worse compounded" summed up the state of the whole Gaelic athletic organisation. Only seven counties attended the 1890 convention. There they learned that the Association was in debt to the tune of £1,000.

Things were to get worse. Ten days before the convention Captain O'Shea was granted a decree for divorce. Charles Stewart Parnell, named as co-respondent, was offering no defence.

On December 7th the majority of Parnell's parliamentary party seceded. There followed a remarkable change of position. The people who were supporting Parnell against an increasingly hostile clergy included many of the old IRB nationalists who had opposed him most vehemently three years before.

The GAA leadership decided to stand with Parnell, resolving: "That this Convention is resolved to support the policy of independent opposition and freedom of opinion under the leadership of Mr Parnell."

There were immediate repercussions. The GAA backed a loser and met the hostility of the clergy. The number of clubs plummeted from 1,000 in 1888 to 220 in 1892. Only six counties were represented at the 1892 convention. Unfortunately, among those who turned against Parnell was the GAA patron, T W Croke. Croke removed a bust of Parnell from his home and described the uncrowned king of a few months earlier as "a moral leper, a measly pig in a litter who infects all the rest."

In Sligo priests were directed to infiltrate and undermine the Association. In Carlow, Louth and Tipperary it was the opposite. In Laois, Kildare and Waterford it was boycotted. In Galway and Mayo it was pulpited by the bishops of Ossory, Elphin, Achonry and Sligo.

Dublin fared better than rural areas as the GAA tore itself apart in the wake of the Parnell split. A quarter of the delegates at the 1890 convention were from Dublin, proclaiming undying support for Parnell. Clubs disbanded and broke up throughout the country. Even in Dublin attendances fell and teams played short.

City clubs had a bad run after the initial successes of the highly trained Commercials and Dundalk teams. But now Dublin Young Irelands were developing a strategic "catch-and-kick" style at practice sessions in the Phoenix Park, near the brewery where the team members all worked. They began their spectacularly successful run in 1892 when they emerged from a rather chaotic Leinster championship.

Arrangements in Leinster were an unmitigated disaster. Kildare champions Mountrice would not play Moyanna of Queen's County because of "the near approach of their sports" (day) and Clane, nominated in their place, did not hear about the match in time. Moyanna would not take the walk-over so Mountrice were eventually enticed to play with the promise of a special train from Monasterevin. After beating Moyanna, Mountrice refused to play Dublin Young Irelands later the same afternoon and conceded a walk-over.

Ulster was no better. The Ulster final at Bailieborough broke up in disarray because Armagh scored a goal after the referee had blown for a foul on one of their players. The referee decided not to give a decision on the incident until the next council meeting.

In the replay Cavan Slashers had to erect the posts when

they arrived for this final against Armagh Harps, using a rope as a crossbar, then scored 1-11 without reply to win the county's first championship. They were heavily beaten by Dublin Young Irelands in the semi-final, by 3-7 to 0-3. Young Irelands went on to play Cork club Clondrohid, who had beaten Kerry champions Ballymacelligott by 2-5 to 0-2 and Waterford's Dungarvan by 3-2 to 1-1 for the Munster title.

The All-Ireland final, fixed for February 21st 1892, was postponed for a week because of snow. When it was played, Clondrohid were declared winners by 2-9 to 2-1. But their second goal was disallowed because a Corkman had picked the ball off the ground. This was not at all clear at the end of the match. Three hours after the game, the referee confirmed that he had disallowed Clondrohid's second goal.

Dublin won little sympathy by their tactics of lining the goal in the second half to prevent Cork from denting their 2-1 to 0-2 half-time lead. At the time a goal outweighed any number of points, so Dublin were now the winners on the scoreline. The inevitable replay was ordered by Central Council.

Young Irelands were eventually awarded the title when Clondrohid refused to travel for a replay fixed for Thurles for April 9th 1893. The matter was further contested and another replay was ordered for September 17th 1894. By that time Clondrohid had disbanded and, although they were probably never officially awarded the title, Dublin are recorded as 1892 All-Ireland champions.

Young Irelands might not have been clear-cut champions, but their contribution to the game was already immense. They had turned their back on the kick-and-rush football of the time. An American emigrant, Father John Devane, recalled the heady mixture of chaos and brute force that 21-a-side football represented in his native Tralee:

> In those days positional play was not in vogue, as we know it today, except at the goal and point posts. Invariably therefore, Captain Jim Foley's instructions to his men before taking the field were brief and simple: "Follie the ball, men," he would say, and "follie it" they did like

Foley's beagles at a fox chase. This form of strategy suited Garrett Landers—the father of the three famous Landers brothers—to a nicety, because his plan of campaign was to throw himself in front of a bunch of players and bring down three or four at a time. Foxy Tom Connor was an adept, too, at bringing down the enemy in a cluster, but Tom, of rugged robust mould, did the execution with his robust shoulders, whereas Garrett was rather slight of build and had to depend more on brain than brawn. Another bone crusher was Denis Kelleher of the Killarney Dr Crokes, who in this fashion rendered great service to his team. In those days it was the practice to play the man oftener than the ball, and the bone crushing style of play was popular with the multitude when the home team was losing. In 1888 we saw Castleisland defeat Tralee in the Tralee Sports Field, but our sorrow was soon turned to joy when we asked one another: "Did you see Foxy Tom throw three Castleisland fellows in a heap over the ropes with his shoulder?"

Skill was only an incidental. The time had come to change the rules, so more of the skills that Young Irelands were pioneering could be developed.

Chapter Three

Survival Games

CLEARING THE FIELD

It was clear that the modified Davin rules were inadequate. Few matches were being played on full-size pitches. Most 21-a-side games ended up as mud-wrestling bouts. Some counties (such as Kildare in 1892) had already taken the initiative, and organised their championships with teams of 16 a side. This enabled smaller clubs to field teams but above all helped clear some space on the playing-field where a footballer could move without fear of disembowelment.

Clubs were persistently selecting players from outside their own area for inter-county matches. There was a growing lobby who proposed that the practice should be legalised. The argument for selected county teams was virtually sealed when one Kerry hurling club, Kilmoyley, disbanded specifically so their best hurlers could join another club, Ballyduff, and win the All-Ireland championship in 1891.

The GAA had another reason to change the rules. They wanted to avoid a repeat of the goal-lining fiasco that ruined the 1891 All-Ireland football final as a spectacle. As early as 1890 Kerry had suggested that a goal should be made equal to five points.

So in January 1892 three important rule changes were made:

Teams were reduced from 21 a side to 17 a side
The goal was made equal to three points
Champion clubs were allowed to select players from any club in their own county for inter-county games.

Matters off the field were not helping the football follower either. Matches were falling through in the aftermath of the Parnell split. The fiasco of the 1892 Leinster championship semi-finals and final, fixed for the same day on March 12th 1892, brought to a head the damaging trend.

The first semi-final went ahead when Young Irelands used their new "catch-and-kick" tactics to beat Kildare who, according to *Sport*, "played genuine Gaelic football and unlike Dublin teams abhor catching."

But because the special train from Queen's County left six minutes early, their representatives Maryboro could only find six players for the second semi-final against Drogheda Emmetts of Louth. Referee J P Cox awarded the semi-final to Louth and asked them to play off against Dublin in the provincial final.

A short while later a band of men arrived claiming to represent Queen's County and demanding a semi-final match against Louth. The referee stuck to his decision (the Queen's County secretary had also conceded the match) and said that a challenge match might be played. Louth protested that the Queen's County team was not genuine and independent observers suggested that there were quite a few Dubliners in the newly recruited team.

The Queen's County "recruits" took possession of the field and refused to leave until they were given a game while spectators stood around in confused groups. Dublin too felt Louth should play a match to even things out. "Feeling ran pretty high," it was reported and "a couple of Queen's County players met with hostile demonstrations from sections of the Dublin supporters."

Late in the day Dublin lined up. Whether Louth had gone home, or whether they still had not cleared the Queen's County recruits from the field is not sure. Dublin got the walk-over and the place in the record books that they would almost certainly have won on the field of play.

Two weeks later Young Irelands were All-Ireland champions, amid more acrimony. A bout of pugilism brought the All-Ireland semi-final the following week to a premature end. Athlone T P O'Connor, who had represented Westmeath

42

against Dublin in the 1890 Leinster championship and lost by 6-11 to 0-2, now came forward representing Connacht as Roscommon champions and were beaten this time by 1-8 to 1-0. Athlone arrived with several bands and a large contingent of supporters for the semi-final, but soon after they had scored their first goal a Dublin player hit one of their players off the ball and Athlone withdrew. The match started late because "some of the Athlone players had to attend Divine Service."

In the final it was Dublin's supporters who caused the problem. According to Cork newspapers the Killorglin visitors found the field was "badly fenced off" and they were surrounded by a hostile mob with no protection. But Dublin newspapers said they had "never seen a match pass off so quietly and orderly" although the usual "knot of wall-climbers and street-urchins" took to booing the referee when he awarded three frees in succession to Killorglin in the first half.

"The crowd encroached on the pitch when Kerry looked like scoring," Kerry claimed afterwards. But the Central Council said the result, a 1-4 to 0-3 victory for Dublin, should stand.

Kerry's Killorglin Laune Rangers created a legend in defeat. They had won their first Munster title when they defeated Dan Fraher's kick-and-rush style Erin's Own club from Dungarvan, and overcame an understrength Cork in the Munster final by 3-6 to 0-5.

Cork's chances of a Munster title were scuttled by an extraordinary series of events in the local championship. Clondrohid's second team won the Cork county football championship, their first team having been beaten in the first round! Confusion over who was entitled to play for the club in the Munster final meant some of the Clondrohid players did not travel to the game.

J P O'Sullivan brought his Laune Rangers north with a powerful reputation, but they ran up against an on-form George Roche in the Young Irelands defence. Kerry started well, scoring two points in the first 10 minutes. Luke Kelly and Bob Curtis scored Dublin points to equalise, then J P himself restored Kerry's lead with a well-taken point. It was 0-3 each at half-time. In the end a defensive mistake let Dublin in for the winning goal with 10 minutes to go after Kerry had dominated during the second half.

Killorglin captain J P O'Sullivan was retrospectively hailed as the father-figure of scientific coaching in Kerry. He won the All-Round athletic event at the 1891 GAA championships (for which he was given a championship belt, boxing-style), was a 120-yard champion hurdler and second in the long-kick championship. He spent most of 1892 training to defend his title but pulled out of the event due to the death of his sister. His free-taking was renowned on the football field. He never tried for a point, but always for a goal. When within range he put the ball in front of the crossbar and left a forward charge by his men to do the rest. He was a fluent Irish speaker and dancer. His father accompanied the County Court Judge on his circuit as interpreter. J P himself worked as paymaster on the railway between Killorglin and Caherciveen when it was under construction, where many of the Laune Rangers made their living. J P played for Firies later on, keeping goal until he was 43 years old. He dropped dead leaving a coursing meeting in Cork. J P's son Eamonn later became the Kerry coach for half of the 20th century and the leading proponent of orthodox fixed-position football well into the 1960s.

MURDER AT PHOENIX PARK

Politics put a stop to Young Irelands' gallop. The great disquiet among the GAA grass roots at the pro-Parnell stand of the Central Council meant that only five counties entered the 1893 championship, three of these in Leinster. Dublin was not amongst them. But just to be sure, Wexford stayed on the field until full-time before claiming victory against them.

Instead another team called Young Irelands, from Wexford town, won the Leinster championships after the most astonishing walk-off in the history of the GAA. Wexford were surprised when Kilkenny captain Dick Kealy took his men off the field, refusing to continue, in protest at

Wexford's "rough tactics"—despite the fact that Kilkenny were leading by five points to one at the time. Kilkenny had two points inside 10 minutes, then led 0-5 to 0-1 at half-time having played with the sun and the wind.

Late in the first half the referee intervened two or three times as "play got exceedingly warm." Kilkenny moaned that five of their players were injured at the time they withdrew, and the rock-hard pitch was not suitable to their style.

In the tradition of the time, Kilkenny expected a walk-over, but the match was awarded to Wexford instead. This is the only time in GAA history that a *winning* team walked off the field! Wexford's other game was an easy 2-6 to 0-1 victory over Westmeath, who scored first despite having to start the game two men short!

In Munster, north Cork club Dromtarriffe reached the All-Ireland final without having played a match. Cork and Kerry were fixed to play in the final three times, twice at Millstreet and eventually at Mallow. But Laune Rangers did not show.

The 1893 All-Ireland final was the most chaotic in the long and bizarre history of the Gaelic football championship. Originally fixed, alongside the hurling final, for the Ashtown trotting grounds, it was transferred to the nearby Phoenix Park because the secretary had forgotten to get the grass cut.

The match was eventually played after the hurling final at the Phoenix Park. Cork scored the first point after 15 minutes of Wexford pressure; Wexford returned with a rushed goal forced from a high ball to go 1-1 to 0-1 ahead at half-time. Cork had a point from a free at the start of the second half.

Then Cork won the ball from a kick-out. The ball was punched back to the goalkeeper's hands, he cleared it to the sideline, and the fun began.

A Cork player fouled a Wexford man and kicked him on the ground. The spectators, never ones in those days to restrain themselves from joining in, invaded the field to exact retribution from the Corkman. Cork, who were playing with what used to be called "the incline," felt they had a good chance before the fracas. They were also becoming incensed at the chants of the Wexford supporters: "North Cork Mili-tia, North Cork Mili-tia."

Dromtarriffe were being taunted with the dastardly deeds of the North Cork yeomen stationed in Wexford in the aftermath of the 1798 rebellion!

Dromtarriffe refused to play on when the referee decided to send a player off from each side and tried to get the teams to resume with substitutes to replace the casualties of the riot.

Thomas Hayes' Wexfordmen got into position and when Cork did not reappear, the match was awarded against them.

Some good points emerged from the disaster. For the first time three brothers played together on an All-Ireland winning team, Tom, John, and Pat O'Connor of Wexford. Nick Lacey emerged as the leading Wexford footballer of his time. Wexford goalkeeper Thomas Maloney-Redmond was one of the first players to turn the position into a specialist area of its own. Thomas "Hoy" Redmond was the star of the side, the epitome of old-style football who campaigned that catching the ball should be abolished when Dublin teams such as Young Irelands developed the tactic.

And this was the first appearance in an All-Ireland final by Tom Irwin of the new pro-Parnellite club Redmonds, the outstanding Cork sportsman of his generation. Irwin won an 1892 All-Ireland hurling medal, played in three football finals, was one of the best cricketers in the country, was in line for an Irish rugby cap at one stage, and later served as Cork county secretary for 21 years.

DESPERANDUM DESPERADOES

In 1894 Irwin joined Nils. Nils Desperandum was a rugby club that switched to Gaelic in 1887 and immediately became a leading force in the game in Munster. In the 1894 Cork county championship their first and second teams met in the county semi-final. They eventually took the title and with players like Irwin and John O'Leary swept through the Munster championship. They went on to beat Tipperary twice. Arravale Rovers of Tipperary (with many Bohercrowe players amongst them) successfully objected to an illegal Kerry team in the semi-final, then found three of the Kerry players playing against them in the final for the Cork Nils selection.

The objection did not do them any good. Tipperary, who were beaten by 0-6 to 0-2 the first day, lost by 2-4 to 0-2 the second day.

Dublin Young Irelands were back in the fold, and they too had to replay the Leinster final as brazen new opposition in Meath began to show its strength.

The two Young Irelands clubs from Dublin and Wexford met in the Leinster semi-final, an initial meeting on August 12th having fallen through because Wexford could not get a special train to Dublin.

Dublin dished out one of the heaviest defeats ever inflicted on reigning All-Ireland champions when they won 1-11 to nil in a clean game where the referee only had to intervene twice "the second time to issue a mild reprimand."

The other semi-final was more rancorous. Kilkenny captain John Fitzgerald was bitter about his side's defeat, and wrote to the papers saying that he did not expect Meath to show and the team "had to select substitutes from the sideline."

Dublin and Meath drew 0-4 each in the final, as Dublin were accused of a lot of dirty play while Meath came back from 0-4 to nil down. The crowd at Clonturk Park was the biggest since Dublin v Tipperary in 1890, and had its problems.

As *Sport* complained:

> No one can blame a schoolboy or a street urchin for climbing a wall to see a game, but it was truly galling and humiliating to see the number of respectable looking men who adopted this means.

Nobody was allowed to stand at the Richmond Road end of the ground.

Fading light prevented the replay in Navan from going into extra time as Meath came back from 0-2 to nil down to draw 0-2 each. After the match Mr McAtumney, who owned the ground, entertained the Dublin team and they were later brought to Nugent's for a meal. A previous tie fixed for November 4th in Navan fell through when captain John

Kennedy withdrew the Young Irelands team.

Dublin had a little luck to help them beat Meath at the third attempt. They played with the wind in the first half, and when the teams changed the wind not only died down but changed sides, leaving Dublin comfortable 1-8 to 1-2 winners. Meath had a little fortune themselves in scoring their goal from a double free-kick, retaken after some play.

The lucky streak continued. Young Irelands were extremely lucky to be awarded the 1894 All-Ireland title, as it was they who walked off the field at a stage when Cork were leading by two points. Dublin withdrew from the replay because the crowd were not "under control." The *Freeman's Journal* would support this view:

> Order was very fair until the last ten of fifteen minutes when the throng in their enthusiasm broke in and as twelve of the Young Irelands (Dublin) players were assaulted by some Cork supporters and the feeling of the crowd getting somewhat heated, disorder then reigning supreme, the Young Irelands refused to continue.

In vain, Cork argued that only the striking of a Corkman by a Dubliner caused the riot. But the Central Council agreed with Dublin and ordered a second replay at a subsequent meeting.

Not everybody was aware that the mammoth contest was to be replayed. When the teams arrived in Thurles they found two club teams ready to take the field unaware that the replay was fixed for that day. Dublin had Jack Kirwan in action for the last time that day. He went on to play soccer for Tottenham Hotspur and was capped 17 times for Ireland.

A record crowd of 10,000 offered the GAA a preview of the days of mass support which were just a decade away. They were attracted by the prospect of another thriller, like the one in Clonturk Park that had resulted in a draw, the finest game in the history of the championship till then. Cork were losing by five points to one when they earned the replay with an easy goal; the Dublin goalkeeper missed the ball completely, mainly due to having to play "with a Corkman hanging around his neck."

It was 13-stone Dick Curtis, six times Irish wrestling

champion, who got Dublin's equaliser after moving to the "extreme forward position." They talked about Curtis with affection in later years: "The longest hour was a holiday to him when men were men."

Then, in the exciting closing stages Cork had another goal disallowed and Dublin's Luke Kelly hit the post. Cork refused to play extra time, claiming that the referee "had played 40 minutes instead of 30 in the second half," and Dublin were awarded the match. Two awarded titles in one year was a record, even by the standard of the times.

THE POINT THAT WASN'T

Cork were not impressed. They struck a special set of "All-Ireland champions" medals for Nils, withdrew from the GAA for 12 months and almost brought the organisation to bankruptcy as a result.

The game thrived locally in their splendid isolation. The number of clubs in Cork increased from 40 to 54, they took affiliations from Limerick and Waterford clubs and it appeared at one stage that they would set up a rival association. Limerickman Pat Ryan, the Mallow Town Park committee, and eventually the Association's patron, Archbishop Croke, worked to bring Cork back into the fold.

Arravale Rovers of Tipperary were the obvious heirs apparent to the Munster title in the absence of Cork. They came through to beat Waterford by 2-7 to 0-1 and Limerick Commercials, who, with not a single survivor of the 1887 triumph on board, had trounced Kerry's Ballymacelligott by 5-6 to 1-1 in the semi-final.

Arravale brought the last one-club selection to play in an All-Ireland final. Their opponents were the Navan O'Mahoneys' Meath selection.

When Young Irelands were beaten by Ringsend club Isles of the Sea in the 1895 Dublin championship, John Kennedy lost his captaincy of Dublin. Isles began the customary clear-out that plagued county teams in the days when the champion club had sole control of selection. This augured well for the prospects of Meath's Navan O'Mahoneys.

Navan was spearheaded by Dick Blake, the polemicist and GAA official who was the cause of much rancour in the GAA at the time, particularly because of his clashes with Cork delegate Michael Dineen. Blake had played a leading role in the suspension of Nils, bringing about Cork's withdrawal from GAA affairs. He was also responsible for steering through a temporary reprieve on the ban on foreign sports, which was removed from GAA rule-books from 1896 to 1906. He also felt that the game needed to be changed.

The 17-a-side formation of 1 full-back, 2 quarter-backs, 5 half-backs, 2 wing men, and 9 forwards caused a continuous scrimmage that moved backwards and forwards along the field. Blake felt that the formation should be broken into clear lines with more space for players to move. Too much importance was still attached to a goal. Blake master-minded the rule changes of February 1896:

> Goal to be made equal to three points.
> Scores direct from a sideline throw to be banned.
> Opposing players to be required to be outside the 21 yard line for kick-outs.
> Players to remain in their own half of the field while the ball is being kicked out from their own goal.
> The forty-yard kick [later the 50] to be awarded when a player sends the ball over his own end line, taken from opposite where the ball crossed the line.
> A goal stopped by a by-stander to be allowed if the referee adjudges that the ball would have crossed the line otherwise.
> A player who gets bottled up to concede a hopped ball.
> The goalposts to be 21 feet wide, the cross-bar 8 feet high, and the point-posts 21 yards on either side of the [still soccer-style] goals.
> Dress to be defined as knee-breeches, stockings and boots.
> Nails and iron tips on boots to be banned.

The 1895 championships were already under way when the rules were decided upon. Cavan made their first and only Leinster championship appearance that year in a handsome rig-out of pink knicks and white jerseys. Cavan, who could find no opposition in Ulster at the time, led 0-1 to nil at half-time against Louth, having pressed for much of the first half.

But three quick points early in the second half upset their hopes of a historic breakthrough and Louth won by 0-5 to 0-1.

Making its last appearance as a venue was Clonturk Park where the second-round match between Kildare and Louth on November 10th 1895 was staged. P P Sutton's report gives a clear idea of why it had to be abandoned in the end:

> Encroachment of the crowd during play was simply deplorable. Non-paying classes of the community scaled the walls. The club that has the greatest following usually gets there in this arena.

Not that Maurice Butterly's Pleasure Grounds on Jones' Road, tried out for the first time a week earlier, were much more successful. The grounds, later to become Croke Park, had only one gate and the crush at the semi-final between Dublin and Kildare reminded one journalist of "boxing night at the Old Royal." Making a first appearance in the Leinster final were the coloured flags for umpires to signal scores, red for a goal and white for a point.

Meath eventually ended the Dublin reign in that final at Jones' road by 1-3 to 0-2, having led 0-2 to nil at half-time and won themselves no friends when they refused to allow a Dublin substitute on the field after Tom Knott was hurt. This was evidently a matter that had to be agreed between the teams at the time. Meath's refusal was couched in defiant terms: "no Isle will come in here." Sportswriter P P Sutton pondered: "This may be just. But is it manly or sportsmanlike?"

In the end Arravale defeated Meath with a controversial point-that-wasn't. The 1895 All-Ireland final made the reputation of Willie Ryan, whose exploits, according to Tipperary papers, included kicking one ball into the air, racing after it, catching it and launching the equalising score. Meath had led by three points to nil at half-time. Ryan scored all of Tipperary's four points, the winning one from a free with seven minutes to go.

One of the Tipperary substitutes, John Luddy, won the All-Ireland long-kick championship at half-time with a punt of 66 yards, two feet and four inches.

The referee, J J Kenny, was puzzled afterwards and wrote to the papers admitting a mistake: one of Tipperary's points should not have been allowed because it was scored from inside the 21-yard line. The much-féted story is difficult to check. But Meath did not demand a replay. Instead, Navan got to play for a set of medals from the Central Council because of the point-that-wasn't. The teams drew 0-5 each (although Meath felt they had scored six) before Tipperary settled the issue by winning 2-13 to 1-4 at the new Jones' Road, where "the rough surface contributed to the high scores."

LIMERICK'S LEAD

The evolution of the playing rules continued when the cross-bar was reduced from 10 and a half to eight feet and a goal was made equal to three points. But the game was still rough, tough and physical.

Dublin Young Irelands' first-round meeting with Wicklow in the 1896 championship was left unfinished because a Wicklow player refused to leave the field when sent off. "The Wicklow men played a game utterly unknown in Dublin," *Sport* commented. "They charged their opponents roughly and with an obvious intention to hurt." When the teams met again in the Croke Cup a special sub-committee was appointed to report on rough play by the teams.

Dublin weathered a great second-half fight-back by Kildare which brought them from 2-10 to nil down back to a respectable four-point defeat; then against Meath in the Leinster final they took control in the first half, went 1-4 to 0-1 ahead at half-time, and recaptured the title by 2-4 to 1-5.

Their All-Ireland opponents were Limerick Commercials, who surprised reinstated Cork by 1-2 to 1-1 and defending champions Tipperary by 2-4 to 0-6 before defeating Waterford by 0-4 to 0-1 in an unfinished provincial final in Mallow. Limerick's fourth point came when the ball rebounded off a spectator and Waterford walked off the field in protest, despite the fact that Limerick offered to forego the score.

52

Training had a lot to do with the Limerick success. Tall, wiry trainer Con Fitzgerald walked his charges six miles to Cratloe every Sunday for a practice match with the local team and then six miles home.

The clash brought a gate of £101/1/- and it was a big surprise that Limerick won by a point, 1-5 to 0-7. Their only goal was scored by Bill Murphy in the first half. The heavier Limerickmen fell back to defend their 1-4 to 0-3 lead. Dublin's star forward, Jack Ledwidge, knocked himself unconscious against massive 6'3" Limerickman Larry Roche, "like spray dashing against the Cliffs of Moher." Roche was a hefty weight-throwing champion who later was instrumental in changing the rules of the game.

Limerick added a free after half-time and played defensively, so much so that "the Dublin goalkeeper was playing in the centre of the field where his presence was often not needed."

Young Irelands spurned scoring chances to go for goals. One 40-yard free by distinguished captain, George Roche, grazed the crossbar. They regretted that miss as they lost by a point in the end. They were unfortunate to lose their best scorer, Bill Conlan, who got the first of two points after just 10 seconds before the players had dashed back into position from the throw-in.

Another massive crowd turned out to see Dublin Young Irelands beat previous All-Ireland champions, Arravale Rovers, by four points to three in the first Croke Cup final. It was a game that the old-timers recalled fondly for 40 years, some maintaining it was better than the 1903 All-Ireland and 1913 Croke Cup finals.

THE INSOMNIA FINAL

Having lost to one set of drapers for the All-Ireland championship, Young Irelands promptly lost to another set in Dublin. C J Kickhams promptly cleared out all except Luke Kelly of the 1896 All-Ireland final team. They also had the advantage of Limerick Commercials star of 1896, William Guiry, who transferred to Dublin and went on to score two goals as the Kickhams selection beat Cork in the All-Ireland final.

Seven of the new Dublin team worked in Clerys, four in Arnotts, and one each in Todds and the Henry Street warehouse.

The Leinster championship started with a hiccup when Longford and Westmeath were included in the draw but subsequently found not to be affiliated. Then Kickhams' new Dublin team ran into problems in the semi-final because one of their players, Canavan, played for both Meath and Dublin in the championship. But they survived to earn a replay because Wexford withdrew 10 minutes from the end of the semi-final in protest at a free awarded against them.

The final was the scene of more controversy. Wicklow, champions for four days in 1889, went three days better in 1897 when they became Leinster champions for a week. The final was fixed for October 30th, alongside the All-Ireland hurling semi-final between Kilkenny and Galway, but torrential rain reduced the track around the Jones' Road grounds to a muddy mess, and the field was not much better. Dublin presumed the match would not be played and went home.

The referee awarded a walk-over to Wicklow but the following meeting of the Central Council ordered the match to be refixed for November 13th. This time Wicklow would not play and sent word to that effect on Saturday evening at 7 o'clock. Dublin easily won the replay on December 18th by 1-9 to 0-3 after leading 1-8 to 0-2 at half-time.

In the All-Ireland final, Dublin's drapers (captained by Cork native P J Walsh who had played against Dublin in the controversial 1894 final) annihilated a defensive Cork Dunmanway selection by 2-6 to 0-2 in the final in front of an attendance that included some special guests—the Irish and English rugby teams. Cork often had a single forward against Dublin's massed defence.

Cork had a good excuse for their defeat. After travelling from West Cork from early Saturday morning, they arrived at 2 a.m. in the city to find that, by accident or design, nobody had booked them into a hotel; various jarveys were bringing them from house to house without showing much enthusiasm for allowing them to sleep. They wandered the streets until 4 a.m. when they gained admittance to a hotel in Amiens St.

LEDWIDGE'S DUO

Defending champions Dublin went through more sweeping changes in 1898. Geraldines took over the team selection, and Matt Rea the captaincy, and Tom "Darby" Errity was back. Dublin faced a protest over an illegal player, but beat Wexford so convincingly by 2-6 to nil in the unfinished Leinster final that it did not matter. The game ended in a brawl, as the referee reported:

> In the second half, after 20 minutes play, a Dublin and a Wexford player had a small row at the sideline which I think could easily have been quelled but for the intervention of an outsider who rushed in and struck the Wexford player.

In the "interests of the Association" the referee called the match off!

Dungarvan club Erin's Hope, one of the dominant clubs in Waterford county since the GAA was founded, won their only Munster title in the most convincing manner possible in 1898. Despite the fact that Dungarvan still had a rival club claiming to be Waterford champions at the time because the county board was split, they beat Tipperary by nine points to nil and Fermoy's Cork selection by 1-11 to 1-3 in a historic final at Lismore. Limerick and Clare were both disqualified for failing to field in a first-round match: they arranged between themselves to play in Limerick rather than Tipperary to cut costs.

Everything was reported to be in order for the final in Tipperary:

> Even the workhouse wall which used to be availed of in the past by visiting non-paying spectators who did not dread the brand of that institution so long as it saved them gate money.

There were to be no more upsets. Dublin beat Waterford

55

by 2-8 to 0-4 in the final, Jack Ledwidge struck just before half-time and again in the second half with goals that foiled the rags-to-riches story. Ledwidge went on to play for Shelbourne and won two Irish caps in 1906. Left wing Bill Sherry, who came from Bellewstown, Co Meath, was followed by a massive group of young fans wherever he played with Geraldines or Dublin.

The Central Council was by now half-considering winding up the GAA and leaving its organisation to the county boards because of financial problems and organisational ineptitude. The 1899 All-Ireland final may have changed its mind, as special trains brought valuable shillings from Dublin, Limerick, Lismore and Waterford.

MESSY END TO THE CENTURY

Cork won back the Munster championship in 1899, thanks to the old custom that each side provide a ball for one half of the match. Cork played with their ball in the first half of the first final with Tipperary. They trailed 2-1 to 0-1 at half-time, cutely demanded Tipperary's ball for the second half, and when Tipperary were unable to produce one said theirs had burst. The referee P J Hayes dispatched a messenger to the town 20 minutes later. He failed to return and the matter ended there although it does appear that Cork agreed that a second half-hour would be played in Cork.

The replay lasted 30 minutes as well: at half-time Tipperary (trailing 1-2 to 0-1 and without their star footballer Willie Ryan) insisted that aggregate scores over the two matches be counted, which would leave them 2-2 to 1-3 winners, and refused to continue. Tipperary did not agree with the decision to stage a second replay, and when 12 Tipperarymen defected, nobody really believed the newspapers when they attributed it to the weather. Cork beat a makeshift Tipperary team by 3-11 to 0-1 in a downpour before a large crowd.

In Leinster, Dublin beat Wexford by 1-7 to 0-3 in the provincial final, thanks to a goal from Pat Fitzsimons after just five minutes that put them 1-4 to nil ahead at half-time, despite "not playing up to standard."

The 1899 All-Ireland final between Geraldines' Dublin selection and the Fermoy's Cork selection was the poorest in the history of the championship so far. Jack Ledwidge scored an early goal and at half-time Dublin led by 1-7 to 0-2. Tom Irwin inspired a Cork comeback in the second half but Dublin won by 1-10 to 0-6. It was poor value for Cork fans who paid a return fare of 1/3.

The championship had fallen into total chaos. The Dublin county secretary, Frank Burke, first learned in the newspapers that his county had been fixed to play Queen's County. And what's more, Geraldines had already represented Dublin there and won!

Wexford were disqualified for not turning up to play Meath (the first they heard about the fixture was their notice of disqualification). To add to the confusion, they were later rescheduled to play against King's County instead!

The malaise reflected the state of GAA organisation generally. Having alienated the clergy in 1891 (although Croke was attending games again from 1895 on, all but two of the hierarchy were still suspicious of the Association and there were allegations of clerical opposition right up to 1906), the Association appeared to have alienated the Fenians as well. Dublin had only 20 affiliated clubs in 1899. It was chronically short of money (for which Blake was blamed). It got a boost from the revival of nationalism that came with the 1798 centenary celebrations, but was in no position to consolidate or build upon it.

In early August 1900 both Wexford and Kilkenny boards threatened to leave the GAA unless the organisation was improved. Watt Hanrahan, a Wexfordman, suggested that provincial councils take over the running of the provincial championships. The September 1900 Congress approved the suggestion, and Leinster Council was formed in October 1900.

And so the GAA survived into a new century. For a young body it had survived a frightening series of crises, a country-wide split caused by the IRB take-over in 1887, the mass defection of rank-and-file members over the 1891 Parnell split, the withdrawal of support by the all-powerful Catholic clergy, the apathy of the politicians, and an attempt by leading officials to wind it up altogether.

SHAM-ROGUERY

Clonmel Shamrocks were entrusted with the task of atoning for Tipperary's humiliation in 1899. They did so spectacularly, winning the 1900 All-Ireland and committing hara-kiri in a row with the Central Council afterwards. Tipperary beat Cork by the hardly extravagant scoreline of three points to one, and then beat Limerick by 2-4 to 2-1. Kerry's Laune Rangers selection, including such strange names as P E Valkenburg, showed "lack of training" in the Munster final, and Tipperary won by 1-13 to 1-3.

Meanwhile, Kilkenny's slate quarries team, and most notably Pat Wall, were winning the county's second Leinster championship comfortably. They beat Carlow by 2-11 to nil, Wexford by five points to four, and in the Leinster final trounced Louth by 12 points to nil.

Defending champions Dublin ran into an internal dispute. The Geraldines refused to travel and Kickhams had to field for the first-round tie against Wexford at short notice, their one-club selection losing by 1-7 to 0-8. After that most attention focused on the Kilkenny-Wexford semi-final, played at the strange-sounding location of Christendom, to where the Slate Quarries team travelled from Carrick-on-Suir by train. Two invasions by the rather unchristian spectators interrupted the game—Kilkenny claimed one of their points had really been a goal and another point should not have been disallowed.

There were other protests: Wicklow objected to Louth in the other semi-final, and Meath felt aggrieved because not one of the Drogheda Independents side that beat Stamullen's selection came from north of the Boyne. They were all technically resident in County Meath!

But the biggest protest of all came from Tipperary after Kilkenny defeated them by 1-6 to 0-7 in the All-Ireland semi-final. Tipperary objected that five of the Kilkenny players lived on *their* side of the border. Tipperary won the All-Ireland final with the help of these five moving quarrymen: Jim Cooney, Pat Wall, Dan Harney, Bill O'Toole and Jack Shea.

When a replay was ordered, Tipperary selected five "Grangemockler" players: the same five, including Jack Shea who had been sent off playing *against* them. Kilkenny refused to turn out.

Theoretically, the beaten "home" finalists Tuam Krugers could have objected to Tipperary and won the title. Instead they offered little opposition, a bitter row over a county final between Tuam and Dunmore led to Dunmore refusing to release their players for the final and Tuam then refused to hand over team selection to the county board. Having qualified for the All-Ireland final without playing a match, Tuam managed just one point with their own club selection, strengthened with a few players from Caherlistrane, Ballinasloe, Galway city and Athenry, and lost by 2-20 to 0-1.

Britain had been declared a province of Ireland at the previous congress with an irony befitting the nationalist GAA and that meant that London Irish got a bye into the All-Ireland final for the first time. The team, which included Sam Maguire and his brother John, arrived at 2 a.m. on the Sunday morning and had a few hours' sleep in the North Star hotel before the match.

Tipperary's Davey Smith scored the goal that started a 3-6 to 0-2 landslide and Tipperary went on to lead 2-2 to nil at half-time.

Distinguished guests at the match included J C Harrington, Lord Mayor of Dublin, and Westminster MP James McCann. The politicians were beginning to support the GAA again. In July 1902 Tom O'Donnell MP attended the Kerry convention. Willie Duffy in Galway, Willie Redmond in Clare, and William McKillop in Armagh all donated cups. Being seen at GAA matches was becoming part of the Irish politicians' survival code.

DUAL-STAR DOLPHINS

Back at full strength under the leadership of captain Dan Holland of Ringsend's Isles of the Sea, Dublin deposed Leinster champions Kilkenny by 3-13 to 1-2 in the first round of the 1901 championship and never looked back. They beat Louth twice in the semi-final, because the match was replayed on an objection, and Wexford by 1-9 to 0-1 in the Leinster final, Michael Whelan having taken the pass from his brother to score a first-half goal.

Before the All-Ireland home final against Cork, played in Tipperary, Dan Holland resigned not just the captaincy but his place on the Dublin team to David "Gush" Brady of Dolphins. At first, this surprise move seemed to have backfired. Dublin trailed Cork 0-1 to 0-3 at half-time but a goal at the start of the second half earned them a narrow victory. The match was delayed because Dublin's train arrived late. Dublin were invited to a reception in the Mansion House afterwards, a sign that nationalists were at last enjoying some political power in Ireland.

Thanks to the Dolphins' influence, this Dublin team was more ecumenical than ever before, enjoying the temporary reprieve of the ban on foreign games. Val Harris of Terenure Sarsfields went on to play for Shelbourne and Everton and was capped twenty times by Ireland in soccer. P McCann played for Belfast Celtic and Glenavon and won seven caps.

But defeated finalists Cork had versatile sportsmen too. Con Walsh, who drove the heavy leather ball of the time 69 yards and two feet to win a long kick championship in 1902, went on to win a bronze medal for Canada in the hammer at the 1908 Olympics.

Mayo took part in their first All-Ireland semi-final, having beaten Galway by 2-3 to 0-3 in the first Connacht final at Claremorris despite a great display by Galway captain J J Nestor.

The Connacht Council was established at a meeting in Ryan's hotel afterwards. R Marsh was Mayo's star, and Willie Parsons captained the side. Tom Patten opened the scoring for Galway who had earlier beaten Roscommon by five points to three. In the semi-final against Cork a Mayo player "got a fit on the field" and Cork got a fit in the second half, running up a scoreline of 4-16 to 0-1 after leading by just 0-5 to 0-1 at half-time. Two players were sent off.

Ulster had their first representatives in action since Cavan played in the 1895 Leinster championship. Dublin led 0-8 to nil at half-time against Antrim and had a Madigan goal at the start of the second half to help them to a 2-12 to 0-2 win. The Ulster championship had been confined to Antrim clubs. In the final Tír na nÓg beat Red Hand by 3-5 to 2-5 at Belfast a week before the semi-final.

BRAY, CO DUBLIN!

The end of Tipperary's greatest era was at hand, although in 1902 they recaptured the Munster title against a county which was emerging as one to watch. The Munster final on October 4th 1903 against Kerry was a draw, 0-4 each. Tipperary narrowly won the replay by 1-6 to 1-5. Three Tipperary veterans from 1889, Willie Ryan, Bob Quane and Dan Quane starred in this last championship fling. Willie Ryan proved the star of the replay.

"Handsome, debonair," P D Mehigan was to say of Ryan, "he was the darling of the time and the team. He stood head and shoulders above great players. A tireless, brainy footballer with craft and pace, he beat whole teams by his own individuality. He would tear through big men on his way to the goal. He could kick at fine length with either foot—on ground, overhead, and across his shoulder."

But the days of Willie Ryan and his "tearing through big men" was coming to an end. Dublin football was considerably more advanced than its country cousins as a result of the efforts of Young Irelands, Isles of the Sea, and Kickhams. Mehigan wrote:

When I went to Dublin in 1900 I found the attractive catch-and-kick style dominant. Players rarely handled a ball in the West Cork fields of my youth. Half the team in those distant days crowded around midfield and swept the ball with them goalward. Rivals met in waves.

Into this fray came a group of Wicklowmen. A tournament in Greystones, where they beat the powerful Terenure Sarsfields, convinced Bray Emmetts that they should concentrate their efforts on winning the Dublin championship. Bill Sherry was among those attracted to the town. Jack Dempsey, born in Monamilla, Co Wexford, captained Bray to their first county title in April 1903. Bray selected nine outsiders on the Dublin team, and, despite the fact that Wicklow have never won a provincial title, went on to win the All-Ireland.

A crowd invasion stopped the Leinster final at Carlow with 13 minutes to go, but Dublin, 2-5 to 0-2 leaders at the time, won the replay by 1-5 to 0-5 in Kilkenny. All 12 counties had competed.

Tipperary's Willie Ryan got the crucial first goal after 15 minutes against Galway in the semi-final and Bill Barrett added a second to go 2-1 to 0-1 ahead at half-time. Defending champions Mayo actually retained the Connacht title later in the year. The Mayo team was selected by Charlestown in 1902 and beat Galway by 2-1 to 0-2 despite Galway claims that one of their points was actually a goal.

The long grass hindered play in the other semi-final in Drogheda, where against Dublin "Armagh's dribbling tactics were spoiled by the luxuriant sward." Dublin led 1-10 to 1-3 at half-time.

Pat "Cocker" Daly was the star of Dublin's 0-6 to 0-5 victory over Tipperary in the home final. An exceptional performance, including the scoring of the two points that helped Dublin come from behind to win, saved his team.

The ball burst in the Dublin square after just five minutes of play. It was Willie Ryan's last fling for Tipperary, and he opened the scoring before Grace, Jack Dempsey and Stephen Mulvey sent Dublin 0-3 to 0-1 ahead at half-time.

The sides were level twice in an exciting second half. A delay to enable Tipperary to find a sub for an injured player "did not help the state of the ground, already considerably diminished in width by the spectators." Tipperary later beat Dublin 0-7 to 0-3 in a testimonial game for Tom Kiely.

Cork's Lower Park was the venue for the final proper,

when Dublin beat London by 1-8 to 0-4.

Thus another era ended with neither a bang nor a whimper. Tipperary and London represented the power-base of 1890s Gaelic football. At the end of 1903 it was Kerry's combination, selected from Tralee and Killarney clubs, which was generating a lot of interest as possible successors to the Willie Ryans and Tom "Darby" Erritys of the time. Their disciplined passing style had won them a lot of admirers in the Munster final, the orders of their Killarney Crokes captain Eugene O'Sullivan being "quickly and heartily responded to."

Ponderous comparisons were made with J P O'Sullivan's Laune Rangers but one sportswriter concluded: "Changes in the rules are so many and the field work so different that such a task could not be attempted." Critics wrote of the Kerry 1902 team: "A fine athletic lot they were, whose very appearance inspired confidence." Much, much more was in store for Kerry GAA.

Chapter Four

Into the Spectator Age

THE 1903 O'THREE

The rule makers had boobed. Instead of working to promote and improve the game, they were arguing over the small print of Irish nationalism and whether British police should be allowed to become members. Meanwhile, Gaelic football in 1902 was only slightly more attractive to watch than the mud-wrestling bouts of 15 years earlier. Young Irelands' practice sessions in the Phoenix Park had shown that footballers could do better. In 1903 the players really took the game in hand.

In preparation for the 1903 All-Ireland home final, they started to try out new experiments, new tactics. Kildare footballer Michael Kennedy tried dropping the ball on to the toe, to be gathered again at stride's end with the hands. His colleagues worked on an open-palmed pass along the ground that enabled a wet, sodden and misshapen leather ball to be propelled much more accurately. And sprints, leap-frogs, and route marches were introduced to increase stamina and flexibility on the playing-field.

Because so many innovations occurred at once, the 1903 All-Ireland home final became the most significant in the history of Gaelic football.

Kildare and Kerry teams started regular three-times-a-week practice sessions for the first time in the history of the game. Kildare's captain Joe Rafferty even brought a football with him on the lands where he worked as a cowherd!

The teams were mirror images of each other. Both buried club rivalries for the honour and glory of the county team. Kerry evolved from Tralee/Killarney club rivalry and Kildare grew out of high-standard contests between Clane and Roseberry (Newbridge) clubs.

Training was first tried for the Kerry team under Eugene Sheehan in 1902, but by the start of the 1903 championship his role had been superseded by the less commanding, but probably equally powerful, Tim Gorman. The county's 10 newcomers included 16-year-old Cork-born scoring forward Dick Fitzgerald. The combined Killarney and Tralee forces had help from Denny Breen of Castleisland and a Kilmacthomas, Co Waterford-born athlete and bank official, Rody Kirwan, who was shifted from New Ross (where he had already been selected for the county team) to Castleisland just in time for the 1903 championship.

Not many people paid attention to the success of this Kerry team in the Munster championship. Kerry beat Waterford by 4-8 to 1-3 in the first round, Clare by 2-7 to 0-3 at Limerick, and Cork in the Munster final by 1-7 to 0-3. The Poor Law elections, in which local politics was given a chance to prove itself in rural areas, had fuelled new nationalism which helped the GAA in the south west. In a natural progression, support for the new Munster champions was then effectively drummed up by the nationalist Tralee newspaper.

Kildare had also the co-operation of a nationalist press. There, a Cork-born county secretary, Dick Radley, had re-organised structures in the county. Newbridge men almost all worked for the Dominicans on the farm and school at Newbridge College. The Clane men were working for the Jesuits at Clongowes College. They played football in their spare time at the colleges.

Their captain, commanding Naas man Joe Rafferty, did not belong to either group, so the rivalry between north and south was stymied. A strong Newbridge man, Frank "Joyce" Conlan accompanied him in midfield. Two speedy Clane forwards, Jack Dunne and Jem Scott, led the attack. Bill Merriman, who was to keep playing into his 40s, was the principal defender. The young Newbridge goalkeeper Jack Fitzgerald was a committed Fenian, intent that fitness and endeavour on the football field were all just a prelude to the eventual fight for Ireland's freedom.

They showed the first signs of things to come when they heavily defeated champions Dublin by 3-11 to 1-3 at Geashill. Dublin had just five of the team that won the 1902 All-Ireland championship, because Keatings had taken over Bray Emmetts in selecting the team.

In the Leinster semi-final Kildare had an easy 4-5 to 0-1 victory over newly-renamed Laois (after a 1903 proposal of J Dooley from Offaly, that King's County and Queen's County be called Offaly and Laois for GAA purposes), and had to play Kilkenny three times in the final. The first match finished 1-2 to 0-5; at half-time in the replay, however, they trailed 1-4 to 0-1, but came storming back to win with a Jack Dunne goal—pending an objection over a disputed Kilkenny point.

Dublin official J O'Shea disagreed with the decision and for the first time in 18 years a referee's decision was overturned in Leinster, by the new provincial council. The dispute only drew further attention to the exciting changes that were occurring in Kildare football. Kildare was better served than most by a network of local stations and the railways of the time. Excursion trains carried 5,000 people who saw Kildare win the championship by 0-9 to 0-1 at the third attempt. Kilkenny's only point, from Tom Hyland, resulted from a Kildare player kicking the ball in the wrong direction!

There were three draws in the Ulster final, too. But this time the explosion in support was curtailed by the hostility of the Great Northern Railway Company. The Great Northern refused to run an excursion for the final between Cavan and Armagh on April 10th so the match was fixed for Easter Monday. The attendance was large, 3,000, the teams drew five points each on two occasions, and although miserable weather kept it down the second day, the estimated 7,000 turn-out for the second replay was a new record. Cavan won by eight points to five at Newbliss.

Ulster could not hope to compete at national level despite the new interest in the game up north. Despite being on the wrong side of an eight points to nil scoreline, Cavan goalkeeper Reilly was the star of the semi-final performance against Kildare. The hurling semi-final was played the same day and it took half an hour to clear the field so the football match could be started.

Considering the fame that the Kerry team has been accorded in retrospect, the Mayomen of 1903 deserve some credit. In the other semi-final Kerry narrowly led Mayo 1-1 to 0-3 at half-time but pulled away in the second half for a four-point victory. Even though Mayo contested the 1903 All-Ireland semi-final they were not Connacht champions. Galway were awarded the Connacht title without kicking a ball, when Mayo and Roscommon were both found to be illegal.

Not much attention was paid to the initial battle between the new powers. When they met in Tipperary the *Freeman's Journal* accorded only 21 lines to the match, most of that describing the confusion at the end. The crowd constantly spilled onto the badly-fenced field. Kildare led 0-2 to 0-1 at half-time, a Kildare goal by "Joyce" Conlan led to a 15-minute dispute with Kerry claiming that the ball had been played along the wing behind the spectators who were well beyond the sidelines, and then a Dick Fitzgerald goal for Kerry with two minutes to go led to another crowd invasion. Although the umpire, Mr Lundon, raised the white flag, his colleague disagreed that Kildare goalkeeper Jack Fitzgerald was over the line when he stopped the ball. With the final score at 1-4 to 1-3 for Kerry, referee Pat McGrath did not give a decision.

In contrast to the match itself, extensive newspaper coverage was given to the aftermath of that game and a lengthy dispute over where the replay should be held. Cork was agreed as a venue for the replay only after two Central Council decisions in favour of Jones' Road, despite complaints that "it was little better than an open plain." Kerry refused to play there. A suggestion that the replay be played in London's Crystal Palace did not gain any support.

Meanwhile the teams were now in special training. Like the news that Blackburn Olympic had gone to Blackpool for special training before the 1883 English FA Cup final, the question of special training raised serious ethical questions for the GAA. The Association effectively sanctioned special training by giving grants to the teams after the matches. But, unlike soccer, professionalism did not result.

Kildareman Jack Murray put his foot through the ball with one almighty kick in that replay! It was the best of the three games, and maybe the best in the history of the game so far. Kerry took an 0-5 to 0-3 half-time lead but Kildare saved the game with a great Jack Connolly goal four minutes from the end, when only four Kildare players touched the ball from the kick-out at the other end. This was followed by an inspirational save by goalkeeper Jack Fitzgerald from Kerry's Jim "Thady" O'Gorman. At first the referee announced Kerry had won but realised his mistake and announced a draw, Kerry 0-7 Kildare 1-4, before the cheering had died down.

There was another bout of council chamber disputes, some rousing "not an inch" speeches from either side, and a couple of delightful newspaper parodies.

Only the third match saw any adequate provision for the unprecedented crowds who came to watch the matches. In contrast many on the special trains travelling to Cork for the second meeting saw only the second half. For the third match it was reported that:

> Players had no reason to fear any encroachment of the ground as the paling was firmly put down and during the course of the game there was nobody but officials and press on the inside grounds.

Third time out there was no mistake as Kerry led 0-3 to 0-2 at half-time, and then scored five points without reply in the second half to win by 0-8 to 0-2, including one from an extraordinarily acute angle by Dick Fitzgerald. Kildare's first point that day was an "own point" scored by Kerry's Rody Kirwan.

Kerry had regrouped intelligently to gain their victory. Joe Rafferty was marked by two Kerrymen the third day. Rafferty had been blamed for sending a free wide off the upright the second day, a miss that cost Kildare victory, by taking the kick himself instead of allowing Frank "Joyce" Conlan or Jem Scott take it.

The phrase "Up Kerry" was invented for the game. According to *Kerryman* writer Pat Foley, it was borrowed from John Baily's local election cry in Ballymacelligott: "Up Baily." It was rare for the teams of the time to acknowledge the difficulty supporters might have distinguishing between them. Many county teams were made up of 21 players in their individual club colours. Kildare and Kerry were tapping on a local pride when they togged out in county colours. As well as a newly established local council, the brethren of Asdee and Waterville had a county team in common. Kildare dyed their boots white to match their white shirts and togs. Kerry wore red.

The GAA must have felt that all of its 21 birthdays so far had come together. After years of penury, the games brought riches beyond the Association's wildest dreams. Gate receipts at Tipperary were £123, at the replay in Cork were £187, and at the second replay at Cork £270. The grateful GAA allocated an extra £25 expenses to each team and presented defeated Kildare with gold medals to mark their achievement. Dick Fitzgerald reminisced: "In my long career I never remember [having] seen more determined games."

Credit must also go to the the first of the great GAA referees: Michael F Crowe, who controlled the games that set such a standard for future generations.

After all that excitement, few people paid any attention to Kerry's victory over London. They won by 10 points to three at Jones' Road.

KINGDOM'S THRONE

Kerry's semi-final tie in the 1904 Munster championship with Cork had taken place midway between the second replay of the 1903 All-Ireland home final and the final proper. Cork objected that a Kerry player who had been sent off rejoined the play, but the objection was overruled and Kerry's 1-4 to nil win allowed to stand. Other Munster teams wanted a share of the action. For their first-round match in Limerick, Clare football supporters hired a steamer to bring them from West Clare up the Shannon estuary. Waterford sank Clare's bid in the semi-final and geared themselves up for greater things.

Then Kerry were almost thwarted in their finest hour. Four weeks after beating London-Irish to win the county's first All-Ireland title, they ran up against Tommy O'Halloran and his Clashmore selection from Waterford that included Paddy Kirwan, a younger brother of Rody's. Waterford took an 0-3 to 0-1 lead over Kerry early in the second half of the Munster final and eventually held Kerry to a draw, 0-3 each, despite having a man sent off. Waterford could have won—had not Tom Ducey missed a vital free kick at the end of the game.

At half-time in the replay Waterford trailed by only 0-2 to 0-1, largely because Kerry had hit the post with their best effort. Then came a goal five minutes into the second half, scored by one of the additions to the 1903 All-Ireland team, Billy Lynch, from which Waterford never recovered and Kerry went on to win by 2-3 to 0-2.

Kerry's All-Ireland semi-final was easier. Cavan beat Monaghan by 0-7 to 0-3 in the Ulster final, lost the title on a Monaghan objection, then won it again on appeal to the Central Council. Kerry defeated them by 4-10 to 0-1 at Jones' Road.

But it was in Connacht that standards were rising fastest. In 1904 Ballina Stephenites took over selection of the Mayo team from Castlebar Mitchels and then staged watershed challenge matches against All-Ireland champions Kerry. To universal surprise, they drew the first 0-1 each, then won 1-2 to 0-4 three weeks before the Connacht final. It became evident that this was a wise move when they beat Galway by 0-7 to 0-4 and Roscommon by 3-6 to 0-1 to win their third Connacht title in four years. When it really counted, in the All-Ireland semi-final, they lost by just two points, 0-8 to 1-3, to Dublin before 10,000 spectators in Athlone.

With selection back in the hands of Kickhams, Dublin got their revenge for the 1903 drubbing by beating defending Leinster champions Kildare by 0-9 to 0-5 in the first round. Kildare goalkeeper Jack Fitzgerald walked off the field because he objected to a free awarded against him. He later publicly apologised in a letter to the papers.

Dublin went on to beat Louth by 0-11 to 0-6 in Dundalk

and Kilkenny by a single point, 0-5 to 1-1, with the help of a few exiled Kilkenny players such as Jack and Pierce Grace. Despite the success of the All-Ireland final, crowd control was as bad as ever. Spectators were so far advanced on one side of the field at the Leinster final in Wexford that wing play was impossible. Kilkenny were enjoying a revival at the time, and were disappointed at not winning out in Leinster to complete a remarkable recovery from the previous year's Leinster final. Lamogue's Kilkenny selection had been formed in 1900, won the 1901 championship and gone to further greatness, coming back from three nil down to beat Wexford in the Leinster semi-final.

Although the glamour of the previous year was missing, the presence of Kerry in the All-Ireland final kept support levels at their new-found high. When the All-Ireland final took place at Cork, Kerry led by four points to two at half-time and Dick Fitzgerald got their second-half point to retain the title, by 0-5 to 0-2, despite having no organised training in the manner of 1903. Kerry also had a point disallowed for over-holding near the end. The match was disappointing, and commenced in a downpour that made the ball difficult to hold and the ground slippery. Within minutes an accident forced John Thomas Sullivan to retire and he was left unattended in the dressing-room for the duration of the game.

MIDSUMMER DREAM

Newspaper coverage, attracted to the new game by the Kildare-Kerry saga, whetted the public appetite for a repeat meeting of the rivals in 1905. Their hopes were realised when Kildare beat Leinster champions Dublin in August 1905, then beat Offaly in Geashill and started against Louth in the final playing with a blinding sun to help themselves into a 0-10 to 0-1 half-time lead, before having to defend it against a Louth onslaught that reduced the final margin to two points, 0-12 to 1-7. Wall and McCourt combined for a Louth goal and Bill Losty and Jem Scott points eventually saved Kildare.

Kilkenny were still struggling on in hope of a breakthrough. They beat Louth in the Leinster semi-final by

0-6 to 1-1, but as they had played an illegal player, a replay was ordered; this only heightened Kilkenny's grievances because the bizarre substitute referee settled all the disputes in this game by hopping the ball between players!

Dublin defeated London by 1-9 to 1-4 as nominees of Leinster in the All-Ireland quarter-final, but were out of the championship by the time the semi-final came round. Although there were no games played in Ulster, the *Anglo-Celt* claimed in 1907: "Cavan have now won the Ulster championship for three years in a row." The lack of competition did not help. Some of the selected Cavan team did not show up as the county went out by 4-16 to 0-2 to Kildare in the All-Ireland semi-final. A *Leinster Leader* columnist concluded: "Cavan would not even win the junior championship of Kildare."

Flushed by the challenge match success over Kerry the previous year, Mayo self-destructed. Roscommon shocked them by 0-7 to 0-5 to win their first Connacht championship. Mayo objected to their first ever Connacht championship defeat because there were no umpires or linesmen, though that does not seem to have been unusual at the time, and also because Roscommon played an illegal player.

Without Mayo, the semi-final was no longer the attraction it promised to be. A Roscommon goal from a free got the All-Ireland semi-final off to a great start but two goals just before half-time sent Kerry into a 2-4 to 1-3 lead and eventual 2-10 to 1-3 victory.

Kerry's challengers in Munster showed none of the promise or heart of Waterford the previous year. Cork initially gave Kerry a walk-over in the Munster semi-final— because the date clashed with a local St Finbarr's v Dungourney fixture! Kerry kept Limerick inside their own 25 for much of the Munster final.

With all of the pretenders out of the way, it was back to real business, Kildare v Kerry. The customary wrangle over the venue for the final took three Central Council meetings to resolve. Kildare refused to travel to Munster to play and at one stage the title was awarded to Kerry on a walk-over. Eventually, on a beautiful June afternoon in Thurles, Kerry and Kildare resumed their by now famous relationship. Kerry won the toss and chose to play against the breeze. That was a mistake. Kildare went 0-6 to 0-1 up at half-time and held on to win by 1-7 to 0-5.

Joe Rafferty's "deft punching" caused havoc at centre-field and Kildare got the game's only goal when Jack Connolly hit the crossbar, only to power his own rebound over the line "after a few minutes of life-and-death struggle." Wing play was credited with the victory. The telephone was used for the first time to send the result back to ecstatic Kildare.

Some letter-writers to the *Kerryman* attempted to blame the referee, but Austin Stack replied:

> I am sure I am voicing the opinion of the whole team when I say the referee's decisions at Thurles were, as they have always been, absolutely impartial.

That was a new departure, too, not blaming the referee when you are beaten. With the Kerry-Kildare rivalry came the first sense of sporting, mutual respect that the new code had found. After learning to bury club rivalries for the good of the county, it was only a step further to bury county rivalries, in victory or defeat, for the good of the game.

PROVINCIAL PUNDITRY

Public enthusiasm to see these deft-punching Kerrymen was responsible for the creation of two more competitions.

Famous 1900s referee, Mick Crowe, was an employee of the Great Southern and Western Railway Company. He prompted his employers to donate shields for an inter-provincial competition in 1905. The shields would remain in competition until they were won twice in succession, or three times in all. The football shield lasted just three years and the hurling four.

The footballers got the shields off to a great start. Leinster hurlers beat Munster in the first semi-final, 3-10 to 1-7, but the football semi-final between the same teams was drawn,

0-7 to 1-4. Three weeks after the 1905 trilogy between Kerry and Kildare in the All-Ireland football championship, Munster (with 11 Kerrymen) met Leinster (with 10 Kildaremen) in the replay. Kildare's Mick Fitzgerald kicked a point from 85 yards during that game, which Leinster won by eight points to five. Wexford's Mike Cummins became the first dual inter-provincial medallist when he played on two winning Leinster teams that year.

Munster footballers won both the 1906 and 1907 Shields and so got to keep the trophy.

The Croke Cup was much older, having been donated by the Association's first patron, Dr Croke, in 1896. It quickly became the GAA's second most prestigious competition. It was first organised on a knock-out basis parallel to the All-Ireland championship but caused so much fixture congestion that after victories by Dublin footballers in 1896 and Wexford footballers in 1897 the trophy was awarded to the All-Ireland champions. In 1904 the competition was revived, and London-Irish were invited to play in the Croke Cup rather than the All-Ireland final of 1904. In 1905 it was confined to the four beaten provincial finalists.

It was eventually discontinued in 1916 and was succeeded by the Wolfe Tone tournaments. Now the trophy is awarded to the National League champions.

URBAN ANSWERS

Dublin took the Leinster title back when they beat Kildare by 1-9 to 0-8 before 5,000 supporters at Kilkenny, with a late goal from Mick Madigan set up by Jack Grace. They had trailed 0-8 to 0-2 at half-time and the crowd spilled onto the field to join in as the match grew to an exciting climax.

By then Kildare had already been in action in the All-Ireland championship, against the Monaghan team that ended Cavan's run. Newblissman Paddy Whelan, Ulster chairman, solved the trains crux by travelling to the Railway Commission hearings in London on March 13th, 1908, to complain successfully about lack of facilities for GAA teams. The result was immediate. When Monaghan played Cavan at

Cootehill, the receipts were £44/12/6. Monaghan trailed 0-2 to 0-3 at half-time, but came back to win by 2-4 to 0-5. Cavan objected to Monaghan afterwards on seven separate grounds, none of which was upheld. Monaghan went on to beat Antrim by 2-10 to 1-2 in the Ulster final before a more typical gate of £12/10/-. The "difference in refereeing was a drawback," it was reported when Kildare beat Monaghan by 2-10 to 1-6 in Belfast.

Dublin got the nomination from Leinster and beat London by 2-7 to 0-3 in the semi-final at Wexford, London having held them to 0-2 each at half-time. In the other semi-final Cork beat Mayo by 0-10 to 0-6 at Limerick's Market's Field. Ballina made up for the previous year's lapse, thrashing both lethargic Galway by 2-16 to 0-1 and champions Roscommon by 2-13 to 0-5. Their star in the Connacht final was Davey Ryder, who ended a great rush "by neatly screwing a goal." Then Mayo gave the crowd eight minutes of excitement towards the end of their semi-final against Cork. Earlier in the game Cork had a player sent off, but a Mayo player followed him to the line after Cork got a score. Kerry were flagging from early in the year. A last-minute point brought them narrow victory over Tipperary, 0-7 to 1-3, in the semi-final. Then Cork stopped Kerry's four-in-a-row bid, by 1-10 to 0-3 at Tipperary. Cork had introduced a league system 12 months before and this contributed a lot to their performance.

In October 1907 Athy showgrounds was the new venue for the All-Ireland final as Dublin came from behind to beat Cork by 0-5 to 0-4 with points from Kelly and Walsh, having trailed three points to two at half-time. Giant Kerryman Paddy Casey, at 6'6" one of the tallest men to play in an All-Ireland final, strengthened the Dublin line-out.

TRAIN TROUBLES

Fermanagh is the only county in Ulster that never contested an All-Ireland semi-final, yet they almost did so in the 1907 championship. They were nominated by the Ulster Council after beating Monaghan in the Ulster championship in

January 1908. The anti-Sunday-sport timetable of the Great Northern Railway made it impossible for them to travel to Dundalk and Monaghan lined out instead. At half-time Dublin led by just 1-1 to 0-2, Monaghan having won the toss, but won eventually by 1-5 to 0-2. Then Fermanagh lost heavily to Cavan by 3-7 to 1-3 in Ulster's new Gold Medal Tournament, and three weeks later went down to Cavan by five points in the championship.

Antrim eventually won the 1907 Ulster championship, ushering in a new successful era. It was due in no small way to the decision in 1908 to set up a league for the city clubs, which gave them regular competition for the first time.

After an uncertain start against Down when they were held to a draw in the quarter-final at Newry, Antrim heavily defeated Cavan by 1-8 to 0-4 in the Ulster final. Cavan changed their selectors between the semi-final and the final. Drumlane players had initially refused to turn out for Cavan, but when Drumlane won the Cavan championship, 12 of the club side were selected to play against Antrim. The new team never recovered from a bad start, and trailed 1-3 to nil at half-time.

A blinding wind and hail storm spoiled the crucial tie in Leinster between Kildare and Dublin. Dublin won 0-11 to 0-7, and Kildare's claims that the Dublin goalkeeper had stepped over his own line were not upheld. Offaly reached their first final, a late goal foiling Meath by 1-6 to 0-4. Hugh Mallin, Jack, Peter and Joe Dunne all starred in Offaly's breakthrough. Dublin retained the championship by 1-10 to 0-4 with their scores coming from Paddy Cox and Michael Kelly.

Meath's quarter-final match with Kilkenny was abandoned in darkness the first day after a long delay caused by a Meath player breaking his leg. An ambulance ferried him to the Mater hospital. Wallis scored the replay goal for Meath.

In Munster, Cork beat Kerry by a convincing six points, 1-9 to 0-6, in the semi-final, scoring a goal just before half-time. Another powerful first-half performance helped them beat a Tipperary team that selected 13 Grangemockler men.

A rushed goal midway through the first half gave them a 1-7 to 0-1 lead. Their semi-final opponents Mayo disimproved, fell 2-10 to 0-2 behind, then walked off against Cork with seven and a half minutes to go when a free was not awarded to them.

Dublin's train was delayed on the way to Tipperary for the All-Ireland final, causing the match to start late for the second time in seven years. Their winning point was scored by Kilkennyman Pierce Grace, Dublin having led 0-6 to 0-2 at half-time.

In the Leinster final Kildare captain Jack Murray won the toss and played with the breeze in the first half and failed to get enough scores. Dublin had a charged goal from Jack Shouldice and Pat "Cocker" Daly midway through the second half for a 1-7 to 0-3 victory. Kildare had struggled against Louth, a last-minute point from Kit Brien forcing an 0-5 each draw where Murray got the vital goal in a 1-6 to 1-5 replay to win. Louth had struggled in the quarter-final against Kilkenny, three late points from Lynch earning a replay. The second meeting was impossible for spectators to follow: "owing to the rushing and swaying of the crowd."

In the All-Ireland semi-final Antrim's Fagan scored a point late in the first half to help them hold Dublin to 0-1 each at half-time, but lost by 1-8 to 0-2. Antrim's selection, from Belfast city clubs, played with a strong breeze in the first half. MacAuley's second-half goal ended their hopes.

Kerry put their 1904 jitters behind them, taking a half-time lead as they beat Waterford, newly reunited after a damaging three-year county board split, by 0-7 to 0-2. Waterford beat Cork by 1-7 to 1-2 with a late goal in the semi-final.

Mayo hoped to build on their achievements earlier in the decade. Players like Andy Corcoran worked to get Ballina's selection to inter-county standard. By 1909 they were probably at their peak but still unable to reach the All-Ireland final. The month after beating Roscommon in the Connacht final they held Kerry to one point to nil at half-time in Limerick but were beaten heavily. The following August they beat Kildare 0-7 to 0-4 in an unfinished Croke Cup final, to bring Connacht its first national trophy.

In the All-Ireland home final Dublin pulled away in the second half to beat Kerry, a 30-yard point from Daly having sent them narrowly ahead 0-3 to 0-2 at half-time. Hugh Hilliard, Martin Power, Tom MacAuley, Hilliard and Tom Walsh set off on a five-point spree in the second half to which Kerry's only reply was a point from Con Murphy too late to bring them back into the game. Dublin went on to beat London easily despite having a man sent off after 25 minutes. Pat "Cocker" Daly, undoubtedly the star of the championship, continued to play football until 1926, when he was 53 years old.

But Kerry were to go the whole way in 1909. They first won an acrimonious meeting with Cork in the Munster final. The first day, Kerry protested that the referee was allowing too much rough stuff and walked off the field. They were persuaded to return and lost the game by 2-8 to 1-7. But immediately afterwards they objected that one of the Cork players, Jerry Beckett, was a native of Kilgarvan who had returned and played for Kilgarvan in a tournament game in Kerry. Beckett argued that the tournament was an unofficial one, but that did not excuse him, and so Kerry earned a replay. In a superb replay at Cork, Cork-born Johnny Skinner scored the winning goal for Kerry. Receipts of £116 from the replay were donated to the family of former Tipperary footballer, Bob Quane, who had died suddenly in October.

In the Connacht final Eamonn Boshell's shot broke the crossbar in Mayo's 1-4 to 0-5 victory over Galway and play was held up for several minutes while it was being repaired. Earlier in the championship Sligo refused to travel to Mohill to play Leitrim "because of the rough treatment they had received on their previous visit to the venue." Kerry beat Mayo by 2-12 to 0-6 in the All-Ireland semi-final at Ennis in November.

The Ulster championship got off to a bad start when an Armagh player refused to leave the field after he was sent off, and the first-round match between Armagh and Monaghan was abandoned. When Monaghan played Antrim in the Ulster semi-final the referee complained that he feared there would be a riot if he sent off any of the Monaghan players!

Monaghan were suspended for 12 months after the match, a suspension lifted afterwards. Gates were still paltry: despite a 6d admission charge they totalled £49/4/10 for the championship. Belturbet's £9/10/- for the final, in which Antrim beat Cavan by 1-9 to 0-5, was the best: 380 spectators.

Kerry had new opponents in the All-Ireland final. Goals from Tom Mathews and Jack Carvin helped Louth beat Kilkenny by 2-9 to 0-4 for their first Leinster title, Kilkenny having led briefly by two points to one. Louth had beaten Dublin by 1-11 to 0-7 in the Leinster semi-final, and went on to beat Antrim by 2-13 to 0-15 in the All-Ireland semi-final, as Antrim put up a good display at Belfast and trailed by only 0-5 to 0-3 at half-time.

Kildare did not even compete in Leinster: a bitter dispute arose out of the Croke Cup final. Kildare were reported for refusing to continue playing against Mayo. They claimed they were waiting for the pitch to be cleared. Some of Kildare's Leinster rivals proposed they be suspended, so Kildare withdrew from the championship.

Against Louth in the final, Kerry completed a comprehensive victory with a brilliant last point from Johnny Skinner. The ball passed through four players without touching the ground...a feat worthy of comment at the time. Louth had started better with three points from Jack Carvin to go 0-3 to 0-1 up but Maurice McCarthy had Kerry's goal soon afterwards and Joe Quinn missed a chance of a goal for Louth in the first half leaving it 1-3 to 0-3 for Kerry at half-time, with the smell of victory everywhere.

When Dublin met London in heavy rain in the quarter-final, it was on one of the wettest days of the year. At the time of the throw-in, there was not a single spectator in the ground but as the rain eased eventually about 200 people arrived to watch. Another attendance record. The wrong sort. It was that sort of decade.

Chapter Five

Kerry's Gold

RULES ROOST

Collecting sixpences at the entrances to the playing-fields was turning into a profitable pursuit for the GAA. The great gate-rushes of the 1900s had shown up the potential of Gaelic football as a spectator sport. In 1909 the Association had collected £317/3/6 from 12,000 spectators at the Kerry v Louth final.

This was still smaller than rival spectator attractions. Dublin was staging an international rugby match each year. Pavilion facilities were better and admission charges were higher, but rugby receipts reached £1,200 on occasions. Soccer matches were being staged with more regularity in Dublin. Gaelic was still regarded as a countryman's game, but was making inroads on the capital. The GAA realised that the survival of the game depended on the organisation of spectator facilities in the city.

But first, there was some more window-dressing to be done. The rules had to be changed to get some of the pulling and dragging out of the game.

The scoring area had been reduced twice in the early 1900s. The old point-posts were 17 feet on either side of the goals, which were 21 feet wide. In 1901 they were brought back to 15 feet on either side of the goal. In 1903 they were fixed at 12 feet on either side of the goal-posts. In 1909 a motion that point-posts be abolished led to the establishment of a sub-committee which reported back to 1910 that point-posts should go, goal-nets should be introduced, and the goals should be 21 feet wide. The old 10-yard line in front of the goals, inside which no scores could be obtained, were replaced by parallelograms. This brought an end to the era of the "whipe," usually a forward of the overweight variety who lurked around the goal-mouth specifically to intimidate opposing backs. He effectively marked the goalkeeper. As one writer commented: "Previous to the change, it was not unusual to see the goalkeeper and the full-forward having a friendly chat together while the ball was thrown down the field."

Another innovation was getting the backs in position when the ball was thrown in. Until now it was possible to get a quick score before the defenders got back to their positions. Collison of Dublin got the last of these "snatch" goals in the opening seconds of the 1910 Leinster semi-final against Wexford. Although M Conlon of Dublin managed a point before the defenders were in position in the 1894 All-Ireland final there was no "snatched" score in a football final as prominent as the goal scored after just five seconds of the 1906 All-Ireland hurling final by Tipperary's Hugh Leonard. Only forwards were required to line up for the throw-in.

Goal-nets helped sort out disputes about scores, although as late as 1929 a Connacht championship match between Sligo and Leitrim was played without goal-nets.

With the rules altered to help the game as a spectacle, there was no doubting who the star attractions to bring the crowds out might be. Louth itched for revenge over their Kerry rivals. They retained their Leinster title in 1910 with an overwhelming 3-12 to 0-10 victory over Kildare (after spectator-winning efforts were all undone by classic Gaelic unpunctuality and the match started an hour and 20 minutes late), and a torrid three points to nil success against Dublin before 6,000 people in Navan. Louth's achievement in holding Dublin scoreless, Tom Burke claimed afterwards, underlined their claim to be the greatest team of the era:

> Kerry took their cue from that and refused to meet Louth in the All-Ireland football final later that year. Let who will put forward any other reason.

The crowd had a lot to talk about. Dublin hit the post twice in that Leinster final, and John Brennan scored the points for victory after Louth led 0-1 to nil at half-time. Jack Grace captained Dublin for the last time in this final: the outstanding player of the previous decade had won five football All-Ireland medals, contested 11 All-Ireland finals, six in football and five in hurling, and played with both Kilkenny and Dublin. Robust rather than speedy, his motto was "give me one yard clear and I fear no man." P D Mehigan recalled: "A thoroughly fair player, he hurt every man that crashed into him. He could run all day, and break up half a team when roused."

Louth, wearing bright green jerseys and captained by Sam Maguire, entertained London in the quarter-final with a great first-half display. London had 1-1 in the opening minutes of the second half, but Louth hung on to win by 2-5 to 1-2. Louth did not play in the All-Ireland semi-final, instead the Leinster council nominated Dublin, who beat Antrim by 3-5 to 0-2.

Kerry were also careering back towards a repeat of the 1909 final. They beat Cork, for whom Charlie Paye was emerging as one of the leading marksmen of the era, by 0-4 to 0-2 in the Munster final. Their semi-final was against Mayo's Stephenites selection. Just before half-time Mayo led 0-4 to 0-1, and even Kerry's point was disputed by Mayo. Kerry hit with a goal, and controlled the second half for a comfortable 1-7 to 0-4 victory.

The Ulster championship was meanwhile staggering through another of its annual outcrops of disorganisation. The first-round match between Cavan and Fermanagh was abandoned when the ball burst and there was no replacement. Then arrangements for admitting spectators to the Monaghan v Antrim semi-final left a lot to be desired: "One man with a bag giving out tickets...one spectator waited half an hour to get the change from 1/-," but the scenes were worse when the match ended and spectators leaving the grounds found they had to pass out the same gate in single file! Antrim beat Monaghan twice, having to replay because of an objection, while Cavan beat Tyrone in the unlikely venue of Bundoran.

But there were good signs amid it all. Antrim eventually settled the issue between themselves and Cavan with an overwhelming 3-4 to 0-1 victory. They used a unique fast handpassing style, developed in training by players who were based close together in Belfast city. The *Anglo-Celt* mourned:

> Cavan were dead slow. You can't cut finished footballers out of a hedge. Muscle in the county is running wild for want of cultivation. Our players have no style, a clumsy catch and awkward delivery.

Antrim's stylists were heavily beaten by Dublin in the All-Ireland semi-final, but had already started their plans for a breakthrough in 1911 at that stage.

There was at least some good news in April 1910 for the Ulster Council, when a meeting between the GAA and the Great Northern Railway Board appeared to secure, at the third attempt, train facilities for teams on Sundays.

The running of trains in Ulster was a sore point. On one occasion, it was claimed, when the Great Northern Railway management discovered that a special train to run on a Sunday was for a football team, they cancelled it! It was also claimed that the GNR had changed their Sunday train schedules specifically to prevent their being used by football teams!

But no sooner was one railway dispute in the North ended, than another erupted in the South. Just as it appeared that Louth would earn their revenge against Kerry, they never got their chance after an extraordinary row over the price of train tickets to Dublin for Kerry's supporters that stopped the 1910 All-Ireland final taking place.

Kerry were furious that the great Southern and Western Railway Company would not give a cheap excursion fare for their followers. Even getting excursion tickets and a carriage for the 17 players and three substitutes was a difficult task. On Thursday November 10th they received vouchers but no promise of a reserved carriage. The following day, Friday, the offer had been extended to a reserved carriage for 20 players and Kerry insisted that they would travel only if vouchers were provided for 12 close supporters and mentors.

Then on Saturday came the bombshell notice in the papers that the match was off, all trains were cancelled, and Kerry stood accused of lowering the GAA's reputation in pursuance of a local dispute with the Railway Company. Despite the fact that Railway Companies and the GAA were going through a rough relationship at the time, the GAA Central Council were livid.

Kerry supporters had a list of complaints against the Great Southern Railway Company, or the "Great Sourface Railway" as the Dublin *Leader* used to call it. They listed excessive fares (compared with round trip fares of 4/- for a rugby match in Cork and 13/- return from Tralee to Cardiff). On two occasions Kerry supporters returning from Thurles were forced to board from the "cattle bank." They never let Kerry players travel by the early train on Saturday from Tralee, the 1.50, forcing them to share the overcrowded 3.20 with market-day passengers who boarded in Killarney. A promise that there would be room on the 3.20 was dismissed by Kerry. Other nationalist organisations, who had difficulty getting train facilities for Home Rule meetings, applauded Kerry's move.

While 800 followers waited for the verdict outside, a delegate proposed Kerry be suspended for five years for bringing the Association into disrepute. Eventually the title was given to Louth, who still said they would prefer to win it on the field of play. Kerry were not suspended, avoiding an 1894-style confrontation, as Cork were threatening to "go into the wilderness with Kerry."

The Central Council lost heavily. Their receipts were paltry: Louth v London in Dundalk earned £46, Kerry v Mayo in Tuam £50, and Dublin v Antrim in Jones' Road £20. When Louth and Kerry eventually met in a 1913 Croke Memorial tournament final, it broke all existing attendance and receipt records.

ANTRIM'S TANTRUMS

The example of Kerry, Kildare and Louth's sudden rise was stirring far-thinking football captains in places as diverse as

Ardoyne, Ardmore, and Ardfert. Both Louth and Kerry made early exits from the 1911 championship.

Waterford, 18-point-losers the previous year, won a famous 1-2 to 1-0 Munster semi-final victory over the Kerrymen, who had been unbeaten since 1908, at Mallow. Waterford conceded the first goal, sent to the net off the post, but scored in an equaliser soon afterwards and picked their way back into the game as a slight drizzle turned into a downpour. While neither side added to their scores in the second half, it was Waterford who did most of the attacking. Waterford were captained by P Lynch, one of 11 Rathgormack players on the side. Kerry had seven of their 1910 selected All-Ireland team, but no Killarney players: the entire Killarney team had been suspended for walking off the field in the county semi-final against Tralee.

The success proved to be more than Waterford could follow, and Cork beat them by 2-5 to 0-1 in the Munster final. As beaten provincial finalists, Waterford qualified for the Croke Cup but were beaten in the final by Meath, who were achieving their first national title. Cork went on to beat Galway 3-4 to 0-2 in the All-Ireland semi-final at Maryboro.

Louth went out to more powerful pretenders, Dublin, by 3-2 to 1-4 in the Leinster quarter-final at Navan. The elated Dublinmen in turn lost to Meath, surprise 1-3 to 0-2 winners in the semi-final. There was a further surprise when Meath went on to lose in turn to Kilkenny by 2-4 to 1-1 in a confusing Leinster final.

Meath were awarded the title at 2.05, because Kilkenny were 20 minutes late. They refused to accept but were beginning to change their minds when Kilkenny arrived at 2.25. By now Meath wanted a challenge match instead. The game went ahead, Meath were beaten in a downpour and their protest afterwards was rejected, so Kilkenny had won their third and last Leinster football title.

For the winners it was largely a family affair. Patrick and Richard Dalton of Knocktopher got Kilkenny's goals, Richard Dalton got two points and William Dalton another point. £100 of gate receipts went to the Wexford Foundry workers who were locked out in a trade dispute. The GAA were identifying themselves with the Trade Union movement at the time, passing rules that their guide books be printed with trade union labour.

Just as the GAA in Connacht and Ulster seemed to have turned the corner, both provinces hit organisational stagnation in 1911. The rise in the standard of football was not being matched by an end to official ineptitude.

Galway and Mayo's proposed clash on September 24th in Claremorris in the Connacht final was postponed as a result of a rail strike and never refixed. Even more extraordinary was the case of Ulster, where the new provincial secretary W P Gilmour was ill for most of the year, and never got around to organising a championship. Getting the 1910 Ulster final played a year late was the height of provincial council activity for the year. A new acting secretary was appointed at the end of the year, and all of the correspondence and minute books collected from Mr Gilmour.

Running the Ulster championship was a loss-making operation; gate receipts were never large enough to cover teams' travelling expenses. The Ulster Council had not any funds to provide their provincial champions with medals until 1919. Even the medals for the 1920s were presented retrospectively in 1930.

And yet Antrim achieved a breakthrough for Ulster by reaching the All-Ireland final. Their surprise 3-1 to 1-1 semi-final victory over Kilkenny resulted in a Central Council investigation into the overt roughness of the game. Kilkenny's James Doyle was suspended for five years as a result. Antrim introduced "toeing off" the ball from goal, which nonplussed the Kilkennymen.

The Ulster joy was short-lived. Cork's record 6-6 to 1-2 score in the final against Antrim caused a lot of comment, but might not have been all that it seems. Newspaper commentators agreed that one of the Cork goals should have been a point.

Nevertheless it was a fine achievement by the Belfastmen, drawn from the Seaghan O'Neill (from which captain Harry Sheehan led their bid), Ollamh Fodhla, Mitchels, Sarsfields, Cuchulainns, and Dalcassian clubs. The first goal of the game fell to Antrim when William Lennon boxed P D Kelly's centre to the net. O'Neill had another Antrim goal disallowed in the second half. By then Charlie Paye, from a Billy Mackessy pass, had helped Cork go 1-4 to 1-0 ahead at half-time, Mackessy followed with a goal at the start of the second half (the first of three by the dual star), and Cork piled in four goals in the last quarter.

Goal-scorer Charlie Paye from Fermoy had once won a soccer medal with Cork Celtic and was one of the first transatlantic players. In 1908 he spent his summer in New York playing for the Cork club. Willie Mackessy, who was born in Buttevant and later played with Kinsale, was a sprinter. Team captain Mick Mehigan, 35 years old at the time of the final, later went on a 24-day hunger-strike at Wormwood Scrubs.

FOOTBALL, FAITH AND FATHERLAND

Not everything had changed with the popularisation of Gaelic games. The GAA was still perceived as a nationalist, almost racist force. As more people played the game, the racial element came to prominence. Cusack cited Meagher's 1840s speeches to assert that the strength and glory of the Celtic race, as against the Saxon and Teutonic traditions, could be asserted by playing games. Croke and Davitt followed. England's racial, imperialist (and even religious in some cases) sporting triumphalism of Victorian times was countered with a Gaelic nationalist Irish (and even Catholic in some cases) mirror-image.

The *Gaelic Annual* of 1907-8 declared:

> The Irish Celt is distinguished among the races, for height and strength, manly vigour and womanly grace; despite wars, and domestic disabilities, the stamina of the race has survived almost in its pristine perfection. The ideal Gael is a matchless athlete, sober, pure in mind, speech and deed, self-possessed, self-reliant, self-respecting, loving his religion and his country with a deep and restless love, earnest in thought and effective in action.

A short-lived GAA journal, *The Champion*, declared in 1903:

> The cause of our national pastimes requires advocacy: firstly because they are a prime necessity to our existence as a race; secondly, because they transmit and conserve the traditions of a great and noble past, and, lastly, because the wants of Gaelic Ireland are systematically suppressed and distorted, its faults paraded, and its virtues ignored.

During the Boer War, the GAA taunted the British with the use of Boer names for their clubs. There were two named after the Boer leader, General de Wet, in Tipperary and Galway. Anti-recruiting leaflets were distributed by the GAA in 1905.

As the GAA got more powerful, this theme did not go away. The ban on foreign games, named specifically as rugby and association football, hockey and cricket, was re-imposed in 1902. Soldiers and policemen were banned in January 1903, the option that county committees could decide on the ban was removed in 1905. The rule caused immense problems for the fledgeling GAA organisation abroad.

Britain's first GAA club had been established at Wallsend, near Newcastle-on-Tyne, and was affiliated in March 1885. In 1896 Britain played Ireland in a football international at Stamford Bridge. In 1900 London Irish were admitted into the All-Ireland competitions and given a bye to the final to play the home champions. London had a shock win in the All-Ireland hurling final of 1901 and the games there grew steadily, led by a small and resolute group of IRB men such as the three Protestant Maguire brothers from Dunmanway and Michael Collins.

London contested the Croke Cup in 1904 instead of the All-Ireland championship. The last "international All-Ireland final" was the football final between Dublin and London in 1908. London footballers competed in the quarter-finals in 1910 and 1913. But the ban was a constant source of problems, and the London board was dissolved in 1912 for failure to observe it. Only four clubs recognised a new board established by the Central Council.

The GAA was also trying to force sportsfield committees to cater for Gaelic sports alone. In 1911 "foreign games" were eventually banned from Jones' Road grounds, as they had already been in Dungarvan, Cork, and Thurles, despite the fact that the GAA did not own any of these grounds. The *Kilkenny Journal* declared:

> The motto of Gaelic fields for Gaelic players is winning all along the line, at these and other places that can distinguish between a hawk and a hand-saw.

The dispute over Waterford sportsfield was long and bitter. At first the GAA split over whether they should boycott the field to force the owners to implement theban (Waterford had a long soccer tradition), but eventually in April 1911 "foreign" games were banned from there too.

In 1912 the GAA took its first step beyond its means; when it ruled that all annual convention proceedings be conducted in Irish, the idea proved unworkable and was dropped in 1917. Ulster Council meetings are still conducted in Irish, but this means that all the relevant business is carried out at sub-committee level instead and just rubber-stamped by full council meetings.

The language provided obstacles throughout the GAA's existence. Moves in 1919 to force players to use only the Irish language on the playing-fields did not get very far.

RAINY DAYS

According to the Met men, 1912 was the wettest summer on record. Rain "destroyed the Leinster semi-final between Louth and Offaly as a spectacle," and caused the postponement of a Dublin—Kilkenny quarter-final replay on August 4th. When the replay took place in Enniscorthy, Dublin dumped the provincial champions by 3-4 to 0-1. Dan Kavanagh, a Wicklow native remembered for playing in his distinctive slouch hat, led Dublin's charge against Wicklow in the Leinster semi-final and reporters complained that the Wicklowmen "could have had more regard for the rules in the second half."

At that stage Dublin looked likely finalists. They were Leinster's All-Ireland semi-final nominees against Harry Hession's Roscommon team at Jones' Road in September. Roscommon missed a first-half penalty, Hession got a goal soon after half-time but F Brady and D Manifold goals made sure Dublin secured a final spot for Leinster by 2-4 to 1-1. Roscommon were surprise Connacht champions after Jim Brennan got the only two points of the provincial final in the first half and they went on to beat Galway by 0-2 to 0-0 at Castlerea.

But in October 1912 in Navan, Louth defeated Dublin by 1-2 to 1-1 to take the title back. They failed to score against the wind in the first half and went in 1-1 to nil behind at half-time. Then Dublin too failed to score against the wind in the second half and Louth squeezed through by a point.

With 15 minutes to go it was 1-1 to 0-1. Then Louth forced a 50 near the corner flag. Joe Mulligan's kick sailed unaided to the net. Louth came back with a long solo run from "Gentleman" Jim Smith, who was exhausted by the time he reached 21 yards from the Dublin goal. Team-mate "Whack" O'Reilly pushed him off the ball and scooped it over the bar.

Again the match was destroyed by what used to be called the "inclement conditions." The rain was so heavy that hundreds who travelled to the match remained in the railway carriages. Many suspected the match would be postponed and four of the players, all from Dublin, cried off because of the weather!

That gave Louth a chance to meet Kerry and gain revenge for both 1909 and the railway ticket fiasco. But Kerry disobligingly lost their semi-final against Antrim on another rainy day by a massive 3-5 to 0-2. Antrim were led by Louth-born Johnny Coburn. Born in Mount Pleasant, he captained Sarsfields from 1908 to 1918.

It was a shock that has gone into legend. Antrim led 0-3 to 0-2 at half-time, having played against the breeze. Early in the second half play became rough and Antrim had their full-back sent off five minutes after half-time. This should have inspired Kerry; instead Antrim came forward for a Joe Mullen goal, followed by two more breakaways as Kerry showed signs of strain. Later Kerry blamed a wedding the day before, but Antrim's great display in the final suggests this much-vented legend is only part of the story. "Antrim have improved in style. They practised for all they were worth," *Sport* wrote.

Antrim ran out of luck before the final, losing a player under the foreign games rule, a rule which hindered the development of the game in Belfast for half a century. It took 14 minutes for Louth's Tom Mathews to open the score. Mullen equalised, Louth led 0-2 to 0-1 at half-time and then Antrim had a goal for the last quarter lead. Jack Bannon, Johnny Brennan, Paddy Reilly and Stephen Fitzsimons got Louth's four points for a 1-7 to 1-2 victory. The attendance included 611 spectators at 1/- a head, 300 at 2/-, and 1,000 at 1/6.

They still had an Ulster championship to defend for a spot of consolation. A week after the All-Ireland final, Antrim lined out in the Ulster final against Armagh in Castleblayney with five changes on the team and won by 2-2 to 0-1.

Armagh had qualified for the Ulster final in the most bizarre of circumstances. Seven Cavan players failed to turn up to play in the semi-final. Cavan were forced to play in their work-clothes in the driving rain which distinguished that summer of 1912, and they included Fermanagh player George Wilson in their line-out. They still won by 1-2 to 1-1, but that illegal player cost them the match afterwards on an objection. Armagh had problems of their own that day: the excursion train went home without most of the players and spectators because of delays in getting the match under way. The county's entire GAA following was stranded in most unblissful circumstances in Newbliss!

Louth had won the championship. But they still had to wait for the Croke Tournament final the following spring to meet Kerry and get a chance of real revenge for the no-show in 1910. When they did so a replayed final set a new GAA attendance record. It is generally reckoned that 30,000 came to watch. The GAA was ecstatic that the attendance record set by a rugby match at Lansdowne Road had been beaten.

The game itself was recalled for two generations

afterwards. The long periods of action in which the ball "did not touch the ground or go out of play" went into the folk memory.

It was Kerry who decided the issue between the teams, winning the replay by 2-4 to 0-5 after an 0-4 to 1-1 draw. Between the draw and the replay Louth introduced full-time training, causing a storm when it was announced that former Scottish soccer international George Blessington and Belfast Celtic trainer Jim Booth were to train them for the final. Since 1905, Kerry players trained separately in Tralee and Killarney and came together on Sundays for practice matches. Kerry now followed suit by bringing their team together to Tralee and Killarney on alternate weeks to train under local athletes Jerry Collins and Bill O'Connor. A 40-year tradition of teams going into full-time training for big matches was begun.

Receipts of £750 and £1,198 at the football finals, and £2,734 in all from just six matches for the tournament, gave the GAA a higher than expected fund for a memorial to Archbishop Croke in Thurles. Much to the chagrin of the Thurles people, who resented the hijacking of their memorial funds, the GAA used the surplus to purchase Jones' Road from their secretary Frank Dineen for £3,641/8/5, and re-name it Croke Memorial Park . The Association paid over £1,641/8/5 in cash! Thurles was given a further £300 towards its confraternity hall to quell its protests.

The new rules were on trial at that replay for the first time, and their success was guaranteed for ever after. The decision to reduce teams from 17 a side to 15 a side gave the game a long overdue boost.

Other new rules included the decision to allow players who had been knocked to the ground to fist the ball away, and to take kick-outs from the 21-yard line after a score.

KERRY ASSERT THEMSELVES

Kerry's Croke Memorial victory was a good omen for the 1913 championship. But surprisingly that was the end of their rivalry with Louth. A new opponent was about to spring from the south-east corner of the country.

Former Dublin All-Ireland medallist, Paddy Breen, had taken over as chairman in Wexford. Under his leadership, Wexford won the Leinster junior championship in 1911, with an impressive 3-1 to 0-2 victory over Dublin. Among the successful juniors were Paddy Mackey, Aidan Doyle, Gus O'Kennedy and Tom Murphy.

In 1912 Wexford had suffered one of their most humiliating championship defeats to date, beaten 4-4 to 1-3 by Wicklow in the first round. In 1913 a new Wexford team, based around New Ross and the county town, gathered together in the spring. Egged on by nationalist journalist Sean Etchingham, and fired by the growth of the local Volunteer group (the Volunteers, said to be entirely a Sinn Féin grouping, even had a Gaelic football club), they selected the county's best-known sportsman as a trainer. Jem Roche had fought Canada's George Burns for the world heavyweight title in 1910. What matter if, at one minute and 28 seconds, it was one of the shortest professional fights on record. Jem's training evidently worked. Wexford were missing a key player, Eamonn Phelan, but they still beat Dublin by 2-3 to 1-0 in the Leinster semi-final in Wexford.

Teenager Aidan Doyle, soon to become a household name, scored the winning goal for Wexford. In the other Leinster semi-final Meath managed to hold Louth down to an 0-2 each draw at half-time but eventually went down by 2-3 to 0-2. Provincial champions of three years earlier, Kilkenny had fallen on hard times. Mascot Peter Dunne was forced to line out for his county against Louth to make up the team and they lost to Louth by 2-5 to 0-1.

Louth were odds-on favourites to challenge Munster for All-Ireland honours. They represented Leinster at the start of the All-Ireland series, travelling to Kensal Rise in early August to beat London. But Wexford surprised even themselves when they stopped Louth's run by 2-3 to 2-2 in the Leinster final in September.

Jim Rossiter, the only player from the Wexford Volunteer club, snatched victory for Wexford five minutes from the end of the final. He had already contributed a goal at the start of the second half. Winning the Croke Cup in June was poor consolation for Louth.

Wexford were therefore Leinster's representatives in the All-Ireland semi-final win over Antrim.

Antrim were in decline. Unrated Fermanagh, with George Wilson back, surprised them with a Cassidy goal and led by 1-3 to 0-1 at half-time in the Ulster semi-final. Then Antrim lost two of their leading players. Both moved away from Belfast the same month. In the circumstances, Antrim barely held their Ulster title by 2-1 to 1-2 against Monaghan, with the help of two soft goals from Ward and Gorman. Frank Duffy got a goal to help Monaghan come back from seven points behind, 2-1 to nil, at half-time, leaving Monaghan with only their goalkeeper to blame for his nervous start.

Goals by Wexford's Johnny Rossiter, Dick Reynolds and Gus Kennedy ensured there would be no giant-killing this time as Antrim crashed by 4-4 to 0-1.

Kerry too were having troubles, this time with Tipperary. In the Munster championship, Kerry's Dick Fitzgerald scored the late equaliser that Kerry needed to draw 0-2 each with Tipperary. Davey Stapleton's goal made life difficult for Kerry in the replay, putting Tipperary 1-0 to 0-1 ahead at the beginning of the second half, but Kerry won by 0-5 to 1-0 and beat champions Cork in the Munster final by the surprisingly large margin of eight points, 1-6 to 0-1, before a record £308 crowd.

It was clear that Dick Fitzgerald, who scored 1-4 in that match, was having his best ever season. Now 26, he was in the process of writing his *How to Play Gaelic Football* which was published at the beginning of 1914 and was giving ample lessons to opponent and spectator alike on the playing-field.

Galway too ran into the Fitzgerald factor as Dick scored 1-4 against them in a 1-8 to 0-1 victory in Maryboro, "as dreary an exhibition of Gaelic football as was ever seen," the *Kerryman* mourned.

For the first time, what a later generation of headline-writers would call "final fever" broke out in advance of the game in Kerry. Thanks to the stand Kerry had taken in 1910, supporters now had ample train facilities to bring them to

Croke Park. Sister Dominick was enlisted to treat an injured Tom Rice, and her nursing skill enabled him to play in the final. Even £1,000-a-year county surveyor Singleton Goodwin was inspired to give a shilling to the Kerry training fund—the *Kerryman* newspaper highlighted it in bold type in their subscription list! A new training camp was established at the residence of Kerry supporter Jack McCarthy in Dunboyne before the All-Ireland final.

Fitzgerald was the outstanding character as Wexford faltered after a promising start in the final. As Kerry beat Wexford by 2-2 to 0-3 before a crowd of 17,000, he scored a goal and a point in the first half, had another goal disallowed (as Kerry led 1-1 to 0-1) and then notched the opening points of the second half. After 15 minutes of the second half Johnny Skinner had a wrap-up goal for Kerry.

Pat O'Shea from Castlegregory gave a wonderful display; his high-fielding earned the comment "'Tis an aeroplane he is," from opponent Johnny Doyle. It earned him a nickname "Aeroplane" O'Shea after the device invented 10 years earlier by the Wright brothers. The *Kerryman* reported that he "did some fine aeroplane turns in midfield, catching the ball at almost incredible heights." His previous nickname with Erin's Hope club had been "Springheel." O'Shea was only 5'8" but was a great judge of the ball. He claimed later: "I'd see the trajectory of every kick and knew when to go for it. Two handed for the reasonable ones, pulling down the high ones one handed; go up like a diver feet together; come down like a hurdler on one foot and kick it with the other. The momentum gave me length and I'd have a map in my mind of where the forwards were."

The political situation was evident in more than the playing personnel, both teams having more than a sprinkling of later rebel leaders. In November Galway delegates proposed that the GAA set up rifle clubs "for the purpose of training an army." More significantly, John Dillon was a guest at the game in what was seen as a bid to forge an alliance between the Irish Volunteer Movement, formed three weeks earlier, and the GAA. Dillon, not knowing his political career would soon be at an end, was certainly not there because of his sporting interests, apologising: "It is so long since I attended a football match I don't know how it is going to start."

The attendance reached 17,000 and the talk on the banks was of replacing the camáns that Volunteers used for drilling with real guns sometime soon. There was a flavour of triumphant nationalism everywhere. James Upton, one of the nationalists who seemed to dominate the sporting press at the time, wrote in the *Kilkenny Journal*:

> Gaeldom is marching today and has attained a position that seemed very remote fifteen years ago, or ten years ago, or even five years ago. And best of all, my brothers, we have reached that position without striking our colours or erasing a single syllable from the principles of an uncompromising faith in Ireland's right to full and independent nationhood.

The Volunteer spirit had seized the GAA. When a challenge match in Drogheda on Easter Sunday 1915 ended with the Louth players calling for three cheers for Kerry, Dick Fitzgerald called for "three cheers for Eoin McNeill instead."

In January 1914 the GAA president James Nowlan called upon members to "join the Volunteers and learn to shoot straight." Delegates finished the April 1914 Congress with a hearty rendition of "A Nation Once Again." By then the UVF guns had landed in Larne and the Irish Volunteers were negotiating to get some of their own.

GUNS AND ROSETTES

Galway County Board was the first GAA body to give official sanction to the Irish Volunteers in 1914. But there were tensions between the competing national bodies, with GAA members claiming that Volunteer training was distracting members from the business of playing games. The Association had passed a "no politics" motion in 1911. The issue of the GAA and politics was not clear-cut, even at that stage. Just three months earlier Dan McCarthy, a leading member of Sinn Féin and later GAA president, said:

> The GAA is not a sporting association alone but above all a
> national organisation to keep the bone and muscle of our
> country from donning the red coat or the black coat of
> England.

In January 1914 Croke Park was refused to the Volunteers
for drilling purposes. Yet some GAA clubs set up Volunteer
branches and dual membership was common. The split in
September 1914 left many of the GAA members on Eoin
McNeill's side against John Redmond, according to police
files.

By then a rivalry of a more familiar, more sporting, but
equally serious type had been resumed. Kerry and Wexford
had been looking forward to a repeat final all through the
season, and a friendship was growing between the counties
that the Kerry-Louth rivalry never achieved. Wexford
entertained Kerry at the county Feis in New Ross and brought
them on a boat trip along the Barrow and Suir. When
Wexford repaid the visit, they were treated to a "motor drive
through Ardfert to Ballyheigue" on Sunday morning, a drive
around Killarney lakes on Monday, and a return by boat.
Among the oarsmen was 1903 Kerry goalkeeper Pat Dillon.
Kerry were relaxing too, by all accounts. Wexford won by
3-5 to 0-2 and, according to the *Kerryman*, "a team of old-age
pensioners would have given a better display of football."

But when the serious business began, Kerry retained their
Munster title by beating Tipperary by 2-2 to 0-2 in
Dungarvan and Cork by 0-5 to 0-1 at Tralee, doing most of
their scoring in the first nine minutes of the second half after
they had gone 0-1 to nil up at half-time. Wexford felt they
were now ready to take the Kerrymen on.

Wexford were now regarded as the aristocrats in Leinster.
They beat Meath, Kilkenny and Dublin in the space of five
weeks to reach the provincial final. But the most ironic event
of an undistinguished championship occurred when, in the
first round, Kildare 1905 star "Joyce" Conlan eliminated his
former colleagues from the championship with a last-minute
goal for Laois (he was working on the railway at Maryboro,
later Portlaoise, at the time). Laois failed to Louth, 5-3 to 0-3,
in the semi-final.

Wexford eventually annihilated Louth by 3-6 to 0-1 after a slow start in the Leinster final. Fittingly, Sean O'Kennedy, their natural leader who cycled a round trip of 80 miles to train the team, got their first goal after 15 minutes. McDonald made it 2-3 to 0-1 at half-time, and Johnny Rossiter got a third in the second half. Meanwhile Louth had the misfortune of having a goal disallowed and then hit the crossbar with another shot.

Ulster had a few surprises in 1914. A record crowd paid £58/13/8 to see Cavan trail six-in-a-row seekers Antrim 1-1 to nil at half-time in the Ulster championship quarter-final, but they took control in the second half and their 2-3 to 1-2 victory ended a winning sequence that extended back to the chaos of 1907. Three weeks later Cavan went down to Fermanagh by 2-1 to 0-4—a surprise considering Cavan had earlier won the Ulster medal tournament by beating Derry 1-3 to 0-2 on May 31st in Newbliss. The Ulster semi-final between Monaghan and Armagh on August 7th at Carrickmacross was a scoreless draw—the only full-length GAA championship match to finish scoreless in 100 years. Monaghan ended a great Fermanagh run when they beat the Teemore selection by 2-4 to 0-2 in the Ulster final.

In the All-Ireland semi-final against Wexford, Monaghan had a second-half goal disallowed as they went down by 2-6 to 0-1 to goals from Gus O'Kennedy and Johnny Rossiter before a paltry 3,000 attendance in Croke Park. Kerry had easily beaten Roscommon by 2-4 to 0-1 in the other semi-final at Maryboro a week earlier. Roscommon had the advantage of having persuaded Connacht's leading player, Harry Hession from Roscommon town, to captain his native county that year, while the Fuerty and Kilbride areas contributed most of Hession's team.

Wexford were back for another crack at the title, and goals from Sean O'Kennedy and Aidan Doyle early on in the All-Ireland final suggested they might succeed this time. But the 2-0 to 0-1 Wexford half-time lead crumbled seconds after the restart when Paddy Breen took Dick Fitzgerald's pass for a Kerry goal. A last-minute point from Fitzgerald earned a replay, 1-3 to 2-0.

Kerry the replay specialists took their time about winning the second time round. Again they trailed at half-time, this time by six points to nil, Paddy Breen repeated his drawn match "psychological" goal to start the second half, Johnny Mahoney piled in another from the kick-out, the irrepressible Dick Fitzgerald kicked two points and Johnny Skinner landed a third. Kerry became outright winners of the Railway Cup by 2-3 to 0-6, having won the All-Ireland twice in succession.

The provincial finalists played off in the Croke Cup semi-finals. Minnows Fermanagh met Louth at Newbliss on November 8th and the 1912 All-Ireland champions only barely survived because Fermanagh missed two penalties; they won 1-1 to 0-1. When Louth lost the Croke Cup final to Cork, by 2-1 to 0-3 in February 1915, it was, to all intents and purposes, the end of the road for Owen Markey and the others.

It was also the end of the road for the Croke Cup itself, after 18 years. With running expenses of £180 and receipts of only £115 it had clearly failed to arouse any interest among the new generation of sports spectators.

Chapter Six

Gael Forces

JOYS OF WEXFORD

Sometime in the spring of 1915, Wexford cracked the formula. Organised selection, organised club football, and organised training could win an All-Ireland. Schoolteacher, sprinter, jumper, hurler and footballer Paddy Breen had proved one of the best wingers on Erin's Hope teams early in the century, at a stage when Dublin had the best footballers and half all the All-Irelands ever played in the bag. At home in Wexford he set up the organisation that would win four All-Irelands in a row. It was only a matter of time before they broke through. When they broke through, it rapidly became a question of who would crack a new formula—the one to stop them.

In the 1915 Leinster championship Wexford brushed aside Kilkenny and Offaly easily enough. Only for a few minutes at the end of the Leinster final did Wexford's provincial three-in-a-row begin to look doubtful—when two Sean Lawlor goals for Dublin forced them to a replay, 2-2 each. Sean O'Kennedy, who scored Wexford's first goal in the drawn match, scored 2-2 in the replay as Wexford eventually triumphed by 2-5 to 1-3. Support was swelling beyond 1913 or 1914 levels. Record crowds of 8,000 (paying £229 in receipts) and 13,000 turned out to watch the Leinster finals.

Two goals, midway through the first half, from newcomer John Wall and team captain Sean O'Kennedy, and another goal from Wall in the second half, helped Wexford to master improving Cavan by 3-7 to 2-2. Cavan at least managed a respectable scoreline, their comeback into the game inspired by Quinn and Rogers goals.

Cavan had a stormy Ulster championship. They had to play Antrim twice on the grounds that they were late on the field the first day, winning 1-3 to 0-2 and 0-3 to 0-1. They drew the final against a Monaghan team in which Eoin O'Duffy was having an increased organisational and playing input, and when they appeared to have won, Monaghan objected to their 0-4 to 0-3 victory on the grounds that "the crowd had been on the pitch for the final ten minutes of the game," that "the goalposts were broken rendering it impossible for them to score," that "the umpire saved a certain Monaghan goal three minutes from the end," and that Cavan's star, Felix McGovern, had played in Leitrim. The McGovern objection was upheld, Monaghan were nominated to play in the All-Ireland semi-final of the following year, and a replay was ordered for October 10th in Belfast. Cavan refused to play and were declared, uniquely, "champions without medals."

Kerry were beginning to falter even before they faced Wexford in the All-Ireland final. M Donovan and young Jack Rice got the Kerry goals that brought them from behind in the second half to beat a Roscommon team captained by future GAA president Dan O'Rourke, 2-3 to 1-1. A week later Roscommon lost the Connacht final to Mayo by 3-1 to 1-3.

Kerry trainer Jerry Collins had been transferred to Limerick, star player Johnny Skinner was working in Clonmel, while Johnny Mahoney had emigrated to New York. Then full-back Jack Lawlor broke his thumb in a trial match in Tralee and was sent on to the field to play with his thumb encased in plaster of Paris and a bandage. This was crucial to the result of the game.

For a third year in succession the outstanding fielding of Pat "Aeroplane" O'Shea of Castlegregory was the highlight of the All-Ireland midfield battle, rapidly becoming the most important sector of the field under the new 15-a-side rules. His skills impressed a crowd of 27,000 who paid receipts of £1,040 to watch, but not Wexford, who got their revenge in the final by 2-4 to 2-1.

Wexford owed their victory, not as might be expected to the O'Kennedy brothers of New Ross, but this time to the place-kicking of Jim Byrne of Wexford town. Byrne kicked two points from 50s, and landed the winning goal from another in controversial circumstances.

The goal was spoken about for years to come. Byrne was not clear about the score as he stepped up to take the third 50. He misread the signal from a colleague indicating he should opt for a point, and dropped the ball in for a goal instead. Full-back Jack Lawlor went to catch the ball with his bandaged hand and then changed his mind. Dinny Mullins tried to save too late and barely touched the ball, which was allowed to strike the underside of the crossbar and drop into the net.

Aidan Byrne had got the first goal that sent Wexford 1-2 to 1-0 ahead in reply to a goal by Kerry's Denis Doyle. Dick Fitzgerald hit the post in the first half and the crossbar in the second half before charging the goalie into the net for Kerry's second goal.

So, Wexford had become champions at the third attempt and collected the new Railway Cup as a reward. Jim Bolger recalled those three Wexford v Kerry finals fondly:

> We had great football but no rough play; and frees were not nearly as frequent as they are today. The meeting of friends was looked forward to from year to year. We talked of things other than football, of events of the future that were in the making. One gained in strength of spirit and hope renewed through contact with these Kerrymen and it did not surprise me when the time came that Kerry ranked high in Ireland's role of honour.

CROKE COMFORTS

It appeared that there was another battle between the finalists in store, this time for the Wolfe Tone tournament, arranged to replace the Croke Cup. But Louth defeated Wexford by a single point, 2-3 to 2-2, in the quarter-final. Kerry had already beaten Cork in another quarter-final by 4-0 to 0-2. By the time the final came to be played political fortunes had changed.

So many of the players found themselves in Frongoch prison camp in Wales after the 1916 Rising that the final was played there and Dick Fitzgerald's Kerry team defeated Tom Burke's Louth team by one point.

A separate tournament was taking place outside the prison camps between four weakened teams, producing victory for Mayo over Kerry and Louth over Monaghan before Louth beat Mayo in the final. The final was the last appearance, at the age of 43, of Jack "Sandman" Carvin. In a career with Kickhams of Dublin, Drogheda Independents, and Tredagh, "Carvin of the 100 battles" was slow to run but had a pair of arms which were reputed to reach down to his knees.

The round-up of insurgents after the Easter rebellion had put several notable GAA players behind bars. Shocked and confused by the unexpected rebellion, the authorities had targeted GAA members because, according to their now hopelessly inadequate files, the GAA was rife with Sinn Féiners. GAA president James Nowlan and prominent Waterford referee Willie Walsh were among the first to be arrested. But they knew nothing about the Rising.

The strongest GAA connection with the Rising was in Wexford, where Sean Etchingham and Seamus Doyle were among the rebels that held Enniscorthy for several days, having used an Easter Sunday GAA fixture to foregather. Kerry GAA man Austin Stack was arrested after the landing of arms for the Rising was bungled. Individual clubs were devastated. The Croke Club had 40 members; 32 fought in the Rising, two were killed. Maynooth Volunteers marched to join the Rising in Dublin, as a result of which the local club could not field in the Kildare championship.

Four Dublin players from the 1915 Leinster final team were among those who fought. Jack Shouldice was sentenced to death after the rebellion. Frank Bourke, the most decorated dual star in Gaelic history, was also in the GPO. Frank Shouldice, P J Walsh and Michael Collins were elsewhere in action, and Con O'Donovan and Harry Boland were rank-and-file GAA members. Among those executed, Pearse was a GAA Colleges Council member and Sean McDermott, Con Colbert, Michael O'Hanrahan and Eamonn Ceannt had GAA connections.

But the GAA responded to the rebellion by denying that it

had any connection, saying that these individual members were acting independently, and distancing itself from the rebels.

There was no stopping Wexford now, especially when Kerry withdrew from the 1916 championship because they wanted "to play matches on their own." As was the case in Galway, arrests had devastated the local GAA scene, and the suppression of the *Kerryman* newspaper cut off communications, bringing club activities to a halt.

Kerry had already eliminated Tipperary by 2-2 to 0-1, so Cork and Clare were left to fight out the final. Somewhat surprisingly, Cork, having led 2-2 to 0-1 at half-time, were forced to hold on grimly and win by 2-2 to 1-4 when Clare came storming back to within a point of them.

Wexford's other main rivals, Dublin, decided to opt out when Frank Bourke and other football colleagues were dispatched to Frongoch in the aftermath of the Easter Rising. Appropriately enough, Dublin won a Leinster championship "final" played inside the camp when they beat Wexford, captained by 1901 veteran John Vize, by 1-8 to 2-3. Under martial law, travel and practice were becoming increasingly difficult. The police banned even training sessions in Cavan, Down and Fermanagh.

Despite losing their Maynoothmen to the rigours of martial law, Kildare still made it to the Leinster final with a new teenage star, Kildare's 19-year-old Larry Stanley, in action: "Stanley, who was taking part in senior football for the first time, covered himself in glory," *Sport* enthused. Wexford won by 1-7 to 0-4, as Aidan Doyle struck with a goal just before half-time to make the score 1-4 to nil and kill off hopes of a Kildare revival.

Although the Leinster final in October attracted an attendance of 10,000, the military was increasingly using its power to cancel special trains within a fortnight, a power often used arbitrarily and late.

The result was that the All-Ireland final and semi-finals drew some of the lowest attendances in years. For the semi-final in Athlone on October 22nd, local businesses prepared to cater for 10,000 visitors to the town but all trains were cancelled at the last minute and the piles of ham sandwiches went unsold.

Mayo were the rising team in Connacht. Some 4,000 attended the Connacht final against Roscommon, Mayo trailed by 0-1 to 0-3 at half-time and their recovery was started by a point from Harry Hession, Roscommon captain and star of 1914!

Mayo won that semi-final by 1-2 to 0-2, and achieved a breakthrough for Connacht, but because one of the Mayo team, Durkin, had lined out in the Cork championship, Mayo were forced to replay, and a Lyons goal and Reilly and Courell points helped them beat Cork by 1-2 to 1-1 the second day in atrocious conditions. The gates were not opened because heavy rain in the morning left a doubt over the game. It eventually went ahead in front of "a few hundred brave enthusiasts" who gained admission at the last minute. The Railway goal was "in the middle of a lake" and there were pools of water inches deep elsewhere on the pitch. Four points from Gus O'Kennedy and three from Jim Byrne helped Wexford overcome Monaghan by 0-9 to 1-1, Joe Keeley scoring the goal, in the other semi-final in Carrick-macross where an impressive total of 5,000 turned out.

Despite the political crisis having brought Gaelic games to a standstill in Belfast and several other parts of Ulster, the championship got under way in June. Down caused a good deal of surprise when they held Antrim to level terms at half-time in the Ulster semi-final, but they failed to score in the second half and lost by 1-3 to 1-0. Monaghan won revenge for the Felix McGovern affair by beating Cavan by 4-3 to 1-5 in the other semi-final, then beat ailing Antrim by 2-3 to 0-2 an anti-climactic Ulster final at Clones.

No special trains were allowed for the All-Ireland final, so the crowd of 3,000 was described by the *Freeman's Journal* as "surprisingly large." The streets of Dublin were sheeted in ice, and overnight frost meant the pitch was extremely hard, despite the fact straw had been spread on it. In later years spectators were better able to recall their journey to and from the game than the match itself.

At 2 o'clock the ground was pronounced playable; the

O'Kennedy brothers quickly established Wexford's superiority and they won by 2-4 to 1-1. John snatched two first-half goals and gave to Gus in the second half for a third. Mayo's reply was a late goal by Tom Boshell and first-half points from Harry Hession and Frank Courell. During the match Mayo's goalkeeper placed his hat against the net behind the goal.

There were attempts to run a rival All-Ireland championship in 1916, by the National Association of Gaelic and Athletic Clubs (the NAGAC, or five-letter-folly, as the GAA ridiculed it). It had its origins in a dispute over the setting up of a separate junior board in Dublin, and one of Dublin's most traditional clubs, Kickhams, seceded from the GAA in 1913. In February 1916 delegates from Galway, Sligo, Tipperary, and Wexford met to join Kickhams delegates and form the NAGAC in Dublin. Among the issues that brought a diverse group of dissident clubs together was opposition to the Volunteer take-over, and also opposition to Dublin control at the expense of Thurles. In 1919 Kickhams rejoined the GAA.

CLARE'S AIRS

As they had difficulty completing local club matches, it was no surprise that Kerry were out again in 1917, but Dublin were back for an impressive 0-12 to 1-4 victory over Louth and an 0-5 to 0-3 victory over Laois to face Wexford in the Leinster final. Their year's absence caused some hiccups. They struggled for 45 minutes in the semi-final against Laois, having trailed 0-1 to 0-2 at half-time.

But they were getting their act together, with the help of a new 6'3" midfielder, Paddy McDonnell of O'Toole's. Wexford needed a dramatic late winner to beat Dublin by 1-3 to 1-1 before 7,000 spectators. Jim Byrne's sideline ball was fisted on by Sean O'Kennedy for the winning goal, again scored by Aidan Byrne. Sean Lawlor got Dublin's only goal in the final, from a drop-kick, after Wexford had held on to a 0-1 to nil half-time lead, despite having played into a stiff breeze.

Wexford missed Tom Mernagh and Val Connolly for their 6-6 to 1-3 semi-final victory against Monaghan but managed to recall former star Fr Edmond Wheeler, unavailable since his ordination. Wheeler played under the pseudonym "J Quinn" to avoid ecclesiastical censure and helped in their victory.

The province from which Monaghan had qualified had, as usual, its fair share of disputes. Most of them revolved around the Ulster semi-final between old rivals Monaghan and Cavan. Monaghan had won by 3-1 to 0-2 but had been late on the field. Cavan were awarded the match by the Ulster Council when Monaghan rejected an offer of a replay. The Central Council ordered a replay but this time Cavan refused, claiming Monaghan had too much influence on the Ulster and Central Councils (a tribute to the persuasive skills of Monaghan's Eoin O'Duffy). The acrimony between the two wasn't doing the coffers any harm: £60 was taken at Cootehill, compared with £10 at the final, where Monaghan beat Armagh by 4-2 to 0-4 with the help of three goals from Joe Keeley as they came back from 0-2 to 0-3 behind at half-time.

There was no such income from the Antrim—Down shambles in the first round, advertised for 3 o'clock "Irish time." Hundreds turned up at 3 o'clock "present time" and when they heard they would have to wait an hour and a half for the match, most went home in disgust. The clock had been tampered with to save fuel during the First World War and this led to total confusion about exact starting times.

Kerry's absence enabled a powerful Clare team to emerge in Munster for their first and only championship 2-6 to 0-3 victors over Waterford, 0-5 to 0-4 victors over Tipperary and massive 5-4 to 0-1 victors over Cork in the Munster final at Tipperary town. The flag they followed on to the field read "Up De Valera." Kilkeeman and Kildare native Jim Foran, all 6'3", of him, organised the training for the side with 1914 hurler Sham Spellisey.

In the All-Ireland semi-final Clare beat Galway by 2-1 to 0-4 at Athlone. Martin McNamara and Ned Carroll got the second-half goals that put Clare into the final, Turlough

"Tull" Considine the point in the first half.

Travel restrictions in the wake of insurrection meant the whole draw in Connacht had to be rearranged. Sligo v Roscommon in Boyle could not be played because of martial law restrictions and the draw was rescheduled so Sligo would play Mayo instead. Galway stopped Mayo in their tracks with a 1-4 to 1-1 victory in the Connacht final at Castlerea, getting the vital goal from Pat Roche.

Because of these restrictions, just 6,500 turned out to watch the final. A group of Wexford players and supporters were fined five shillings with costs at Arklow petty sessions for defying restrictions and using a motor car to travel to the game. Driver Jim Fortune commented: "Had the members of the RIC, who halted us on our way home from the game, made a search of the car, instead of taking us as mere football enthusiasts, the story would have been different."

Wexford were expected to complete the three-in-a-row rather easily. As it happened, they needed a lot of luck to prevent a shock Clare victory, although the 0-9 to 0-5 scoreline was a comfortable one in the end.

Wexford led 0-6 to 0-4 at half-time and after a dispute over a disallowed goal by Aidan Doyle, they came under pressure in the second half. Turlough "Tull" Considine from Ennis, one of the outstanding GAA personalities of his generation and a player in the All-Ireland hurling final as late as 1932, broke through but was tripped from behind; then Clare had a goal disallowed and Wexford held on for a four-point victory, thanks mainly to Jim Byrne's sharp-shooting, while Martin McNamara of Clare was doing some of his own.

Clare players turned to a different kind of shooting in the years that followed. Two of them lost their lives during the War of Independence.

BALLS VERSUS BATONS

There were signs that all the political problems that the GAA had narrowly avoided so far would eventually catch up with them in 1918.

Kerry signalled their return to championship football in

1918 by beating defending Munster champions, Clare, by 5-3 to 1-3. But in the Munster final, they failed to Tipperary by 1-1 to 0-1. Tipperary started with a goal from Bill Grant minutes after the throw-in. Con Clifford scored a Kerry point before half-time but Davey Tobin scored a winning second-half point for Tipperary. A tiny attendance watched at Cork.

Leinster provided the shaggy-ball story of the championship. The ball burst before the Laois—Kildare match could get under way on June 30th. The game lasted only 10 minutes as numerous attempts to repair it proved fruitless.

But everywhere politics was bubbling to intervene. Public meetings were banned in 13 counties on July 4th, with the rules framed to include GAA, but not cricket or lawn tennis games. With the RIC demanding permits for the holding of football matches under the Defence of the Realm Act and the GAA refusing to apply for them, a confrontation was inevitable. During the long, hot month of July soldiers baton-charged matches in Offaly and Down, took down goal-posts in Kildare, and occupied playing-fields in Cork.

The biggest show-down took place before an Ulster championship match between Cavan and Armagh at Cootehill in July, where a large body of troops occupied the playing-field where 3,000 had gathered. Local parish priest, Father O'Connell, addressed the crowd, asked them to disperse quietly and no incidents occurred. A match was fixed for the same field on the following day. This time police attended but bayonets were not drawn and the game took place.

On August 4th the GAA replied by mobilising 54,000 players at games throughout the country. All the matches started at the same time, parishes and townlands which had not fielded a team for a generation lined out, and there was no RIC interference. The permit issue was allowed to die.

The championships quickly swung back into action. Antrim and Derry played at a new Belfast venue: Celtic Park, home of the Belfast Celtic soccer club. Cavan were sulking and had to be persuaded to enter the championship at all. Following the objections saga of 1917 they had considered

109

playing in Connacht instead. Then they proposed a new fifth province of Tara, to include themselves and Longford, Westmeath, Louth and Meath! The proposal was not taken seriously.

As it happened. Cavan totally dominated the final against Antrim and won by 3-2 to nil. They had first-half goals from John Malone and Pat Fay while Antrim managed to get across the halfway line only once. In the second half Antrim managed just one dangerous attack, while Cavan had a third goal from J P Murphy. Gate receipts were only £5/17/4!

Wexford faced a renewed challenge from Louth in Leinster. Louth had already beaten Meath, Dublin, and Kildare. Louth's attempt to stop Wexford was not helped by the fact that four of their players never made it to Croke Park because the car in which they were travelling broke down. In October Louth were Leinster's last nominated semi-finalists and needed two second-half goals from Frank Byrne to beat Cavan 2-4 to 0-4 before a smallish attendance of 3,000.

But Wexford were not finished yet. In January Jim Redmond and Gus Kennedy's first-half goals sent Wexford into a commanding interval lead of 2-3 to 0-2, and they held on to beat Louth by 2-5 to 1-4 before a 10,000 attendance. Noel Butterley got the goal that brought Louth back within two points midway through the second half. Politics, not football, was the conversation piece among spectators. The first Dáil met the following day.

Having survived the political crisis of 1918, the GAA faced an even more serious one, a killer influenza epidemic carried back from the trenches of France by the returning soldiers from October on. All-Ireland finalists Tipperary were badly hit by the 1918 flu. Davey Tobin scored two goals that gave Tipperary the cushion to pip Mayo in the semi-final by 2-2 to 1-4. He was one of the flu victims who missed the final.

Then, nine days later, came the Solohead shootings, which kicked off the War of Independence on January 21st 1919. Tipperary training had to be halted as a military clampdown followed.

Sport enthused that Wexford's team was "the best ever"

after the Leinster final. Nevertheless Wexford had the closest victory of their four in the All-Ireland final, by 0-5 to 0-4 in front of a replenished attendance of 12,000. Tipperary could have won. Gus McCarthy, scorer of two Tipperary points, had another disallowed for "whistle gone." Former Kerry footballer Jack Skinner and Tommy Ryan got the other Tipperary scores as Byrne, Pierce and Redmond put Wexford 0-3 to 0-2 up at half-time, and Pierce and O'Kennedy went on to complete a historic victory.

At the tail-end of the game Gus McCarthy was inches wide with a 30-yard free and Tipperary also claimed the ball bobbed across the line before a Wexford back scooped it away. Wexford had created a record by winning four in a row, but only by the skin of a whitewash line.

CLEAN AND MANLY

When Wexford ran out of steam it was not Louth or Kerry who succeeded them. Dublin's star, in an 0-11 to 1-2 semi-final victory over the seven-in-a-row seekers, Wexford, was midfielder Paddy McDonnell. Dublin were under threat from a proposed ban on all Civil Servants who had taken the oath of allegiance. It had already been used against one of McDonnell's clubmates and could have caused large headaches for the GAA if Dublin had gone on to All-Ireland level. But Dublin were shocked in turn, by 1-3 to 1-1 by Kildare in the Leinster final.

Kildare were inspired by 22-year-old midfielder Larry Stanley who demonstrated his legendary "one-handed catch" against McDonnell. Rugby star Jim O'Connor was Kildare's goal-scorer in the final, he had scored 4-1 in the semi-final against Westmeath.

Louth's bid was short-lived. In the first round Meath came back from six points down to earn a draw with Louth, forced another draw, and beat them by 2-5 to 2-4 in a second replay.

In Ulster Cavan won the championship while the Ulster Council celebrated the province's first £100 gate receipts. Armagh beat Monaghan and then lost to Antrim in turn. The Council had thought of a unique way of getting rid of their financial problems, having started the year £230 in debt. It organised three meetings between the finalists, at first arranging that the "best of three matches" would decide the championship.

As this would be of doubtful legality, the first two meetings were redesignated "build-up friendly matches," to boost interest in the game and, more importantly, the funds of the Ulster Council. Cavan won the first match by 5-3 to 1-4 in Belturbet, the second meeting resulted in a draw, Cavan 2-4 Antrim 1-7; and when Antrim rejected Belturbet as a venue for the final proper, it was staged at neutral Clones. Cavan won by 5-5 to 0-2. Council receipts soared from £144 in 1918 to £359 and the Ulster champions were presented with medals for the first time!

Kildare beat Cavan by 3-2 to 1-2 in the semi-final at Navan. Frank "Joyce" Conlan, a survivor from 1905, scored 2-1 for Kildare in the first few minutes of the game, and had a breakaway shot from the throw-in barely saved.

Kerry took back the Munster title after five years and also had a new star, marksman John Joe Sheehy. Kerry ousted champions Tipperary in the first round by 2-4 to 2-3, and Sheehy got the first-half goal that sent Kerry 1-7 to nil ahead of Clare at half-time in the Munster final at Ennis. Then he started the second-half goal-rush that led to a massive 6-11 to 2-0 victory.

But Kerry lost to the Connacht champions in the All-Ireland semi-final. Michael "Knacker" Walsh was to become Connacht's best-known forward of the 1920s. In 1917 he scored one point for Galway, in 1919 he turned the match around just when Roscommon had gained an 0-5 to 0-1 lead, scoring a dramatic goal and a point immediately afterwards to give Galway a 1-6 to 0-5 victory in the Connacht final before 3,000 spectators at Tuam. Walsh's exploits continued in the All-Ireland semi-final, as Galway drew 2-6 to 3-3 with Kerry when J Egan got two goals in answer to two from Baily and a lucky Kerry goal from O'Connor, and then won the replay by 4-2 to 2-2 three weeks later. In the replay Walsh's sixth-and 16th-minute goals helped Galway into a 3-0 to nil lead with another goal from John Hannify, while Michael

Flannelly scored a fourth 12 minutes from the end. Kerry's two goals came late in the game.

Kildare devised a plan to keep Michael "Knacker" Walsh from upsetting their All-Ireland prospects. The goalkeeper and full-back would change places, and the goalkeeper would body-charge Walsh while the full-back stood on the line. As the goalkeeper was the massively built veteran from 1903, Larry "Hussey" Cribben, whose giant physique would tear up the Croke Park turf like a bullock as he paced the goal-mouth, the body-charge was expected to work. After one near miss there was a crunch of body-to-body impact, and after that Galway's only point in the game came late in the second half from John Egan.

Meanwhile Larry Stanley, playing at midfield with Mick Sammon, helped Kildare dominate the game while Galway's placing was described as wretched. For the final, Kildare's goals came from another 1905 survivor, Frank "Joyce" Conlan, after 17 minutes, and Jim O'Connor who tipped a Mick Sammon 50 to the net nine minutes after half-time. Kildare had taken a 1-2 to nil half-time lead. Kildare newcomer 19-year-old Paul Doyle, who played his first championship game because Peter Grady had flu, proved one of the finest lifters of the ball so far.

Stanley, one of the contenders for the tag of "greatest ever," was to play just 17 times for Kildare, and failed to line out in 1920 because he was disgusted at being suspended for "not trying" in a match.

The suspicion was that he was helping someone win a bet. Bookmakers were common at GAA matches until the 1920s. One of the best stories of a betting footballer was told about Johnny Brennan, who asked a friend to put 7/6 on Dublin at 6/4 in the 1913 Croke Cup competition. Brennan then kicked seven frees to help Louth *beat* Dublin by 0-7 to 0-5. After the game he found out his friend had forgotten to lay the bet in the excitement!

But bookmakers were a minor threat to the GAA compared to what was coming. A new round of bans had just been introduced, against Sinn Féin, the Irish Volunteers, Cumann na mBan and the Gaelic League. The GAA had escaped, but on the eve of the All-Ireland final, the *Freeman's Journal* complained that the authorities: "place every obstacle in the movement of devotees to Irish native games." But, for Gaelic football, the political obstacle-course was only beginning.

Chapter Seven

And When the War Is Over

TAN TRAUMA

The GAA braced itself for a new round of political problems in 1920. At least Leinster's problems were born of old-fashioned football rivalry.

Kildare's threats to withdraw from the 1920 Leinster championship, after Larry Stanley had been suspended for allegedly "not trying" in a challenge against Kerry after the 1919 All-Ireland, brought out the old county rivalries within Leinster and Central Councils.

While old rivals proposed that Kildare be suspended for anything up to five years, Stanley played for Belfast Celtic and, although he lined out for the 1924 All-Ireland final with Dublin, he was not to play for Kildare again until 1926.

When Kildare were eventually persuaded to enter, tragedy resulted. Their first-round match with Wexford resulted in an injury to William Hodgins from which the Wexford player later died due to a complication.

Kildare met Dublin in the Leinster final on August 29th, losing by 1-3 to 0-3. St Enda's headmaster and successor to Pearse, Frank Bourke, scored the final point against his native county, having set up a first-half goal for Paddy Carey.

The All-Ireland semi-final took place on September 9th, and Dublin beat Ulster nominees Cavan by 2-6 to 1-3. Cavan had just beaten Dublin 2-6 to 0-6 in a challenge match in Virginia on September 5th. Then, to Cavan's chagrin, the Central Council postponed the match from September 12th for two weeks. When it went ahead John Synnott killed off Cavan with two early goals while Frank Bourke scored a third at the beginning of the second half. J P Murphy got

Cavan's goal just before half-time.

As it happened, despite the argufying, Leinster was one of only two provinces to complete their championship in 1920. While less sporting troubles brought competition to a halt in Munster and Ulster, seven days before the Leinster final Connacht had completed their championship when Mayo beat Sligo in the final at Castlerea before 2,000 spectators.

Tom "Click" Brennan, Paddy Colleran and Mick Kilcoyne were the stars of the Sligo team which beat Mayo in the final of the "other" Connacht competition, the Railway Cup of 1920. Sligo were soon to make a big impact on the championship itself, but not for two more years. Mayo were eventually saved by first-half goals from P Robinson, from a free, and D F Courell, with a fine overhead effort, to defeat Sligo. A group of Sligo supporters from Templeboy commissioned a motor lorry to bring them to the game.

Ulster's championship had reached the final stages by then, but the final between Cavan and Armagh was not played until August 1923. In a noteworthy championship, Down shocked Antrim, now just a shadow of their former strength, and a run-of-the-mill motor breakdown depleted Tyrone's team for the match against Armagh.

But it was Munster which felt the winds of war the most. Kerry had beaten Cork in the first Munster semi-final on June 20th before play came to a stop there. Tipperary were due to play Waterford but did not get a chance to do so until February 19th 1922. By then all had changed utterly.

Several closed days had disrupted the GAA calendar, and Tipperary had long been out of action when a letter from the secretary and captain of the Tipperary football team appeared in the *Freeman's Journal* on November 1st 1920:

> We understand that Tipperary's superiority over Dublin
> in football, despite two decisive victories by Tipperary,
> is being questioned by Dublin. We therefore challenge
> Dublin to a match on the first available date, on any
> venue, and for any objective.

Dublin replied. The Central Council fixed a match for November 21st, in aid of an injured Gael. The Gael was not named, but in Dublin Castle they had no doubt that the game was to raise funds for the IRA.

The day was to become known as Bloody Sunday. Early in the morning groups from Michael Collins' squad entered eight separate houses and shot dead 12 British officers and wounded several others. The IRA claimed the British were agents sent to assassinate Republican leaders.

In the afternoon soldiers and police went to Croke Park and fired upon the crowd as a reprisal. Twelve people died on the day, and a thirteenth later in hospital. Nine people, including three children, were shot dead. A woman was crushed to death in the panic. Another man died of shock. Among the dead was Tipperary footballer Michael Hogan. The GAA immediately accepted its crown of martyrdom in the cause of Irish freedom. Hogan entered the mythology of the Association. The Hogan Stand at Croke Park was named in his honour in 1925 (the present stand was built in 1959).

The outrage brought Gaelic games to an end for the first half of 1921. On July 11th 1921, a truce was declared between the Irish Republican and British forces, but it was another 10 months, 18 months after Bloody Sunday, before the Munster championship resumed.

Tipperary beat Kerry by 2-2 to 0-2 in the provincial final. Meanwhile, the country braced itself for a Civil War which would tear both counties apart.

So the All-Ireland semi-final eventually took place on May 7th 1922 and Tipperary beat Mayo by 1-5 to 1-0 before a surprisingly large crowd of 15,000. Tom Powell got the goal at the end of the first half. William Lydon got Mayo's goal. Pat Robinson was Mayo's best player as Sean Lavin did not reproduce his Connacht championship form.

When Tipperary started out in the 1920 championship, Dan Breen was on the run. By the time the All-Ireland final was played between Tipperary and Dublin 18 months later, Dan Breen was a hero of the revolution and invited to start the match by throwing in the ball before a crowd of 17,000.

Tipperary won by 1-6 to 1-2. Frank Bourke, another hero of the revolution, scored a magnificent 30-yard goal for Dublin to send them 1-2 to 0-3 ahead at half-time, but

Tipperary came back to equalise 18 minutes into the second half and go ahead with a Mick Arrigan point before Tom Powell got a clinching goal. Ned O'Shea was the best of their backs; Tom Powell, Gus McCarthy, Mick Tobin and Vincent Vaughan the best forwards.

The following week Dublin beat Monaghan by 2-8 to 2-2 in the 1921 All-Ireland semi-final.

Leinster had completed their championship by September 1921 despite a drawn final, but some teams were badly prepared for championship action. Kildare's 9-8 to 1-1 annihilation of Carlow stood as a record for 58 years. Both counties expected the game to be prohibited by the British authorities, but it went ahead and the better-prepared Kildare were sent on course with a goal from local man Ed "Sapper" O'Neill, later to star on New York and USA Tailteann teams.

Leinster found the going tough throughout 1921. The attendance at many early-round matches did not cover the costs of the games, as motor cars had to be used because the railway system had broken down. The salvation came from a £2,974 windfall from the replayed football final. The drawn final drew an estimated 20,000—the biggest attendance since Bloody Sunday.

The inactivity of the months since had been used to carry out £12,000 of improvements to the ground with a view to staging the Tailteann Games, now a real possibility since the Dáil had given it the go-ahead. A new stand had been erected in Croke Park (or Crow Park, as it was called in the British House of Commons after Bloody Sunday) and the length of the pitch increased by 15 yards.

Albert O'Neill got Kildare's goal for a 1-3 to 0-6 draw and "Joyce" Conlan, the 1903 All-Ireland final goal-scorer who was still going strong, missed the chance of a winning point. Dublin won the replay by 3-3 to 1-3 and went on to beat Monaghan. There was an early goal from Bill Fitzsimmons, Dixon scored a second after 10 minutes, and Dublin led 2-3 to 1-0 at half-time before going on to win by six points. Michael Deery scored both Monaghan goals.

Monaghan's preparations for the semi-final included six weeks spent in jail after they were kidnapped by B Specials in

Dromore, Co Tyrone, on January 14th 1922 while on their way to play in the Ulster final against Derry.

Half of the team were in the old IRA, including Dan Hogan, Officer-in-Command of the 5th Northern Division, and brother of Bloody Sunday footballer-victim Mike Hogan of Grangemockler. But the War of Independence had ended with a truce the previous July and the IRA was now the army of the new Free State. They were travelling in six cars in convoy to Derry for the game. Documents were found on them relating to plans to release three prisoners due to be executed in Derry jail. Pro- and anti-Treaty factions united in the efforts to get the players released.

Then things turned nasty. In February 42 loyalists were kidnapped by the IRA and held as hostages for the footballers. Eventually the three prisoners were reprieved and the footballers released on February 16th, after Michael Collins, had intervened and instructions had been passed to Sir James Craig from Winston Churchill.

The match was postponed while the players spent those six weeks in jail, but in the confusion afterwards arranging a replay proved difficult, and Monaghan represented Ulster in the All-Ireland semi-final against Dublin in June. The final was eventually played (after the 1922 and 1923 finals had been completed) on October 28th 1923 when Monaghan beat Derry by 2-2 to 0-1 to confirm their nomination to represent Ulster as provincial champions that year. "The Ulster Council are nothing if not persistent," *Sport* commented. Their persistence had to extend to locating their entire funds. The account had been transferred so often from bank to bank that the treasurer claimed he had mislaid it!

And according to the *Anglo-Celt* of May 13th 1922, the prize for a game between two local teams at Ballyjamesduff the following day would be a machine gun!

In Connacht Mayo played one match each year, beating Roscommon in November 1921, Galway in June 1922, and Roscommon in March 1923 to win the Connacht championship. A Roscommon v Sligo match fixed for Tubbercurry fell through—both districts were controlled by anti-Treaty forces during the early stages of the Civil War.

Mayo got a walk-over from Tipperary in the semi-final.

Munster Council got through their fixture pile-up and wriggled out of an impasse with some ingenuity, deciding that the 1920 finalists should play the 1921 provincial finals. This was really designed to get over a difficult objection by Limerick hurlers to a Cork player. It suited the hurlers, but Tipperary and Kerry still had not played before the Civil War took full effect from July 1922. With fighting especially severe in the Kerry mountains and around Carrick-on-Suir, a November Munster Council meeting decided to postpone all championships until 1923.

The Civil War issue would not go away in Munster. In April 1923 Tipperary finally conceded a long-fought, on-again, off-again All-Ireland semi-final against Mayo on the issue of the Republican prisoners, officially because they found it "impossible to field a team."

Eventually in June 1923, Dublin beat Mayo by 1-9 to 0-2 in the All-Ireland final. They had the game sewn up when Bill Fitzsimmons scored a late goal to augment their scoreline. Dublin took 15 minutes to open the scoring and led 0-4 to 0-1 at half-time.

The spectators watched a new tactic in operation that day. Mayo point-scorer Sean Lavin was one of the first to perfect the hand-to-toe technique, and was later to represent Ireland in the sprints at the 1924 Olympics, at which Dublin and Kildare midfielder Larry Stanley competed in the high jump. Ireland had a flag of its own by then. The birth of the nation had been painful.

BACKLOG BREAKING

The rest of 1923 would be spent clearing up the backlog of fixtures. Leinster alone of all the provinces completed its 1922 provincial championship on time, as tensions mounted.

Anti-Treaty forces had seized the Four Courts in April 1922, British troops began withdrawing from the barracks on May 17th, and the Four Courts bombardment started the Civil War on June 28th. As a result the Dublin—Kildare semi-final was postponed from July 9th to October 1st. When the game got under way "local incidents and prevailing circumstances" caused five of the Kildare team not to turn up and they lost by 2-5 to 0-1.

For the Leinster final, Kilkenny called their 1911 goal-scorer Paddy Dalton out of retirement to play in goal, but were missing two of their current players because of a motor breakdown. It was Kilkenny's last appearance in the Leinster final, as they lost by 1-7 to 0-2 to rampant Dublin. Paddy McDonnell ran up 1-4 without interruption at the start of the second half, breaking the dogged Kilkenny defence open after Dublin were held 0-2 to 0-1 at half-time.

Inside Newbridge internment camp, where 1,200 anti-Treaty campaigners were imprisoned, Kildare had defeated Dublin by 3-6 to 1-5 in the internees' Leinster final in October 1922. The campaign to get those prisoners released was increasingly intruding on Gaelic games throughout that summer of 1923.

Munster was the scene of the worst excesses of the Civil War. South Tipperary was reorganised in August 1923, but Kerry was still undergoing post-war confusion. Tipperary had a walk-over from war-torn Kerry, but different types of walking were involved before they beat Cork in the Munster semi-final. They had to walk part of the way, travel partly by car, and partly by rail past blocked roads and blown-up bridges on the way to Cork. After all the exertion, Jim Ryan got the vital goal as Tipperary beat Limerick by 1-7 to 0-1 in the Munster final. That the final was played at all was regarded as a triumph for the GAA as a unifying force over the bitterness of the Civil War.

Monaghan won the Ulster championship with a last-minute goal from Mickey McAleer to put them 2-7 to 2-6 ahead of Cavan. Armagh managed to field a team for the semi-final against Monaghan at Ballybay, despite the fact that they had no county board at the time and half their team was on the run on both sides of the border. The newly established border was causing more than a little discomfort for GAA followers and most of the matches in the championship were held south of the border.

Monaghan failed to get a single score against Dublin in the

semi-final at Dundalk in July 1923, and lost by 2-5 to nil. John Synnott got both Dublin's goals in the second half after they led 0-3 to nil at half-time.

But the talking-point of the 1922 championship was the saga of how Sligo won an All-Ireland semi-final and never played in the final. In the Connacht final, Sligo beat Galway by a point, 3-2 to 1-7, thanks to goals from Tom "Click" Brennan, Mick Kilcoyne and Vincent Cunningham. Objections dogged Sligo through the campaign—they had to beat Roscommon twice in the first round. The inevitable objection from Galway eventually cost them their hard-won Connacht title.

Sligo had beaten Tipperary in the All-Ireland semi-final by the time that Galway's objection was upheld. Three points down at half-time against Tipperary they took the game by storm and won by 1-8 to 0-7. Michael Kilcoyne got three points, James Colleran added another, a Sligo goal was disallowed and with 10 minutes to go Nick Devine scored the winning goal.

The Connacht final replay acted as a curtain-raiser to the All-Ireland hurling final. This time Galway won by 2-4 to 1-5, as Pat Roche and Denis Egan struck for goals in the first half on front of a not very impressed 20,000 crowd. Bernie Colleran replied for Sligo, who were short James Colleran, Peter Harte and Ned Colleran.

So Galway got straight into the All-Ireland final and Sligo remain the only team to have won an All-Ireland semi-final and never to have played in a final.

Galway went down in the final anyway. Dublin came from behind to beat them by 0-6 to 0-4. Captain Paddy Carey scored the last point from a 50. Joe Synnott, Paddy McDonnell and Frank Bourke also scored before Martin Walsh and Leonard McGrath pushed Galway ahead. The game was played on September 9th 1923, and for the first time there was a real possibility of getting the 1923 series out of the way and bringing the championship back up to date.

The little comedy left the Connacht Council with egg on its face. But what war had done to disrupt the GAA was nothing compared with what the Connacht Council would achieve over the next three years.

GETTING THEM OUT

Ulster was a model of efficiency in 1923, in probably the most adverse circumstances of all. Three Ulster finals in all were played in 1923, four if you count the drawn 1922 final, including the 1921 final played in October before a gate of £7/15/-! Derry, contestants in that delayed 1921 final, had been kicked out of the 1923 championship for playing an illegal team and Donegal given their place in the semi-final. Donegal failed to show, and eventually Cavan beat Monaghan by 5-10 to 1-1 in the 1923 Ulster final at Cavan before a a gate of £104. This gates bonanza meant the Ulster Council could grant a set of medals to internees on the Argenta in Larne and at Ballykinlar camp in County Down, as the troubles began to die away.

Dublin were managing to continue a normal GAA life in the midst of all the trouble, and were favourites to retain their All-Ireland title in 1923 as the effects of Civil War inactivity were felt in the rural counties. Kilkenny ousted an out-of-practice Kildare rather spectacularly from the 1923 championship by 2-3 to 2-1, after the sides were level 1-0 each at half-time. Dublin beat Meath by 3-5 to nil in the Leinster final!

Dublin beat Mayo by 1-6 to 1-2 in the All-Ireland semi-final with a goal from Frank Bourke at the start of the second half in reply to one by White, on another cold, miserable, semi-final day.

In Munster, the memories of Tipperary's semi-final no-show and the return of Kerry would be sure to test the frayed nerves of GAA followers. Kerry's pro-Treaty team won the Munster championship without any help from their interned colleagues, beating Limerick by 4-5 to 1-3, Cork by 3-4 to 0-3 and Tipperary by 0-6 to 0-3. But all was not well. Only two players had turned up for Kerry's first training session of the year and three players had to be recruited from the sideline to make up the 15 to play Cork in the semi-final.

In April 1924 Kerry defeated Cavan by 1-3 to 1-2 in the

All-Ireland semi-final. Kerry had to endure an enthralling finish in their semi-final against Cavan in terrible weather conditions. Tom Egan got Cavan's first-half goal that put them two points ahead.

With six minutes to go they still led by two points when, in the quagmire that passed for a Cavan goal-mouth, the ball was forced over the line demolishing netting and almost demolishing Cavan goalkeeper Jack Heslin. Amid protests the goal was awarded. J P Murphy's equalising point for Cavan came seconds too late. Cavan had the help of Kildare stars Paul Doyle and Jack Higgins stationed in the army in Cavan.

But playing off the 1923 All-Ireland finals was now proving to be more difficult than at first thought. The Free State Government continued to hold in gaol a large number of prisoners. In August de Valera joined them. An October hunger-strike created a public hysteria and in Waterford GAA games were halted to draw attention to their plight. Grounds in Cork were vandalised by sympathisers. Although the hunger-strike was called off on November 23rd, two days later several delegates walked out of a Kilkenny County Board meeting when it refused to stop all matches until anti-Treaty prisoners were released.

For six months of 1924 there was no sign of a mass release of political prisoners. Dublin would not accept a walk-over awarded in June 1924 when Kerry refused to travel for the All-Ireland final in protest at the imprisonment of County Board chairman Austin Stack, among the last Civil War prisoners released alongside Eamon de Valera in July 1924.

Most of the Munster GAA backed the anti-Treaty side. After hasty suspensions were dished out to football finalists Kerry, hurling finalists Limerick and junior hurling finalists Cork for refusing to fulfil All-Ireland fixtures, Munster Council joined the protest by refusing to participate in the Tailteann festival and Connacht followed suit. Only a special congress in August 1924 prevented a split in the GAA.

Kerry benefited in the end. When the internees were released they beat the county team by 12 points in a replayed challenge match. There were 11 changes in the team for the

All-Ireland championship!

The 1923 All-Ireland final eventually got under way on September 28th. A 20,000 attendance paid receipts of £1,622.

Although Dublin won by 1-5 to 1-3, Kerry started with a storm. Con Brosnan crashed home a 50-yard shot to give them a 1-2 to 0-1 half-time lead, but Kirwan had a goal for Dublin from John Synnott's cross on the restart and Paddy McDonnell, Jack Murphy and Joe Stynes (2) got the points to secure a four-point win.

Whereas Brosnan, later to stand for Cumann na nGaedheal in the 1932 General Election, and many of the Kerry team were pro-Treaty, John Joe Sheehy, Kerry's second-half scorer was definitely anti-. When Sheehy was hiding out "on the run," he had heard the land-mine blast in Ballyseedy when nine prisoners were killed in one of the most horrific episodes of the Civil War, and rescued a survivor, Stephen Fuller, from the scene. He was on the run constantly from August 1922 to May 1924. When he emerged from his Cnocán dug-out to play in a match in aid of Republican prisoners in Tralee (700 from the town were in internment camps), no attempt was made to arrest him. In Kerry football was helping to dress the wounds of Civil War.

Paul Russell, who was 17, had never played before for Kerry at any grade when he was selected to play in the final.

KINGDOM RETHRONED

A year in internment camps had sharpened up the Kerrymen. They halted Dublin's bid for four in a row at the last hurdle in the 1924 All-Ireland final, not played until April 1925.

Three weeks before the 1923 All-Ireland final, two first-half goals from Bill Landers helped Kerry's reunited team beat Cork by 4-3 to 2-1 in the Munster semi-final. Then, a fortnight after the All-Ireland defeat, they beat Clare by 3-10 to 2-2 in the Munster final. Con Brosnan dominated midfield and three Kerry goals insulated the champions against two late goals in reply by Clare for an 11-point victory.

Kerry had a Dublinman on board. Jimmy Bermingham later went on to play for Bohemians in their record-breaking

1927-8 sweep of FAI Cup, League of Ireland, Shield and Leinster Cup.

Reaching the final was an achievement for still-divided Clare, whose county board had split after the execution of county secretary Pat Hennessy and fellow GAA activist Con MacMahon by the Free State forces in January 1923. By the time the 1924 Munster final was played, the two county boards were suspending players who played in the other board's competitions. It was the summer of 1925 before the situation was resolved.

Kerry continued their comeback march as winter closed in. In December 1924, John Ryan scored a goal at the end of the first half of Kerry's semi-final against Mayo for a 1-4 to 0-1 victory before a £460 crowd. Mayo had won the Connacht championship after a unique 0-1 each draw with Galway when the final was first played.

Meanwhile, Wexford reappeared in the forefront in Leinster. Martin O'Neill scored their 1-1 total in the semi-final to help them beat another re-emerging county, Kildare, for whom 1903 hero Frank "Joyce" Conlan was making his last appearance. In the other semi-final Dublin had a man sent off in a 2-6 to 2-4 victory over Louth and also missed their adopted midfielder, Larry Stanley, who competed with the first Irish Olympic team in Paris in May.

It took Dublin two efforts to beat Wexford in the final. The first day a late goal from another internee, Joe Stynes, saved Dublin from defeat, 1-4 to 1-4. In the replay, Dublin took an early 2-1 to 1-2 lead with goals from Joe Stynes and M O'Brien. In fact, Dublin led by nine points approaching the end of the replayed final before Martin O'Neill's goal for Wexford cut back the margin to five points, 3-5 to 2-3.

The only controversy was, thankfully, an old-fashioned "biased referee" football dispute. Dublin objected to ex-Kerry footballer Dick Fitzgerald being appointed to referee their semi-final against Cavan because of his decision, as an umpire, to allow a Mayo goal against them in 1923. Despite J P Murphy's scoring a second-half goal from a free he followed up himself, Dublin won easily by 0-6 to 1-1. Cavan's goalkeeper R Black was outstanding.

Dublin's run came to a halt as rejuvenated Kerry defeated them by 0-4 to 0-3 in a fabulous game, watched by 28,844 spectators. The gate receipts of £2,564 became a cause of a libel case against the *Freeman's Journal* who claimed that "there was surely 40,000 at the match."

Kerry's man of the match was Con Brosnan, who scored the winning point after a tremendous match. It took 20 minutes to open the scoring. Dublin's Joe Synnott pointed the first free of the game from 40 yards, Landers punched an equaliser for Kerry. Peter Synnott restored Dublin's lead two minutes later; John Baily and then Con Brosnan gave Kerry a 0-3 to 0-2 half-time lead. Joe Synnott pointed an acute-angle free to equalise. In a final enthralling sequence Baily had a goal disallowed for "whistle gone" before Brosnan's winning point.

Spectators paid five shillings to sit in the newly erected wooden Hogan Stand, named after the Tipperary footballer who died on Bloody Sunday. A new scoreboard on the railway wall was in use for the first time. It was a tremendous game which was probably the best in Gaelic football history to date.

So good was it that it reminded the *Sport* correspondent of Arravales v Young Irelands. This was an achievement, because Arravales never played Young Irelands in the All-Ireland championship during the 1890s heyday of both teams, just in a forgotten 1894 Croke Cup final. Even in 1924 nostalgia was not what it used to be!

Chapter Eight

Renewing a Rivalry

DECLARATION CONSTERNATION

Just when the GAA had apparently extricated itself from a political minefield, it carefully constructed a home-made one which promptly blew the 1925 championship out of the record books.

A sad and confused championship resulted from a motion to the 1925 congress that players could opt to play for their native county. It was designed so that rural counties could plunder the wealth of talented footballers who migrated to Dublin and were debarred from championship football. At the 1925 Congress, Barney Fay of Cavan won the case with a plea: "We only ask for a chance that players who are not wanted by Dublin teams to assist counties where they have trained." The motion was accepted with a small amendment.

Rural teams scrambled to reclaim their exiles. Dublin, whose three-in-a-row had helped bring the motion about, went out of the championship at the first hurdle, 2-4 to 1-6 victims of Wexford. Two goals inside the first minute of the second half, from Martin O'Neill and Jack Lucey, turned a five-point deficit into a lead that Wexford never surrendered. Ironically Martin O'Neill was one of the declaration players but he was not living in Dublin, he resided in Bray at the time. He went on to score four goals for Wexford against Meath. Wexford went on to take the title. Kilroy and Synnott got the goals in a 2-7 to 0-3 victory over a shaky but promising Kildare team in the final.

After Kerry beat Cavan by 1-7 to 2-3 and Mayo beat Wexford by 2-4 to 1-4 in the All-Ireland semi-finals, things started to go wrong. Cavanman James P Murphy, ironically from the county which first proposed the rule change, was the new rule's first casualty because of his somewhat complicated life-style.

He had played with Dublin club Keatings in 1924 but with Cornafean in 1925, while he was living in Mullingar! It emerged that he went home at weekends and had taken a month's sick leave before the All-Ireland semi-final. On a 9-5 vote he was found to be illegal because the declaration rule was not clear enough in defining a player's home, one Galway delegate pleading that "a man's home is where he earns his bread and butter."

Murphy's contribution to the All-Ireland semi-final had been outstanding, particularly his innovative hand-to-toe solo runs, the first time the tactic had been seen by many Kerrymen (although it had first been used by 1903 Kildare footballer Michael Kennedy, and was also used well by Sean Lavin of Mayo).

Kerryman Phil Sullivan was next on the doubtful list. He played for his college UCD against the Civic Guards in a Dublin hurling league match and for Faughs in the Dublin hurling championship, so Kerry too were eliminated on spurious grounds.

Kerry demanded a special congress to sort out the crux but the GAA stuck to their rule-books, and meanwhile Connacht muddled their way through an 11-match championship that fell hopelessly behind schedule. When a Connacht application to postpone the All-Ireland championship was refused by Central Council early in the year, the Provincial Council nominated Mayo to take part.

So when Kerry and Cavan were thrown out of the championship everyone assumed Mayo became champions by default. Defeated semi-finalists Wexford had a go on the objection merry-go-round as well, but their claim that Mayo player, Michael Mulderrig, had played for Tipperary against Kerry in the Munster Junior championship failed on another 9-5 vote. It was a pity because the semi-finals had both been exciting: Jack Henry and Williams got Mayo's first-half goals to beat Wexford by a goal, and John Joe Sheehy's 10th-minute goal spurred Kerry to a one-point victory over Cavan.

Connacht's championship was still plodding along. Roscommon and Sligo played six times. Despite the fact that Sligo qualified in the end, two of the matches were won by Roscommon. After the first meeting in Boyle, Sligo objected that a disallowed goal of theirs should have been allowed. Sligo's Mick Noone forced a draw with a late goal the second day. Sligo's Tom "Click" Brennan forced a second draw with a late point, and Sligo forced a third draw with two second-half goals after they trailed 1-3 to nil at half-time. Roscommon won the fifth match with a disputed goal on which the referee "reserved judgement" until the next council meeting, and eventually Sligo won at the sixth attempt by the decisive margin of seven points, 2-3 to 0-2.

Leitrim forced Galway to two draws, refused to play extra time, and were eventually beaten 2-3 to 1-4 at the third attempt.

Mayo had already been declared All-Ireland champions when the Connacht final was played. Galway beat them by 1-5 to 1-3. A free from old 1919 warrior, Michael "Knacker" Walsh, at the start of the second half hit the net in response to a similar goal from Mayo's Jack Henry.

Galway (who reportedly had not trained) were now Connacht champions. But even they were surprised by the news that the All-Ireland title had been awarded to them at a Central Council meeting on October 23rd. A Galway delegate proposed that Galway become champions after Sean T Ruane of Mayo left the meeting and the motion sneaked through.

Galway were champions for two weeks before anyone knew anything about it. An *Irish Independent* newspaper report on November 7th leaked the information that sometime after midnight at the October 23rd 1925 meeting of the Central Council the All-Ireland championship had been awarded to Galway. In the 1925 championship, a council chamber lobbyist proved more important than 15 men on the field.

The embarrassed Central Council organised an "in lieu" competition that had no real credibility because Kerry refused to compete. Galway did save some blushes by winning it with two three-goal sprees: from Bannerton, Egan and James as they beat Wexford by 3-4 to 1-1 in the semi-final against Wexford, and from Roche (2) and Egan as they beat Cavan by 3-2 to 1-2 in the final. Kerry instead replayed their 1924 All-Ireland final against defeated Leinster finalists Dublin in a much-heralded challenge match but lost 2-6 to 1-6.

Galway got their only dual medallist out of the chaos: Leonard McGrath who had forsaken rugby to play in the 1925 championship (and may have been illegal if anybody had bothered to object against Galway). Once claimed as a native of Australia, McGrath was claimed as a native of Leitrim, a parish between Athenry and Ballinasloe, in the 1967 *Our Games Annual* by Seamus Ó Cualláin. The GAA suffered from more than a tarnished image: funds were down from £2,553 to £1,553 because the "in lieu" tournament was poorly supported.

It was not all bad news, however. The 1924 Tailteann Games had seen the revival of inter-provincial competition, when Munster, captained by Phil Sullivan of Kerry (he had eight colleagues, with four Claremen and one each from Limerick and Cork on his team) beat Leinster, captained by Dublin's Paddy Carey. And the unhappy mess might have helped boost interest in a new Central Council competition, the first "secondary" competition since the Wolfe Tone tournament of 1916-17.

While the declaration rule was being introduced, another motion to the 1925 Congress established the Leagues. A four-county League set up by Louth, Monaghan, Cavan and Meath, proved highly successful in 1924. National Leagues were proposed by Sean McCarthy of Cork and seconded by Liam Clifford of Limerick (both were to become presidents of the GAA).

The Central Council set up a sub-committee to formulate the League and they presented their findings on Sunday, August 8th 1925. The competitions were seen as a threat to the traditional power-base of the GAA, the club and club competition, and the club structure has had a stormy relationship with the League at times in the years since.

The competitions began in 1926. Unlikely group winners emerged: Antrim, Laois, Longford and Sligo, as well as

Dublin and Kerry. Laois footballers won their first national competition: they beat Kerry by 1-6 to 1-5 in the semi-final and eventually beat Dublin before 1,000 spectators in New Ross in the first final.

Until 1935-6, the Football Leagues were run on a regional basis with three divisions and a series of play-offs between the divisional winners.

JACK MURPHY'S MEDALS

Kerry and Kildare restored pride and funds to the GAA with another classic replayed final in 1926.

The year had not started well for Kerry, still seething over the declaration fiasco of 1925. Cork shocked Kerry in the Munster semi-final with two early goals from Jim Fortune and Duggan, but a Paddy Farren goal left the teams level at half-time, and Jackie Ryan, Joe Barrett and Tom O'Mahoney points gave Kerry a 1-9 to 2-1 victory and a final against Tipperary—which was just as well, because the final was advertised on Railway Company posters before the semi-final had even been played!

Kerry beat Tipperary by 0-11 to 1-4 with the help of six points from John Joe Sheehy and would have won by more if it hadn't been for Barrett's late goal for Tipperary. Kerry's Jeremiah Moriarty and McCarthy of Tipperary were sent off for fighting in the first half, at the end of which Kerry led by 0-5 to 0-3.

In the semi-finals Jackie Ryan's first-half goal and four points was enough to exact revenge for Kerry over Cavan, the last nominated team in an All-Ireland semi-final, who "abandoned their old aggressive game" only to be mesmerised by Kerry's deft quick-passing and lost by 1-6 to 0-1.

The news that their opponents were going to be old 1903 and 1905 adversaries Kildare was greeted with delight by old-timers. Kildare began their comeback by hammering Louth by 5-8 to 1-5 in Leinster. A good first-half display (with Joe Curtis and George Higgins goals) deposed Dublin by 2-5 to 1-2 in the Leinster semi-final. They had Bill "Squires"

Gannon in goal-scoring form (he scored both goals as they beat Wexford by 2-8 to 1-5 in the final) and Larry Stanley back under the declaration rule.

A 12,000 crowd watched the Leinster final as Kildare built up a seven-point lead and Patsy O'Connor's goal came too late to save Wexford. Kildare looked even more impressive as they tore apart All-Ireland champions Galway by 2-5 to 0-2 with goals from Curtis and Ryan, although some Michael "Knacker" Walsh scores had given Galway an early two-point lead.

The final survived the threat of another 1910-style boycott: North Kerry players were asked not to travel to the match in a protest over the quality of train services.

This match was worth waiting for. Bill Gorman got one of the most dramatic equalising goals in GAA history after 29 minutes of the second half, five minutes short of the final whistle, and forced a 1-3 to 0-6 draw.

Jack Murphy of Kerry played an excellent game at centre half back, but apparently put on his clothes without bothering to take off his playing-gear afterwards. The following Wednesday a selector, Euge Ring, noticed he was in pain. A doctor was summoned, and he was sent to hospital in Tralee where he died of pneumonia the following day, leaving his colleagues to win an emotional All-Ireland by 1-4 to 0-4 in his honour.

Larry Stanley became embittered by the grilling he got on the field from Phil Sullivan in the replay. Curtailing Stanley in the final paid off for Kerry: he was regarded by now as the greatest player to have pulled on a Gaelic football jersey.

Each of his three scores in the drawn match came from frees. Eight minutes into the second half he pointed a free kick from an angle so acute he had to remove the corner flag to kick it. He also scored a point in the replay, despite some rough treatment.

Tom O'Mahoney scored Kerry's valuable second-half goal in the replay. Kildare hit the woodwork three times as the squashed followers cheered the match to the echo. P D Mehigan relayed the match to a couple of thousand radio listeners. "Pirate" programmes were on sale for the first time.

Attendance figures brought a bonanza for the impoverished Central Council. The drawn match drew 37,500 spectators paying a total of £3,540; 35,500 turned up for the replay, paying £3,374. The GAA could pay its bills again.

SHORT GRASS SUCCESS

Kildare and Kerry's rivalry had been passed on to an enthusiastic new generation. Revitalised and filled up with "if only" stories from one of the greatest finals ever, Kildare stuttered back into action in the 1927 championship. Meath led Kildare 0-3 to 0-1 at half-time before succumbing in the semi-final before Kildare came back to win 1-5 to 1-2.

Kildare retained the Leinster title by 0-5 to 0-3 as sharp-shooter Paul Doyle scored four of his side's points. He was resuming an old free-taking rivalry with Kerryman Paul Russell, captain of Dublin for the year.

Russell changed allegiance because his club, Garda, had won the Dublin championship. It was rumoured that Garda sought a declaration from all its team that they would play with Dublin to help win the 1927 All-Ireland championship. The outcome of all of this was that Larry Stanley, the most famous Garda of them all, opted to play for neither Dublin nor Kildare.

Paul Russell helped Dublin defeat Wexford by 0-8 to 1-1 in a replayed semi-final, one of the last matches at Kilkenny's old St James' Park. The venue certainly left its mark on those who occupied the specially rented grandstand. It collapsed beneath their weight, and sent six-inch nails protruding through an occasional backside, with not a whisper about public liability insurance in those innocent times. The man who would be responsible for all aspects of organisation at the game, the Leinster secretary, was unaware of all this. Instead Martin O'Neill was busy in the Wexford attack. He and Seamus Hayes had scored Wexford's first-meeting goals as they drew 2-5 to 0-11 and Dublin's Mohan was forced to save the match with a late equalising point.

Hayes surprisingly did not score any of the record 13 goals

in Wexford's previous game as they beat Longford by 7-10 to 6-2 in the first round. Longford had just been suspended for 12 months as a result of a row over a challenge match with Dublin in 1926, and at one stage the Connacht Council asked that Longford be allowed to join them!

Kildare reached the final once again, but had to recover from their customary slow start to beat Monaghan by 1-7 to 0-2 with a second-half goal from newcomer Tom Keogh, later to star with Laois.

In Ulster, Monaghan were tired of losing replays to Cavan, so they spiked Cavan's five-in-a-row bid in style, 2-6 to 1-6, thanks to two early goals from Shevlin and T J Weymes and a penalty save by goalkeeper Tommy Bradley. Bradley stopped Jim Smith's kick splendidly when there was three points between the teams minutes from the end. After that, the final should have been easy against the previous year's All-Ireland junior champions, Armagh. Not so. Monaghan were forced to come from behind to win 3-6 to 2-5.

Connacht resumed its traditional histrionics. Mayo and Sligo's first-round match lasted just three minutes, before the crowd invaded. One angry newsman wanted to know why the crowd did not wait until three minutes from the *end* before they invaded and allow everybody to get their money's worth! The referee had changed his mind and disallowed Sligo's goal after Mayo defenders protested and two Sligomen, George Higgins and Mickey Noone, left the field in protest. Sligo were disqualified from competition for 12 months, a punishment that was to have extraordinary results for the Sligomen.

But 1927 was the year of Leitrim's breakthrough. Leitrim's good displays of 1925, when they drew twice against Galway, stood them in good stead as they captured their only Connacht title in 1927 with the help of Sean O'Hehir's training (Sean was father of the veteran radio commentator, Michael) and with a little good luck.

Their Connacht semi-final opponents Roscommon had to line out without five players whose motor car had broken down and Leitrim won a replay encounter by 0-7 to 1-0. Roscommon deserved a replay as some of their team had been recruited from the sideline when Leitrim beat them 1-3 to 0-2 the first day. "Nipper" Shanley led the Leitrim attack to a 2-4 to 0-3 victory over Galway in the Connacht final, and earned a place on the Irish team to play America in the Tailteann tournament.

Contacts with American GAA structures had reached an advanced stage in 1926, and Kerry played Cork earlier than usual in the Munster championship to allow time for a prestigious first ever US tour.

The GAA had been set up in America as early as 1886, when the Irish Athletic Club in Boston was founded, and in June 1886 staged the first Gaelic sports in the United States. The idea of a tour was an old one, too. In 1888 the GAA's American promotional tour, the ill-fated "Invasion," brought the Association's finest athletes on an exhibition tour across America. Of the travelling party, 17 never returned.

Branches of the GAA were formed in New York in 1891, and Brooklyn Wolfe Tones beat the Irish Americans in the continent's first hurling final in 1892. In 1904 the Irish Counties Athletic Union took control of GAA affairs in New York. It was superseded in 1914 by the New York GAA, which was affiliated to the GAA in Ireland. Chicago had a 15-team club league in operation in the 1890s, while Philadelphia, San Francisco and Detroit had GAA organisations from early days. In 1911 a team of Chicago hurlers toured Ireland.

New York's GAA teams first played in Celtic Park in Queens, but the present Gaelic Park located in the Bronx area was first used in 1928. It is the property of the Transport Authority and the lease has been held ever since by individuals closely associated with the GAA in New York. In 1926 Tipperary were the first Irish team to tour the United States, and it was inevitable that they would be followed by Kerry footballers, who embarked on an 11-week tour in 1927.

It was a shock to the Gaelic followers in Ireland that Kerry were beaten so comprehensively by the exiles. New York beat Kerry by 3-11 to 1-7 before 30,000 spectators in the 55,000-capacity New York Giants' baseball stadium, the Polo Grounds, with Mayo's Sean Carr, Tipperary's Martin

Shanahan, and Kildareman Joe Stynes all in action for New York. New York went on to beat Kerry by 12 points to three for the "World's Championship." Even at home, with the Central Council infuriated by the manner in which the New Yorkers advertised the games, it was acknowledged that by now New York had the best Gaelic football team in the world.

Outside New York, attendances were meagre. Only 6,000 showed up in Boston, 8,000 in Chicago, and 4,000 in Springfield, Massachusetts. To the disappointment of the players a promised match in San Francisco fell through for lack of finance.

The tour ended in controversy. On the morning after the final match, the promoter, a former baseball manager in his 80s called Ted Sullivan, disappeared from a New York hotel with all the receipts from the tour. A third match was hastily arranged for Celtic Park. New York won again, this time by 2-5 to 2-1. That, and a donation from the New York Kerry Association helped get the team home.

Part of the motivation in organising a full international between Ireland and the United States as part of the 1928 Tailteann games was to restore Ireland's pride, which the international team duly did with a 2-9 to 1-4 victory.

But the time spent together in America stood Kerry in good stead when they came home and they had an easy run in the championship, beating Cork by 1-7 to 0-1, Tipperary by 2-6 to 1-1, and Clare by 4-4 to 1-3, and then facing Leitrim in the All-Ireland semi-final.

Leitrim's only appearance in a semi-final was a stormy affair in Tuam: as Kerry won by 0-4 to 0-2 the referee did not send anyone off. He stayed out of controversy, ironing over the awkward situations by getting two players to shake hands. Two John Joe Sheehy frees gave Kerry the cushion they needed to go 0-2 to 0-1 up at half-time and gradually wear down the outsiders.

The All-Ireland final between the old rivals was exactly what the spectators ordered. A record 36,529 of them turned up to see Kildare beat Kerry by 0-5 to 0-3, in a game that failed to live up to 1926 levels, but had enough to talk about all the same. Kildare trailed by three points to nil early in the game but Tom Keogh, Paul Doyle, Bill "Squires" Gannon, Joe Curtis and Doyle again scored points to restore Lily White pride.

It was not a classic but the inevitable comparison with the previous year was not entirely inappropriate. Kerry again broke through with five minutes to go but this time John Joe Sheehy hit the post. This time it was Kerry who counted the "if only"'s.

HANDPASS FOR SAM

Immediately, Kerry began strengthening their hand for the 1928 championship. One of their first moves was to attract back their exiled Garda, Paul Russell, now a veteran at 20 years of age.

Russell hit the headlines early in 1928, when he found he was picked by both Munster and Leinster inter-provincial teams! Because he had declared for Dublin in 1927, having already played for Munster in the 1927 Railway Cup, Leinster thought he would be eligible for them. Munster picked him because he had declared for Kerry for the 1928 season, but Central Council ruled he should play for Leinster in the end. It enabled him to win his second Railway Cup medal in two years with different teams.

Meanwhile his Munster colleagues stormed off the field because of a dispute over a goal by Ulster in the semi-final. Ulster took a quick throw-in and scored a goal that gave them a lead of 2-8 to 2-6, but Munster players refused to kick out the ball, claiming that the throw-in to Ulster should have been a Munster throw-in instead. Their walk-off led to a six-month suspension, but the controversy gave the new Railway Cup competition a welcome boost.

The successful Railway Shields experiment was just a memory when Pádraig Ó Caoimh proposed that inter-provincial competition be resumed in 1926. In 1927 the Railway Cups were inaugurated, again donated by the Great Southern and Western Railway Company, to be held annually between the four provinces with the finals to be played on St Patrick's Day. A crowd of 10,000 turned up to see Munster beat Connacht in the first final, despite the fact that Connacht underwent a special course of training in Ballinasloe. For nearly 40 years this formula was to prove highly successful.

Kerry had Russell. Now they wanted revenge for their defeat in the 1927 All-Ireland final. But they had to wait two years to get it. In the 1928 Munster championship, Tipperary inflicted a famous 1-7 to 2-3 semi-final defeat on the six-in-a-row seekers, Kerry's first in a semi-final since 1911. Kenny's goal sent Tipperary 1-7 to 0-3 ahead at half-time, and goals from Kerry's Jack Sheehy and Paul Russell came too late in the game to make any difference.

Then Tipperary were heavily beaten by 4-3 to 0-4 in a one-sided final as Cork's two footballing physicians, Doctors Kearney (who got two) and O'Callaghan scored goals.

Kildare were meanwhile unimpressive in their first outing in Leinster as a boxed Laois goal from Harry Browne had them in trouble in the first round before Kildare won by 0-4 to 1-0.

Meanwhile in Leinster, the recently suspended minnows Longford qualified for the Leinster semi-final with their first ever victory in a senior championship match: Gilleran (2) and Clarke got the goals that beat Meath by 3-4 to 0-11. That match started a tradition, Longford's hex on Meath would be confirmed at the most surprising times over the history of the Leinster championship.

The Leinster final brought Kildare a dramatic narrow-squeak 0-10 to 1-6 victory over Dublin. Kildare went seven-nil up at half-time, Dublin came back. Mick Durnin got a goal, Paddy McDonnell was sent off, and the champions squeezed through. As the referee left the field, chased by a screaming horde of Dublin players, the man who came to his rescue was the Dublin captain Paddy McDonnell. It ensured clemency for McDonnell—and eligibility to play for Ireland in the Tailteann Games. It was a bitter disappointment for McDonnell and his 12 team-mates from O'Tooles who fancied their All-Ireland chances after a big win over Wexford.

For the first time since 1900, Leinster and Munster were paired in the All-Ireland semi-final. As it happened, Kildare had an easy task against Cork and won by 3-7 to 0-2 at Cork Athletic Grounds. Paddy Martin got two of their goals and Joe Curtis the third as they raced 1-5 to nil ahead at half-time and eventually won by 14 points.

That left Connacht and Ulster teams with a great opportunity. In Connacht, Sligo won an overdue title that counted, unlike the 1922 affair, and did it the hard way. After the three-minute mess in 1927, they had been suspended for 12 months and showed the splendid isolation had done no harm by beating Roscommon 1-5 to 0-1 on their comeback on May 13th. They then drew with All-Ireland champions Kildare in a challenge at Sligo showgrounds.

Leitrim too were still contending, beating Galway by 0-7 to 0-3 in a replay after a unique goal-each draw in Roscommon. But Sligo had an easy 1-5 to 0-2 championship win over Leitrim. Nickey Devine delivered the pass to Milo Flynn for Sligo's crucial goal as they beat Mayo by 1-4 to 0-6 in the Connacht final.

Armagh avenged the previous year's defeat by Monaghan, winning 0-4 to 0-1 in a semi-final that was played at 5.30 in the evening to allow Commissioner Eoin O'Duffy's car to travel north with four Monaghan players who had played in the Army v Garda challenge earlier in the day. Regular bulletins were issued from the Garda barracks in Castleblayney as to how the journey was progressing. A four-point objection by Monaghan to Armagh failed afterwards.

When Cavan met Armagh in the Ulster final, brothers Charlie (Armagh) and John (Cavan) Morgan played in opposing goals. Cavan won by 2-6 to 1-4 despite the fact they were without their international star Jimmy Smith.

Cavan trailed by 1-2 to 0-2 at half-time, thanks to Gerry Arthurs' goal for Armagh. A breather in the second half, when Armagh led by 1-4 to 0-5, helped them. The ball was kicked into an adjoining field of oats and it took seven minutes to find it before play resumed. The interruption saved Cavan. J P Murphy and Andy Conlan had the ball in the Armagh net twice in the space of two minutes when play was restarted.

Cavan had home advantage in the All-Ireland semi-final,

yet trailed Sligo by a point at half-time; two quick-fire goals from Andy Conlan and Patsy Devlin at the start of the second half put them into the final, by 2-5 to 0-4.

Cavan were robbed of a breakthrough title. The open-handed pass was the source of much controversy in its day but never more than the Handpass for Sam in 1928. After Kildare won the title by 2-6 to 2-5, P D Mehigan produced one of the most damning lines in GAA history when he wrote: "Let it be written quickly: P Loughlin threw the ball into the Cavan net."

It won a new cup for Kildare captain Bill "Squires" Gannon. There had been no cup for All-Ireland competition for 12 years. A group of friends of the London-based Intelligence officer for Irish forces during the War of Independence (and All-Ireland captain), Sam Maguire, presented a silver cup based on the Ardagh Chalice in his honour.

Paddy Loughlin's goal was not the last scored in the match: it provoked a retaliatory goal from Devlin for Cavan and Bill Mangan scored the winning point for Kildare minutes later. Kildare had led 1-2 to 0-3 at half-time with a Mangan goal and Patsy Devlin had scored the Cavan goal that brought them back into the match immediately before the Loughlin handpass.

Patsy Lynch of Cavan is said to have been the youngest player to play in an All-Ireland final, he was 16 years and six months when he was selected for the game. The attendance was 24,700, receipts £2,007.

Kerry, aggrieved, watched from the wings. But they had the satisfaction of beating Kildare by 2-4 to 1-6 in a National League final that drew 10,000 excited spectators to Croke Park and infused new life into the competition. Another Kildare—Kerry final was on the cards. There would be no slip-up in 1929.

KERRY TO THE FOUR

As the 1920s drew to a close, weaker counties were getting a look-in.

Inspired by Sligo and Leitrim, Longford led Dublin twice in the Leinster quarter-final of 1929 but were stunned by a Paddy McDonnell goal with 10 minutes to go and eventually lost by 3-7 to 2-6. Kilkenny's physically strong team won their last ever senior championship match by 0-10 to 0-4 with a great first-half display against Louth. They then held Kildare level at half-time in the semi-final before succumbing to two last-quarter goals from Albert O'Neill, 2-11 to 0-3. Meath too gave notice of changing times: attacking theologian Fr MacManus scored a late point to earn a replay, 1-5 to 1-5. Bad luck was promised to Kildare when they committed the cardinal indiscretion of objecting to the priest before winning the replay by 3-5 to 0-9. "Ye will never win another All-Ireland," they were told—and they never did.

In the Leinster final Kildare got another fright from a maturing Laois team, before winning by 2-3 to 0-6. They trailed 0-1 to 0-2 at half-time, but two Peter Pringle goals and a series of great saves by goalkeeper James O'Reilly came to their rescue.

Laois showed their capabilities when they beat Wexford by 3-3 to 0-7 in the quarter-final, using an unprecedented five substitutes, and then qualified for the final by beating Dublin by 5-5 to 3-10. O'Shea secured their historic final spot with a doubtful looking final point. Dublin had already been shaken by goals from Jack Delaney, Harry Browne, McDarby, a Dublin defender's own goal and Callanan at that stage.

Derry re-established their county board in 1929, and once more there were 32 counties in competition. But the 1929 Ulster championship is remembered for a tragic incident in the Ulster semi-final between Cavan and Armagh, as Cavan's Jim Smith clashed with Jamesy Kiernan of Crossmaglen. Kiernan died two days after the incident, and a storm erupted around the affair.

Kiernan's death was due to peritonitis following an operation, the doctor in Belturbet having made light of Kiernan's injury after the match. During the inquest Smith was implicated by the questions of an RUC Head Constable and charges were initiated against him in Cavan. Smith was cleared when preliminary evidence was heard, but the incident cast a shadow over Ulster football for several years.

When Monaghan and Cavan met again in Ulster the match was a draw, 1-4 each. In the replay Jim Smith was barracked throughout the match as a consequence of the Jamesy Kiernan incident. To add to Cavan's problems, Monaghan won by 1-10 to 0-7 thanks to a goal from T J Weymes with 10 minutes to go, following up his own shot that came back from an upright. Monaghan faded early against Kildare in the All-Ireland semi-final, were 0-6 to 0-1 down at half-time, and lost by 0-9 to 0-1.

But Kildare's old rivals were stirring. Cork led Kerry by 1-2 to 1-1 at half-time but Kerry avoided another semi-final exit by 1-7 to 1-3 with a John Joe Landers goal. When Kerry met Clare in the final for the fourth time in seven years Clare showed their strong defensive qualities, but precious little else. Kerry went 0-10 to nil up at half-time despite having a goal disallowed, and raced away to a 1-14 to 1-2 victory as Miko Doyle made his debut for the team.

In the Connacht championship, Sligo and Leitrim played the last senior championship match to take place without nets on the goal-posts—after they lost by 1-4 to 0-6 Leitrim's objection was ruled out of order because it was not on Irish watermarked paper. Meanwhile Mayo laid the foundation of a great 1930s team by winning the provincial title. Six D F Courell points, combined with a goal from Kenny, helped them beat Galway by 1-6 to 0-4 after mauling unfortunate Roscommon by 20 points in the semi-final. Mayo went into three weeks full-time training under Garda boxing instructor Tommy Moloney at Enniscrone, but they were crushed in turn by Kerry in the All-Ireland semi-final, by 3-8 to 1-1. The closest they got to the final was shortly after half-time when they came within two points of the Kerrymen.

In the All-Ireland final Kerry survived a rattling second-half comeback by Kildare that kept the record attendance of 43,839, paying receipts of £4,010, on their feet to the end.

Ned Sweeney's first-half goal, shot in off the upright after a Jackie Ryan free, proved enough. John Joe Sheehy and Paul Doyle scored five points each in a duel of free-taking. Paddy Martin landed a 30-yard drop-kick into the net at the start of the second half to inspire Kildare.

John Joe Landers and John Joe Sheehy points killed off the challenge when Kildare came back to within a point of Kerry, against the sun and the wind. But instead of Kildare's three-in-a-row, Gaelic football braced itself for Kerry's four.

In the National League, Kerry beat Kildare, again by a single point, 1-7 to 2-3. The rivals had much more to offer. But first an interlude.

BULLFIGHT

The Kerry v Kildare rivalry had not passed its peak. The sides should have met again in 1930—but things started going wrong. Just as Kerry's concentration had slipped in the run-up to the big match in 1928, Kildare's slipped in 1930. The result was a breakthrough for Monaghan that had such humiliating results that Monaghan supporters wondered was it worth the effort.

Monaghan had no real opposition in Ulster. They qualified for a final meeting with Cavan when they beat Armagh by 2-2 to 0-5 with a goal each from Mason and, in the last minute, from Charlie McCarthy. The fearful referee had to be escorted from the field by RUC men after he sent off Armagh star Jack Corrigan. At least they only had to play one team in the Ulster semi-final.

Cavan, on the other hand, had to play the Ulster semi-final twice against two separate opponents! Antrim did not include Patrick Gunning in the list of players handed to the referee when they beat Fermanagh 3-3 to 2-5, with the help of two(!) own goals by defenders. Then Cavan faced two separate opponents in two Ulster semi-finals. They had already beaten Antrim in the semi-final when the objection was upheld, so they had to beat Fermanagh as well.

The final was endangered when Cavan objected to travelling to Carrickmacross' showpiece grounds, opened two years earlier, because of the abuse Jim Smith suffered there in 1929. The Ulster Council secretary, Cavanman Benny Fay, and colleague Standish O'Grady recruited a rebel Cavan team on the morning of the match, mainly from

Cornafean and Crosserlough.

It was heavily beaten, trailing 3-3 to nil at half-time and eventually losing by 4-3 to 1-5, to goals from Fischer (2), McCarthy and P J Duffy. Cavan County Board reacted by suspending all of the rebels, and "selectors" Fay and O'Grady. Cavan were in turn suspended for failing to turn up at the Ulster junior final two weeks after the senior final. They also missed a National Football League match against Down on August 3rd. As confrontation loomed, a special convention on September 27th tried to defuse the situation and reinstated Cavan.

Monaghan were underdogs for their All-Ireland semi-final. But it was a good year for underdogs. In the Leinster semi-final Dublin were already struggling against underdogs Meath in the semi-final before Tom McGennis' goal plunged them seven points down; P Colclough added another goal in the dying minutes for a 3-6 to 1-4 surprise win for Meath.

Larry Stanley had been called out of retirement to help Kildare beat underdogs Meath in the Leinster final. Tom McGennis had forced them all back to Croke Park with a goal near the end of the final. They needed two meetings before Meath eventually succumbed by 2-6 to 1-2, to goals from Jack Higgins and Larry Stanley at the tail-end of the first half.

Monaghan's win over Kildare in the All-Ireland semi-final ranks as one of the shocks of the century. A breakaway goal midway through the second half left the score 1-6 to 0-3, but Kildare were not unduly worried...until their comeback efforts went wrong. A Harry Burke goal was disallowed for "whistle gone." Another Burke pile-driver was stopped by a dazed goalkeeper. And rain bucketed down as Monaghan held on to win by two points, 1-6 to 1-4.

Ulster did not have the monopoly on objections. Galway beat Mayo by 0-7 to 0-1 in the Connacht semi-final, but Mayo got to the final anyway on an objection. There they beat Sligo, too, after some anxious moments. Sligo had a great start, at half-time it was 0-4 to 1-1 and M Moran got Mayo's goal soon afterwards to bring about a 1-7 to 1-2 victory. In the All-Ireland semi-final, Mayo tried to do a Monaghan, and took a four points to three lead against Kerry at Roscommon but

John Joe Sheehy's goal and his second-half sharp-shooting sorted out all suspicion of a shock with a resounding 1-9 to 0-4 win.

The upsets ended when Kerry hammered an unfortunate Monaghan team by 3-11 to 0-2 without their goalkeeper touching the ball! P D Mehigan described this as "the best Kerry team since 1925."

It certainly managed to play with a swagger in this match. Jack Riordan was the goalkeeper; Dee O'Connor, Joe Barrett, and Jack Walsh kept the full-back line; Paul Russell, Joe O'Sullivan, and Tim O'Donnell played in the half-backs; Con Brosnan and American-born Bob Stack were at midfield. Jackie Ryan scored three points from right wing; Miko Doyle was at centre-half and scored 0-2; athletic champion Eamonn Fitzgerald played left wing; Ned Sweeney scored a goal from the right corner; John Joe Landers scored 1-2 from full-forward, and John Joe Sheehy scored 1-3 from the left corner.

And they beat Kildare 0-9 to 0-2 in the specially arranged Count McCormack challenge match after the All-Ireland, just to prove the point.

A Monaghan County Board official described the final as a "bullfight." Monaghan scored first and a second point made it 0-4 to 0-2, then John Joe Landers punched over the goalkeeper's head, making it 1-6 to 0-2 at half-time. Sweeney punched another goal eight minutes into the second half, Sheehy got a third almost from the kick-out, and the crowd invaded the pitch near the end after an altercation between two players.

It was a rough one, four Monaghan players retired injured, and Sean O'Carroll had his leg broken. Matadors' luck.

HOME ARE THE HEROES

Kerry set off on another triumphant United States tour. Their appearances in Yankee Stadium, New York (with a capacity of 82,000, much larger than the Polo Grounds) brought out crowds of 60,000 and 55,000. There were 45,000 in Comiskey Park, Chicago, to watch them play. Kerry won all their matches this time, the tour promoter was rumoured to have made £20,000 without taking the trouble to abscond, and Kerry came home with enough profit to purchase Austin Stack Park in Tralee.

This time Kerry, never ones to exaggerate, came home with a "Champions of the World " tag by virtue of their wins over Irish-American teams and hammered Tipperary by 5-8 to 0-2 in the Munster final, having been given a bye because of the tour.

Kerry's next opponents were to prove more difficult. New scoring star Gerard Courell scored 2-4 to help Mayo fight off Roscommon's best challenge in 15 years before 6,000 spectators in the Connacht final at Sligo, Mayo winning by 2-10 to 3-2. In the All-Ireland semi-final Jackie Ryan got a goal for Kerry against Mayo in the very first minute, Kerry led 1-5 to 0-1 at half-time and Culkin boxed a Mayo goal at the restart to cause Kerry a lot of worry. Mayo had a goal disallowed and the pitch was invaded before Kerry eventually won by 1-6 to 1-4.

Cavan beat Armagh by 0-8 to 2-1 in the Ulster final, the first meeting between the teams since the Jamesy Kiernan fatality in 1929. Dundalk was chosen as a safe venue, a nasty situation was averted when an attempted invasion of the field after an Armagh player was injured did not come off, and all ended peacefully. Unhappiest team in Ulster of 1931 were Donegal, thrown out of the championship for being late on the field after a breakthrough victory over Antrim, their first major win in senior football championship history.

Back in the All-Ireland semi-final with a full team, Cavan threatened to avenge 1928. Their attempt to "do a Monaghan" on Kildare started with a Colleran goal at the end of the first half which left the score 0-2 to 1-4, but Kildare's "Peter and Paul" combination (Pringle and Doyle) linked up with Pat Byrne and Paddy Martin to storm back to victory by two points, 0-10 to 1-5.

So Kerry had familiar opponents in the All-Ireland final. After drawing with Meath for a record third year in a row, Kildare reached the final thanks to Paul Doyle's contribution of 1-3. Rain spoiled the Dublin—Louth match and caused the initial Meath—Louth game to be abandoned on one of the wettest days in Irish meteorological history: the Boyne burst its banks and large areas of east coast river valleys spent days under water. Kildare had new opponents in the Leinster final. Westmeath, the 1929 junior champions, thwarted Dublin in the Leinster semi-final with goals from P Bracken and J Smith and had a shock 2-4 to 1-4 win. Kildare started with a sensational goal from Paul Doyle, shot to the net from 40 yards, and won by 2-9 to 1-6, but another Doyle, from Westmeath, kept Westmeath in the reckoning throughout their first Leinster final with a vital goal at the start of the second half.

Kerry were missing John Joe Sheehy and Ned "Pedlar" Sweeney. Somewhat dramatically, Johnny O'Riordan was dropped in the dressing-room minutes before the final was due to begin and his place in goal given to Dan O'Keeffe.

Kerry settled the argument by 1-11 to 0-8 in the final, thanks to a somewhat lucky goal from Paul Russell and a series of ingenious switches at half-time.

A good second-quarter performance helped Kildare to lead 0-6 to 0-4 at half-time. Paddy Whitty was switched to left wing, Jackie Ryan to full-forward, Eamonn Fitzgerald to right corner forward and Stack and Brosnan switched sides.

Kerry had already taken a 0-10 to 0-7 lead as a result of those switches when Russell's long shot was allowed to drop in the net because the goalkeeper and the full-back misread each other's calls.

TRICK OR TREAT

Of the '20s twosome, Kildare ran out of steam first. Leinster had new champions in 1932.

The question was, who would succeed them? At first Wexford looked like becoming Kildare's successors. Wexford's Nick Walsh and Martin O'Neill got the goals to thwart Kildare's seven-in-a-row bid at the semi-final stage by 2-8 to 2-5—despite conceding an own goal in the first minute when a back fly-kicked into his own net. Davey Morris set a new individual scoring record with 5-1 for Wexford against Laois.

There were two other hopefuls. The previous year's finalists Westmeath eventually ran out of steam after leading Dublin by two points in the semi-final. Willie Bracken and P Doyle got the Westmeath goals. Meath also led Dublin by two points in the quarter-final before collapsing in the second half.

In the end it was Dublin that took on Wexford in the Leinster final: and old-timers Paddy Synnott (2) and Paddy McDonnell scored the goals to give them a 13-point half-time lead (3-5 to 0-2) and sure victory over Wexford by 3-7 to 2-5 in a bad-tempered replay. Wexford's Nick Walsh had earned that replay with a spectacular late point from near the half-way line for a 2-5 each draw. Only one Dublinman had made the Leinster team for the Railway Cup that spring!

As Kerry found no clear-cut rivals in Munster, Clare beat Cork by 3-5 to 1-6 with the help of a new hero. Georgie Comerford's best football, however, was to be with Dublin with whom he won a Leinster medal two years later. But Kerry beat Tipperary in the final and faced another much-heralded Munster—Leinster semi-final, against new champions Dublin.

It merited the full-blooded build-up, as the new *Irish Press* and older *Irish Independent* competed for the GAA readership with far more extensive coverage. Both teams played a remarkable scoreless first half. Dowd got a Dublin goal, another Dublin goal was disallowed, and Kerry were in serious trouble before Paul Russell got their winning goal with four minutes to go. It was a lucky goal: Russell's long speculative shot caught the goalkeeper unawares and put Kerry into the All-Ireland final. The *Irish Independent* eulogised:

> This was one of the greatest displays of football ever witnessed in Croke Park or elsewhere. It was a wonderful struggle, packed with thrills from start to finish, and as an exhibition of speed and dash, grit and vigour, and all the best qualities that contribute to the best that there is in the Gaelic game, new heights were reached. Dublin, beyond a shadow of a doubt, are unlucky losers.

That left Connacht and Ulster to fight out the other semi-final. In Ulster Cavan were set for their 2-9 to 0-2 victory in the provincial final from the moment an unfortunate Armagh defender dropped the ball over his own line. Jack Smallhorne added a second-half goal and the match ended prematurely when the crowd invaded three minutes from the end with Cavan leading by 2-9 to 0-2.

According to the Ulster Council, a Detective Garda had produced a gun, triggering off the invasion. Ironically, earlier in the year a storm was created when Antrim proposed a motion debarring Garda members and Free State soldiers from GAA membership! Against Cavan in the first round, two Donegal players had failed to turn up and four others were involved in a motor accident in Clones and unable to play.

Mayo had begun to show the innovative style that captured six National League titles in the 1930s. Paddy Moclair of Mayo was reputedly the first "roving" full-forward. They won their fourth Connacht title in a row, beating Galway by 3-5 to 1-3 at Castlerea before a record 11,000 attendance, and Sligo by 2-6 to 0-7. When the provinces met, Mayo won by 2-4 to 0-8. Moclair's two goals against a disallowed goal by Smith of Cavan was enough to protect their semi-final lead.

Mayo had a boxer on board. Substitute Dick Harris was seven times Irish light heavyweight champion and won 173 of his 198 amateur bouts. In a startling football career he played inter-county with Roscommon, Longford, Donegal, Cork, Dublin and Mayo.

Kerry almost let the four-in-a-row slip. They were three points down at half-time, 1-1 to 1-4, Paul Russell getting the Kerry goal, Courell the Mayo goal and Moclair most of the points. The Kerry selectors switched Jackie Ryan and Tim Landers at half-time. On the restart Bill Landers struck for a lightning goal, Con Brosnan had another disallowed, and Forde's goal with only four minutes to go was shell-shocked Mayo's only score in the second half. Courell missed two late frees, the second from just 30 yards range, that might have saved the day for Mayo.

Kerry were missing Eamonn Fitzgerald, chosen to

represent Ireland in the triple jump at the Los Angeles Olympics. He finished fourth, missing the bronze medal by just over four inches. Three Landers brothers played together in the final. Bill Landers, who had returned to Ireland from America in May as part of the touring 1932 American GAA team, came on as a substitute for the injured Con Geaney to join brothers Tim and John Joe on the team. Youngest of the three brothers, Tim, was undoubtedly the man of the match, according to P D Mehigan: "Elusive as an eel, hopping like a rubber ball, quick to strike as a serpent in attack, he made bohereens through the Mayo defence." He was probably the first Kerry player to turn down an offer of a professional soccer contract. Among the Kerrymen who played on all four winning teams was Miko Doyle—he was not yet 21!

Heavy rain delayed the start of the match and kept the attendance down for the final: 25,816 spectators paid receipts of £2,247. They watched the end of Kerry's greatest era to date. Being Kerry, the target of four-in-a-row served to inspire, rather than intimidate, future generations of footballers.

Chapter Nine

North West Awakens

TWO MINUTES SHORT

Who would beat Kerry? Evidently nobody in Munster. Kerry got another bye to the provincial final because of a US tour. They travelled to another new venue, Clonmel, the seventh in eight years for what was among the worst-attended of the Provincial finals at the time. This time it was not so easy. The teams were level three times in the first half, and Tipperary took the lead early in the second half before two goals put Kerry back in the driving-seat and they won by 2-8 to 1-4. Paddy Foley concluded in the *Kerryman* that victory was "not due to superlative merits on their part, but rather to the home team's inefficiency."

Not a good sign. Leinster would appear to provide the main contenders.

Meath were destined to succeed Kerry as 1932-3 National League champions, beating Cavan in the final by a single point, 0-10 to 1-6. But when it came to the championship, Meath came back to equalise against Dublin before a late P Perry goal saw them off, 1-8 to 1-4.

Laois forced a replay against Kildare with late goals from Chris Delaney and Johnny Brennan but Tom Keogh (later to play with Laois) scored a last-minute goal for Kildare to win the replay, 2-11 to 1-5.

Louth were disappointed and scoreless during the second half of their match against Dublin as they watched their one-point lead dwindle into a nine-point defeat.

Wexford led Dublin by 2-7 to 0-3 at the three-quarter stage then saw their lead reduced to three points before beating Kildare by 2-8 to 1-8. Wexford led through a Martin O'Neill goal, 0-4 to 1-4 at half-time.

In the end Dublin came back to equalise with 11 minutes to go and won by 0-9 to 1-4. Dublin became Leinster champions with an eye on the title they last held 10 years earlier.

Connacht had two contenders. Mayo were National League semi-finalists (and were not to be defeated in the competition again until 1946), but Galway had been threatening for two years to depose rampant Mayo. It happened as Mick Donnellan sprang a surprise early goal to give Galway a 1-5 to 0-2 lead. Mayo got a goal at the start of the second half and Gerald Courell reduced Galway's lead to a point shortly before the end, but Galway went on to win by two, 1-7 to 1-5.

Cavan had the advantage of having the first sniff at an increasingly vulnerable Kerry team after they ran away with the Ulster championship. To get there Cavan beat Armagh by 1-8 to 0-2 and Tyrone by 6-13 to 1-2 in the provincial final.

That was not too difficult. Tyrone's Dungannon players had all defected an hour before the match and stormed out of the Railway Hotel in Cavan, leaving the county board to scout for replacements to make up their 15 players.

The Cavanmen who faced Kerry had just five survivors from the 1928 near-miss. The 1928 goal-scorer, Willie Young, was in goal; Willie Connolly, Patsy Lynch, and Mick Denneny were the full-backs; Tommy Coyle, team captain Jim Smith (an international in the 1928 and 1932 Tailteann Games), and Packie Phair were the half-backs; at centre-field were "Big" Tom O'Reilly from Cornafean and Hughie O'Reilly; converted goalkeeper Donal Morgan, Patsy Devlin and Jack Smallhorne were the half-forwards, while Vincent McGovern, Louis Blessing and "Son" Magee were the full-forwards.

On August 27th, 1933, a crowd of 17,111 looked on in Breffni Park as Cavan stopped Kerry's run. Kerry were within two minutes of the five-in-a-row. Vincent McGovern booted to the net after Devlin had laid on a ball previously received from Smith, making the score 1-5 to 0-5. Tim Landers was just wide on an equalising mission for Kerry and the crowd went wild.

The excitement had boiled over earlier when the crowd raided the field after a Cavan player was fouled.

That put the All-Ireland up for grabs between the weaker provinces who sought to break the Munster-Ulster stranglehold on the championship. A week earlier Galway too had a tight-squeeze victory as they watched their 0-8 to 1-2 half-time lead get whittled back to a single point, 0-8 to 1-4, and Synnott had a Dublin goal disallowed before a 7,596 attendance at Mullingar.

The public loved the change. Despite blinding rain, a record 45,180 crowd showed up and 5,000 were locked out when the gates were closed 20 minutes before the start. They listened to the match on loudspeakers outside the grounds.

Radio listeners had an unexpected interruption. At half-time, a group of men bustled commentator Eamonn de Barra away from the microphone and called for the release of Republican prisoners. Engineers at the various broadcasting stations realised what was happening and turned the microphones off. Athlone acted more quickly than Dublin or Cork.

"The standard of play was dull for half an hour," but that did not disturb the fans who watched Cavan win Ulster's first title by 2-5 to 1-4 with two first-half goals. Louis Blessing put Jim Smith's 50 into the net after 22 minutes, and sent a pass to Michael "Son" Magee for the second in lost time at the end of the first half. That gave Cavan a 2-3 to 0-2 half-time lead.

Galway played better in the second half, but struggled to come to terms with that deficit. A goal two and a half minutes into the second half was variously credited to Mick Donnellan and Brendan Nestor. Fly-kicking and rushes from midfield made Cavan worry, and Dermot Mitchell hit the post. But Cavan held on in a finish broken by several stoppages for injuries.

Cavan returned on Monday to a parade through the town to the Farnham hotel, led by the Cavan Labour band. Jim Smith, twice Cavan's only representative on Ireland's Tailteann sides, said: "My life's ambition is now realised. After fourteen years of struggle I have what I want at last."

The *Anglo-Celt* did not understate the significance of this win, describing it as "an event of international importance."

TROUBLE AT TUAM

That description was accurate when applied in New York, at least. When Cavan went on tour to America in May 1934 Mayor La Guardia welcomed them to City Hall, wishing them "everything in the world except victory, after all I am from New York." The welcome did not extend to the exile Gaelic footballers. When there was a heavy tackle on Jack Smallhorne towards the end of the match against New York before 40,000 people in Yankee Stadium, it took police, firemen and stewards to clear the ground and mounted police stood by in anticipation of a wholesale riot.

As All-Ireland champions, Cavan had found the going much tougher in the 1934 Ulster championship. They appeared to lose to Tyrone in the first round, but qualified on the official scoreline of 2-5 to 2-4. When the match ended, Tyrone celebrated, thinking they had won by two points. As the Tyrone players were chaired off the field by jubilant supporters, it was pointed out that one of Tyrone's second-half goals, by Seamus Campbell, had not been allowed so it was Cavan who had won.

Allegations that Tyrone had deliberately shortened the pitch were withdrawn. Other allegations were made that Tyrone had "deliberately roughed up" the Cavanmen. In reply to that, the referee said "it was the cleanest match I ever refereed." That shenanigans over, Cavan set off on their triumphant American tour and returned for an impressive win over Fermanagh by 3-4 to 1-3.

When Cavan eventually beat Armagh by 3-8 to 0-2 in the Ulster final, a record crowd for the province (£511 worth) walked in procession along the two miles from Castleblayney to the field in the Hope Estate, where the Ulster final got under way somewhat late. The second half did not start until 5.20!

Galway had that rarity, a dual goalkeeper, Michael Brennan, in action. They, too, were convinced they could go a step further in 1934, particularly after Michael Donnellan

155

captained Connacht to victory in the Railway Cup for the first time. Donnellan retired immediately and missed another honour, although that hardly seemed likely as Galway got a shock from Roscommon in the first round of the Connacht championship when they trailed 0-1 to 0-3 at half-time before they came back to win by 2-7 to 0-4. They heavily beat Mayo in the Connacht final at Castlerea before a 16,000 attendance. John Dunne and Kerryman Martin Kelly got the goals for a 2-4 to 0-5 victory.

The show-down between Cavan and Galway, a repeat of the 1933 All-Ireland final, was fixed for Tuam on August 12th. There was no banking whatsoever to facilitate the 28,000 spectators who turned up. The impending crisis was evident from an early stage. The sideline seats were filled from half-way through the curtain-raiser, a hurling match. The racecourse stand was unusable, as it was 200 yards away from the pitch. Entrepreneurial locals were charging 5/- for a box to stand on.

When the match got under way the ground was hopelessly crowded, with spectators 15 yards over the east sideline. The despairing linesmen started giving throw-ins wherever the ball hit a spectator. Rain at half-time made the situation worse, as thousands were pushed on to the field by late-comers with poor views. At times it was possible to shake hands across the field, so close were the spectators to each other.

The pitch had to be cleared five times in a fragmented, scattered match, that one Cavan official, T McCormack, described thus: "I saw five minutes of the game and three glimpses of the ball in the second half." Six Central Council members convened at half-time to decide whether the match should continue. Galway were 1-5 to 0-5 ahead at that stage, about to face the wind, and agreed. Cavan's captain apparently said no, although this was disputed vociferously by Cavan at a council meeting afterwards, claiming that they wanted the match to go ahead as a friendly, saying:

> The question arose at half-time whether the game
> should be continued and we understand that the Galway

officials and their team were unanimous though holding the lead at half-time to have the game declared off and replayed at Croke Park if Cavan so wished. They consulted among themselves and captains of teams and the Cavan side expressed a desire to have the match finished in Tuam.

The match went ahead, Sonny Magee missed a late penalty and at 6.10, two hours and four minutes after the throw-in, Galway emerged winners by virtue of Dermot Mitchell's early goal, 1-8 to 0-8. Not everybody thought that the game was out of control. John Joe Sheehy claimed: "I never saw the sideline at all but the encroachment was not a serious handicap."

In contrast Tralee set a great example in the other semi-final four weeks later: with brand new banking adequate to cope with a record 21,438 attendance. Everything went according to plan except the home team's performance. They went four points up before they succumbed to goals from Georgie Comerford in the first half and Michael Wellington and Paddy Colleran in the second.

Dublin had a hard, tough, mixture of natives and blow-ins in action. Goalkeeper was John McDonnell, the only survivor from the last victory in 1923; full-backs were Des Brennan, Michael Casey from Clare, Seamus O'Shea from Kerry, and Frank Cavanagh; half-backs Paddy Hickey, Ned McCann, and Paddy Cavanagh, brother of Frank of Dolphins; midfielders Bobby Beggs (Finglas-born, but later to win All-Ireland medals with Galway and Railway Cup medals with Connacht), and Kerry-born Martin Kelly; and forwards Gearóid Fitzgerald from Kerry, Georgie Comerford from Clare, Mick O'Brien, Michael Wellington, Willie Dowling, and Michael Keating from Wicklow. All were expected to prove more than a match for their Leinster opponents.

Yet in the Leinster final Dublin and Louth went to three meetings, Louth appeared to have won at the first attempt when Mort Kelly struck back with 1-1 towards the end and Louth relied on a Sean Cullen equaliser for a 0-5 to 1-2 draw. Eventually, in the second replay, Dublin came from behind to win by 2-9 to 1-10 at Drogheda, having trailed 1-9 to 2-2 early in the second half. Sligo-born Paddy Colleran's first-half goals laid the foundations of victory.

Dublin never recovered from a bad start in the All-Ireland final, and before 36,143 spectators Galway brought Connacht its second title and answered the critics of the 1925 muddled title by a decisive 3-5 to 1-9. Most of the triumphant Galway team were in their early 20s. They won with two first-half goals from 23-year-old Kerry-born UCG student Michael Ferriter. The 28-year-old Martin Kelly got the third at the start of the second half before Dublin began to edge their way back into the game. The 10.8-second sprinter from Miltown Malbay, Co Clare, George Comerford slotted over four of Dublin's final five points as they pushed the margin back from eight to two points. This was as near an All-Ireland medal as Comerford came. It was once wrongly claimed he had won a Railway Cup medal alongside 14 Kerrymen. Comerford's contribution to football history was as an outstanding player in the wrong counties at the wrong time— he played for six inter-county teams in all.

CAVAN RETURN

Fermanagh have always been regarded as the weakest GAA county of them all. They have, as one county secretary called it, "the population of Leitrim divided by two because of sectarianism" to choose from. Under-age games were organised at 11 a side and 13 a side for many years because of the shortage of players. Poor pitches, the difficulty in getting land because of the hostility of the Unionist community, and dispersed population all combined to leave it the sole Ulster county which has never won an Ulster championship.

In 1935 Fermanagh had their best championship run for a generation with the help of Northern wandering star, Jim McCullough. The former Armagh player also played with Tyrone as his job with the Northern Ireland Electricity Board brought him through several different counties in a 12-month period, confusing officials and incurring suspensions (which he always seemed to avoid by moving to another county) with his meanderings.

Fermanagh had won the McKenna Cup in 1933, then McCullough had helped Fermanagh reach the 1935 League final in the most momentous year in their history. He was an inspiration for their great championship run. Fermanagh beat Tyrone by 1-11 to 2-6 at the second attempt and Armagh by 3-4 to 2-2 at the second attempt to face rampant Cavan in the Ulster final.

It was David and Goliath stuff, especially when "Son" Magee scored a seventh-minute goal; Louis Blessing hit another, and Cavan led 2-3 to nil approaching half-time. But McCullough switched between centre-field and centre half back, Bill Maguire got a goal before half-time, Eddie Collins got another in the second half and after Fermanagh's defeat, they reminisced on Maguire missing another chance with the goal at his mercy.

Munster were weaker than usual. Kerry county convention decided the county should withdraw from all championships in protest at the treatment of Republican prisoners at the Curragh. As an uneasy alliance between the IRA and de Valera fell apart from the time the Cumann na nGaedheal military tribunal was re-established in August 1933, Kerry GAA was once again drawn into the political controversy. They had withdrawn from a December 1933 National League match because 12 Tralee youths were arrested on the night that Blueshirt leader General Eoin O'Duffy visited Tralee.

So Tipperary beat Cork by 2-8 to 1-2 to win their last Munster championship and Cavan's "last-minute goal" survival technique had another trial against Tipperary in the All-Ireland semi-final. Tipperary had made their way back from five points down to lead 0-8 to 0-7 when they faced a Jim Smith 50. There was silence as Jim Smith sent the ball in to Louis Blessing, who punched through to "little" Tom O'Reilly (from Mullahoran), who tipped it to the centre of the net for a sensational goal and 1-7 to 0-8 victory.

Smith's place on the Cavan team had not been secure right up to the throw-in. Dublin County Board were meeting in Croke Park almost until the throw-in to consider whether he should be suspended over a club incident. O'Keeffe had a Tipperary point disallowed in the second half. Tipperary objected but to no avail.

The Leinster championship had a changed look about it, as Westmeath and Meath defied tradition by playing their Leinster quarter-final tie on a Thursday night and 1933 junior champions Carlow had a historic 5-7 to 1-6 victory over Wexford. Kildare eventually retook the Leinster title. Christy Higgins and newcomer Paul Mathews combined to take control of midfield for Kildare against Mathews' native Louth, and they won the provincial final by 0-8 to 0-6.

Mayo protested about the Connacht Council's choice of Roscommon as venue for the provincial final, then won out the much-heralded clash between National League (Mayo) and All-Ireland champions (Galway) by a comfortable 0-12 to 0-5 before 26,000 spectators. Mayo then went down to Kildare by 2-6 to 0-7, thanks to goals from Geraghty and Keogh in the first 10 minutes of their semi-final.

Four points was the end margin in the final. Cavan got revenge for 1928 by 3-6 to 2-5 before a record 50,380 attendance, and Kildare simmered for months afterwards over the dropping of regular goalkeeper Pa "Cuddy" Chanders. Although he had not conceded a goal in the championship he was replaced by a converted corner-back, Jim Maguire, who had never played in goal, because of the belief that his nerves would not be up to it after he let in six goals in a challenge match against Meath. But, according to a *Leinster Leader* correspondent there was more to it than that:

> Chanders, a pick and shovel man but a good goal-keeper, was turned down to make room for Maguire, a cuff and collar man and a bad goalman, because in the eyes of the selection committee the game was already won—a trip to America was contemplated, and the newcomer to the goal would be a more suitable traveller and more deserving of All-Ireland honours.

Legends still survive in Kildare, that an attempt was made to reinstate Chanders on Saturday night, that Kildare full-back Matt Gough announced "We'll test this goalkeeper," at the start of the game to his own backs, that a section of the team left the bus and refused to travel to Croke Park, that instead of Tom Keogh's usual rousing song on the team bus he sang an old mourner that summed up the melancholy mood of the Kildaremen. It was all very petty in view of the fact that none of the three goals could be blamed on the goalkeeper, and that Cavan put three goals past Chanders when they won a November League match in Newbridge.

None of this deterred the fans. An official 50,300 turned up, and when the gates were locked at 2.50 some 5,000 more waited outside to listen to the match on the loudspeaker relay.

Cavan won the match in the first half, when the O'Reilly pair, Hugh from Cootehill and "small" Tom from Mullahoran, took control at midfield. "Kildare were put off their game by faster and fitter footballers, who were a transformed team since their last appearance against Tipperary."

Michael J "Son" Magee scored a point after just 20 seconds, the fastest opening score since 1896. Packie Boylan landed 24th-and 31st-minute goals in the first half and Tom Reilly a third in the second half to make amends for the tragedy in Tuam in 1934. Kildare improved in the second half, and fought to regain the lost ground with 1-3 in the last quarter, Mick Geraghty's goal complementing one by Tom Mulhall just before Boylan's second in the first half.

"It is possible," P D Mehigan wrote, "that Kildare's change of goalkeepers was ill-advised, for Chanders never had a goal scored against him in the championship. Through the second half Maguire cleared good balls, and he was opposing a much-improved group of forwards." What is left unsaid is that Cavan's first two goals should not have been scored.

MAYO JOIN THE CLUB

Newly crowned champions Cavan were given a bye to the Ulster semi-final because they decided to follow the 1930s tradition of taking an American tour. On their return they beat Armagh and Monaghan to recapture the Ulster title by 1-7 with the help of an early goal from Louis Blessing. Monaghan's Christy Fisher missed his side's best chance when he put a penalty over the bar at a stage when Monaghan trailed by 1-7 to 0-4 midway through the second half. Both goalkeepers gave a series of great saves late in the game.

Cavan's run was ended by Laois, who had taken back the Leinster title after 47 years, when it seemed Kildare had won the *real* final against Louth. The semi-final was attended by 15,576 who saw Kildare win by 1-8 to 1-4. For the final, just 13,567 showed up, and they watched in surprise as John O'Reilly engineered Laois' 3-3 to 0-8 victory with three goals. In the All-Ireland semi-final, Laois came from three points down at half-time for a Chris Delaney penalty to launch a second-half comeback fired on by former Kildare player Tom Keogh to victory.

Back in the Munster championship, Kerry lived dangerously. They fell 0-1 to 0-5 at half-time against Tipperary but won by 1-5 to 0-5. Kerry then fell 0-1 to 0-2 behind against Clare. Clare blew their chances with a bewildering series of misses, and Kerry got through by a comfortable 1-11 to 2-2.

Mayo became Connacht champions in a replay after Galway's Brendan Nestor engineered a thrilling 2-4 to 1-7 draw, almost causing a riot in the process. Galway trailed by three points when Nestor forced the ball over the line. A Mayo defender punched it back, the umpire hesitated, and Nestor raised the flag himself.

The crowd invaded the field, and it took several minutes to clear it so the last few seconds could be played. After that excitement it was back to Roscommon where first-half goals from Josie Munnelly and Paddy Flannelly settled the issue 2-7 to 1-4 in Mayo's favour. Roscommon was the venue for the All-Ireland semi-final, too, where Paddy Flannelly scored the vital goal in the first half as Mayo beat Kerry by 1-5 to 0-6.

The 50,160 who attended the final did not expect to see Mayo hammer a stage-struck Laois team by 18 points, 4-11 to 0-5. Cause of the disaster was an unfit player. Laois midfielder Bill Delaney limped through the game with two broken bones in his foot while Mayo's Paddy Flannelly cleaned up at midfield:

> He raced through and shot to the square, to the net, and high between the posts—he seemed to inspire his side

who played runaway football...Flannelly fielded and raced to either wing, paving the way for Munnelly's and Moclair's overwhelming scores.

"A temperamental team always, the Western champions opened so brilliantly they were always on top of the wave. Speed to the ball was their trump card." Paddy Munnelly had goals in the 10th and 12th minutes of the first half, Paddy Moclair followed 10 minutes into the second half, and Paddy Munnelly scored again after four minutes of injury time.

Laois had four Delaney brothers from Stradbally, Jack, Chris, Mick and Bill, in action. Their uncle Tom played at full-back. Goalkeeper Tom was no relation to the others. The four brothers were to win 17 Railway Cup medals. A legacy of the defeat was a superstitious horror of getting a trainer from outside the county to help future Laois teams, a reluctance that lasted until 1981. "Laois were beaten for pace and seemed stale and over-trained," was the verdict. "Never handling a ball confidently, they muffed many openings."

Mayo's team had matured. Their team was worth more than one All-Ireland: throughout the 1930s they solidly dominated the National League, winning six titles in a row between 1934 and 1939, opting out (for Galway to win it in 1940) and coming back to regain the title in 1941. They had Tom Burke in goal; John McGowan, Paddy Quinn, and Purty Kelly in the full back line; Tommy Regan, J Seamus O'Malley (captain), and George Ormsby in the half-backs; Patsy Flannelly and Henry Kenny at centre-field; Jackie Carney, Peter Laffy, and Tom Grier in the half-forwards. Paddy Moclair scored 1-5 in the final from right corner. Josie Munnelly who scored 0-3 from full-forward was back 21 years later to win an All-Ireland junior football medal in 1957. Paddy Munnelly scored three goals from left corner.

THE MISSING POINT

Nine years had passed since a goal-that-wasn't was scored against Cavan to deprive them of the All-Ireland. In 1937, in a cruel role-reversal, Cavan saw a point of their own disallowed, depriving them of another.

Two Cavan newcomers caught the eye as they romped through the Ulster championship, a corner-back Paddy Smith and a wing-back from Cornafean, John Joe O'Reilly.

They had to look to Connacht for a semi-final opponent. There All-Ireland champions Mayo won another classic final by 3-5 to 0-8 as Galway refused to give up against overwhelming odds. Mayo's first goal came from a mêlée in the opening minutes, their second from Josie Munnelly at the start of the second half and their third from Peter Laffey near the end clinched the issue.

The Connacht semi-final between Galway and Sligo degenerated into what was described as a "miniature riot" near the end. The referee had failed to show and Jim Farrell of Roscommon was recruited as stand-in from the sideline. He probably regretted his readiness to do so afterwards as he was forced to make a speedy exit as soon as he had blown the final whistle, chased out of the ground in his togs by a horde of screaming spectators.

At Mullingar in front of 26,000 spectators, Cavan eliminated All-Ireland and League champions Mayo in a much-interrupted All-Ireland semi-final by 2-5 to 1-7 with late goals from "Son" Magee and Louis Blessing. It ended a remarkable run of 57 games without defeat by Mayo.

The other semi-final was turning into a dogfight between Kerry and Laois. In Leinster, Laois had surprised their critics with a good championship run. Tom Keogh put his old colleagues from Kildare out of the championship by 2-10 to 2-7 with a last-minute goal, just as Frank "Joyce" Conlan had done in 1914.

But Laois had some troubles of their own. Twice against 1935 junior champions Offaly, Laois found themselves in a crisis situation. First they trailed at half-time, retook the lead, and Byrne's dramatic last-minute free earned a draw for Offaly, 1-9 to 2-6. Then came two late goals to beat Offaly in the replay, 2-7 to 1-7; the first by Keogh led to a crowd invasion and several minutes of confusion...when order was restored Keogh passed to Harkins for the last-minute winning goal. Laois eventually beat Louth by 0-12 to 0-4 before a

15,317 crowd in the Leinster final.

Laois could have gone farther than their eventual semi-final defeat against Kerry. They had regrets after travelling to Cork to draw 1-6 to 2-3 thanks to a late goal for Kerry from Con Geaney, then had more after losing the replay by 2-2 to 1-4 in Waterford to a similar late Kerry rally. Laois made a great second-half comeback in that replay, inspired by a fabulous left-footed drive into the corner of the net from "Boy Wonder" Tommy Murphy, a 16-year-old Knockbeg College student. But Kerry's "tall, young rear-guard of six-foot striplings" thwarted their efforts to go further.

Kerry struck back to win the semi-final with a Tim Landers goal at the end. The full-back failed to come out to meet O'Sullivan's long ball, Landers snatched it, and for the second time in a fortnight Laois saw their three-point lead against Kerry snatched away in the dying minutes. Then Jackie Lyne added the winning point to send Kerry into the final.

The final brought old warriors Kerry up against the new Cavan team, as one commentator put it: "Kerry's tall backs against Cavan's brainy forwards." Some of the tall backs were mere striplings of lads. Tadhg Healy and Joe Keohane were still eligible for minor. Cavan did the celebrating, but only because they had been announced as winners on the radio and the Croke Park loudspeakers. The referee had other ideas, however. He said that he had disallowed Cavan's winning point.

Cavan goal-scorer Packie Boylan was the scorer of what should have been the the winning point, disallowed for throwing, three minutes from the end. Few of the spectators noticed a free out was taken instead of a kick out; it was announced over the loudspeakers that Cavan had won, radio commentator Father Michael Hamilton told the nation that Cavan were the champions, and many supporters were at home in Cavan before they realised a replay was needed!

Cavan had shown great sparkle in coming back after an appalling start to draw 1-8 to 2-5, after John Joe Landers had the ball in the net twice from beautiful swerving raids in the first 13 minutes for Kerry. In the 21st minute of the second half a great solo run by Jim Smith sent Cavan's Packie Boylan through for a dramatic goal—"the thrill of the hour"—that put Cavan ahead by the odd point in 19. Kerry launched two scintillating counter-attacks, from returned exile Gearóid Fitzgerald to level and Tim O'Donnell to regain the lead. Michael "Son" Magee put the sides level again with six minutes to go, and then Boylan and Magee changed places at the corner and with "Kerry's young backs showing signs of wear," Boylan flung the ball over the bar from close range for the winner-that-wasn't.

A massive 52,325 crowd nearly got squashed to death in their attempts to see the game. The Cusack Stand had not yet been built, and when the gates were forced open by the crush at 2.45 anything up to 10,000 more could have got in.

Kerry won the replay rather easily, by 4-4 to 1-7. Mehigan complained:

> The play was broken too frequently by minor accidents to compare with the drawn match as a continuous and gripping sporting spectacle. It was too earnest, too fierce to be a classic. It was more severe as a test of men than the drawn match, and it introduced us to a young team of footballers who would do credit to any nation.

The tackling was indeed "robust." Cavan's Tom O'Reilly and Jim Smith were both injured. Timmy O'Leary flicked Kerry's first goal to the net after 12 minutes, it was 1-0 to 0-3 at half-time, Miko Doyle got the second six minutes after half-time, O'Leary the third 12 minutes into the second half, and John Joe Landers the fourth after 28 and a half minutes.

Inflating the bladder of an early Italian *pallone* or football. Until the pneumatic ball was invented in the 1860s, inflating the bladder was a complicated task and most Irish villages used bladders stuffed with hay.

[Established over a Century.]

THE COMMERCIAL AND FAMILY HOTEL,

Between seven and thirteen people gathered in the billiard room at Hayes's Hotel, Thurles, on November 1st 1884 to found the Gaelic Athletic Association.

Limerick Commercials were dispersed around the world and many were dead by the time they were presented with medals for their 1887 All-Ireland victory.

The Cork Examiner was the first newspaper to produce action photographs of GAA matches. These come from the "Games that made the GAA," the 1903 final between Kildare and Kerry, with Kildare on the attack.

The parade around the field in 1913 brought Kerry and Wexford into opposition for the first time. Wexford went on to win four in a row, while Kerry's captain, Dick Fitzgerald, was renowned as the best footballer the game had seen up to then.

Action from the 1921 Leinster final between Dublin and Wexford. The match came soon after Bloody Sunday and Leinster was the only province to carry out championships reasonably punctually during the war years.

Kerry's 1928-1932 team won four in a row and qualified for the 1933 All-Ireland final before this goal from Vincent McGovern put them out of commission at Breffni Park.

Galway defeated Kerry with this goal in 1938, but when the referee blew the whistle prematurely, Kerry had to recruit ten substitutes to play out the final minute.

The triple-decker stands of the New York Polo Grounds provided a fascinating backdrop to the 1947 All-Ireland football final. Not so fascinating was the baseball diamond that interfered with play. Kerry's Batt Garvey has just crossed it to shoot (above). Mick Higgins gets in a shot at the other end (below).

Roscommon progressed from junior to senior champions in four years. Jimmy Murray, leading the parade, and Donal Keenan, in third place, were their stars when they beat Kerry in 1944.

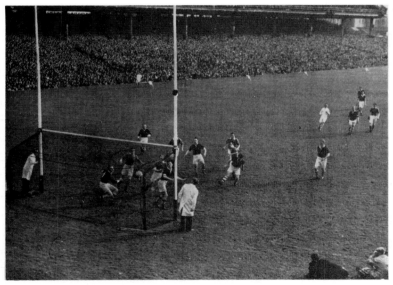

J D Benson and Brian O'Reilly watch Tom Langan's shot enter the net for a Mayo goal in the 1948 All-Ireland final. The wind that day led to the two most spectacularly different halves in All-Ireland history before Cavan won by a point.

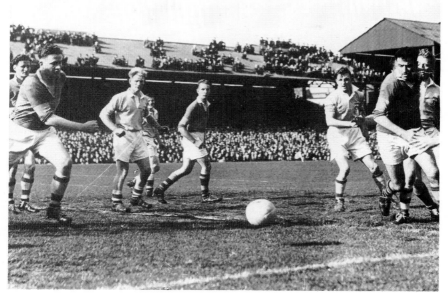

The first battle between the new and old style game came when Kerry's purist football defeated Dublin's unorthodox game.in 1955. Des "Snitchy" Ferguson, Paddy "Jack" Haughey, Kevin Heffernan and Ollie Freaney tussle with Kerry players, Ned Roche and John Cronin.

Frank Stockwell of Galway was one of the scoring stars of the 1950s. Here he closes in to beat Kerry goalkeeper Johnny Culloty for a Galway goal in the 1959 final.

Down came form nowhere to surprise Kerry in the 1960 final. Eamonn McKay, Pat Rice and Leo Murphy in action at the Kerry goalmouth.

Galway perfected the punch-pass game in the 1960s. Here Mattie McDonagh scores against Kerry in the 1964 final, despite the efforts of Kerry's Niall Sheehy, Paud O'Donoghue and Seamus Murphy.

Two greats of the 1960s, Sean O'Neill of Down and Mick O'Connell of Kerry rise with John Purdy of Down in the 1968 final.

Offaly goalkeeper Martin Furlong comes out to meet Kerry's Mick O'Dwyer in the 1969 final.

Martin Furlong, the greatest goalkeeper of his generation, dives to save Dan Kavanagh's shot as Offaly beat Kerry in the replayed 1972 final. Furlong was to thwart Kerry again ten years later.

Paddy Cullen became the first goalkeeper to save a penalty in a All-Ireland final when he tipped Liam Sammon's kick around the post. He also secured the first of three Dublin successes in a four-year period.

The greatest of them all? Kerry's babes were to win eight All-Irelands in twelve years. Back row: Paud Lynch, Paud O'Mahony, Pat Spillane, Tim Kennelly, John O'Keeffe, John Egan, Brendan Lynch and Ger Power. Front row: Denis "Ogie" Moran, Páid O Sé, Mike Sheehy, Jim Deenihan, Michael O'Sullivan, Pat McCarthy and Ger O'Keeffe.

When Paddy Cullen argued with the referee in the 1978 final, Kerry's Michael Sheehy lofted the ball into the empty net. 1. Cullen about to clear. 2. Cullen clashes with Ger Power. 3. Cullen disputes the whistle. 4. Robbie Kelleher politely hands the ball to Sheehy. 5. Sheehy bends to place the ball and Cullen begins the race to the line. 6. Sean Doherty joins the race. 7. The ball begins to overtake Cullen. 8. The ball in the net, Cullen in disarray.

The purists criticised the style of the 1970s, but some of the finest fielding was seen in these games. Kerry's Sean Walsh goes higher than Dublin's Brian Mullins in this 1979 encounter.

Seamus Darby of Offaly, extreme left, watches in delight as his shot beats Charlie Nelligan with two minutes to go in the 1982 All-Ireland final and deprives Kerry of the coveted five in a row.

Dublin star Barney Rock was the talk of the 1980s with his goal-getting exploits. He scored a last minute equaliser in the 1983 semi-final, the winner in the 1983 final against Galway, and several Leinster final goals. This one in the 1984 final was not enough, however, to beat Kerry.

In 1985 Timmy O'Dowd tucked a breakaway winning goal to give Kerry the clinching victory over Dublin.

For three minutes in 1986 Tyrone thought they were going to win a dramatic All-Ireland title, after Paudge Quinn snatched a second half goal. Kerry won in the end, but only after the most enjoyable All-Ireland final of the decade.

Tears of defeat from an under-14 player at Croke Park. Gaelic football in the 1990s would be unrecognisable to the founding fathers

Chapter Ten

Three-in-a-row Won,
Three-in-a-row Lost

THE FIND-A-SUB ALL-IRELAND

Kerry lost their title after another replay in 1938. They had only three players over 25 on the team that beat Cork by 20 points in the Munster final. Then they met Laois in the semi-final for the second year in a row. After this happened it was decided to rotate the semi-finals among the provinces.

The semi-final saw the new Cusack Stand opened with a blast of community singing by Sean O'Síocháin. Kerry's Con O'Sullivan and Mick Kelly eliminated Laois from the championship by 2-6 to 2-4 with two goals in 90 seconds early in the second half.

Offaly had been surprise semi-finalists in Leinster: Hughes got the goal that started their comeback from six points down against Wexford to win their first-round tie by 1-9 to 1-5. His declaration to play for Offaly was found in order by an appeals board just 24 hours before the match! But it was Laois who gave a classic display in beating Kildare by 2-8 to 1-3 in the Leinster final.

Galway took the Connacht title back from Mayo by 0-8 to 0-5. They also felt sore at having a goal disallowed. But they kept their heads. Their "Kerry recruit," Jack Flavin, started popping over the points and Galway collected their reward in the All-Ireland final at Croke Park.

There was a surprise in Ulster as Monaghan interrupted what would have been a 15-in-a-row run for Cavan, for the only time in an incredible 30-year period from 1927 to 1957. Before 8,000 people, Armagh beat Cavan in the semi-final by 2-7 to 1-4. After Monaghan beat Armagh by 2-5 to 2-2 in the Ulster final the referee, Cavan star Hughie O'Reilly, had to be escorted off the field. An objection by Armagh that Monaghan's team list was not complete and the referee was not impartial failed.

When they met in the All-Ireland semi-final at Mullingar, a new 18-year-old radio commentator was describing the match on the airwaves. Dubliner Michael O'Hehir was to earn the nickname "the voice of the GAA" during a 40-year career relaying games on radio and television. O'Hehir was not a full-time commentator until 1959. At first he worked in the Civil Service and was paid a guinea a game for his services. He replaced a number of commentators such as Paddy Mehigan, Eamonn de Barra, and Father Michael Hamilton who had given out the wrong scoreline at the end of the 1937 All-Ireland final. The best story about O'Hehir, that he was in hospital listening to a commentary on radio and felt he could do better, is not true.

Galway beat Monaghan by 2-10 to 2-5, thanks to two quick-fire goals, from Mort Kelly and a Jimmy Burke 50, to qualify to meet Kerry in the final.

When Kerry drew with Galway, 2-6 to 3-3, the final whistle went early and a would-be winning point by substitute John Joe Landers was disallowed. Kerry complained no time had been added for stoppages. A goal five minutes from the end by Timmy O'Leary had left them counting down to the championship, but Bobby Griffin propelled Brendan Nestor's free over the line for Galway's breath-saving goal three minutes from the end. Ned Mulholland and the outstanding Nestor got the other two for Galway.

The replay was even more bizarre. When the crowd invaded prematurely, the whole match had to be restarted in bizarre circumstances. Galway, "the more uniform, the more secure, the more united team," broke Kerry's knack of winning replays (they had previously won three), despite having a penalty claim turned down in the first half. Goals from Galway's Ned Mulholland and Martin Kelly set up their 2-4 to 0-7 victory, confirmed after 10 minutes of total confusion.

The crowd mistook it for the final whistle when the referee blew twice for a free two minutes from the end. The free had been awarded to Kerry, a Galwayman stood too close to the ball, and when the referee whistled again the crowd swept across the field. Even the Kerry players were fooled: nine of them went away to tog off at the Central Hotel. Four more had gathered around John Walsh, who was having hip and shoulder injuries dressed, in the new Cusack Stand dressing-room. Sean Brosnan and Tim O'Leary were still on the field and probably the first to hear loudspeaker pleas for the players to resume. Myers, Casey, Dillon, and Paddy Brosnan had gone.

Mort Kelly, the injured Joe Keohane (who had watched the rest of the final from the stand, dressed in his Sunday suit), Murphy, Ned Walsh and Jack Sheehy filled some of the places but Kerry finished the match without their complement of 15. Despite this they scored a point in the remaining minute!

Moyvane-born Johnny Flavin won his second All-Ireland medal in successive years, first with Kerry, then for Galway against Kerry!

Styles had changed completely from the fast handpass days of the 1920s. Now shoulders were to the fore.

SPRING IN THE AIR

Galway fell at the first hurdle in 1939. Connacht football had outgrown its facilities—when Mayo met Galway in the Connacht final the old Roscommon grounds could not hold the 20,000 crowd. It took 30 minutes to start the match and the spectators overflowed onto the pitch in the second half. Mayo were clear 2-6 to 0-3 leaders at that stage, thanks to Paddy Moclair's 7th-and 23rd-minute goals and 1-3 in a vital seven-minute spell which gave them a 2-5 to nil half-time lead. The match ended prematurely in an invasion with two minutes to go.

In Munster Kerry went off on another American tour so they were given a bye into the provincial final, where Tipperary qualified to meet them by beating Cork 1-9 to 2-2 and Clare 4-5 to 1-6. Goals at the start of each half from Tom McAuliffe and Michael Kelly secured the title for Kerry, 2-11 to 0-4, on their return.

Ulster provided another unfinished final. Cavan were leading Armagh by 2-6 to 2-4 in the unfinished first match, fought out on a steadily shrinking pitch in Castleblayney, as the crowd (receipts £693) advanced further and further beyond the touchlines. They invaded, eventually, when Conaty got an Armagh goal in the first half. And when Armagh captain Jim McCullough (the Fermanagh wanderer) was punched by one of the crowd as he was taking a throw-in, a mêlée followed. The referee abandoned the match when the pitch was not cleared. It had been rough going, the match had started at 4.15 and was called off at 6.45, the crowd having swept across the field four times in all.

Cavan won a sedate replay in the unfamiliar surroundings of Croke Park with goals from T Clarke and Tom O'Reilly in a two-minute spell in the second half.

Spectators joined in a previous fight in Castleblayney during the Monaghan—Armagh semi-final as well, as Loughman scored a late equaliser for Monaghan and had to repeat the performance when Armagh went ahead again. Armagh finished the 1930s, despite their reputation, stranded in the middle of their most barren spell, having lost three Ulster finals in a row, and a total of eight finals in 12 years. The 1938 and 1939 McKenna Cups were poor consolation for their woes. Gate news was good for the Ulster Council: £693 for the abandoned match and £400 to the Ulster Council from the All-Ireland semi-final gate of £2,615, where the replay acted as a curtain-raiser.

Leinster had new champions. Meath had been one of the easier opponents in Leinster football since Dick Blake's days. Ten years after first showing signs of changing that with priestly help, they got the Leinster title they deserved, beating Laois by 1-9 to 1-7, Kildare by 2-10 to 2-8, and Wexford by 2-7 to 2-3. Last-minute goals featured in the 1939 Leinster quarter-finals: Louth went out to one by Somers of Wexford, Laois to one by Willie Brien of Meath.

Meath's semi-final victims Kildare protested that

Cummins' goal for Meath should not have been allowed, calling their defenders to give near-identical statements before Leinster Council insisting in turn that they had "stopped playing when they heard the whistle" for a free-in. The referee had changed his mind to award the goal. Peter Clarke scored another goal against the disoriented Kildaremen, and Meath ate away a nine-point half-time lead. When the Council refused to reverse the referee's decision Kildare withdrew from the National League in protest.

When they fell behind in the Leinster final against Wexford, it was 24-year-old Tony Donnelly who started the revival. He had starred since a debut against Cavan in the 1932-3 League at the age of 17. Matty Gilsenan and Peter Clarke (with a second-half goal) brought Meath back from behind in the final against Wexford, who had struck with two timely goals from Smyth and Roche immediately before half-time.

The troublesome tradition of 1939 was continued at the All-Ireland semi-final between Kerry and Mayo, as Kerry came back from two points down at half-time to draw amid displays of pugilism and considerable trouble for Fermanagh referee Dunne, who was dispossessed of the ball after the match. After the teams drew 0-4 each, the replay was, at least, an improvement, and Dan Spring and Charlie O'Sullivan goals in the dying minutes of the first half and another from Walsh within a minute of the restart saw Kerry through by 3-8 to 1-4. The first goal confused many people (Spring was a late call-up to the team in place of Miko Doyle) including radio commentator Michael O'Hehir, who was passed an illegible slip of paper telling him about the team change, and described the full-forward as "Dan Shine" throughout the game.

A great first-half display and a Cummins goal to start the second half brought Meath through the first of many famous local derbies with Cavan, by 1-9 to 1-1, and into their first All-Ireland final.

Meath won the toss to wear their familiar green jerseys, so Kerry won their 13th All-Ireland in the red jerseys of county champions Dingle.

171

There, Kerry had to fight to beat off the new challenge of Meath. Dan Spring got two goals for Kerry in a 2-5 to 2-3 victory. The first was awarded only after some hesitancy on the part of the referee, who consulted his umpires. Then, one of the best goals in GAA history from Mattie Gilsenan just before half-time, and another from Jim Clarke midway through the second half brought Meath back into the reckoning.

After kicking 11 wides Meath lost by two points in the end. The first goal, a lucky effort awarded only after the referee had consulted the umpires, saw Kerry through in a match described euphemistically as one where "hard knocks were given and taken." According to the *Kerryman*, "it was a triumph of backs over forwards."

This was the spirit of the 1930s. No elaboration, but hard knocks and hard shoulders.

GREEN AND GO

Despite Kerry's successes, support for football in Munster was not very high: a crowd of about 2,000 (Gate £90) turned out for the 1940 provincial final in Waterford city, which meant football in Munster was now running at 10 per cent of hurling final support. With Cork losing to Tipperary in the first round, and Kerry beating Limerick at a temporary pitch in Glin (4-9 to 0-2), Tipperary (4-8 to 1-5) and Waterford (1-10 to 0-6) by big scores, the disinterest was perhaps justified. Despite this Waterford led 0-5 to 0-2 at half-time after playing with a strong breeze. After that, a scoring spree from Sean Brosnan, who finished with 1-4, ended their dreams.

Perennial Ulster champions, Cavan, trounced Antrim in a replay by 6-13 to 0-4 after Antrim had drawn with a skeleton Cavan team in Corrigan Park 3-3 to 0-12, then met two aspirants, Donegal (0-12 to 3-2) and Down (4-10 to 1-5) in the semi-final and final before a crowd of 6,000. Down were on the way up: they had astonished the Gaelic football world by reaching the National League semi-finals in 1940 and again in 1941.

Down's first appearance in a final began with a flourish

when J Carr scored a goal and Michael Lynch a point before Cavan settled down. But a Vincent White penalty before half-time sent Cavan in with a five-point lead, and when Pat Boylan, Donal Morgan and Joe Stafford added goals in the second half, Down's dreams were demolished. Down felt the war-time travel restrictions and abnormal times unfairly penalised them, and protested over the fact that the match was fixed for Breffni Park in Cavan, but to no avail. Earlier in the year Down settled their long-standing dispute with Armagh over the border areas around Newry.

Munster and Ulster met in the semi-final thanks to the rotation system. Kerry had an exciting 3-4 to 0-8 win, having fallen 0-2 to 0-5 behind 10 minutes into the second half. Jim "Gawksie" O'Gorman's two easy goals and another immediately afterwards from John Walsh destroyed Cavan's bid to avenge 1937. On the same day, in a double bill semi-final that brought 33,251 spectators to Croke Park, Galway defended their six-point half-time lead against a Meath onslaught in the second half to win by 3-8 to 2-5.

Mayo may have made a mistake when they opted out of the National League after winning six in a row in 1940. Galway won the League in their absence, and their inactivity led to troubled signs when Mayo played Sligo in the Connacht semi-final and were held to a draw, 1-7 to 2-4, as only a last-minute goal struck by Mick O'Malley from 20 yards out saved Mayo embarrassment against Sligo, for whom McLoughlin scored two goals. Paddy Moclair with two goals and a third from Jim Laffey settled the issue in the replay, 3-2 to 0-7.

When the Connacht final came around Galway showed that their League victory was well-merited. Bobby Beggs gave one of his best ever displays as they beat Roscommon by 1-7 to 0-5 in Roscommon. Few turned out to see it, probably because they had been half-crushed to death the previous year. Galway trailed by two points at half-time, levelled mid way through the second half, and then took control with a Brendan Nestor goal.

To retain their Leinster title before 29,351 spectators against Laois, Meath had to come back from three points down at half-time. Dan Douglas got a goal for Laois midway through the first half, but J Mayo struck twice in the second half for a Meath victory, by 2-7 to 1-7, as Tony Donnelly tacked on the winning points.

Laois were on to something. Their semi-final defeat of Offaly by 2-7 to 0-7 started with a 2-4 scoring spree in six minutes at the start of the game—observers noted that "their handpassing resembled Kildare at their best."

Dublin's first ever all-native selection were seven points down at half-time in the quarter-final against Louth, but came back to win by one and bowed out to Meath in a bad-tempered semi-final. With Galway's victory over Meath, that left Kerry with a chance of revenge for 1938. They got it by a solitary point—0-7 to 1-3, as 60,821 spectators roared them on.

After touring the United States together in 1938, these teams knew each other well. Perhaps too well. "The game was not productive of great football. The play was scrappy all through and hard knocks abounded."

There were more fisticuffs. Jimmy Duggan's goal for Galway set the game alight, booted to the net from a tangle of players after a John Dunne free just before half-time. Then, when Galway added just one point as they lost their 1-2 to 0-3 lead in the second half, tempers began to boil. John Burke's attempt at a winning point for Galway came back off the post and was cleared. Soon afterwards Charlie O'Sullivan shot the winning point for Kerry with a left-footed shot from 40 yards, after 37 minutes of second-half play.

The introduction of Paddy "Bawn" Brosnan set Kerry away on the trail of the four points they needed to win. Galway were awarded 38 frees to Kerry's 24, a total of just over a free a minute. One report claimed that the number of times Galway players slipped when going for the ball indicated that their boot studs were faulty!

Despite the tough edges to the game and the pouring rain, there was a marvellous moment when a duck, clad in green and gold, was let loose to waddle across the field.

That left Kerry within sight of the three-in-a-row for the second time in 14 years.

KERRY'S THIRD

Like Cavan in Ulster, the lack of opposition in Munster did not seem to deter Kerry. They were given a bye into the provincial final while the other Munster counties played off for the McGrath Cup which was recently presented by Munster Convention. Tipperary were certainly no longer a threat. They barely survived a first-round championship match with Waterford when Ahearne had a last-minute goal disallowed. Tipperary decided to concede a walk-over to Clare because foot-and-mouth worries sent the county into quarantine. Clare won the mini-competition, and despite the efforts of returned football nomad, 1934 Dublin star Georgie Comerford, Clare trailed 1-3 to 0-3 at half-time and went down by 2-9 to 0-6 thanks to a Murt Kelly goal at the start of the second half.

But any of the provinces could mount a challenge to Kerry at the semi-final stage, and Dublin's "native players" policy was paying dividends in Leinster.

Dublin started with a draw, Matt Fletcher scored Dublin's last-minute equaliser against Louth which left the score 2-7 to 3-4. Even the referee was confused that day: he initially announced Louth 3-5 to 2-6 winners, then consulted his umpires and admitted his mistake. Fletcher popped up again in the replay for the winning goal near the end. Then Dublin ousted champions Meath by 1-8 to 1-6 at Drogheda.

Fletcher got both goals for Dublin as they survived a late Kildare comeback in the semi-final to win by 2-11 to 2-10.

It was a year of replays in Leinster. Surprise packets Carlow survived a four-match marathon against Wexford, eventually winning by 2-8 to 0-3 with goals from Rea and Byrne. They looked home and dry the second day but Wexford came back from eight points down.

Dublin could have gone the whole way. In the semi-final, which resulted in an 0-4 each draw, only a late Murt Kelly free saved Kerry from defeat.

Dublin ran into transport problems when they replayed the semi-final in Tralee. Those who travelled from Dublin on Sunday morning arrived to discover that the other half of the team had not arrived—the ones who thought it would be a bright idea to overnight in Limerick were still snailing along en route to Tralee by turf-train. Dublin failed to reproduce their Croke Park form and went down by 2-9 to 0-3.

Dublin were therefore out of the championship by the time the Leinster final was played, thanks to the foot-and-mouth cattle disease scare. Fletcher, Fitzgerald, O'Connor and Banks scored the goals to beat Carlow by 4-6 to 1-4.

In Ulster Tyrone made their bravest bid yet. They beat Armagh by 3-13 to 0-1, 1940 surprise team Down (who had fairly hammered Antrim by 5-4 to 0-4) by 1-10 to 1-9, and went into full-time training with Belfast Celtic trainer Joe Devlin for the final, only to meet with massive disappointment when they had to field without captain and inter-provincial star Peter Campbell whose father died on the morning of the game. Cavan won easily, 3-9 to 0-5. Few Cavan supporters travelled to the final in Armagh, as it was difficult to go north without identification during the war, yet the gate of £525/13/8 was twice the 1940 figure.

For the first time in nine years of the Connacht championship, the 1941 final wasn't a Galway—Mayo affair. When the old rivals met in the semi-final before 15,000 spectators at Tuam, Galway came from behind to beat Mayo by 0-10 to 1-5, thanks to a superb save from goalkeeper Jim McGauran in the dying minutes.

Avoiding Galway and Mayo in the Connacht semi-final helped Roscommon's case. The 1940 junior champions, were on the way up, and were clearly no respecters of reputations, and were to add a 1941 minor title to that of 1939.

Galway scraped through by a single point in the final, 0-8 to 1-4, when Eamonn Boland scored a late goal for Roscommon. Hugh Gibbons, later a Fianna Fáil TD, had another Roscommon goal disallowed in the first half.

Galway defeated Cavan in the All-Ireland semi-final by 1-12 to 1-4, but fared no better against Kerry than in 1940 as they went down by four points, 1-8 to 0-7. According to P D Mehigan: "Kerry were outmanoeuvred by Galway's grand team for fully twenty minutes of the first half and it was a miracle that Galway weren't goals in front."

Again Galway lost the lead; as Kerry had trailed by two points four minutes into the second half, six minutes later came a turning-point goal from Tom "Gega" O'Connor, and with the game getting steadily rougher, Kerry secured their three-in-a-row with two Murt Kelly points: "It was one tremendous finish where hard knocks were taken as they came and the thud of men's eager bodies left many prone again and again as herculean athletes heaved their weight and unbeaten spirit into the mighty fray."

Emergency restrictions affected the attendance. Some 45,512 spectators paid £3,540 in receipts, with 11,000 coming by turf-fired train and two hardy Kerrymen arriving by tandem from Killarney.

Brawn, more than brain, characterised the Kerry three-in-a-row team. They are certainly not recalled with affection by lovers of the game in the manner of the 1929-32 team. Dan O'Keeffe still held the goalkeeper's spot he had taken from Johnny Riordan in a last-minute dressing-room reshuffle nine years earlier; the full-back line consisted of Bill Myers, Joe Keohane (it was said of army officer Joe that you had to have a written permit before he would let you approach the parallelogram), and Tim Healy; the half-back line of team captain Bill Dillon, Bill Casey, and Eddie Walsh could also handle themselves in a skirmish.

Sean Brosnan and Paddy Kennedy were the classy midfielders with a simple high-catching approach to the game; half-forwards Johnny Walsh, Tom O'Connor and Paddy "Bawn" Brosnan, skipper of the fishing smack "Rory," were also known for a solid shoulder; while Jim O'Gorman, Murt Kelly, and Charlie O'Sullivan were lighter and more athletic. O'Sullivan once scored a point in a colleges final while lying on the flat of his back on the ground.

Brosnan summed up the philosophy of those teams: "In our day we had a few farmers, a few fishermen, and a college boy to take the frees."

GALWEGIAN GAFFE

Despite the failures, it was Galway who put a stop to Kerry's quest for another four-in-a-row, a decade after the first had been accomplished. Only a fumbled 50 kayoed Kerry. One by Galway's Dan Kavanagh was tipped to the Kerry net by an unsure back and Kerry bowed out in the semi-final by 1-3 to 0-3 before 20,420 astonished spectators.

Meanwhile Dublin were growing in confidence, a new threat to Galway's breakthrough. In the first round they were lucky as McGoey missed an open goal for Longford when they drew with Dublin at Mullingar and a late Banks free forced the match into a replay which Dublin won with an O'Connor goal early in the second half. After beating Longford by 2-15 to 1-3, Dublin ousted their principal rivals Meath by 3-5 to 1-10 and points from Banks and Joy clinched victory by 0-8 to 0-6 in the Leinster final at Athy after Carlow had equalised near the end. Half-time score was a remarkable two points to nil in favour of Dublin.

Carlow were somewhat lucky to reach their second final in three years: Doyle scored a last-minute equaliser against Offaly in the semi-final. The replay ended in total chaos as the referee blew for full-time 10 minutes before time was up by accident. Carlow were leading by 1-9 to 0-6 and when he tried to restart the match, he was threatened by the spectators, Offaly refused to continue and were subsequently suspended for six months. This was not the only bizarre event of the 1942 Leinster championship. Kildare had to recruit players from the sidelines for their first-round match against Offaly.

Dundalk staged its third Ulster final, on Down's insistence, as access to venues north of the border was difficult for southern supporters during the war. Down's semi-final with Armagh was ended three minutes early by a crowd invasion, with Down leading by 0-7 to 0-6, and forced to a replay which Down won by 1-12 to 2-5. The attendance was a large 7,000, paying £430 in receipts, but the final was disappointing. Cavan won by 5-11 to 1-3 having weathered 15 minutes of Down pressure, then switched Tom O'Reilly to centre half forward. They quickly gained control, led 1-8 to 0-2 at half-time as a result of a Donal Morgan goal just before the interval, and then shot four more goals in quick succession after the break, from Paddy Smith, Pat Boylan,

Cahill and T P O'Reilly.

War-time restrictions were costing the GAA dear. Only 8,059 watched the All-Ireland semi-final where another fumbled 50, this time taken by Dublin's Paddy Kennedy, was helped to the Cavan net by a defender. The performance of Dublin's Kerry-born captain Joe Fitzgerald and defender Peter O'Reilly decided the game as Dublin came through by 1-6 to 1-3.

Galway ended up with three-in-a-row lost as Dublin's first All-Ireland win since the days of the declaration rule came with the help of a goal from Paddy O'Connor after just 10 minutes. As they came back from three points down with a devastating second-half performance, Dublin had late points from a Tom Banks 50 and Matt Fletcher. The attendance of 37,105 was the lowest since 1934.

Dublin had refined their "native" policy. They could also train a team more cheaply than any of the rivals, by bringing them together after work in the evening. They had Charlie Kelly in goal; Galwayman Bobby Beggs, Paddy Kennedy, and Caleb Crone in the full-backs; Paddy Henry, Cavanman Peter O'Reilly, and Brendan Quinn in the half-backs; Mick Falvey and team captain, Kerryman Joe Fitzgerald, in centre-field. A native of Dingle, Fitzgerald had been on the last of the great Garda teams under Killarney Inspector P Cryan. When Garda broke up their club Joe joined Geraldines where he was later joined by Kerry midfielder Paddy Kennedy. Another Kerryman, Jim Joy from Killorglin, joined Paddy Bermingham and Gerry Fitzgerald in the half-forwards; goal-fiend Matt Fletcher, Paddy O'Connor, and Tom Banks were the full-forwards.

Chapter Eleven

Installing the Handpass

ROSCOMMON RISE

The clash between Mayo and Galway in the semi-final of the Connacht championship brought its lowest attendance in 16 years, 3,000, to Kiltimagh. Times had changed. Galway won easily, 3-6 to 1-5, but they had new opponents to worry about.

Firstly, the 1941 provincial junior champions, Leitrim, had three first-half goals from McMurrough in beating Sligo, their first victory in a championship match since 1928. But Leitrim's revival was soundly destroyed, 2-12 to 1-3, in their own Carrick-on-Shannon grounds by Roscommon, who felt their year had come. By 2-8 to 0-8 at Roscommon on July 18th 1943, Roscommon took their long-awaited fourth Connacht title at the third attempt. Knockcroghery business man Frank Kinlough and UCD medical student Donal Keenan, from a sparkling handpassing movement midway through the second half, got the historic goals.

Handpassing played its part in the re-emergence of Louth from the Leinster championship. Louth defeated local rivals Meath by 2-10 to 1-8 with the help of a doubtful goal from Fanning and another from substitute Keogh in Drogheda before a £323 crowd that was a sign of things to come. Then they stopped Dublin's run by 1-6 to 1-5 at the same venue. Coyle's second-half goal gave them a relatively narrow 1-9 to 2-3 win over Offaly in the semi-final. In the final against Laois, Louth recovered from an early Harkins goal set-back. Goals from Coyle and Corr (who scored 1-7) brought them success by 3-16 to 2-4 after nine years of near misses.

Earlier, Kilkenny forced back into the senior championship when the junior championship was abolished, earning the distinction of being the last team to fail to score in a championship match when they went out to Wexford by 3-6 to nil.

But when the breakthrough teams met, Louth's handpassing tactics came unstuck in their semi-final against Roscommon as Frankie Kinlough timed two vital goals for the opening and closing minutes of the game and Roscommon won by 3-10 to 3-6.

Amid all the surprises in the championship, Kerry's exit was probably the most remarkable. In 1942 Kerry's half-time lead against Clare in the semi-final was an unimpressive two points but they still went on to win by 1-8 to 0-2 and hammer Cork by 3-7 to 0-8 with second-half goals from Murt Kelly, J Gorman and Paddy "Bawn" Brosnan for seven-in-a-row. Going for eight in 1943, they were foiled by a late goal in the Munster semi-final at Cork and went out to Cork by 1-5 to 1-4 after a pre-emptive 2-3 to 0-9 draw at the same venue. In the drawn match Cork had made most of the running before a late Murt Kelly point saved Kerry. In the replay, Kerry led 1-5 to 1-3 when a Kerry back made a mistake in fielding the ball; Eamonn Casey smashed it into the net then followed up with two points for Cork's first victory over the ould enemy for 36 years as Kerry's defence fell into disarray.

Kerry had not been beaten in Munster since 1928. Had they not opted out in 1935, they might have been chasing 15-in-a-row. They could blame Munster's convention, which decided to make the same draws for hurling and football. Cork went on to beat Tipperary by 1-7 to 1-4 in the Munster final at Fermoy.

Cavan too had a case for the monopoly commission. They beat Tyrone (by a colossal 4-10 to 1-3) and Monaghan (by four points, 2-3 to 1-5) to win yet another Ulster title. In the final Cavan trailed 0-4 to nil during the first half, and seemed to miss absentees John Joe O'Reilly and Donal Morgan badly. But they came back with a T P O'Reilly goal before half-time, and took control of the second half with a second goal from Joe Stafford. Morgan came on as a substitute and was back for an exciting one-point win over Cork in the All-Ireland semi-final by 1-8 to 1-7. Joe Stafford got the vital

Cavan goal 14 minutes after half-time.

The final was one of the great occasions of war-time Ireland. Before a record 68,023 spectators, Cavan led 1-4 to 0-3 at half-time, thanks to a great Stafford goal, but a spectacular reply by Jimmy Murray two minutes into the second half started Roscommon's comeback. Cavan regained control by bringing Tom O'Reilly to midfield and John Joe to centre half forward and forced a draw, 1-6 each. The referee asked the teams to play extra time but they refused.

In the replay, Roscommon completed their sudden rise from junior obscurity to put a new name on the Sam Maguire Cup. Cavan's resistance was eventually broken with goals by Frank Kinlough after 10 minutes and Jack McQuillan after 12 minutes, but finally with a Phelim Murray point after Cavan had fought back to two points behind.

Roscommon went on to win by 2-7 to 2-2. Annoyed Cavanmen tried to prevent the umpire from signalling the winning score, the crowd rushed the field as a Cavan player felled the referee with a blow, and the trouble took several minutes to clear up.

The sending off of Cavan's semi-final and final goal-scorer, Joe Stafford, for a blow on Roscommon's Owensie Hoare 10 minutes into the second half started the row. The referee was attacked again after the match and two players were subsequently suspended for life by Central Council. It was a sad end to a a great series.

All around neutral Ireland, sports competition had ground to a halt as Europe worried about more serious matters. Missing from the VIP section of the stand for the first time since 1941 was Italian envoy Signor Bernardis as Mussolini's government had been defeated. German minister Eduard Hempel and British minister John Maffey sat a few seats apart in the Cusack Stand.

CONFIRMING ROSCOMMON

Connacht was once more offering an intriguing provincial championship, this time with three contenders for the first time in 30 years. Roscommon took no chances, went into full-time training early, and became the first team to spend over £1,000 defending their All-Ireland title.

Mayo came back out of their four-year doldrums to take on Roscommon in 1944—an early Joe Gilvarry goal helped them beat Galway by 1-11 to 1-3 in Castlebar. Sligo, too, promised a return to the big time. In the semi-final, A McMurrough scored a surprise equaliser that forced the new All-Ireland champions to a replay. Second time out Sligo took the lead at half-time and only the wisdom of the Roscommon mentors who sent on John Joe Nerney for Frank Kinlough helped Roscommon win in the end by 0-13 to 1-6. In the Connacht final at Tuam, Roscommon surprised the begrudgers by holding on to their title by a convincing 2-11 to Mayo's 1-6. They led by just one point at half-time, but won by eight thanks to Hugh Gibbons and Jimmy Murray goals in the second half, while team captain Jimmy Murray thrilled the crowd with his hand-to-toe runs. Liam Gilmartin was man of the match.

Monaghan continued to give Cavan a run for their money in Ulster. Cavan trailed 0-4 to 1-2 at half-time when the Ulster final was played before 10,000 spectators at the not yet officially opened St Tiernach's Park in Clones, a few hundred yards from the border. D McGrath gave Monaghan an early three-point lead. Tony Tighe started the revival, T P Murphy shot a goal and three points, and Cavan went on to win by three points, 1-9 to 1-6. Gaelic football was allocated just 20 footballs by the Belfast Ministry of Supplies under war-time regulations. The smuggling of balls kept the game going in the north.

The repeat of the All-Ireland final had none of the previous year's ugliness or uncertainty as Roscommon won by 5-8 to 1-3. Frank Kinlough started Roscommon's goal-rush and was joined by Hugh Gibbons (2), Jackie McQuillan and John Joe Nerney.

But Roscommon had the most traditional rivals of all to face in the All-Ireland semi-final.

When Tipperary ousted Cork by 1-9 to 1-3 in the Munster semi-final, Kerry gathered strength and won back the title with a strong defensive display, 1-6 to 0-5. Tipperary should have kept the ball on the ground, according to reports, where they had Kerry on the run. Instead Paddy Kennedy got Kerry's vital first-half goal, Murt Kelly and Paddy Brosnan picked off the points, and Kerry's defence held firm in atrocious conditions.

Kerry had new semi-final opponents. Carlow defeated Kildare, Laois and Wexford in an impressive run to the final, then celebrated a monumental breakthrough with two J Doyle goals early in the second half that brought them back from 0-1 to 0-5 down to beat Dublin by 2-6 to 1-6 and win their sole Leinster Championship in Athy. In the previous four years they had suffered near misses in two finals and a semi-final. But the difference between Carlow in 1944 and their previous teams in 1941 and 1942 was in centre-field: the Kelly-Morris midfield combination gave Carlow a valuable advantage.

Longford, too, inspired by the success of next-door neighbours Roscommon, made a brave bid to reach the final: beating Offaly and taking a 1-3 to 1-1 lead against Dublin at half-time, only to succumb by 2-2 to 1-4 to a second-half goal from Paddy O'Connor. O'Connor got the goal in lost time that helped Dublin depose champions Louth by 2-10 to 3-6 in the Leinster quarter-final. But nobody at that stage expected Carlow to make it to the big time.

By the All-Ireland semi-final the 40,727 who turned out to see them play Kerry were not so sure that Carlow were out of their depth. Carlow celebrated by going two points up against Kerry but conceded an unfortunate penalty goal to Murt Kelly just before half-time. When Paddy "Bawn" Brosnan scored Kerry's third goal 10 minutes into the second half it looked all over. But Doyle and Moore helped Carlow back to a respectable score, 3-3 to 0-10, just two points behind.

That left the test to Roscommon. How good were they? Could they rise to the task of beating the county that had won nine of the previous 16 All-Ireland titles, in an All-Ireland final, and show they were really entitled to the status of champions?

A record 79,245 watched Roscommon succeed by 1-9 to 2-4. Frankie Kinlough scored the goal from Nerney's pass after 11 and a half minutes. Then things went wrong. Roscommon defenders got in each other's way as Kerry's Eddie Dunne landed a goal 11 minutes into the second half and with Roscommon two points in arrears Donal Keenan took over. He scored two points to equalise with five minutes to go. Kinlough and Keenan slotted over two winning points and Roscommon bonfires were ablaze.

CHAMPAGNE CORK

Two generations of Cork footballers had waited in the wings. In 1945 Cork struck back, won their revenge from Tipperary by 1-7 to 1-6, and beat Kerry for the second time in three years. A 7,384 attendance turned out to see them beat the home team by 1-11 to 1-6 at Killarney. Eamonn "Togher" Casey did the damage again with an early goal and Cork led 1-6 to 1-2 at half-time. Jim Cronin got their Munster semi-final goal against Tipperary, when the side looked far from All-Ireland championship material.

The Cork team went into full-time training after winning the Munster championship under renowned hurling trainer Jim Barry, first in Clonakilty and then in Cork city.

Pint-sized Derry Beckett gave Cork the start they needed with a goal after eight minutes of the All-Ireland semi-final against Galway and added four valuable points in the second half. Cavan kicked 12 wides in the second half of their semi-final against Wexford and had to rely on a Jim Stafford goal to pull them through.

Roscommon were going for three All-Irelands in a row when they came a cropper in the Connacht semi-final against Mayo. Mayo led 0-4 to 0-3 at half-time, Billy Kenny and Mulvey both scored Mayo goals in the third quarter, and Eamonn Boland's goal for Roscommon at the tail-end of the game succeeded only in cutting the margin to a more respectable five points, 2-8 to 1-7.

Mayo and Galway went to Roscommon to play the final. Galway held out for an exciting two-point victory, 2-6 to 1-7, as a final 20-minute siege on the Galway goal thrilled the 8,000 crowd. Paddy Thornton's goal gave Galway a half-time lead of 1-4 to 0-1. Then Kilroy and Co arrived to pick off Mayo points.

Galway goalkeeper Eamonn Mulholland was charged to the net but no goal was given. Eamonn Mongey eventually scored the goal Mayo needed, but it was too late: Sean Thornton had got one at the other end for Galway.

By now Leinster had the most open championship of them all. A trend was started at Navan when Meath beat Louth by 2-9 to 2-7 with a Willie Halfpenny goal. Louth were soon to replace Carlow as Meath's great championship rivals. Carlow failed to Kildare by 2-13 to 2-10. Longford's hopefuls went out to Offaly. Meath needed extra time to dispose of Dublin by 2-16 to 1-10 after a 3-6 to 4-3 draw: Snow got their winning goal in the first period of extra time, Culhane scored the equalising goal for Dublin a minute from the end of the first match. But a poor start to the semi-final saw them fail to Offaly by 1-8 to 0-5.

The eventual champions, for the last time in their football history, were Wexford, who beat Kildare by 5-5 to 0-6, Laois by 4-5 to 1-11, and Offaly by 1-9 to 1-4 in an unusual Leinster final that drew a 9,873 attendance to Portlaoise.

In the final, Wexford timed their winning move well. Joe O'Connor scored a vital goal just before half-time as Offaly were trying to run the ball out of defence. Offaly were leading by three points at the time, thanks to a J Byrne goal, and dreaming of their first title. But stars such as Bill Goodison and a teenage full-forward called Nicky Rackard, who fought a thrilling duel with Offaly full-back J Kelly, put an end to that. Rackard had got two out of four goals against Laois and J O'Connor two out of five against Kildare.

They had seen off aspiring Antrim by 2-11 to 2-3 in the first round and new challengers, Fermanagh, with an early goal in the Ulster final from their own star newcomer, Peter Donoghue from Crosserlough. Others followed from Joe Stafford, P A O'Reilly and P J Duke in the second half for a 4-10 to 1-4 victory. Cavan's handpassing style was leading to an increased number of fouls, and occasional bouts of fisticuffs kept spirits high, but Cavan's control of centre-field meant the issue was never in doubt.

Fermanagh's rise from junior success in 1943 to the Ulster final was completed when Durnin and Breslin goals gave them a one-point victory over Armagh. Their forward B Lunny, a 1943 Colleges star, was the hero of their championship bid.

Central Council, disagreeing with the handpass and the effect it was having on the game, took matters into their own hands. At a Council meeting they banned the handpass, an extraordinary decision for which there was no justification under the constitution of the GAA. Cavan were hampered by this decision. They needed a great save from goalkeeper Brendan Kelly to beat Wexford narrowly by 1-4 to 0-5 in the All-Ireland semi-final, having shot 12 wides in the second half. It now appeared that Cavan might have a chance of their third All-Ireland title after 10 years.

The new game excited post-war fans. The driver of one express train from Glanmire must have had a bet on the match because he made the journey in four and a half hours.

Cork completed their happy ending after 34 years in the wilderness with a 2-5 to 0-7 win over Cavan in the All-Ireland final, and gave Jack Lynch the fifth of six All-Ireland medals in succession (the others were in hurling). P D Mehigan complained:

> The crossing wind put perfect football out of the question; there was too much misfielding and wild shooting for a classic game, and the highlight from a spectator's point of view was the stern passage near the three quarter way when Cavan forced the pace and stormed in on Cork's tall backs in one of the finest rallies in many years.

Clareman Mick Tubridy sent a rising, thundering shot that hit the lower edge of the crossbar and rebounded to the net after six minutes, and Derry Beckett, one minute from the end, got the victory goals. But despite the margin they were assured of victory only after Cavan had come back to one point behind, "against the win in the second half they tore in in waves and shook Cork backs to their foundations," and jittery Cork had missed three scoring chances.

Derry Beckett made the issue safe with a goal 29 minutes into the second half. Jack Lynch and Eamonn Young managed to bear the ball out to his corner. He fielded, slipped around Barney Cully and let fly a rising ball to the net. P D Mehigan quoted from *The Man with the Velour Hat* in his account of the game:

> What Cavan man could score dat goal of Derry Beckett an' he not the size uv a sod o' turf, wit big Tom Riley and Barney Cully tryin' to drive him down tru' the groun'. An' what about Weesh Murphy of Beare Island—me sonny boy, de Cork full back dat pulled de whole side of a boat agin four strong men in Bantry Bay regatta.

Cavan corner-back "Big Tom Riley" was now a TD. Trained in the debate of the GAA council halls, he was elected as an Independent in 1944 with a remarkable vote of exactly 5,000, when Fianna Fáil transfers helped him oust former Unionist John J Cole. He joined Fine Gael before the 1948 election, and lost two-thirds of his vote and his seat. Cork's Jack Lynch had more luck. He turned down an offer to stand in the 1946 Cork by-election, turned down another from Clann na Poblachta before opting to stand for Fianna Fáil in the 1948 General Election, came in in second place, and went on to become Taoiseach between 1966 and 1973.

The character of the Cork team was goalkeeper Moll Driscoll. On the night before the final he offered Mick Finn a shilling for a song, and 19 to stop.

A crowd of 60,000 greeted the Cork team's return to the city, the greatest welcome in football history. One speaker demanded that Dublin Corporation take down Nelson's pillar and put up a new one to Cork trainer Jim Barry.

The handpass might have helped Cavan win in 1945. The issue of palmed passing would just not go away.

PASSED MASTERS

Handpassing is as old as the GAA itself. The handpass was not invented. It evolved from a looseness in the old rule which stated that "the ball, when off the ground, may be struck with the hand."

It was used by early teams: Dundalk Young Irelands in the 1887 All-Ireland final, Erin's Hope in the 1887 Dublin championship, Clane in the 1888 Kildare and Leinster championships, Monaghan in the 1888 Ulster championship. The 1903 Kildare team are said to have "handpassed the leather along the ground." Dublin used a short handpass, involving two or three men, successfully against Kerry in 1923 and 1924. Kildare took it up with a longer and more frequently used handpass against Kerry in 1926, and in 1928 Kildareman Paddy Loughlin threw the ball illegally into the Cavan net for a vital goal in the All-Ireland final. Mayo used it from 1936 on in National League and championship campaigns. Full-forward Paddy Moclair moved outfield and slung the ball to both wings as the forwards came forward. Cavan used the short-pass even more frequently, and critics claimed that many of their movements broke down through over-elaboration.

A 1939 commission, reporting on the rules of Gaelic football, recommended that it be abolished or "alternatively that the player receiving the ball from a hand-pass be forced to kick the ball." Michael Ó Ruairc of Kerry was among those who argued at the 1940 Congress that "hand-passing gives rise to rough play and makes the task of the referee more difficult." The motions to abolish it were short of the two-thirds majority by just one vote.

Then came the 1941 Railway Cup final between Munster and Ulster. Ulster further developed the Mayo technique, using the centre-forward, Alf Murray of Armagh, instead of the full-forward as a pivot of the handpassing movement: "a mixture of basketball and rugby," as horrified *Kerryman* writer Paddy Foley described it. Ulster soared 1-6 to 0-1 ahead without kicking a single score. Munster came back to draw and won the replay. But Ulster stuck to the new handpass technique, and when Murray was joined by another handpass master, Simon Deignan of Cavan at full-forward, they came back to win the Cup from Munster in 1942 and beat Leinster by a point in a 1943 final that is still remembered as the best ever.

A Kerry motion to the Congress of 1945 got a simple majority, but not the necessary two-thirds majority needed to abolish the handpass. In August 1945, however, the Central Council conferred with referees and ruled that the ball must be struck with the fist only.

That move, of doubtful legality, may have cost Cavan an All-Ireland, but when it was forced back onto the rule-book by an Antrim motion to the 1946 Congress, at least the issue was cleared up for once and for all.

Antrim had been masters of the tactic 35 years before. Well beaten by Cavan in 1944 and 1945, their Belfast-based players in particular had perfected the technique for the 1946 Ulster championship. Antrim beat Down and Armagh to become Cavan's fifth new final opponents in six years.

Ulster Council benefited from the excitement that Antrim brought to their championship, earning a record £1,051 from 15,000 spectators at Clones. They seemed to have their work cut out for them. Cavan, seeking eight-in-a-row, hit Tyrone with seven first-half goals in Omagh, and won by 8-13 to 2-4 in the Ulster quarter-final.

But in the Ulster final Antrim, with Kevin Armstrong acting as their handpass "pivot," showed they meant business with three scores in the first three minutes. The third was a goal from Joe McCallin; he added a second five minutes before half-time, and Antrim had only to defend their 2-5 to 0-4 lead in the second half. When Cavan sub Tom O'Reilly got a Cavan goal and had another disallowed, Harry O'Neill swarmed into the backs to relieve the siege and Antrim won by 2-8 to 1-7.

Kerry had no time for such niceties. They deposed All-Ireland champions Cork by 1-6 to 0-7 in the first round of the Munster championship at Ennis, with the help of an own goal from a Cork defender at the start of the second half. It was the last time Munster's great football rivals would meet outside the final.

Clare put in a strong challenge in the semi-final against the eventual champions, Tadhgie Lyne's second-half goal sent Kerry through by 1-6 to 0-7. In the final, Kerry's 2-16 to 2-1 rout of Waterford was largely due to Tom O'Connor, who scored all of the first-half points that sent Kerry 0-6 to 1-1 ahead. There to throw in the ball was former Kerry player Redmond "Mundy" Prendiville, who had sneaked out of the seminary to play in the 1924 All-Ireland final and became the church's youngest ever archbishop when he was appointed at the age of 31 (a stand in his diocesan capital, Perth football stadium, is named after him).

Johnny Clifford, who was born in Kerry but played on the beaten Galway team in the 1942 All-Ireland final, was now stationed in Cork. He declared for Kerry in 1945 when they were beaten by Cork. Now he declared for Cork only to end up on the losing team again.

The clash of styles between Antrim and Kerry in the All-Ireland semi-final was the horror story of a football generation. Still smarting with the memory of the 1942 defeat of a Munster team that contained 14 Kerrymen by Ulster handpassers in the Railway Cup final, Kerry devised an unashamed tactic to short-circuit Antrim's mobile hand-passing style: "Never mind the man in possession, hit the man in position to take the pass" tactics. Two players, Kerry's Bill Casey and Antrim's Harry O'Neill, were sent off. The radio commentator diplomatically ignored the warfare despite a chorus of boohs from most of the 30,051 spectators which almost drowned him out.

Within seconds of the throw-in Antrim were in the midst of a weaving handpass movement when Bill Casey halted Kevin Armstrong in his stride. Willy O'Donnell sent a low ball to the net for Kerry after 90 seconds. A late Batt Garvey goal sent Kerry through by 2-7 to 0-10. "Antrim's short passing and swerving methods were hampered by the weather, the greasy topped sod and a slippery ball," P D Mehigan mentioned, adding later that:

Antrim's movements broke down on Kerry's stonewall defence. O'Keeffe and his six backs in front were determined not to let those flashing speed merchants through. As Armstrong was swerving away on a solo run, Casey had him down; O'Neill rushed in and there was a brief ruggy—over in a flash, but Casey and O'Neill were marched off. Casey's loss at this stage almost cost Kerry the game. But there was no mistaking Kerry's all-round proficiency in skilful, orthodox Gaelic football of the very best kind.

One *Kerryman* writer recorded that:

> The Antrim men stormed through from the centre of the field on dazzling attacks, but they persisted in trying to walk the ball to the net and this was something that just wouldn't work with backs like Joe Keohane, Bill Casey, Teddy O'Connor and Eddie Walsh around.

Joe Keohane compared the barracking and general condemnation Kerry got after the game with the Nuremberg trials! A unique Antrim objection that Kerry had brought the game of Gaelic football into disrepute with their tactics failed by 19 votes to 10. The two who were sent off were suspended for two months.

The second semi-final was going to be eventful, with Laois breaking through in Leinster and Roscommon successfully defending a three-point lead throughout the second half against champions Galway to win the Connacht semi-final 0-7 to 0-4 and winning back the Connacht title almost as dramatically as they were to lose the All-Ireland, beating Mayo by 1-4 to 0-6.

There was almost another Connacht final riot. Jimmy Murray scored the winning goal entering the fourth quarter, with many spectators speculating that the ball had hit the umpire, with Jimmy chasing it, before he pushed it inside the post for the vital goal. In the confusion, Jimmy raised the green flag himself, just as Brendan Nestor had done for Mayo in 1936. Mayo came back for two points from 17-year-old Padraig Carney, but it was too late.

Laois had relied on a series of goals: by Tom Keogh against Dublin to win by 1-3 to 0-5; by Connolly just as they trailed by two points at the second half against Offaly; and by Bill Delaney as matters were even worse off, 0-1 to 0-8 down at the start of the second half against Louth (they won by 1-9 to 0-10). They eventually beat optimistic Kildare by 0-11 to 1-6 before 27,353 spectators in a famous final with 0-8 from

Tommy Murphy, no longer the "boy wonder" but a full-grown force to reckon with in championship football. Murphy's frees kept Kildare's bid for recovery at bay in the second half after Thomas Ryan got Kildare's goal in the first half.

Kildare's optimism stemmed from the fact that they had beaten reigning champions and hot favourites Wexford by 3-3 to 0-10, having trailed by eight points before Bob Martin, Tom Fox and Mick Geraghty got their vital second-half goals. Laois were the third county in succession to win a Leinster title that have not won one since.

So the second All-Ireland semi-final not only drew a bigger crowd than Kerry versus Antrim, 51,275 (partly because the interminable 1946 summer rain seemed to break for the day), but it was much better to watch. Tommy Murphy led a storming Laois comeback and Hughes went for the winning goal, shooting narrowly inside the post only to see Roscommon goalkeeper Gerry Dolan make one of the most spectacular saves ever seen at Croke Park. Roscommon held on to win by one point, 3-5 to 2-6. Surely a great series...with an interruption.

The All-Ireland final was postponed from September 19th because of the "save the harvest" scheme, designed to prevent crops from being ruined after a bad summer, and lost to an economy still curtailed by war-time conditions. This enabled the suspended Bill Casey to play in the final. With Kerry and Roscommon back in opposition after two years, it was clearly a case for a new record attendance, now the transport situation had improved, and 75,771 showed up, paying £6,190 in receipts to a grateful GAA.

They saw Gaelic football's most extraordinary finish. Roscommon led by six points with three minutes to go in the drawn final. They had suffered the loss of star Jimmy Murray 14 minutes after half-time and seen three Donal Keenan shots rebound off the woodwork.

Then, with Murray's hair combed so he would "look right" for accepting the cup, Kerry struck: Paddy Burke landed a goal. Two minutes later Tom Gega O'Connor sent an easy goal past a confused defence and Kerry had pulled off a remarkable 2-4 to 1-7 draw.

Kerry made sure in the replay by 2-8 to 0-10. Paddy Burke took a Gega O'Connor goal for Kerry to come from behind again. Gus Cremin came on to the field 15 minutes from the end and Kerry hung on by their fingertips until a second goal was bundled over the line in a last-minute mêlée.

NEW YORK, NEW YORK

Getting the 1947 All-Ireland final played in New York's Polo Grounds was one of the the great achievements of Canon Michael Hamilton's active career (he had been a radio commentator in 1937). Almost everyone opposed the idea when he first mooted it. Skilful lobbying eventually convinced a controversial Central Council meeting at Barry's Hotel that it was worth carrying through.

Relations with New York had cooled somewhat from the heady days of the 1930s. After the fiasco of the 1927 tour by Kerry Footballers, when the promoter made off with all the money and the team had to be rescued from their hotel, and because of bad feeling over the way the series had been billed "the championship of the world," Central Council refused an application to tour from Kildare footballers. In 1931 Kerry toured again, this time successfully, and a world record attendance for a GAA match was set at Yankee Stadium when 60,000 watched them avenge a 1927 defeat by New York.

Immigration restrictions imposed after the Wall Street Crash meant that New York teams never again achieved the level of dominance over the touring footballers from Ireland that they had in 1927. But the tourists came more and more enthusiastically and often throughout the 1930s.

After Kerry toured successfully in 1931 and came home with enough money to purchase Austin Stack Park in Tralee, Mayo followed in 1932, Kerry again in 1933, Cavan and Galway in 1934, Cavan again in 1935 and 1937, Galway again in 1936, Laois in 1937, and Mayo again in 1937 (when Leitrim player Johnny McGoldrick defeated them almost single-handedly and then collapsed in the dressing-room with pneumonia). Kerry and Galway travelled together in 1939 and played exhibition games across the United States.

Much of the touring, particularly in Mayo's case, was due to the influence and money of Bill O'Dwyer, the Bohola-born judge. When he was elected Mayor of New York in 1946 the GAA now had the necessary clout to stage an All-Ireland final.

Suddenly the entire championship sprang to life. The trip to New York became a prize in itself. Nowhere was this more apparent than at the Munster final in Cork where 32,000 spectators turned out to watch Kerry beat Cork by 3-8 to 2-6.

American fever had helped Kerry give Clare a 33-point Munster semi-final thrashing, 9-10 to 0-4, in the semi-final that would not be exceeded for 32 years.

Kerry's passage to New York was helped along by a famous penalty miss by Cork 10 minutes from the end. Kerry full-back Joe Keohane argued with the referee for two minutes, standing on the ball and sending it deeper and deeper into the sticky Cork Athletic Grounds mud. When Jim Ahearne took the kick it rolled harmlessly along the ground. Keohane was to claim afterwards: "All the time I was arguing I could see the skyline of New York getting clearer and clearer."

Meath too had their eyes on a trip. Leinster spectators turned out in their masses, 41,631 paying £3,636 to watch Meath beat Laois by 3-7 to 1-7. Meath newcomer Bryan Smyth scored a goal before half-time and Peter McDermott got the first and third goals for a rather easy victory in that game. Paddy O'Brien was the hero of an 0-9 to 1-4 semi-final win over Louth, when Meath came from three points behind after a Jim Quigley goal for Louth. Paddy Meegan got the goal to beat a fighting Westmeath by 1-8 to 0-5, and McDermott celebrated the first-round victory over Wicklow by scoring 4-2.

Ulster too had an attendance record, 34,009 paying £2,268 to see Cavan take on Antrim at Clones. Cavan introduced full-time training for an Ulster final for the first time in preparation for this crunch game. Two soft goals early in the second half had similarly served Cavan in the semi-final against Tyrone. A slip-up in the twice-played quarter-final against Monaghan provoked this decision. Cavan were foiled by a saved penalty in the drawn match by the Monaghan goalkeeper, and Monaghan regretted a dramatic last-minute save by Cavan's goalkeeper in the replay that sent Cavan through by 1-11 to 1-9.

In the provincial final Cavan got their title back by 3-4 to 1-6, with three goals inside 11 minutes, and when Antrim lost Kevin Armstrong through injury the record attendance thought the final was over. But Frank Dunlop got a goal midway through the second half, and only Antrim's over-carrying the ball and a missed chance, when an equalising goal looked on, thwarted their comeback in a rain-drenched thriller. Antrim's downfall started when one of their defenders put the ball into his own net. Peter O'Donoghue scored the second, and Joe Stafford got the third.

That same day Roscommon announced their candidature for New York as well, beating Sligo by 2-12 to 1-8 with goals from Jack McQuillan and John Joe Nerney as Sligo eventually made back into the final after 15 years: beating Galway by 2-6 to 1-6 with the help of Eamonn White's 1-2 near the end. White missed a penalty early in the second half of that semi-final, but when he scored one in the early stage of the final it failed to inspire his colleagues.

The run of attendance records continued in the semi-finals. When Cavan beat Roscommon by 2-4 to 0-6 60,075 paid £5,448 to see man of the match Tony Tighe score a goal in each half to help end Roscommon's run.

The new record lasted just seven days, as the following Sunday 65,939 paid £5,693 into GAA coffers to watch Teddy O'Connor's midfield performance inspire a Kerry win over Meath by 1-11 to 0-5.

The players travelled the gruelling 29-hour flight from Rineanna to New York via Santa Maria in the Azores, Gander and Boston, the Monday before the game. An advance party of 25 officials and substitutes had already journeyed by ocean liner, the *Mauritania*. A cavalcade of 30 cars, 18 motor-cycle policemen escorting them with sirens screaming, drove the awe-stricken footballers through the streets while Irish

Americans gave a scaled-down version of the New York ticker-tape parade. Lord Mayor Bill O'Dwyer, a native of Bohola, Co Mayo, received them with a party of 5,000 people at City Hall. On the morning of the game Cardinal Spellman welcomed the teams from the pulpit at St Patrick's Cathedral and was photographed with the team captains on the cathedral steps afterwards.

This was to become one of the most romantic finals of them all. The New York Police Band played three anthems, Amhrán na bhFiann, Faith of our Fathers, and the Star-Spangled Banner;then Cavan won the famous victory on the playing-field, by 2-11 to 2-7, in what was described as "pitiless heat," but nobody was quite prepared to admit what a disaster the whole experience was.

When GAA officials got to New York they found the match was poorly publicised, and had been fixed for a bumpy pitch that was only 137 yards long by 81 yards wide. A big patch of grass had been worn away by the feet of baseball players. Grass on the remainder was scorched by the blistering sun. The ground was as hard as concrete, with a baseball mound in the middle of what should be the playing-field for an All-Ireland final.

This strange cairn proved important in the build-up to two of the goals that came in the first half. Kerry went eight points up with Batt Garvey and Eddie Dowling goals, a six-man move led to T P O'Reilly getting one back for Cavan, and when Mick Higgins struck just before half-time Cavan were a point ahead.

Four points in each half earned Peter Donohue the plaudits of the three mainline American sportswriters (from the *New York Times*, *Herald Tribune,* and now-defunct *New York Journal*) who bothered to attend. He was variously described as the Babe Ruth or Dead Eye Dick of Gaelic games, but others wrote of Cavan winning a "rough Irish game." Commentator Michael O' Hehir suffered the indignity of having to appeal over the airwaves to the New York telecommunications people not to cut off the commentary to the ears of excited fans at home.

Only Irish influence with the telegraphic unions and an

appeal to the Mayor got the radio equipment linked up in the first place. Lastly the attendance was only 34,491, fewer than anticipated in the 55,000-capacity stadium. It was bigger than only the Connacht final of the big matches at home that year.

New York's efforts to bring the 1950 All-Ireland hurling final to the Polo Grounds were unsuccessful. The prize trip to New York was confined to League champions for another 25 years.

As for the Polo Grounds themselves, they are no more. They were sold off for development when the New York Giants upped and moved to San Francisco in 1957.

Cavan did not heed the begrudgers. The event lives on in the folk memory. The winning team was photographed with the Stars and Stripes. When the team reached home, 15 bands waited for the bus on the outskirts of Cavan town.

Chapter Twelve

Fêtes of Nationalism

JOHN JOE'S RETURN

When the All-Ireland final came home, it was as a pageant.
The GAA had big plans for what was increasingly being seen
as a celebration of Irish nationhood.

After 20 years of Irish government, parliament and civil
service, and the triumph of nationalism in the 26 counties, the
players of Irish games could claim that there was nothing
more to accomplish. Defiant gestures such as the playing of
the Irish anthem and the flying of the tricolour at matches in
the six counties were just one side of the story. A campaign in
the south to drive the last remnants of imperialism was still
underway. In 1946 the author of a short GAA history urged
the GAA to forget the American tours, the 70,000 crowds at
All-Ireland finals, and concentrate instead on the grass roots
parish games.

Parish football was in crisis. The drift from the land, the
growing practice where towns with bakeries and industries
were offering regular jobs to good footballers from rural
parts, and slackening of the old parish rules, were killing the
game. The annual "high-class gladiatorial shows" with their
glamour and publicity, meant that too much big business
attention was being drawn to a part-time rural pursuit. In
every county, it was claimed, two or three glamour clubs
were getting all the publicity and luring players from weaker
clubs. In most counties clubs found they were only offered
half a dozen matches a year and local competitions were
running up to four years late. The writer concluded:

Only by cultivating the mediocre, by having more

people playing the games instead of watching others play, will a general and even standard of excellence be maintained.

The call went unheeded. The gladiatorial shows were growing even bigger. The 1947 New York experience had convinced the GAA that they had a valuable nationalist pageant on their hands. In 1948 and in subsequent years, there was going to be no mistaking the symbolic importance of All-Ireland day. The presence of a Tyrone team from the "severed six" in the 1948 minor final especially helped boost that image. "Faith of our Fathers" joined "Amhrán na bhFiann" as a pre-match hymn. Locking the gates half an hour before the throw-in was a matter of pride. The crowds were way beyond what Croke Park could handle. But it was still the GAA in a depressed Ireland. It would be 10 years before anyone would think of extending the grounds to handle the new crowds.

Cavan's efforts to become the leading football team of their generation continued in 1948. They suffered the indignity of losing an eight-point lead when they met Cork in the 1948 National League final and were forced to come back for a draw in injury time from a 45-yard free by Pete Donohue. The replay was delayed until after the championship, and Cavan won easily, 5-8 to 2-8.

By then Cavan were Sam Maguire Cup holders as well, after a frenetic campaign. Alongside Antrim, they had transformed Ulster's football final from an irrelevancy that merited three paragraphs in the national newspapers into a national event.

Clones station could not handle 14 special trains in the same hour for the 1948 Ulster final, but the new park there was proving such a favourite an Antrim proposal that the match be held in Croke Park was turned down.

When the arguments stopped and the football started, Cavan were stung into action when a second-half goal by Antrim's Joe McCallin was equalised. Cavan tacked on five points and had a late goal from Peter Donoghue for a convincing 2-12 to 2-4 win. Goals had been exchanged in the first half by Edwin Carolan of Cavan and Brian McAleer of Antrim. Tyrone had a new star when they hammered Fermanagh to reach the semi-final—a diminutive player called Iggy Jones.

Leinster was in flux before facing Cavan in the semi-final. Four Leinster semi-finalists all felt that they could take the Leinster title in 1948.

A Louth goal from White helped beat neighbours Meath by 2-6 to 2-5 in a thriller while Wexford saw off the last Carlow bid for honours by 3-9 to 4-5, with a Padge Kehoe goal in the very last minute.

Cavan built up a massive first-half lead against Louth in the semi-final. They went 1-10 to 0-1 ahead before another series of shocks. Fagan, Mick Hardy and Ray Mooney got three Louth goals in quick succession. Another was disallowed. Ray Mooney was narrowly wide and eventually Hardy got Louth's fourth goal. With Louth needing a goal to draw Casey tried to fist the ball over Benson's head only to see the goalkeeper make a dramatic fingertip catch. The 51,117 spectators breathed out, and Cavan went through by 1-14 to 4-2 with the phrase "by the fingertips" on everybody's mind.

In Connacht, Mayo and Galway served up two and a half finals of the finest quality after Galway newcomer Frankie Stockwell helped see off champions Roscommon with his first championship goal. In that watershed semi-final E Keogh got two more and Galway saved a late Roscommon penalty to win by 3-4 to 1-4. When they met Mayo in the final, Galway trailed 2-3 to 0-3 at half-time thanks to Tom Langan and Peter Solan goals for Mayo. Then Canavan started Galway's revival in the second half and Stockwell scored the equalising point to make it 2-4 to 1-7. The replay was coming to a close when Galway's Tom Sullivan, from a penalty, and Mayo's Peter Solan exchanged goals in injury time. The thrills continued in extra time. Sean Mulderrig landed the winning goal for Mayo and Padraig Carney added a point to make it 2-10 to 2-7.

Ageing Kerry had their lead cut back to two points in the Munster final before 40,000 spectators in Killarney, after

J Ahearne scored a Cork goal in the closing stages. But Maurice O'Connor and Tom O'Connor goals in each half saw them through by 2-9 to 2-6.

Throwing in the ball for the Munster final was Catholic war hero Hugh O'Flaherty, the monsignor who used the Vatican to smuggle POW escapees and refugees out of fascist Italy during the Second World War, immortalised in J P Gallagher's book, *The Scarlet Pimpernel of the Vatican*, and Jerry London's 1983 film, *The Scarlet and the Black*.

Kerry trailed by three points at half-time in their semi-final against Mayo, then collapsed completely in the second half, failed to score and went out by 0-13 to 0-3. It was the last appearance in Croke Park of a clatter of Kerrymen. Goalkeeper Dan O'Keeffe had won most honours of all, eight All-Ireland medals, and played until he was 41. He was born in Fermoy and his family moved to Tralee when he was nine.

The final was a game of two extraordinarily diverse halves, one of the most extraordinary in football history. Cavan allowed Mayo to come back from 12 points down to equalise, then won by 4-5 to 4-4 with a late point. Cavan's sharp-shooter Peter Donohue suffered an unprecedented attack of the jitters.

Tony Tighe got two goals, Victor Sherlock another and Tom Byrne had a goal disallowed as Cavan went 3-2 to nil up at half-time. Mick Higgins struck the fourth early in the second half but by the time John Joe O'Reilly was carried off with a shoulder injury Peter Solan had already jolted Mayo into action.

Goals from Tom Acton (2) and Padraig Carney followed, Eamonn Mongey got the equalising point and Cavan watched breathlessly as Peter Donohue missed three scoring chances before landing the winning point. Carney had a miss from a Mayo free. Donohue missed another for Cavan. Carney's penalty goal was the first in a final since the 1940 decision to introduce the goalkeeper v kicker situation.

This was the finest hour of the new Cavan team. Goalkeeper John Dessie Benson had the most valuable fingertips in Gaeldom; full-backs Willie Doonan, Brian O'Reilly, and Paddy Smith prided themselves on their first-half display; half-backs P J Duke, team captain John Joe O'Reilly and Simon Deignan were the most formidable half-line seen to date; Phil "Gunner" Brady partnered Victor Sherlock at midfield; two-goal Tony Tighe, balding 1930s hero Mick Higgins, and John Joe Cassidy were the half-forwards; while the front-line marksmen were Joe Stafford, Peter Donohue and Edwin Carolan.

Opposition teams were trying to do it "the Cavan way." Mayo's Sean Flanagan, speaking later, said that Cavan brought handpassing to its ultimate perfection and Down, Galway and Dublin later built on their style. But successful handpassing needs pacey forwards, and Cavan's were not getting any younger.

NEIGHBOURS BITE BACK

Cavan's three-in-a-row dream creaked. Their closest call in many years in Ulster came when they faced an Armagh team bolstered by the near-successful juniors of 1948 in the provincial final. Peter Donoghue sent a 14-yard free to the net for a 1-2 to 0-3 half-time lead, then an Armagh comeback was prompted by S McBreen's goal from a high ball that deceived the goalkeeper. Foxy Cavan held on to win by 1-7 to 1-6.

Antrim had tested Cavan's mettle by coming back from 11 points behind to a more respectable 3-7 to 2-6, although even a Brian McAleer goal disallowed near the end for "whistle gone" would not have given them victory in the end.

Kerry went out of the Munster championship in dramatic circumstances. Clare scored their most spectacular victory in championship history when they beat Kerry in the semi-final at Ennis.

At half-time Clare trailed 0-2 to 0-5 and it seemed to be the same old story over again, but when Kerry had a goal at the start of the second half from Gerald O'Sullivan to go seven points up it was Clare who ignited. J Murrihy had a point, T Kelly sent to Murphy for a goal, Daly came through for a point, and Niall Crowley and Pat Crohan struck for goals to complete the shock.

Thus came to an undignified end a formidable Kerry team. Long-serving goalkeeper Dan O'Keeffe was the one who made the record books. His eight medals went unequalled for 40 years.

Kerry affections were reserved for Paddy Kennedy of Anascaul, however. In 1984 he was still rated as Kerry's greatest midfielder ever against competition such as Pat "Aeroplane" O'Shea, Mick O'Connell, and contemporary Jack O'Shea. Kennedy appeared as a tall and slim Tralee CBS student when Kerry were completing four-in-a-row in 1932. He won two Munster Colleges medals, played minor in 1933 and 1934 and also played for Kerry juniors in 1934. He made his senior debut at 19 but Kerry did not compete in the 1935 championship for political reasons. Initially he had difficulty holding down a place in the half-forwards and was dropped for the replay of 1937.

Paddy was just six feet tall but looked much taller because he was so slim. In 1939 he came to work for the Gardaí in Dublin and joined several Kerry colleagues on the Dublin Geraldines team. They won three Dublin championships and he continued to play with them through the 1940s. When Gus Cremin was dropped for the 1946 replay, Paddy Kennedy took over the captaincy. Despite a name for not being able to handle harsh opponents, Kennedy dominated midfield in the 1946 replay, earning a reputation that outlasted him.

Munster's other semi-final was hectic for other reasons: the referee had to be escorted by Gardaí away from the ground after Cork's four-point win over Tipperary. Cork easily beat Clare by 3-6 to 0-7 in the Munster final as Cork's first goal from P O'Donnell proved the turning-point of the game.

As Cavan beat Cork by 1-9 to 2-3 in the All-Ireland semi-final, Simon Deignan was the inspiration and Peter Donohue the marksman. Donohue scored five of the Cavan points and J J Cassidy the goal at the start of the second half.

Brainwave of the 1949 championship belonged to Kilkenny: they played their *second* team in the senior championship against Wicklow and their *first* in the junior championship! What that was supposed to achieve was anybody's guess. They lost the senior tie by just 16 points, a point less than their last first team to compete in 1945!

Westmeath won their second Leinster final place, also in a replay; Peter Mullaly scored seven points as they totally dominated three-quarters of the match against Offaly to win by 0-8 to 1-2. Mulloy scored 2-2 in the second half of the first game. Smallest man on the field Johnny Ward scored three goals when Westmeath gave the first signs of their great run to come. A shock win over Carlow followed, and Ward got the second goal against Laois to reach the semi-final.

But the Leinster cup stayed in Navan. Meath beat Kildare by 0-11 to 1-5, Wexford by 0-14 to 4-0, and Louth in a thrilling replayed semi-final. The first match resulted in a draw, 1-5 each, a swollen 31,845 attendance watched the replay being drawn 2-9 to 3-6, before Meath eventually won by 2-5 to 1-7 at the third attempt before a 39,034 attendance, almost 2,000 more than at the Leinster final. The incidents from those games went into football folklore: Meegan's equalising point for Meath in the drawn match, Louth's dramatic equalising point in the replay, Quigley's goal at the end of the second replay for Louth and P O'Connell's lost-time point for Meath when it seemed a third replay would be necessary.

Meath beat Westmeath by 4-5 to 0-6 in a disappointing Leinster final, scoring three goals at the start of the second half for an anti-climactic victory.

Matty McDonnell was the star of Meath's 3-10 to 1-10 semi-final win over Mayo, snatching two of his side's three goals in the second half. Mayo's Peter Solan had gone on a scoring spree in Connacht. He scored a record 5-2 against Sligo in the semi-final, and 2-1 as Mayo trounced surprise finalists Leitrim in the final by 4-6 to 0-3. Eamonn Boland's three goals helped Leitrim come back from 1-2 to 1-4 down to beat Galway by 3-3 to 1-7 in the semi-final before 9,000 spectators at Carrick-on-Shannon.

The final had all the trappings of the new All-Ireland spectacle of the 1950s. A group of supporters in Donegal hired a private plane to come down for the game. Another group flew over from New York with P J Grimes, former hurler and organiser of the Flying Gaels tour, complete with banners.

When attention turned to the playing-field, Meath stopped the Cavan run in the end, as Bill Halfpenny proved his worth with the second-half goal that prevented the three-in-a-row by 1-10 to 1-6 in a poor final. It was his third goal chance. He missed one and hit the side-netting with another in the first half as Meath went 0-7 to 0-3 ahead.

Cavan tried to come back after Halfpenny's goal, Mick Higgins got a goal in reply but nothing was added to Peter Donohue's total of six points, five from frees. Jim Kearney, who had played on the 1939 All-Ireland final team, was brought out of retirement to partner Paddy O'Connell successfully at midfield for this game.

The neighbours met again in the 1950 League final. This time Cavan won by 2-8 to 1-6 and Phil "Gunner" Brady played his greatest game. Shortly before the game Cavan team member P J Duke had died at the age of 25.

HANDPASS CONFUSION

The handpass had been abolished by the Central Council in August 1945, but forced back onto the rule-book by an Antrim motion in 1946. They may not have invented it, but it appeared that Antrim had patented the handpass. Surprisingly, in 1950, an Antrim motion to abolish the handpass was passed.

Antrim was still regarded as the home of the handpass at this time. Internal power struggles between the rural and urban clubs in the county are blamed for bringing the Antrim motion to Congress. Passing with the closed fist was retained but open-palm passing was banished for 25 years.

The confusion was immense. The 1950 championship was full of instances of handpasses which were ruled illegal. Carlow's Jim Rea forgot the rule and handpassed the ball to the net in the Leinster quarter-final against Louth. The goal was disallowed, Carlow lost by 1-7 to 1-6, and shortly afterwards Michael Reynolds scored a soft goal for Louth, leaving Carlow to ponder on might-have-beens as Louth went to the All-Ireland semi-final. Kildare's P Lyons was luckier: when he handpassed a goal against Dublin in the first round, this time it was the referee who forgot! Kildare went through by 2-11 to 1-9.

Contrary to expectations, specialists Antrim seemed to be unaffected by the ban imposed on the handpass. In the Ulster semi-final Antrim narrowed the gap by two points in a great second-half comeback against Cavan, only to lose 1-12 to 2-6. Cavan got through to face Armagh, who were lucky to get to the final at all. Cole missed an equalising chance for Down as Armagh beat them by 1-8 to 1-7 in the semi-final. When they met in the Ulster final, a match with scarcely a breeze and scarcely a foul provided a great day for 30,000 excited spectators, the *Anglo-Celt* declared.

Armagh stoked the bonfires with their first Ulster title since 1902 on a score of 1-11 to 1-7. Bill McCorry got the goal from a penalty near the end; it provoked one in reply by Cavan's Phil "Gunner" Brady. But by then it was "all over bar the shouting"—and there was lots of that, as busloads returned to bonfires all over Armagh.

Another relatively new rivalry, between Louth and Meath, was sprouting into one of the most even matches in the history of the game. In 1950 the whole nation sat up when the neighbours met in the Leinster final. The semi-finals from which they qualified were equally full of drama. Roger Smyth got Louth's winning goal to beat Kildare by 1-10 to 1-8, but only after Kildare had equalised. Brian Smyth's early goal for Meath sufficed for a 1-5 to 0-6 victory as Wexford missed several chances of winning the other semi-final.

Crowds of 36,202 and 25,000 turned out on successive Sundays to see the games. With the teams level at 1-3 each, the final whistle was greeted with boohs the first day because only 29 minutes of the second half had been played. McDonnell (Meath) and Reid (Louth) exchanged the goals for a result that the referee appeared over-anxious should finish as a draw.

Louth won a crunching physical replay by 3-5 to 0-13 with a late point by Roe, the same player who had just got their second goal minutes earlier. Mick and Hugh Reynolds got first-half goals as Louth avenged the previous year's defeat, but only by a single point.

Louth followed this up with a great semi-final victory over Kerry, by 1-7 to 0-8. Sean Thornton made a fine first-half double save to keep the half-time deficit down to 0-2 to 0-6, and Jim Smith snatched the goal and Jim McDonnell the point that brought historic two-point victory.

Kerry were still recovering from the shock of '49, especially as Clare almost did it again in the 1950 Munster semi-final: two goals in two minutes from Lynch sent them into a 2-2 to 0-4 half-time lead, but they lost it when McMahon scored a Kerry goal in the second half and Kerry came back for a 1-6 to 2-3 draw.

Kerry won the replay by 5-6 to 2-4 in Limerick in terrible conditions, Griffin's first-minute goal eventually breaking down Clare's resistance, and Kerry had to come from behind to beat Cork by 2-5 to 1-5 in the Munster final when Dan Kavanagh struck for goals twice in two minutes, in the 10th and 11th minutes of the second half.

Cork managed to stay in contention until Kerry's last point from Teddy O'Sullivan, four minutes into injury time. Niall "Toots" Kelleher scored Cork's first-half goal to take a 1-5 to 0-3 half-time lead. With nothing but an unsuccessful League final and an unsuccessful Munster final appearance to show for five years of hoping, Clare faded back into oblivion.

Mayo were clearly the team to watch with Meath and Cavan's elimination. An easy draw in Connacht gave Mayo the chance to win the Connacht final by 1-7 to 0-4 from Galway's conquerors, Roscommon, having led by just 0-3 to 0-2 at half-time. Then a goal by Mick Mulderrig and great combination play between Eamonn Mongey and Padraig Carney saw that one-point lead grow to six during the second half.

Mayo easily outpaced Armagh's Croke Park debutants with two goals from Sean Flanagan and another from Peter Solan to win a disappointing semi-final by 3-9 to 0-6.

Experience won the All-Ireland. Mayo snatched the title by 2-5 to 1-6 with the help of a freak goal five minutes from the end. Sean Boyle tried to clear, Sean Flanagan charged the ball down and ran 20 yards to score a goal. Mick Mulderrig added a point and Louth's dreams lay in tatters.

Mayo had waited a long time for their success. Goalkeeper Willie Durkin; the full-back line of John Forde, Paddy Prendergast, and team captain Sean Flanagan; the half-back line Paddy Quinn, Henry Dixon, and John McAndrew; Padraig Carney and Eamonn Mongey at midfield; goal-scorer Mick Flanagan, Billy Kenny and Joe Gilvarry at half-forward; Mick Mulderrig, Tom Langan, and ace scorer Peter Solan in the full-forwards made up the team who achieved the breakthrough. They wanted more.

MAYO MAGICIANS

In 1951 it dawned on Mayo that the Connacht championship was no longer a serious contest. With Eamonn Mongey joined by 6'4" John McAndrew for a dominant midfield partnership, they crushed Galway's resistance by 4-13 to 2-3 before a 27,000 crowd in Tuam in one of the poorest ever Connacht finals.

As Mayo's Peter Solan scored three goals, Galway's only source of consolation was the performance of Sean Purcell, who had starred for Galway as they overwhelmed Roscommon in the semi-final. He also got Galway's first goal in the final but to no avail as Mayo won by 16 points, their biggest victory over Galway in a final since 1907.

Mayo were still accepted as one of the country's premier teams, if only by virtue of their six League titles and one All-Ireland in the 1930s. They had announced their revival by winning the 1949 League, beating Louth in the final.

Kerry were still struggling to replace their 1940s combination. They squeezed past Cork into the All-Ireland semi-final by 1-6 to 0-4 only when future senator Des Hanafin palmed the ball to the net in the last minute after a long Cork onslaught in search of a winning goal, during which C Duggan hit the crossbar, and Martin Cahill (who scored four goals against Clare) and D Murray were wide with great chances. Veteran Paddy "Bawn" Brosnan had one of his greatest days in defence for Kerry.

Then, when Kerry seemed to have faded from the scene, they came desperately close to ousting reigning All-Ireland champions in a drawn semi-final. Mayo trailed by four points as the game entered injury time. Brosnan's kick-out fell to Eamonn Mongey who got the ball to Tom Langan for a snap goal with the full-back out of position, and Irwin added a point a minute later to force a 1-5 each draw and earn a replay.

Mick and Sean Flanagan got Mayo's goals as they won the replay by 2-4 to 1-5 before a record attendance for a semi-final of 57,345, but Mayo had to sit uneasily on their two points lead through the nail-biting nine minutes of lost time.

Without the benefit of the handpass, Antrim came through for their last Ulster title. D Forde's early goal was enough to beat Cavan by 1-7 to 2-3 in the Ulster final, concluded with a difficult Ray Beirne free from 35 yards in injury time. It was Antrim's third close one of the series. Joe McCallin provided the valuable winning point to beat Donegal by 1-6 to 1-5 in a quarter-final replay (Brogan's goal and Brennan's equalising point for Donegal brought the teams back for a second meeting). In the Ulster semi-final McCallin scored 1-4 in a second-half burst when Antrim were trailing by four points to beat defending champions Armagh by 1-8 to 0-5. But it was unrated Derry who supplied the shock of the series: McCann's goal beating Monaghan by 1-3 to 0-5.

Leinster's "real final" was between Meath and champions Louth in the semi-final, when a Taaffe equaliser forced the match to a replay, the fourth between the teams in three years. The replay, before a record for Leinster of 42,824 spectators, was the best of the entire championship and one of the best matches ever seen in Croke Park. Brian Smith and Paddy Meegan scored the late points that sent Meath through by 0-7 to 0-6. Ironically all but three points from both matches were from frees.

What was technically the 1951 Leinster final had a smaller crowd, 32,484, and few thrills as Meath had their fifth title sewn up at half-time; they had two goals before Laois had scored, and eventually won by 4-9 to 0-3.

Against Antrim in the semi-final Meath amassed a 2-6 to

0-2 lead with a goal at either side of half-time from Paddy Meegan and Jim O'Reilly, before Antrim came storming back with five points and a disallowed O'Hara goal, only to lose by 2-6 to 1-7. O'Neill was Antrim's goal-scorer, too late to save the game.

The All-Ireland final brought fine weather, and also brought two Mayo goals in the first half which left them a nose ahead, 2-3 to Meath's 0-8. But they still needed Padraig Carney's three points in the last five minutes for a 2-8 to 0-9 victory.

The first Mayo goal came when a Joe Gilvarry pass set Tom Langan off on a double-swerve solo run in the 10th minute to crack the ball high into the corner of the net. The second came before half-time when Mick Mulderrig floated the ball into the square, it broke between Langan and two Meath defenders, and Joe Gilvarry pounced on the ball to drive it home.

Mayo's Mick Flanagan lost control of the ball as he almost careered through for a third at the start of the second half. Paddy Mehigan concluded:

> After Langan's goal in the tenth minute, these nimble men of the West left no doubt whatsoever of their superiority. At times they were really brilliant and in the second half often made Meath look a mediocre side. Their final winning margin of five points hardly represented their marked superiority in every department of the game—defence, midfield and attack.

REPLAY CAVAN

At Castlebar in July 1952, Mayo's three-in-a-row seekers came unstuck. Under pressure from early on in the game, they succumbed to three Roscommon goals from Shevlin, O'Malley and Fallon late in the second half and Roscommon took the Connacht title back by 3-4 to 0-6. Sligo too had pressurised Mayo in the first half of the Connacht semi-final and led 0-5 to 0-2 at half-time but the champions had recovered in that game to win by 0-9 to 0-6.

Kerry too faltered. Cork knew they had what it took to beat

their ageing rivals, having done so in the National Football League the previous November and again in March on their way to the League title.

This time they won in style, finishing with three great Con McGrath points to end up 0-11 to 0-2 ahead, their biggest win over the old enemy since 1906. In the semi-final Waterford, too, led Kerry at half-time by 1-4 to 0-6. But this time the Kerrymen pulled away in the last 15 minutes and Waterford had to wait five more years for a historic victory.

That left Cavan and Meath. Cavan beat defending Ulster champions Antrim by 3-6 to 2-6 and then Edwin Carolan scored the winning goal nine minutes from the end of a close final with Monaghan that saw the teams level five times in all. Monaghan's semi-final over Armagh had almost been halted by a crowd invasion 15 minutes from the end, but the pitch was cleared and Monaghan went on to make their last appearance in a final for 27 years. Meath beat old rivals Louth by 1-6 to 0-8, with Paddy O'Brien starring and Brian Smyth getting the goal midway through the second half when they trailed by two points.

The neighbours did not stop at that. Mick Higgins, who had probably his best ever game against Down in the first round of the 1952 Ulster championship, scored three of Cavan's 10 points in the semi-final as they passed Cork with five points in the last 10 minutes for an 0-10 to 2-3 victory. But first they suffered a set-back goal in each half from Tom Moriarty.

Meath too had their problems when they chose to play with a strong first-half wind in their semi-final against Roscommon. Only a Paddy McDonnell goal prevented them trailing at half-time, but Paddy Meegan and Jim O'Reilly saved them in the end with points against the wind to go through by 1-6 to 0-7.

It took two All-Ireland finals to send the cup back to Cavan. Cavan earned a 2-4 to 1-7 draw with one of the most bizarre points in GAA history. Edwin Carolan chased a ball that appeared to go over the end-line, kicked it across the goal. It hit the far post and rebounded over the bar. Much to everyone's surprise the umpire signalled a point: some speculated that Carolan had been merely kicking the ball back for the kick-out.

It had appeared that Peter McDermott's late goal had secured Meath's victory over Cavan at the time. The drawn match was played in a downpour, and one casualty of the wet ground was Cavan's Mick Higgins who slipped as he was taking a free at the start of the second half.

Meath's Jim Reilly and Cavan's Tony Tighe both hit the post from goal chances, Paddy Meegan hit the post with a point shot in the second half, and Paddy O'Brien of Meath missed a 50 at the end of the game.

Despite more rain, Cavan could thank a more sure-footed Mick Higgins for a cherished 0-9 to 0-5 replay victory. While Paddy Meegan missed three frees he should have scored, Higgins scored five and another two from play for a four-point win. Meath's Peter McDermott missed a great chance towards the end when he shot wide with only the goalkeeper to beat.

An anomaly of the final: the Maguire brothers played for opposite teams. Liam and Dessie played for Cavan while Brendan played for Meath. Brendan was to create another record after he emigrated to the United States. In 1986 he was elected sheriff of San Mateo County, California, with an overwhelming 81,769 votes. After the count it was discovered that he had died two months earlier!

Chapter Thirteen

Tradition Wins Out

BILL'S MISS

Cavan's celebrations were tempered with tragedy. On November 1st 1952 recently retired team captain John Joe O'Reilly died at Curragh military hospital. "Through the length and breadth of Breifne they are singing one refrain/ God rest you John Joe Reilly, the pride of Cornafean."

That was a landmark of sorts. Cavan never won another All-Ireland.

In general, champions had a bad time in 1953. Louth beat Meath by 1-7 to 1-6 with a 47th-minute goal from Jim McDonnell, then won by 1-7 to 0-7 against Wexford. Offaly reached the Leinster semi-final in the strangest of circumstances. Alo Kelly arrived late and breathless in a borrowed car for the quarter-final meeting with Carlow, then scored a first-half goal and crowned it with the winning point.

There were other championship incidents. Wexford hurler Nick Rackard scored Wexford's winning goal in the quarter-final against Laois with a spectacular left-footed shot. In the first round Westmeath had a goal disallowed against Louth because the Louth backs stopped when somebody in the crowd blew a whistle!

Two weeks later Kerry took their title back from Cork by 2-7 to 2-3. Tom Ashe was the name on everybody's lips after he came on as a sub, scored the winning goal, and then got sent off! When Waterford met Tipperary in the first round of the Munster championship they had to wait for 30 minutes for a score—eventually Ormonde scored a goal for Waterford!

Then All-Ireland champions Cavan bowed out. After 40 minutes of the Ulster final in Belfast Art O'Hagan grabbed a

Mel McEvoy free and put it in the net 10 minutes after half-time for a 1-6 to 0-5 victory for Armagh over Cavan. The newly opened Casement Park in Andersonstown, West Belfast, was crammed with 30,000 spectators for the occasion. A Cavan goal by Jim Cusack was disallowed for over-carrying at the tail-end of the game. Armagh's early conquests included Antrim, when an extraordinary total silence greeted Armagh's winning goal in the quarter-final against Antrim at Lurgan as a Mal McEvoy 50 dropped into the net.

That left only Roscommon of the clubs of '52. After beating Mayo by 1-6 to 0-6, they had to survive the last great objection saga in GAA championship history.

Mayo had their fair share of problems that year. Short several players for the semi-final against Sligo they had to recruit four subs from their junior team, but when they lost a three-point lead in the dying minutes of the Connacht final they saw red.

Mayo objected that five players: Aidan Brady, Ned Ryan, Regan, Seamus Scanlan and T P Cullen were not born in Roscommon. Roscommon counter-objected that Eddy Moriarty had been born in Boyle and not properly transferred to Mayo, and that five Mayo players were illegal because they had attended foreign games.

Objections were the great bugbear of four generations of GAA followers. A major championship result had not been changed since Galway had a Connacht semi-final win taken from them in 1930 and Tipperary hurlers were thrown out of the 1938 Munster championship under the foreign games rule.

But at club level the objection was part and parcel of GAA life, especially after a suicidal 1920 decision that all correspondence should be on Irish watermarked paper. All over the country GAA secretaries strained their eyes to see if team lists and objection slips were on Irish watermarked paper, because if they were not, they were invalid.

Some objections were legitimate complaints against clubs importing players from outside areas. Techniques included asking football impostors the name of their local parish priest to see if they were really from the catchment area of the club they had played for. But the objection had become an art-form of its own before it disappeared practically without trace in the 1950s. A whole army of GAA amateur lawyers roamed the council chambers, upturning results and frustrating the best results of the footballers.

One of the jokes of the era went: "Are you going to the match? No, I'm waiting for the objection." It was an example of how GAA followers found a funny side to the most painful thorns in the side of their sports body.

On August 5th 1953, only four days before the Connacht champions were due to play Armagh in the All-Ireland semi-final, the objections were heard in Castlerea. Crowds converged outside the council meeting in the local technical school, the same place that Roscommon players were in full-time training. Close to midnight the objections were settled: some counter-objection points were lost and the rest withdrawn, and Mayo withdrew their objection.

Roscommon went out anyway. Ger O'Neill was Armagh's big scorer as they pulled 0-8 to 0-7 ahead of Roscommon in the second half of the semi-final. Kerry beat Louth in the second semi-final with three first-half goals, two by the ubiquitous Ashe, for a comfortable 3-6 to 0-10 win.

Nobody anticipated the gate-breaking interest that Armagh's appearance in the final would arouse. Armagh supporters outnumbered Kerry supporters, according to one estimate, by five to one. The official attendance of 86,155 counts only those who got through the turnstiles before the gates at the Hill 16 end were forced. When the gates were closed again, some 5,000 more stood outside, listening to the match on the radio, or on loudspeaker relays around the city centre.

Almost all of the 86,155, and even those who were locked outside, were quick to claim afterwards that they were directly behind the goal where Bill McCorry had one of the most famous penalty misses in Gaelic history.

McCorry was given the chance because goalkeeper Johnny Foley handled the ball on the ground (illegal until 1960) 24 minutes into the second half. Armagh trailed by two points,

0-10 to 1-5, at the time, and claimed a goal at first, asserting that Foley had fumbled the ball over the line. But they seemed happy enough when they got a penalty instead. Foley had been given a horseshoe before the pre-match parade. He now needed all the luck he could get.

McCorry hit the ball left and wide. Armagh panicked, and went goal-hunting in their remaining attacks, while scores from John Joe Sheehan and Jackie Lyne put a relieved Kerry four points ahead. Brian Seeley took a point back for Armagh, but Sheehan's third point put the margin back to a heart-breaking four points and Armagh supporters muttered prayers for McCorry.

Would Kerry have won anyway? John D Hickey, writing in the *Irish Independent*, reminisced:

> In the light of the fact that Armagh failed to score from a penalty and that subsequently they squandered many golden chances of points, it may seem ungracious to say so but, everything considered, I have no hesitation in putting on record that Kerry deserved their triumph.

At that stage, Armagh badly needed another boost like Mal McEvoy's goal. It had come from long range, helped to the net by a defender, after 18 minutes of the first half, and gave Armagh a two-point lead which they lost and regained.

Kerry, who might have run away with the game in the first quarter had not the Armagh full-back line held steady, trailed by two points 10 minutes into the second half, then Tadhgie Lyne started to pick off the points. Jackie Lyne scored another and John Joe Sheehan the rest for a four-point win. Armagh lost Sean Quinn from defence through injury and had to play with three different goalkeepers at stages of the game.

CUP OF MEATH

Armagh were shaken by the experience but survived a hairy first-round tie in the 1954 Ulster championship against Antrim. As they trailed by a point in "lost time" at Casement Park Joey Cunningham burst through on a 25-yard run and sent a long 50-yard shot bouncing to the net.

Luck ran out for Armagh in the Ulster final, where they went out to Cavan by 2-10 to 2-5, having fallen six points behind in the first eight minutes. A Gerry Keyes centre dropped into the net after just two minutes; Paddy Carolan shot a second goal through the goalie's legs; Cavan went 10 points ahead, then J McBreen and Art O'Hagan goals revived Armagh's pride. The crowd invaded the field near the end but play resumed.

Meath also had their lucky breaks in defending the Leinster title; in the quarter-final against Wicklow Paddy Meegan scored the winning point in the ninth minute of lost time, Wicklow having led by two points at the end of the 60 minutes. The "long count" went into Wicklow folklore and Meath went into a semi-final against Longford where Kevin Lenehan rallied Meath to overtake Longford's lead early in the second half after an early Arnold Maher goal put the underdogs on top until early in the second half.

Their Leinster final opponents Offaly were getting a reputation for coming back, especially when they beat Dublin by 2-5 to 2-4 with goals from Sean Kinehan and Mick Furlong after the early double set-back of goals from Kevin Heffernan and Des Ferguson.

Meath beat the Offalymen by 4-7 to 2-10 with goals from Moriarty, Meegan and veteran Peter McDermott (who came on at midfield when Tom Duff broke his leg), to barely survive an Offaly rally that almost brought them a first ever title after Paddy Casey and Sean Kinehan scored goals in the dying minutes. Offaly were left to ponder on might-have-beens, particularly Paddy Casey's missed penalty in the first half.

It would now be customary for provincial champions to retire to Mountnugent or Killarney for full-time training at this stage. Except that full-time training had been banned in a controversial decision by congress the previous April. Since Louth had introduced it in 1953, almost every county had gone into full-time training for major games. Counties such as Kerry and Galway, whose teams were separated by vast distances, were most affected by the ban. But within two years the now more prevalent motor cars were being utilised for twice-a-week evening training, sustained over a longer period than was previously the case, by even the rural counties.

Meath's lucky run continued in the All-Ireland semi-final. Against Cavan, they came back from three points down at half-time with a Brian Smyth goal early in the second half and hung on to their one-point lead, 1-5 to 0-7, as Brian Gallagher missed a 30-yard free with the last kick of the match.

Galway beat Connacht championship favourites Mayo in the provincial semi-final by 2-4 to 1-5 with goals from Halliday and McHugh in a three-minute spell at the end of the first half. Mayo ended Roscommon's reign by 4-9 to 1-7 in the first round with four extraordinary goals from a John Lynch own goal, Mick Flanagan, Peter Solan and Dan O'Neill.

Galway were now expected to canter through a final against Sligo, but when they conceded midfield they almost paid the price. Sligo had an equalising goal disallowed and a free-out awarded instead. Mick Gaffney and Mick Christie goals brought Sligo back into the game in the second half, but Galway held on to win by 2-10 to 3-4.

Kerry retained the Munster championship with a 4-9 to 2-3 victory over Cork as Cork's star forward Neilly Duggan was sent off with Kerry full-back Ned Roche. They then weathered a Galway comeback to win the All-Ireland semi-final by 2-6 to 1-6.

Gerry Kirwan stormed past two defenders only to miss a great goal chance after 58 minutes. Frank Evers, too, went for points from close-in frees in the 43rd and 55th minutes. Greaney's goal came in the second minute of injury time, leaving Galway three points behind. Paudie Sheehy and Tadhgie Lyne got Kerry's valuable first-half goals.

Houdini team Meath won the final, by 1-13 to 1-7. The crowds were less boisterous, and they got a blast of Brian MacMahon pageantry at half-time to quell their rebellious spirits: "Éire's Four Beautiful Fields," with Mother Ireland calling her four provinces to a united Ireland.

At that stage Meath trailed by a point, 0-7 to 1-5, but piled on the pressure in the second half and eventually Tom Moriarty's 20th-minute goal sealed victory. Michael Grace had a brilliant match for Meath.

John Sheehan got Kerry's first-half goal, two minutes before half-time, when he lashed out with his boot after missing a high ball. Meath deserved their goal in reply. It came when Peter McDermott's shot was saved by the goalkeeper but rebounded for a quick interchange between McDermott and Moriarty before entering the net.

P D Mehigan concluded:

> Lack of their usual collective training in camp hurt Kerry. Of that I have no doubt. Some restricted but more controlled training may be introduced. They were too bad to be true. Meath, in my opinion, played the best football in recent years—most deserving winners.

Kerry lined out in blue, and a little terrier joined their first attack as he chased the play. The Kerry blue terrier, it was often said, fights best when he is on his back.

TRADS TRIUMPHANT

Gaelic football was extremely short on instructional literature. Kerry player Dick Fitzgerald wrote the first instructional book on Gaelic football in 1914. This slim volume was the sole work to serve a generation of footballers. Larry Stanley wrote a fascinating instructional manual for Gaelic footballers in the 1940s, but it was only distributed among Garda members. In effect little changed between the 1913 Fitzgerald tactics and the 1950s.

In the days of full-time training, Kerry's trainer for 13 All-Ireland victories after 1924 was J P O'Sullivan's son, Dr Eamonn, a fourth-placed triple jumper in the 1932 Olympics, and the man whose philosophy summed up the first 30 years of the 15-a-side game. Dr Eamonn's way of winning an All-Ireland was to bring the team away for two weeks' sharpening up before the big day. Employers were asked to release players. It was suspiciously professional-sounding for an all-amateur game. Some counties did it for provincial finals; Kerry waited until the All-Ireland, until the system was abolished in 1954.

Four years later Dr Eamonn produced a book, *The Art and Science of Gaelic Football,* but the game technique he described was also becoming outdated.

He preached that players should stick rigorously to their field positions, because:

> Close adherence to positioning by the forwards opens up play and gives more scope to each player for the development of scoring opportunities. What has been described as machine forward play is based entirely on positioning and is incapable of development when indiscriminate wandering to other sectors leads to bunching.

Dr Eamonn elaborated on a whole variety of basic skills:

—follow the centre line of the ball in catching and kicking;
—follow through a kick;
—never hesitate;
—clasp ball to the chest;
—pass only when necessary;
—cover opponent's kicks;
—hop the ball only to gain time;
—train on the weak foot.

He was sticking to traditional methods as Kerry set out on their 1955 campaign, determined that, even without full-time training, they could continue their winning streak. They were lucky to get out of Munster. In the provincial final before 23,403 people in Killarney, Jim Donovan gave Cork a goal-start to each half but his colleagues shot 17 wides. Kerry, who had just eight wides of their own, survived by 0-14 to 2-6.

Dublin had no need for full-time training, and they now had a new trainer who was to challenge the orthodox methods. Peter O'Reilly had coached Kildare in the 1930s. He was originally from Cavan, and in the 1950s was involved with the Dublin team. He tinkered with the traditional 3-3-2-3-3 positioning of players.

In the 1955 Leinster final, Dublin scored five goals against All-Ireland champions Meath. Dublin full-forward Kevin Heffernan roved out of position and took Meath's full-back Paddy O'Brien with him in one of the most famous instances of the "roving full-forward" tactic. Heffernan scored one goal himself and started the moves for three others as Dublin ran riot, and beat the All-Ireland champions by a record 20 points, even larger than the fêted Kerry v Dublin match of 1978. Heffernan was not the first "roving" full-forward, but never had a legendary name in football been so completely outfoxed by a wandering forward.

Not since Wexford in 1894 did All-Ireland champions make as dramatic an exit as Meath did in the 1955 Leinster final. Gaelic football was shaken to the backbone.

Meath had been lucky to survive the Leinster quarter-final too. Kildare showed signs of revival and were forced to a replay only by Patsy Ratty's free which came back off the post and was sent to the net by the same player—it should not have been allowed under the rules. The teams were level seven times in all in the replay, before Meath went through by 1-9 to 0-11 after extra time. Then Meath had to rely on a late point from Michael Grace to beat minnows Westmeath by 0-10 to 1-6. Mick Scanlon was Westmeath's hero for a beautiful 44th-minute goal, and villain for a last-minute miss that would have put them into the final.

The country was now looking to Mayo to see if the Dublin forward machine would be as efficient again. Youth was not on Mayo's side. Captain Tom Langan was now 33 and Sean Flanagan, also 33, came out of retirement. As Mayo beat Roscommon by 3-11 to 1-3 in the Connacht final, Langan got two goals and Sean O'Donnell scored the other from a defensive mix-up. Roscommon had spent £40 flying Gerry O'Malley home from Denmark.

In Ulster, Cavan's Peter Donoghue, too, came out of a three-year retirement and scored 0-8 to help beat 1953 junior champions Derry in the Ulster final as Charlie "Chuck" Higgins missed a 28th-minute penalty for Derry.

Both All-Ireland semi-finals were drawn. Veteran Langan got Mayo's goal in a drawn semi-final by 1-4 to 0-7, putting the Dubliners under pressure within 90 seconds of the start of the second half. Mayo shot eight wides, three from easy positions. Forwards were in short supply again in the replay. Jim Curran was the only Mayo player to score and he missed just one shot and scored his team's 1-7 against Dublin's 1-8. Freaney scored the 25th-minute goal that sent the Dubliners on their way.

Cavan seemed destined for the final after a Gallagher goal and four Peter Donoghue frees before John Cronin launched a high ball which Tadhgie Lyne battled into the net for a late Kerry goal. Cavan got the point that earned a replay but went down to four second-half goals from John Sheehan, Johnny Culloty and two from Mick Murphy before a record semi-final attendance of 71,504 for the replay double bill.

After the escapes of the semi-final, it is hard to work out why Dublin were such firm favourites. In the final Kerry shocked a fancied Dublin side by 0-12 to 1-6. But they had to survive a goal from Ollie Freaney five minutes from the end and a desperate four-minute onslaught in search of the equaliser.

Tadhgie Lyne scored six of the Kerry points. Flying fair-haired Jerome O'Shea made two spectacular second-half saves. Kerry captain John Dowling recalled:

> It was one of the most shattering defeats ever inflicted on a team in an All-Ireland final. Dublin could make all the excuses they wanted to afterwards but the simple fact was that we had proved our football to be superior. We were in peak condition and we were determined that we would break the back of this so-called mighty football machine.

The old school held sway.

TERRIBLE TWINNERY

The clear-out of 1955 champions started on June 17th 1956 when Mayo's team of warriors all grew old together. They crumbled by 5-13 to 2-5 against old rivals Galway. Gerry Kirwan and Frankie Stockwell shared the goals, and Sean Purcell kicked eight points.

Roscommon were left equally humiliated after Kirwan's goal helped send them crashing by 3-12 to 1-5. Sligo's promise of 1954 had never been fulfilled, but on-form Galway did not offer them an opportunity as Sean Purcell's inspired performance on a slippery sod made him man of the match in the Connacht final.

Cork were upset that they had been left behind as Kerry took another All-Ireland. Convinced that they were the second-best team in the country, they ousted the All-Ireland champions at the second attempt, despite their habit of giving away last-minute goals to Kerry.

The first meeting started disastrously for Cork when their goalkeeper thought a lob from D O'Shea was going wide until it dropped into the net. Cork led 0-6 to nil at half-time in that game, and it could have been more had not a goal by Neilly Duggan adjudged to have been thrown to the net. But they still led by three points with just a minute to go when Kerry's Jim Brosnan snatched an equalising goal to draw 2-2 to 0-8. Then in the replay, Cork were leading by three points when Jack Cronin scored a dramatic equalising goal through a crowded Cork goal-mouth: 1-7 each.

It looked like Cork had blown their chance. But there were 30 seconds still remaining, and corner-back Paddy Driscoll kicked out to Neilly Fitzgerald who soloed through to the 21-yard line for the winning point for Cork. Fitzgerald had been a teenage protégé and played for four years on the Cork minors.

The replay was played on the same bill as both of the Munster junior finals, and Ardfert player Tom Collins played in all three games! He lined out for Kerry junior hurlers in their historic first title win over Waterford, for Kerry junior footballers in another win over Waterford, and then came on as a substitute for Mick Murphy towards the end of the senior football final!

As Meath faded out in the first round to Kavanagh's goal for Offaly by 1-14 to 1-5, Louth went out to a Ned Treacy goal for Kildare by 1-9 to 0-9, and Dublin followed in the semi-final, goals by John Ryan and Padge Kehoe sending Wexford through by 2-7 to 0-7. Leinster had to choose their new champions between Kildare and Wexford.

Kildare won the title by 2-11 to 1-8, with a clinching goal five minutes from the end by Ned Loughlin, son of 1928 All-Ireland winning goal-scorer. Ned Treacy got the first after a great solo run 10 minutes before half-time when Kildare looked like losing touch with a rampant Wexford team which had been triggered into action by Mick Byrne's seventh-minute goal.

Leinster provided the accident of the year. A spectator upset the Dublin—Wicklow quarter-final when he blew a whistle. The crowd thought it was full-time and invaded the pitch and the referee didn't get the ball back to restart the match!

No "new" county had won an Ulster title since 1900—but it was about to happen three times in four years. Tyrone were first through. They beat Derry by 3-7 to 2-4 and Jody O'Neill was their semi-final star as M Kerr and F Higgins' first-half goals helped to beat Monaghan by 2-9 to 0-7. More traditional counties, Cavan and Armagh, had a player each sent off as their semi-final was fought out in a downpour. Cavan qualified for their 18th successive Ulster final by four points.

In the final, Tyrone triumphed in the rain: Jackie Taggart caught the Cavan defence out of position after two minutes, Donal Donnelly had a second-half shot fumbled to the net by the goalkeeper, and Iggy Jones saw his shot drop between the goalkeeper's legs. It all came together for a first ever Ulster title.

A second-half downpour didn't help the Croke Park debutants in the All-Ireland semi-final. It came just as Tyrone were overcoming their big-match nerves. Purcell was again the hero of the semi-final, as Galway took a five-point lead and defended it ferociously to win by 0-8 to 0-6. Ten of the 14 scores in that game came from frees, five of Galway's from Purcell, and Tyrone's mainly from Frankie Donnelly.

Cork's 0-9 to 0-5 victory over Kildare was featureless: according to sportswriter John D Hickey the worst he had ever seen. Cork kicked 21 wides, Kildare five, and two great saves from Kildare goalkeeper Dessie Marron were the only highlights.

A polio epidemic in Cork city caused both All-Ireland finals to be postponed, the hurling for three weeks to September 23rd, and the football final by two weeks to October 7th. Because the camogie final was played in-between, it meant that Cork lost three All-Ireland senior finals in Croke Park in a three-week period in 1956!

The All-Ireland football final was a vast improvement on the semi-finals, bringing five goals and one of the greatest punch-pass partnerships seen in Croke Park. Galway were using the closed fist as skilfully as any of the 1940s handpassers, and Frankie Stockwell—"the will-o'-the-wisp, waltzing, jinking Stockwell"—emerged as the hero of a 2-13 to 3-7 victory.

He scored 2-5 and had another goal disallowed for a record which was to stand for 20 years. Stockwell was just half of the story. His "terrible twin" Sean Purcell sent in the line-ball which allowed him to skip in to sidefoot the first goal; Purcell's punched pass gave him the second, and a third was disallowed before half-time.

But a deflected Cork shot was not held by the defence and was tipped in by Johnny Creedon, another was sent sizzling to the net from 20 yards by Niall Kelleher, and then a low Kelleher shot which had been half-stopped by the goalkeeper trickled across the line for Cork's third second-half goal. It inspired Cork back to within a point of Galway and it was left to the twins, Purcell and Stockwell, to wrap up victory with a point each.

Hickey even forgot that Cork—Kildare semi-final:

> Never, I feel certain, was there an All-Ireland Senior Football Final so completely satisfying as the 1956 decider. The game had just everything. The splendour of the football was inspiring, if not awesome, the tenseness of the closing stages simply beggars description; there were individual displays to rank with the greatest I have seen; and yet, despite the supercharged atmosphere of the combat, the conduct of every one of the contestants was a model of good sportsmanship.

LITTLE BEATS LARGE

"We gave them some fright," said the Corkmen, but it was not enough. Cork needed another chance. They got it almost by default. National League finalists Kerry lost the Munster semi-final to Waterford in one of the most astonishing championship games of them all.

Kerry were understrength, but, contrary to rumour, stand-in goalkeeper Tim Barrett was no novice. He had Munster minor and Colleges medals. Kerry still suspended first-choice goalkeeper Marcus O'Neill for six months for not turning out. Kerry, short three of the full-time team in all, led 0-6 to 0-2 at half-time and had gone six points ahead when Noel Power scored a Waterford goal after 45 minutes. Stand-in goalkeeper Tim Barrett was shouldered over the line for a second goal with five minutes to go, and Tom Cunningham struck the winning point in the last minute for Waterford.

It was a breakthrough Waterford had promised since Cork scraped by them with a flukey goal in 1953. A two-year suspension on the two top clubs slowed the progress down.

In the Munster final, Jim Timmons started the scoring with a Waterford point but Waterford disappeared after that, and failed by a massive 0-16 to 1-2, Cork having to survive a rough-and-tumble second half after leading 0-6 to 0-2 at half-time. Waterford never got into the game after Kerry's Jackie Lyne was selected to referee the final and did so wearing a green-and-gold Kerry jersey with Number 4 on the back!

Cork avenged the 1956 defeat against impressive Connacht champions, Galway, in the All-Ireland semi-final. By beating Roscommon by 0-13 to 0-7, Galway got a chance to stage a gala opening of their new Pearse stadium in Salthill which was opened for the provincial final where they beat Leitrim by 4-8 to 0-4.

In the All-Ireland semi-final Galway started with four points without reply, but Cork got their own back with goals from Fitzgerald and Duggan in a seven-minute period in the second quarter of play. They fell a point behind in the second half, but two late points by Eric Ryan, the first allowed to hop over the bar, gave Cork a one-point victory, 2-4 to 0-9.

Leinster champions Kildare crashed to Louth in the semi-final by a massive 5-8 to 1-9, thanks to three Jim McDonnell goals and one each by Roe and O'Brien. Louth had trailed by five points at half-time against Wexford in the quarter-final, but were stung into life by a superb Stephen White solo-run goal which ended with him punching the ball 25 yards into the net, and won by 1-12 to 0-9.

Wicklow won their first Leinster semi-final place in 60 years, with John Timmons scoring two goals against both Laois and Meath. Dublin ended Wicklow's run with a goal from Conroy, two from Boyle and a successful guard on Timmons. To add insult to injury, the following year Timmons won an All-Ireland medal in Dublin colours!

Dublin now had unfinished business from 1955 to look after, but Louth took command of the Leinster final in the second half to win by 2-9 to 1-7. Dublin's Kevin Heffernan and goal-scorer Des Ferguson managed to hit the posts while Jim McDonnell got a Louth goal in each half. Showband star Dermot O'Brien set up the second and Louth swept from four points down to a four-point victory.

For the first time since 1938, Cavan missed the Ulster final. Derry got revenge for 1955 in their semi-final against Cavan with a Roddy Gribben goal six minutes into the second half to win by 1-10 to 1-9. But Tyrone held off optimistic Derry's challenge in a final that would have been unthinkable five years before, the first between two of the "six counties" since partition. Frank Higgins got a Tyrone goal midway through the first half; with 13 minutes to go scores were level; Jackie Taggart and Frank Donnelly got the points for Tyrone's 1-9 to 0-10 victory.

But Tyrone's second All-Ireland semi-final was no more successful than the first. They went 0-5 to 0-1 up, trailed by just 0-6 to 0-5 at half-time, but lost 0-13 to 0-7 to Louth who turned on a great second-half display, despite a penalty miss by Stephen White.

Louth, Ireland's smallest county, had missed out in 1950 and 1953. They were not expected to go the whole way against biggest county Cork in 1957. Their 1-9 to 1-7 victory came thanks to Sean Cunningham's goal five minutes from the end. Kevin Beahan sent in a line-ball, placed neatly for Cunningham to punch past Liam Power into the net.

Beahan, Jimmy Roe and Cunningham had picked off the scores to bring Louth back from three points down shortly after half-time. A switch between Stephen White and Peadar Smith helped thwart Cork, whose goal had come two minutes before half-time from a long Neil Duggan lob that entered the net with Tom Furlong and Denis Kelleher harassing the defence. Louth were the cheers.

SIEGE OF DERRY

That left Dublin wondering where they had gone wrong. Since 1955 they had brought new techniques, innovative tactics, and a new mobility to the game of Gaelic football. Now they were backing that up with more physical presence.

They showed erratic shooting in the 1958 Leinster quarter-final against declining Meath: one shot hit the corner flag, but Des Foley got the vital goal in the end and three first-half goals saw off surprise semi-finalists Carlow. They defeated Louth in the Leinster final at Navan by 1-11 to 1-6, with such ease that they wondered why they had waited so long.

Kevin Heffernan's team augmented their 0-8 to 0-1 half-time lead in driving rain in the second half, and the match was well over before Heffernan scored a goal five minutes from the end. Kevin Beahan got a Louth penalty goal in reply, but only Beahan and McDonnell (and he only once) managed to get scores from the Louth forward sector.

In Connacht, Galway fought off Leitrim's best challenge in 30 years with a rugged, disruptive game. Galway's victory was 2-10 to 1-11 on the scoreboard, but the moral victory belonged to Leitrim. Packie McGarty got a Leitrim equaliser 16 minutes into the second half: Sean Purcell, Frank Evers and Mattie McDonagh notched Galway frees before Cathal Flynn pulled one back for Leitrim, and Galway held on to win a great final by just two points. Galway led 2-4 to 0-6 at half-time before the brilliant McGarty inspired Leitrim's revival.

He roamed around the field and caused havoc for his Galway opponents, one of whom ripped his jersey in an outrageous foul. McGarty gave Cathal Flynn the pass for a goal 14 minutes into the second half, but as Leitrim drew level in the last quarter it began to rain and their game fell apart.

The last alias to play in a provincial finals was Mike "Smith" of Leitrim. His real name was Michael McGowan, a brother based in Cork who was defying monastic rules by playing. E "Dowdican" had played for Sligo in 1956. The Leitrim display removed pretensions of "the real final" from the Galway—Mayo semi-final which had been decided by two Sean Purcell goals. In the other semi-final Cathal Flynn's six points helped Leitrim beat over-confident Roscommon for the first time since 1927.

In Munster, Tipperary tried to do a Waterford, and might have done so after they led 0-4 to 0-2 at half-time on a blustery day but for Kerry newcomer Mick O'Dwyer's display. Garry MacMahon's two goals helped Kerry take the Munster title by 2-7 to 0-3 against Cork.

Cavan survived two replays against Monaghan in the quarter-final, the first abandoned in extra time when the crowd invaded the pitch, but their great days were over. Derry put them out of the semi-final by 4-7 to 3-6, Sean O'Connell (scorer of all but two of Derry's points in 1957) scoring two goals. Tyrone too went out at the semi-final stage, thanks to 1-5 from Down's Paddy Doherty.

Derry eventually became champions by beating up-and-coming Down by 1-11 to 2-4 in the first final since 1890 in which neither team had previously won the Ulster championship. Christy "Chuck" Higgins scored a Derry goal at the start of the second half, and Down were far too late when they came back with a goal from Jim McCartan and another penalty goal from Paddy Doherty, stopped by the goalkeeper but at the wrong side of the line, according to the umpire.

Derry were not expected to go any further, but Sean O'Connell had other ideas. A brilliant display by Jim McKeever in the rain pushed Derry into a three-point lead early in the second half; Kerry equalised. O'Connell put Derry a point ahead, and then Smith sent in a free which O'Connell fielded and smashed into the net. Tadhgie Lyne got a goal back for Kerry but only to cut Derry's victory margin back to a point, 2-6 to 2-5.

Dublin too scraped through, beating Galway by 2-7 to 1-9. Johnny Joyce was Dublin's double goal-scorer towards the end of the third quarter of the semi-final. Ollie Freaney kicked the winning point from a free after the referee told him it would be the last kick of the match.

As could be expected, Derry were not up to the task of beating Dublin. They entered the field to the most thunderous reception anyone could remember. Then they lost by 1-12 to 1-9. But with 20 minutes to go Derry had drawn level and were still in the hunt.

Owen Gribben shocked Dublin with a goal after the goalkeeper had saved brilliantly twice. But disaster struck for Derry two and a half minutes later. Des Ferguson's centre hopped 25 yards from goal, the full-back slipped, and Paddy Farnan was left with a clear run for goal.

Johnny Joyce got Dublin's second goal at the call of time. It was the closest that Columcille's county got to an All-Ireland. Events in Ulster were soon to overtake Derry too.

KERRY'S RETURN

After Derry's breakthrough came Down. Down's revolutionary approach was to shake Gaelic football into the modern age, adapting and developing the Dublin game. Even in 1959 they tried to play with six interchangeable forwards and introduced off-the-ball running.

Not that they had it easy in Ulster. Brian Morgan scored a morale-boosting goal just before half-time to help Down beat Tyrone by 1-12 to 0-4 in a replay. The first day it was Tyrone who led at half-time and Jim McCartan's goal with 10 minutes to go saved Down.

It put Down into the final against traditional champions, Cavan, although Derry's shock conquerors, Armagh, felt they were done an injustice in the other semi-final.

Eddie O'Neill had got the Armagh goal that ousted the champions just before half-time in the first round. Then in an Ulster semi-final replay against Cavan, Phil "Gunner" Brady struck for a Cavan goal, eight minutes from the end, when there were three men in the square and the umpire tried in vain to bring the referee's attention to the breach of the rules. The goal stood and Armagh went out by two points.

Down were leading Cavan by six points to two in the Ulster final when in a twinkling, the scoreline changed to 2-10 to 0-2. Brian Morgan hit a goal, Paddy Doherty lofted over three points, and 90 seconds into the second half Tony Hadden shot a second Down goal. Cavan never recovered, and, eventual winners by 2-16 to 0-7, Down became the seventh county to take an Ulster title and Mourneside supporters' dreams were realised in the sweltering heat of Clones.

Hopes for a shock in Connacht the same afternoon were not realised, despite Leitrim's best efforts. Four weeks earlier Leitrim had their first ever win over Mayo. In a thrill-packed semi-final at Roscommon, Leitrim went 2-6 to nil up at half-time with the help of a strong wind and two goals from Seamus Brogan and Michael Mullen just before half-time. Packie McGarty gave another outstanding midfield display and Cathal Flynn notched up seven points.

Leitrim hoped to go one better than 1958 but lost to Galway again in the Connacht final, and this time the margin was 11 points. Galway already had three goals at half-time from Frank Stockwell and Sean Purcell (2). Leitrim brought the margin back to seven points before Joe Young and Michael McDonagh struck twice more. Joe Dolan missed a Leitrim penalty.

Having stopped Leitrim, Galway also deromanticised Down by 1-11 to 1-4, with the help of a crushing Sean Purcell penalty nine minutes after half-time when Galway already led by four points.

Laois appeared to have Dublin on the rack in the Leinster final. They led by six points at the start of the second half before Ollie Freaney punched the goal that changed the course of the game. Cathal O'Leary was man of the match and Dublin so dominated the second half they could afford to kick eight wides despite coming back from 2-6 to 0-7 behind to win 1-18 to 2-8. Noel Delaney and Mick Phelan scored

Laois' snap goals before half-time.

There followed one of the greatest games of the decade, in which Kerry beat Dublin by 1-10 to 2-5 in the All-Ireland semi-final. Mick O'Connell ranked the 1959 semi-final between Dublin and Kerry as one of the fastest, most open and best to watch in his entire career:

> It was no accident that some of the best games of the 1950s and early 1960s were those in which the Dublin team was involved. Their attractive brand of combination football was almost totally constructive and they were never wont to adopt spoiling tactics to beat the other side. This was probably their undoing in not harvesting more championships but it was certainly conducive to open, continuous football.

O'Connell came to prominence for his display in that game, running riot in the first half when Dan McAuliffe got the vital goal. Cathal O'Leary moved to mark Mick O'Connell, Paddy Haughey and Ollie Freaney got goals, and Dublin's revival failed by two points.

Kerry went on to beat Galway in yet another disappointing All-Ireland final, thanks to a great display at centre-half-back from Sean Murphy and a series of switches at half-time. After five minutes Frank Evers stabbed the first Galway goal in from six yards after he seemed to lose possession running through, and it was 0-5 to 1-2 at half-time.

"So close was the charge and counter-charge that there was little spectacular football," Paddy Mehigan reported. "Over-anxiety brought many wides. Yet there were some very fine bouts of football which the critics seem to have forgotten."

Then came the switches, followed by three Kerry goals. A punched Tom Long ball was forced into the net by Dan McAuliffe and when goalkeeper Jimmy Farrell caught a long John Dowling shot McAuliffe thundered in on top of him, forcing him to lose possession and drop the ball on the wrong side of the line. A third followed from substitute Garry McMahon, who slipped as he sent the ball to the net five minutes from the end. Man of the match was a Kerry defender, wing-back Sean Murphy.

233

Off the field, followers had plenty to talk about. Kerry sharp-shooter Tadhgie Lyne had been married on the previous day. Mick O'Connell left the cup in the dressing-room in the excitement.

Chapter Fourteen

Twentieth-Century Down

DOWN'S CROWN

Faster, fitter, first to the ball, that was the football played by twentieth-century Down. Schooled on the Queen's University stylists of 1958, they took a clean Ulster championship in 1960. Nobody could match their finesse, starting with a spiritless 0-14 to 1-4 victory over Antrim, a 2-11 to 0-7 victory over Monaghan which showed just how superior they were in terms of fitness, and a 3-7 to 1-8 victory over Cavan before a 33,000 crowd in Clones.

They owed success to their blitzkrieg starts. Down dashed away to a great start in that final with a Paddy Doherty goal after just 30 seconds and another from James McCartan before Cavan had settled down. The final, a repeat of the National League final in which Down had beaten Cavan before 49,451 spectators in Croke Park in May, was still full of drama.

They owed success to their tactical astuteness. When Cavan recovered rapidly, and six minutes into the second half the sides were level, largely through the efforts of Con Smith, Down started breaking the ball at midfield rather than trying to catch, Doherty added another goal and Down's big lead was restored.

Leinster had its revolution too. Midland minnows did well in 1960. Westmeath had their best run in 30 years. They reached the semi-final with two goals against Laois to win by 2-10 to 1-11, and two more against Kildare for a 2-9 to 2-8 victory, all scored by 19-year-old Georgie Kane, and then blew their big chance against Louth. Westmeath took a 1-1 to 0-1 half-time lead, Mick Carley scoring the point from the throw-in and the goal from a penalty after just eight minutes, then kicked 13 wides in the second half as Louth demolished their lead. Longford too, beat Meath for the second year in succession with a late Roger Martin goal.

Dublin's Johnny Joyce was the score-finder of the year; he scored a record 5-3 for Dublin against Longford, forced another goal off a defender, and had a rebound finished by Ferguson as Dublin won by 10-13 to 3-8. Kevin Heffernan got one of the most remarkable goals in championship history when he was lying unmarked in the square, recovering from an injury; he climbed slowly to his feet, received a pass and shot to the net!

In the end Offaly captured their first Leinster title, one final and 10 semi-finals later. They trailed by four points at half-time against Louth because a defender picked up the ball in the square and Kevin Beahan goaled the penalty. But team captain Donie O'Hanlon scored a winning point with six minutes to go for a 0-10 to 1-6 success.

Offaly seemed to have a knack of conceding penalties. Against Dublin in the semi-final they gave another away but it was missed by Kevin Heffernan. Offaly hit back in that game with two Donie Hanlon goals and a third by veteran Paddy Casey to win by 3-9 to 0-9.

Down's semi-final matches against Offaly did not show many signs of their impending triumph: when they first met Offaly they trailed 2-4 to 0-3 at half-time thanks to Offaly goals from Mick Casey and Sean Brereton. Down's equalising goal was not a clear-cut affair, either. Dan McCartan could have been whistled for over-running but got a penalty instead and Paddy Doherty sent it to the net eight minutes from the end; an exchange of points left Down with 1-10 to Offaly's 2-7. Peter McDermott of Meath was invited to help coach Down after that match.

In the replay Down came from behind again to win 1-7 to 1-5. Brian Morgan got the vital goal after the goalkeeper parried the ball 13 minutes into the second half.

For the fourth year in a row Leitrim reached the Connacht final and lost to Galway, this time by 2-5 to 0-5. Frank Kyne scored the first goal after just two minutes, the second was punched into his own net by a beleaguered Leitrim defender as the defence panicked in the last 10 minutes. Sean Purcell's shot had seemed destined for a point at the time. The own goal was indicative of the Leitrim jitters, another ball was punched over the Leitrim bar by a defender.

In the Connacht semi-final against Roscommon, Leitrim went into a 1-4 to nil half-time lead but needed Liam Foran's goal to kill off a Roscommon comeback. Mayo too started with a flourish and went 1-5 to 0-1 ahead before Galway caught them on the proverbial hop with two Sean Purcell goals.

Waterford did a 1957 to Cork. Cork back Eamonn Sullivan dropped the ball in the square, Donal Hurley tried to belt it clear, the ball hit the post, and Tom Kirwan slapped the rebound into the net.

But when they met Kerry in the Munster final Waterford got a 16-point drubbing, 3-15 to 0-8. Waterford trailed by just one point, 1-5 to 0-7, at half-time in that final. But they had to face the wind in the second half and a goal from a Kerry penalty by Paudie Sheehy, one of three footballing sons of 1926 and 1930 captain, John Joe, started the rout. It could have been worse. Kerry shot 27 wides and Waterford goalkeeper Denis Corcoran stopped plenty more goals with a brilliant individual performance.

A fumbling Galway defence let Kerry win the All-Ireland semi-final: Garry McMahon got the ball through a mix-up just before half-time and turned the game in Kerry's favour. Kerry went on to win by 1-8 to 0-8.

That left it up to Kerry and Down. The climax was uproarious. When Tadhgie Lyne grabbed Dr Morris' throw-in and had to elbow his way through two photographers who had lingered a little too long in taking the traditional throw-in shots, the referee awarded a free to Kerry! A record 87,768 turned out to see Down take on Kerry in the final. Two quick-fire goals in the third quarter brought the cup across the border.

There were emotional scenes as Down's 2-10 to 0-8 victory put a new name on the Sam Maguire Cup. Jim McCartan turned the game around 11 minutes into the second half when he took Kevin Mussen's line-ball and sent in a high 40-yard lob. According to Paddy Mehigan:

> Down's fairy godmother must have been flighting around Croke Park. The ball travelled dead but Johnny Culloty covered it with great confidence. The ball dropped just under the bar and Culloty put his hands on it. There were no Down attackers in, but by one of those accidents common in sport the ball dropped from his hands into the corner of the net.

Two minutes later Paddy Doherty was pulled down in the square. He scored the penalty to put Down six points up with 18 minutes to go.

Kerry supporters blamed the selectors who had sent John Dowling on to the field limping badly with a leg injury. Even in the parade it was evident he would be unable to play, yet he stayed on the field until midway through the second half. There were also a few near-misses for Kerry. Early in the second half, soon after Kerry had drawn level, Paudie Sheehy sent a low shot screaming a foot wide of Down's right-hand post.

Down too had chances, as they showed the knack of opening wide spaces directly in front of Kerry's goal. Paddy Doherty had a great breakaway chance in the early stages which he cannoned off the post. In another incident Tony Hadden raced clear of the defenders for a spectacular point. Faster, fitter, and first to the ball, the sight of Down forwards running on to collect the ball with Kerrymen in pursuit was a common one during the match.

RED HAND REVOLUTION

Old GAA men joked in the early 1960s about when the team coach used to run on red diesel. Down players were talking about coaching as if it was a totally new concept to Gaelic football. Team sports were changing. Coaches were realising that there was a lot to be gained by putting more effort and better and faster players into defence.

Everybody realised Gaelic had its tacticians for generations. The earliest Gaelic football teams had captains who coached. Some had non-playing captains. Clearly, being a captain in the early 1880s meant more than accepting the cup and making the "Is mór an onóir dom" speech after the game. Men with military experience, usually in the American rather than the British army, were sought out. They would train the men, bringing them on route marches to toughen them up. J P O'Sullivan, who captained the Killorglin 1892 footballers that contested Kerry's first All-Ireland final, was a 120-yards hurdles champion and an all-round athlete in the days when the GAA's "all-round" events formed a precursor to the decathlon. Young Irelands teams in the 1890s developed catch-and-kick football in the Phoenix Park under the watchful eye of John Kennedy.

The *Freeman's Journal* described in 1902 how Eugene Sheehan was in charge of the Kerry team for the replayed Munster final against Tipperary: "He has his men under command. His orders or rallying cries are quickly and heartily responded to."

Much of what was written about the 1903 games between Kerry and Kildare was later romanticised by sportswriters who were not even at the matches, so whether the Kildare and Kerry teams of 1903 *really* invented the toe-to-hand, the long low handpass along the ground, and the art of "scientific" Gaelic football, will never be confirmed. But it is certain the teams were coached. Kildare had a captain who led his team with authority, Joe Rafferty: "When Kildare fought for All-Ireland honours, Gaels will remember how Joe Rafferty's voice resounded over the field instructing the Kildare men and calling for greater effort from them," a *Leinster Leader* correspondent wrote 14 years later.

After the 15-a-side game was introduced, midfield became the key to dominating a game. Tall fielders of the ball, probably beginning with Pat "Aeroplane" O'Shea, were selected for midfield positions by four generations of selectors. Controlling midfield was the key to winning from 1913 on.

For two generations, players were taught to stick rigorously to their field positions by coaches such as Dr Eamonn O'Sullivan of Kerry. Doctor Eamonn's own position was that of coach, manager and trainer all rolled into one. But coaching was by now becoming a personality business. In American football, Knute Rockne as coach of the "Fighting Irish" football team at Notre Dame had become one of the game's best known and loved personalities. In English soccer Matt Busby won a personal battle against the directors of Manchester United and established the independence of the English soccer manager from about 1948 on.

But Doctor Eamonn's traditional ways won out. When Antrim in 1946 tinkered with the traditional game with a running style, using the handpass, Kerry solved that problem by tackling the man before he got the ball.

In 1955 Kerry stopped Dublin's machine forward play with a more acceptable style of direct catch-and-kick. Tom Woulfe concluded afterwards: "If Dublin had won in 1955 Gaelic football would have developed more rapidly."

Peter O'Reilly coached Dublin in a style that was fast and open. By 1959 Down's team, based on the Queen's University team of 1958 that had won the Sigerson Cup, won the Ulster championship by taking O'Reilly's game a step further. They used their new game to defeat Kildare's O'Reilly-trained team in the 1968 National League final.

Down's tactic was to bear down on the player in possession and to leave players unmarked everywhere. This was certainly not Dr Eamonn's game. When in 1960 Down won the League, they beat a stronger Cavan team in the Ulster final by breaking the ball in midfield rather than attempting to catch. This was bunching of the type that would give Dr Eamonn nightmares. It worked.

Down's approach was regarded as revolutionary. They wore tracksuits, until then a sign of doubtful masculinity in the realm of team sports. Joe Lennon wrote:

> There is a need to think about the game...not in the way we have been thinking for the past sixty years but in a way that is in keeping with the tenor of mid twentieth century life. It is only by keeping the game up with the progress of social, educational and scientific reform that we can hope to make it acceptable to the age in which we live.

The position of midfield is probably wrongly blamed more often than any other position on the field. There is a tendency to lay too much stress on the comparative influence of midfield play. Although strength in midfield is often the key to success, it is seldom acknowledged that the amount of good a midfielder does depends to a large extent on the play of the rest of the team.

Lennon's 1963 *Coaching Gaelic Football for Champions* preached interchangeability for full-backs, speed to back up the forwards for half-backs, a block system of midfielders arranging back-up for the breaking ball, a more roving role for midfielders, half-forwards who are prepared to back-pass and help out defence as well as range in on the opposition goal, and speedy full-forwards with lots of free movement among the forwards but little or none among the backs.

Lennon admitted that the idea, which "sounded original", was already being practised by the best players, even if subconsciously.

But the very mention of coaching made the GAA sit up. Lennon directed the first GAA national coaching course in 1964. Their opponents' response to the fluid Down game was predictable.

DOWN'S DESSERT

Down's open football could be stopped with punch, rather than with pace. The 1961 Ulster final ended in a mêlée 30 seconds from the end when the ball appeared to cross the line for an Armagh goal. The referee turned down Armagh's claims for a score and had to be protected from raging Gaels on his way back to the dressing-room after Down won by 2-10 to 1-10.

It was a close shave for Down. Armagh's M McQuaid scored a goal that gave his side a valuable lead against Down, 1-7 to 1-2 ahead at half-time. Brian Morgan and Jim McCartan got Down's goals and Paddy Doherty, Sean O'Neill and P J McElroy contributed a total of eight points in the second half that secured victory for Down.

Kerry drew with Cork in the Munster final, 0-10 to 1-7. They then won the title so easily that they wondered why they needed a replay in the first place. Worse, that first day, Joe O'Sullivan had sent Cork into a shock lead when he bundled the ball into the net after just five minutes and Kerry trailed by six points at half-time but Mick O'Connell completed a great comeback with a carefree equaliser in the last minute of play.

The replay was disappointing. Kerry were well ahead before a punched goal by Gerry Clifford at the end of the first half and another by Brian Sheehy at the end of the second turned the victory into one of gargantuan proportions, 2-13 to 1-4. That sent them through to meet Down in a repeat of the 1960 All-Ireland final.

The prospect brought a new record 71,573 attendance for a semi-final, a few dozen more than had attended the 1955 semi-final replay double bill.

Again a penalty was at issue. This time Doherty's miskick was easily saved by Johnny Culloty, but Down went through anyway, 1-12 to 0-9, thanks to a Sean O'Neill goal in the very first minute. Midway through the second half, with the score 1-8 to 0-7 in Down's favour, Kerry dropped five 50s in quick succession into the Down goal-mouth but to no avail.

The no-nonsense approach had also defused Dublin. The Leinster final was fixed for Portlaoise, the last time it was held outside Croke Park. Offaly's chances of retaining their title were increased immensely. It turned out to be a rough game.

Tommy Greene got the clinching goal for Offaly seven minutes before half-time. Mickey Whelan got one back for Dublin 10 minutes after half-time, then things started getting out of hand. One of the Dublin players threw a stone into the crowd in one of the most reckless acts by a player in Gaelic history. After the match, a Dublin player struck an Offaly player. And, according to the *Irish Independent*: "Immediately the pitch was the scene of a hundred battles."

Offaly were used to battlefield strategy after a rough arrival in the Leinster semi-final. Their match with Kildare was stopped 68 times for frees. Kilkenny reappeared after aspiring to a Leinster junior title, and came close to their first senior first-round win in 31 years when Paudge Butler (2) and John Nash scored three goals against Kildare. But they lost by 3-8 to 3-4 in the end, and still haven't won a Leinster senior tie since 1929.

In Connacht, Roscommon retrieved the title after nine years by shrewdly moving Eamonn Curley to midfield eight minutes after half-time in the final. At the time they trailed 0-5 to 1-6, then Mick Shivnan scored a goal with a low drive. Cyril Dunne replied with one for Galway and eventually T Kenny got the winning point in the dying seconds for a 1-11 to 2-7 victory.

Roscommon were a poor match for Offaly in the All-Ireland semi-final. Des and Don Feeley helped them nose 0-6 to 1-2 ahead at half-time, but man of the match Tommy Greene scored two goals and Harry Donnelly a third to give Offaly a 3-6 to 0-6 victory.

Croke Park did not really have the capacity to accommodate the 90,556 spectators who paid in to see the final, but thankfully nobody was killed in the crush. The record will never be beaten unless some vague GAA plans for a 100,000 capacity super-stadium see the light of day.

This time the blitzkrieg start was Offaly's. A first title seemed on the cards for Offaly after just six minutes of the All-Ireland final. Mick Casey took a Har Donnelly pass and sent in a dropping ball from 20 yards out that arched into the net, and Peter Daly snatched a second goal from a defensive mistake. But Offaly lost their six-point lead, and had a famous penalty request turned down. Harry Green was apparently dragged to the ground by two Down defenders as he raced into the smaller parallelogram four minutes after half-time.

Down got three goals of their own before half-time, from Jim McCartan (11th minute), Sean O'Neill (23rd minute) and Brian Morgan (30th minute). These sent Down 3-3 to 2-3 ahead at half-time. Apart from the non-penalty, Offaly's grievances included Har Donnelly's decision to go for a point from a 21-yard free at the end when his side clearly needed a goal. So Down held on to win by 3-6 to 2-8.

YAWN OF A NEW DECADE

Down's three-in-a-row aspirations were stopped by a teenager. Cavan's 19-year-old Raymond Carolan was man of the match in a surprise Ulster final that saw the defending All-Ireland and National League champions go down by 3-6 to 0-5.

Down tried five men on him, but never quite coped. Charlie Gallagher placed Jim Brady for the 16th-minute goal that started Down's downfall and foiled their four-in-a-row. Jim Stafford got two more goals for Cavan, while at the other end Jim McCartan missed Down's best chance. Carolan's concerto meanwhile scuppered Down's centre-field.

In Leinster, Dublin's Wicklowman John Timmons narrowly escaped being sent off, then gave a great semi-final display as Dublin beat Laois. An extraordinary last 10 minutes in the other semi-final saw Kildare concede two freak goals to Offaly's Mick Casey (53 minutes) and Tom Furlong (57 minutes) as goalkeeper Kieran Dockery lost his nerve.

A record 59,643 crowd turned out to watch Offaly and Dublin resume their all too volatile hostilities in the Leinster final. Dublin regained the title by 2-8 to 1-7, with an early goal from Paddy Delaney and another in the second half from Bob McCrea after Offaly failed to turn their first-half dominance into scores. It was a thrilling game, despite stoppages for the game's 52 frees.

The splendid memory of Dublin's clash with Kerry in 1959 was still fresh in everyone's mind. But there was bad news from Munster. Kerry's second massive win in successive Munster finals, this time by 4-8 to 0-4, led to bottles being thrown, some cars attacked leaving the ground, and sods thrown at the players. Kerry's Noel Lucey and Cork's Joe Sullivan were sent off near the end. On the positive side, Mick O'Connell showed his genius with a beautiful narrow-angle goal near the end, followed by a beautiful catch from the kick-out and another magnificent point.

And that set for the tone for the All-Ireland semi-final, watched live on the new RTE television channel all over the country. O'Connell was superb, fielding in masterly fashion and scoring one point direct from the kick-out. First-half goals from Tom Long and Garry McMahon helped Kerry gain a clear-cut 2-12 to 0-10 victory. It was another classic, which was just as well, considering the mind-numbing nonentity that passed for an All-Ireland final.

Roscommon retained the Connacht final with the help of some shrewd switches when, with 15 minutes to go, they trailed 1-4 to 2-7 against Galway. They moved Gerry O'Malley to midfield, then Cyril Mahon punched a timely goal. Don Feeley shot to the net for a 60th-minute equaliser, and a romping solo run by 33-year-old O'Malley set Des Feeley up for the winning point in injury time for a 3-7 to 2-9 victory. The only spot of bother in the course of the victory was a delay when Aidan Brady broke the crossbar.

Sligo beat Mayo in a first-round replay and, in the semi-final, a 19-year-old newcomer, Michael Kearins, scored 1-7 and should have had a penalty before he went off injured with a gashed forehead.

Roscommon pulled off a surprise when a 25-yard shot from Tony Kenny gave them a winning goal in the All-Ireland semi-final against Cavan, after Don Feeley had a first-half penalty saved. That gave them an All-Ireland final against Kerry.

Garret McMahon got Kerry's only goal after 35 seconds, punching to the net after two defenders let a Mick O'Connell free fall to him unmarked at the edge of the small parallelogram. Roscommon, disoriented and demoralised, eventually lost by 1-12 to 1-4. Jim Lucey fielded the kick-out and Timmy O'Sullivan had Kerry's first point within seconds.

By the time a foul on Cyril Mahon allowed Roscommon to get back with a 20th-minute penalty goal from Don Feeley, Kerry had added five points to their total. Sean Óg Sheehy, whose father John Joe captained Kerry in 1926 and 1930, was presented with the cup.

At half-time it was 1-8 to 1-1 and wellnigh over.

"Undistinguished, unexciting, cheerless and insipid," sportswriter John D Hickey bemoaned.

CAMERAS IN CROKER

The worst All-Ireland final since 1930 was the first to be seen live on television. The All-Ireland semi-finals, finals and Railway Cup finals were to be broadcast live under a new agreement (for a nominal £10 fee) with the new Teilifís Éireann Head of Sports, Michael O'Hehir. Although attendances at finals would not be affected, within five years those at All-Ireland semi-finals would plummet, and the Railway Cup would be wiped out as a viable competition. Broadcasting came into conflict with Gaelic football for the second time in a long and otherwise harmonious co-existence.

After the state broadcasting service, 2RN, was started, the GAA entered the electronic age in 1926 when, on the instigation of hurling supporter and radio director, P S Ó hEigeartaigh, the second replay of the Munster hurling final was broadcast by Paddy Mehigan. The All-Ireland hurling semi-final between Kilkenny and Galway and both All-Ireland finals were also broadcast.

The GAA authorities were suspicious of this innovation and the effect it might have on gate receipts. Radio technicians were refused entry to the 1927 All-Ireland hurling final.

The first GAA match to be televised was a hurling match in Gaelic Park, New York, in 1951. The previous year a Birmingham television crew recorded a match between John Mitchels of Birmingham and Naomh Mhuire of London for showing the following weekend. But the only record of All-Ireland finals during the 1940s and 1950s were poorly edited films with voice-over commentaries compiled by the National Film Institute.

From the 1960s on, television brought Gaelic football into homes where the game was unknown. It was also bringing soccer into homes where it was unknown. The days of the ban on foreign games were numbered; surprisingly, it was to survive another decade.

BUBBLIN' DUBLIN

Roscommon went into deep decline, after that humiliating All-Ireland defeat. They lost to lowly Leitrim in the 1963 championship. Leitrim, who were still pondering on their four-in-a-row loss, had already beaten Sligo and ousted Roscommon by 1-8 to 1-5 with the help of a Cathal Flynn penalty and five frees.

In the Connacht final Galway made short work of Leitrim, winning 4-11 to 1-6. Mattie McDonagh eventually won the duel with his old bogey man of 1957-60, Josie Murray. And when Liam Foran fluffed a Leitrim goal chance after just two minutes, a predictable pattern was emerging. This match was to prove the genesis of greater things to come for Galway.

All-Ireland champions Kerry reshuffled their team madly in Munster. They trailed by five points, 0-2 to 1-4, at half-time in the provincial final against Cork, but came storming back to win by 1-18 to 3-7 with the help of Mayoman Frank O'Leary and former Kildare minor Pat Griffin. The sides were level 11 times in all before Tom Long robbed a Cork defender and laid on the winning goal for Mick O'Dwyer.

Kerry threatened to run Galway off the park in the All-Ireland semi-final. At half-time they had a lead of only four points to one, having run up 11 wides. Eight minutes into the second half, Kerry led 0-7 to 0-2. Galway were struggling, they needed a lucky break.

Then a Galway player saw that Pateen Donnellan was unmarked. Donnellan had been having an injury tended in front of the Kerry goal.

He lofted the ball upfield, Pateen retrieved it, evaded the goalkeeper's tackle, and tapped the ball into the empty net. It took seven more minutes for Galway to wake up to what was happening; they equalised with two minutes to go, and Seamus Leyden kicked two winning points for a 1-7 to 0-8 victory.

Dublin brought Des Ferguson out of retirement in their bid to retain the Leinster championship. When Offaly star

Tommy Greene failed to return from London as expected for the Leinster semi-final, Laois ousted them by 2-7 to 0-9 to bring a new pairing to the Leinster final.

Dublin beat Laois by 2-11 to 2-9 with goals from Brian McDonald and Gerry Davey. This gave them an eight-point lead. Suddenly Noel Delaney struck with two goals in the last eight minutes. There were frequent bouts of fisticuffs throughout this final, but no names were taken.

Dublin's opponents in the All-Ireland semi-final were Down, and the prospect brought 70,072 people to Croke Park. Down had an easy run in Ulster. Defending champions Cavan crashed out of the Ulster semi-final by 4-5 to 0-6, their bid collapsing as Donegal's Harry Laverty scored two goals and hit a third that crashed off the upright, Des Houlihan punching the rebound to the net. Then Down ambled to victory in the last Ulster final to be staged at Breffni Park. Donegal failed to score in the first half and lost by 2-11 to 1-4. Only the Ballybofey brothers Frankie and Brendan McFeely showed signs of not being overwhelmed by the occasion.

But that was all that Down could expect in 1963. Brian McDonald and Gerry Davey goals dumped them out of the All-Ireland semi-final by 2-11 to 0-7 and Dublin qualified to meet Galway in the last of the huge-attendance All-Ireland finals.

Some 87,106 showed up to see Dublin's 1-9 to 0-10 victory. Gerry Davey got the winning goal nine minutes into the second half. It was an untidy affair. Brian McDonald sent a line-ball to the goal-mouth. It was touched on by Simon Behan, and Davey powered it to the net with Noel Fox backing him up. Six defenders and four attackers fought for possession in the parallelogram.

Galway managed to cut the margin back to one point near the end, but John Timmons finished the game with a Dublin point. The game produced 52 frees, and at one stage the referee seemed to award a penalty to Galway, then changed his mind.

Galway went West to plot a comeback.

Chapter Fifteen

Corrib Canters

GALWAY'S HAUL

The forward machine malfunctioned. On a pleasant July afternoon in Belfast's Casement Park in 1964, a Cavan substitute, the 20-year-old Peter Pritchard, destroyed Down's defence of the Ulster title. Pritchard struck twice for goals in a four and a half minute spell late in the game, after one of the most dramatic comebacks in Ulster championship history. Down, the one Ulster team who appeared to be able to hold up their heads in Croke Park, were out of the 1964 championship.

Pritchard disappeared. Dentist Gallagher was one of the finest free-takers of his era. He was taken off the field during the 1969 All-Ireland final. If he had been on the field to the end, Cavan might have made the final.

Cavan trailed by four points when Pritchard was placed by a pass from his former teacher Jim O'Donnell and right-footed it into the net. Charlie Gallagher added a point and then Gallagher had a shot redirected to the net by an ecstatic Pritchard.

There had been an omen. Down had been in trouble in the Ulster semi-final too. They scraped through by 2-8 to 1-9 against Antrim with the help of a controversial goal: Jim McCartan's punched ball was slammed against the upright by Antrim goalkeeper Pat McKay but the flag went up anyway.

While Down were clattered in Clones, 30,000 spectators in Tuam were watching Galway machine-gunning Mayo out of the championship in a four-minute spell that same afternoon. After 33 minutes Mayo's Mick Ruane had a goal disallowed and in the 36th minute Seanie Cleary rounded the goalkeeper for Galway's first goal. Cyril Dunne got eight points and Tyrrell the second goal in a 2-12 to 1-5 victory.

A week later the news came from Leinster. Meath had beaten Dublin by a convincing 2-12 to 1-7. A goal from Ollie Shanley (after 10 minutes) gave them a one-point half-time lead; then they dominated the second half so completely that they could afford to shoot nine wides to none by Dublin. The championship was up for grabs.

Kerry were convincing Munster champions, and when Tom Long had a goal after four minutes against Cavan in the All-Ireland semi-final it emerged that they were the most likely candidates for a 1964 All-Ireland championship that would ultimately decide who would dominate Gaelic football through the mid-1960s. Kerry won by 2-12 to 0-6.

It had seemed that the Galway-Meath semi-final would decide the championship. Before 52,547 spectators, Galway managed to take the lead for the first time in that game from a Mattie McDonagh goal just before half-time. But Meath's Jack Quinn kicked an equaliser with 10 minutes to go and it took two late points from Mick Reynolds and Sean Cleary to send Galway through, 1-8 to 0-9.

It turned out though that, as suspected within the county, Kerry's team was not up to the standards of their predecessors. Galway won an unpatterned final by 0-15 to 0-10, taking a four-point lead in the first 10 minutes against Kerry and defending it throughout the game.

Cyril Dunne got nine of their 15 points, Mick O'Connell seven of Kerry's. But despite the free-taking duel, this was an impressive Galway display—the best of the three-in-a-row. Their distinctive punched-pass game, developed from the days of Stockwell and Purcell, led them through the Kerry defence. Four of Galway's points were fisted over the bar.

After John Donnellan collected the cup he learned that his father, Mick, captain of the 1933 losing team, had died watching the game in the grandstand. Mick Donnellan was a pioneer, on and off the field. A player in 1919, 1922, and 1925, he captained Galway unsuccessfully in the 1933 All-Ireland final and Connacht successfully in the 1934 Railway Cup final before retiring at the age of 34. In 1938 he founded

Clann na Talmhun, was elected to the Dáil in 1943 and was leader of the party for a year. He stayed with Clann na Talmhun until his death, one of the Clann's last two deputies.

John, as son and All-Ireland captain, was an obvious candidate to succeed him. He was invited to stand for Clann na Talmhun, for Fianna Fáil by Brian Lenihan, but eventually stood for Fine Gael at the request of Paddy Cooney. He won the seat and was the first footballer TD since Tom O'Reilly in 1945 when he played in the 1965 and 1966 All-Ireland finals.

SECOND COURSE

Galway's wave almost broke in the north west. Sligo arrived in the 1965 Connacht final on the crest of a wave after beating Mayo by 2-11 to 2-8 at Charlestown.

New Sligo star Michael Kearins scored 1-6 in that historic victory over Mayo, and Bill Shannon's ground shot with 10 minutes to go proved the decisive score for Sligo as Mayo were denied a last-minute penalty.

There were high hopes of an upset in the final too when Mickey Kearins scored Sligo's equaliser with eight minutes to go. As the crowd held their breaths Cyril Dunne got two points for Galway, and Mattie McDonagh a third, for a 1-12 to 2-6 victory. Sligo made most of the running in the game. Dan McHugh and Mickey Durkan scored goals to give the outsiders a 2-3 to 1-2 half-time lead.

Sligo were not the only ones to come close to upsetting the status quo.

Limerick had re-entered the senior championship for the first time since 1952 with trepidation, having lost the first round of the 1964 junior championship. It didn't augur well for their chances until they fired a 16-point salvo across Waterford. The semi-final brought an unexpected breakthrough when they beat Cork by 2-5 to 0-6. Eamonn Cregan scored both goals against Cork, the first from a Mick Tynan centre. The Limerick duo were to become well-known as a result of that 1965 championship.

In the Munster final, Limerick got the start they dreamed about. They had goals from Mick Tynan, after nine minutes, and a second from Pat Murphy after 13 minutes. With the breeze they led 2-5 to 0-6 at half-time and were looking superbly fit and confident, with John Ahearne and David Quirke in control at midfield.

As 16,943 spectators looked on in anticipation, Kerry switched their team around and drew level with Vincent Lucey and John Joe Barrett points by the 40th minute. When Mick O'Connell sent them ahead Eamonn Cregan gave Limerick their last taste of the lead with two points. John Joe Barrett's goal didn't kill off Limerick; only some great goalkeeping from Johnny Culloty prevented further goals from Mick Tynan and Eamonn Cregan towards the end. Bernie O'Callaghan's last-minute goal eventually gave Kerry the breathing-space they needed and a comprehensive-looking 2-16 to 2-7 victory.

Limerick's impetus burned out within 12 months. They were the last "outsiders" to reach the Munster final. Kerry's disorganised team now saw the rest of the 1965 championship as a frantic battle for survival. But in fact they came close to winning the All-Ireland.

And in Leinster Longford were matching Limerick's exploits. Sean Murray and Bobby Burns were Longford's stars as they defeated Offaly by 1-5 to 0-6 (Burns set up Murray for a tenth-minute goal) and beat champions Meath by 2-6 to 1-7 in the semi-final. Dublin stopped the run, defeating Longford in the Leinster final by 3-6 to 0-9 with two goals in a three-minute spell.

Both were inspired by Des Foley, between the 47th and 49th minutes, to kill off a Longford comeback which had just cut the deficit back to a point. Brian McDonald and Jimmy Keaveney were the crucial goal-scorers. It had all started going wrong for Longford as early as the seventh minute, when Sean Murray missed a penalty. Two minutes later their goalie misjudged a long ball from Foley and let it slip to the net.

In Ulster, Down secured revenge from Cavan by 3-5 to 1-8, thanks to Jim Fitzsimon's late breakaway goal. Cavan were caught out when Cavanman J J O'Reilly had a kick blocked down in midfield and Fitzsimons finished the movement to the net with five minutes to go.

The talk of the 1965 Ulster championship concerned an earlier round. Cavan took two replays to eliminate Donegal in a controversial quarter-final; it was followed by the last serious objection and counter-objection in senior championship history. Donegal had refused to play extra time the second day, and a squabble over the date of the McKenna Cup final was dragged into the argument.

Kerry and Dublin served up their last great game of football for 10 years in the 1965 All-Ireland semi-final. Five minutes after half-time Dublin led by 1-5 to 0-4, but Mick O'Dwyer had come into the game and he sent in the pass for an O'Shea equalising goal after 36 minutes. Bernie O'Callaghan scored a second entering the last quarter, and O'Dwyer scored two himself in the last nine minutes for a 4-8 to 2-6 victory.

Galway and Down could not throw up a goal between them in the second semi-final. Galway, who trailed by two points with 11 minutes to go, had a point from Sean Cleary and four from Cyril Dunne without reply to win by 0-10 to 0-7. John Donnellan's switch to left half forward in the third minute of the second half was crucial in establishing the trend of the game.

Galway struggled to put Kerry away in the All-Ireland final and had their lead cut back to just one point with 20 minutes to go. It could have been worse, had John Joe Barrett scored the probable goal rather than the possible point he ended up with from a breakaway move five minutes after half-time. But Pat Donnellan curtailed Mick O'Connell, and four points in five minutes from Galway restored order for an 0-12 to 0-9 victory.

Towards the end Derry O'Shea (Kerry) and John Donnellan (Galway) were sent off and John O'Shea followed them off minutes later. It was the first time that three players were sent off in a final. The only previous sending-off incidents in an All-Ireland final were an unidentified Dublin footballer in the 1908 final against London and Cavan's Joe Stafford in 1943.

THIRD PARTY

The fourth county to win three-in-a-row in 1966, Galway found the going got tough as the trio beckoned. Take the Connacht final. A great goal from M J Ruddy sent Mayo 1-6 to 0-4 ahead after 10 minutes of the second half. Joe Langan was dominating centre-field for Mayo and Galway's reign looked all over. Then Mayo missed three goal chances. Galway sensed the opportunity. They chipped away at the lead, and Liam Sammon scored the winning point in injury time for a narrow-squeak 0-12 to 1-8 victory.

Take the All-Ireland semi-final. Cyril Dunne's goal gave Galway a five-point lead against Cork 10 minutes after half-time. Niall Fitzgerald was sent on with instructions to get back a goal for Cork. He shot appallingly wide with 12 minutes to go. Then he jinked right through the defence with nine minutes to go, only to produce an appallingly weak shot right in front of the goal. Galway reached the final by 1-11 to 1-9.

West coast championship rivals for both legs of Galway's two-in-a-row, Kerry, ran out of talent just 10 minutes short of a record nine-in-a-row in Munster. Two flashes of red in a 90-second period, 10 minutes before the end, gave Cork a 2-7 to 1-7 victory. Jerry Lucey sent to Eric Philpott, who passed to Johnny Carroll for the first. Gene McCarthy tossed in the second. Kerry, reduced to 14 men when Seamus Fitzgerald was sent off shortly before half-time, were facing a new Cork goalkeeping star in Billy Morgan.

Kildare, 1965 under-21 All-Ireland champions, were expected to provide a new challenge in Leinster. With the entire population of the country pondering what happened Kildare after their fourth and last All-Ireland in 1928, the usual bar-stool solution is that internal power struggles and personality clashes prevented Kildare from ever achieving the level of organisation that winners require.

In 1966 Kildare seemed to have found both the players and the balance. They defeated champions Dublin by 3-9 to 2-5 with the help of 3-2 from under-21 star Pat Dunny, but ran out of time against Meath in the Leinster final. Another Ollie

Shanley goal from a 30-yard solo run gave Meath a 1-9 to 1-8 victory.

Kildare believed they could have drawn, inspired by a Tom Walshe goal with the third-last kick of the match, they were pressing for an equaliser when the whistle blew for a foul. Kildare protested that time should have been extended to allow Jack Donnelly's late free to be taken, but the referee claimed he had already accidentally overplayed time by five minutes so that even Walshe's goal should not have counted.

Donegal, too, had high hopes, but went down to Down by 1-7 to 0-8 in the Ulster final at Casement Park. Donegal were unlucky. They presented the opposition with a Sean O'Neill penalty goal, after the Donegal full-back picked the ball up in the square three minutes from the end. A ragged 57-free match presented a dreadful advertisement for the game—especially as it was the first Ulster final to be televised live on BBC. Donegal had objected to the venue too, which was chosen to facilitate the TV cameras.

Meath displayed a soon to become familiar slow start against Down in the All-Ireland semi-final. They got two goals in three minutes from Jack Quinn and tacked on 13 points for a 10 point win.

Meath's slow start cost them the final. As Galway won by 1-10 to 0-7, all was decided in the 10 minutes before half-time. A long clearance found Mattie McDonagh unmarked at the edge of the square in the 21st minute and he thundered the ball to the net. At half-time Meath were eight points behind, 1-6 to 0-1. With eight minutes to go they had cut it back to 1-8 to 0-7 but that was as far as they got.

A conclusion: Galway's three All-Irelands of the 1960s were forgettable affairs.

CONNACHT MYSTERIES

Most of the Galway players agree that their team fell in 1967 because of a trip to America. They crashed to Mayo by 3-13 to 1-8 at Pearse Stadium in the 1967 Connacht semi-final, five weeks after a transatlantic hop to play in the National League final. There was no arguing with the defeat, when it came.

P J and Willie Loftus gave Mayo the possession at midfield and Seamus O'Dowd, Johnny Farragher and Mick Ruane scored the historic goals for Mayo.

As if Connacht had not provided enough talking-points, Leitrim provided another upset. They beat Roscommon in remarkable circumstances to reach the final for the last time.

The mystery of the disappearing minor had defied Gaelic selectors for over three decades. An All-Ireland under-21 competition was eventually introduced to help clear the matter up in 1964. With a great flush of enthusiasm the competition that would save the best under-18 players for the senior grade was played out before 10,497 spectators at Croke Park on September 13th 1964. All it supplied was a delusion that an All-Ireland was just around the corner for some of the early champions, Kildare in 1965 and Roscommon in 1966, Mayo in 1967 and Derry in 1968.

Hence in 1967 Roscommon fielded five of the previous year's under-21 champion team, who had been promoted *en masse* in one of those bouts of enthusiasm which accompanied the introduction of the under-21 grade. They would have won the semi-final had Dermot Earley's goal from a 14-yard free from the last kick of the game been allowed.

Leitrim goalkeeper Mick McTiernan punched the ball en route to the net and the goal was disallowed as it was not scored direct. Leitrim went on to lose the most one-sided final in Connacht history by 4-15 to 0-7, their 20-point defeat breaking a 60-year-old record. Leitrim got just one point from play. Mayomen like Joe Langan exploited Leitrim's lack of depth with long solo runs and midfielder Willie Loftus played as an extra half-forward, picking up a goal for his trouble.

The argument in Munster ended with Cork retaining their title by a single point, but they had to survive sustained shooting practice from most of the opposition team, including the Kerry goalkeeper! Cork started triumphantly by forging 0-6 to 0-1 ahead 16 minutes into the first half, only to lose the lead 90 seconds after half-time. They eventually nudged ahead again with seven minutes to go. Kerry goalkeeper

Eamonn O'Donoghue narrowly missed the equalising point when he was called up to take a free from 35 yards out with three minutes to go. He would later win an All-Ireland medal as a forward.

Cavan beat Down by 2-12 to 0-8 in another torrid, mauling final thanks to a brilliant first-half goal from J J O'Reilly and a great individual goal from Michael Greenan six minutes after half-time.

But a penalty that Cavan conceded with nine minutes to go, sent to the net by Cork's Denis Coughlan, cost Cavan a place in the All-Ireland final. A goalkeeping error had let Flor Hayes in for a Cork goal in the first half, Cavan still built up and lost a 0-8 to 1-3 lead, and were narrowly ahead, 0-11 to 1-7 when they conceded the penalty. Cavan's Charlie Gallagher narrowly failed to equalise with a 55-yard free into the breeze.

In the Leinster final Meath stopped Offaly's comeback by drafting substitute Frank Duff to midfield. As Meath won by 0-8 to 0-6, another sub Paddy Mulvaney scored a point, but the referee disallowed it because he had not been informed that Mulvaney was on the field!

Offaly had flown army lieutenant Larry Coughlan back from security duty in Cyprus for the semi-final victory over Longford, but not for the final. Meath went on to beat Mayo comfortably by 3-14 to 1-14, thanks to Peter Moore and Tony Brennan goals in the 17th and 18th minutes of the second half, when they had just taken back the lead by 1-10 to 0-12.

Another slow start almost cost Meath the All-Ireland. Their first-half lethargy left them 0-1 to 0-3 behind at half-time. Then from a Matt Kerrigan centre six minutes into the second half, Terry Kearns managed to sneak unnoticed behind the back-line to punch the ball to the net from five yards out on the right-hand side.

Some good scoring by Cork's Con O'Sullivan and another last-minute goal bid, pulled up because Con O'Sullivan's short free to Flor Hayes was too short, could not save Cork. It was, on the whole, a forgettable final.

Meath's pride was to be shattered within a month of their triumph by surprise opponents, from even further south than

Cork, as the GAA grasped a straw of hope for real international competition.

DOWN UNDER

The get-together of Australian and Gaelic football in 1967 was an unusual one. To all intents and purposes, the decision of the Melbourne and Geelong football clubs to replace the round ball used in their Gaelic-style game with the oval ball had put Australian football beyond the bounds of any international contact with Gaelic football. Australian teams had tried matches against a touring English Rugby Union team under Australian rules in 1896.

Australian Rules had adopted Gaelic-style point-posts in 1897, but just 13 years later the GAA abandoned them. Unlike Gaelic, point-posts were a success down under. Scores rocketed to 150 or 200 points per match, and the crowds loved it. They rose to high-catching heroes; in 1914 ANZAC troops at Gallipoli had a battle-cry: "Up there, Cazaly," after a tall Tasmanian ruckman called Roy Cazaly.

Professionalism crept in in a way that it never had in Gaelic, but it was never possible for anyone but the most accomplished players to make a living from the game.

An 18-year-old player, Haydn Burton, was banned for a year in 1929 when Fitzroy were discovered to have offered him a pair of boots as an inducement to sign. Undeterred, Burton went on to become the game's most elegant and subtle star of the 1930s. Just as famous was Jack "Captain Blood" Dyer of Richmond, a legendary figure said to have broken the collar-bones of a dozen opponents. Goal-scoring hero was Ken Farmer of South Australia. By 1938 these star players had pushed the attendance at the Victoria Football League grand final at Melbourne Cricket Ground to 96,834. Twenty years later, until seat reservation was introduced in 1957, fans were prepared to camp for a week outside the ground to get seats for the final. In 1970 when Carlton came from behind to beat Collingwood (known around Melbourne as the traditionally Irish "Fenian" team) a record 121,696 showed up.

Just as Alf Murray, Kevin Armstrong and Simon Deignan had brought the handpass to perfection in the 1950s, Australian rules in the 1950s saw the introduction of a new technique by the part-Aborigine ruckman, Graeme "Polly" Farmer. Until Farmer's day "hand-balling" was a defensive measure, used in desperation when a clean catch was impossible. He turned the handpass into a devastating tactical weapon. When the punch-pass was brought into more use by Down and Galway in the 1960s, the Australian and Gaelic codes were looking more alike than at any time since the 1890s.

The explosion of jingoism that followed England's soccer World Cup triumph in 1966, watched on television in Ireland, left the GAA longing for a world competition of their own. Gaelic competitions between Irish and American teams were hastily renamed "The World Cup," but the only real possibility of a world cup lay in the Australian game.

Australian football had long been looking for an international outlet too (its only international match was staged between North Queensland and Papua in 1957). In the 1960s Australian rules games were staged in Tokyo, Honolulu, San Francisco, and Bucharest. In the autumn of 1967 Harry Beitzel brought a selected Victorian Football League side to Ireland.

The term "Galahs" was originally applied to them as a taunt, comparing the manner with which they wore their "digger" hats with a rather vain parrot-like Australian bird. The name caught on, and the Galahs dumbfounded an attendance of 23,149 by beating All-Ireland champions Meath by 3-16 to 1-10 and Mayo by 2-12 to 1-5 (before a 20,121 attendance for a first ever Saturday afternoon fixture in Croke Park) in Gaelic football matches. The only concession in the rules was that Australian players could pick the ball directly from the ground. The only solace to Gaelic football was a victory by an over-robust New York team in Gaelic Park by 4-8 to 0-5. Aussie star Ron Barrassi had his nose broken. Hassa Mann was so badly injured that six Victorian clubs refused to release players for future matches against Gaelic teams. "Not only did we lose the match"

Beitzel commented, "but we lost the fight as well."

Irish pride was restored by Meath the following spring; they beat Victoria's semi-professionals by 3-7 to 0-9 in front of a 26,425 crowd in Melbourne.

In 1970 Kerry followed this with a world tour, and beat the Victorian selection in a Gaelic game. In Adelaide Kerry agreed to play half the game with an oval ball. The theory was that at half-time the Australians would be so far ahead that it would make no difference. In fact the match was a draw at half-time, Kerry 2-2 South Australia 1-5, and Kerry took over when the round ball was introduced in the second half and won by 7-13 to 3-5. Talk began immediately about devising a compromise set of rules, but it was another 14 years before this would come to fruition.

TWO GOALS DOWN

The revolutionary year of 1968 brought the last "new" provincial champions in Leinster.

Longford had come close for several years. Roger Martin scored their winning point to beat Meath in 1960. They had almost repeated the trick when they whittled back a six-point lead against Meath in 1961. Heavy defeats put a stop to their gallop against Laois in 1962, Offaly in 1963, and Westmeath in 1964. But they had beaten Meath *en route* to the 1965 provincial final, won the National League home final (but lost to Louth in the championship) in 1966, and beaten Kildare in 1967 to reach the provincial semi-final.

When they went the full way in 1968 it was at the expense of Dublin, beaten by 1-12 to 0-12 at Tullamore (Jackie Devine scored the crucial penalty three minutes before half-time), Meath who were back from their Australian conquests, by 0-12 to 0-7, and Laois by 3-9 to 1-4.

Jackie Devine organised two goals in the last six minutes to beat Laois in an unusual Leinster final: Sean Donnelly and Jim Hannify were the scorers. Longford became the 10th of the 12 Leinster counties to win the provincial championship. Only Westmeath and Wicklow remain waiting in the wings for their first title.

The team got a hero's welcome home to Longford. Jim Hannify and Mick Hopkins starred in Longford's semi-final win against Offaly, having earlier dumped optimistic League finalists Kildare from the quarter-finals with three goals between the 18th and 22nd minutes of the first half from Lalor, Fennell and Dunne.

Then Longford almost added Kerry to their list of scalps. In winning back the Munster championship, Kerry had found a new star as they beat Cork by 1-21 to 3-8. A 19-year-old converted goalkeeper, UCC player Brendan Lynch notched four points from as many kicks at goal. Cork too had a new star; debutant Ray Cummins got their first goal. Old stars helped too. Mick O'Dwyer and Mick O'Connell had both been coaxed out of retirement after the shock of seeing Wicklow almost beat Kerry in a National League match!

Longford showed no respect for tradition, and took the lead against Kerry by one point with 10 minutes to go. This they did by switching Jimmy Hannify to midfield. Then Tom Mulvihill and Jackie Devine, from a penalty, put Longford a point up. Kerry recovered to win by two points, 2-13 to 2-11. It was not a bad showing for Longford, considering what Kerry had done in the first half, racing 2-7 to 0-6 ahead with goals from Pat Griffin and Dom O'Donnell.

In a drawn Connacht semi-final against Roscommon, Galway stuttered again. Cyril Dunne missed a penalty and a couple of goalkeeping errors kept them within reach of Roscommon, for whom George Geraghty scored a frenzied equaliser in the nick of time.

Galway won the replay by 2-8 to 1-9 and got their title back by a solitary point, 2-10 to 2-9. Midfielder Keenan kicked seven points, three from 50 yards out, and a goal from a free 55 yards out after just nine minutes. Mattie McDonagh added another Galway goal to contain Mayo's comeback when Joe Langan landed an inspirational 50 in the net eight minutes from the end.

Six points without reply between the 40th and 47th minutes helped Down to secure their seventh Ulster title in 11 years. They beat Cavan in Casement Park by 0-16 to 1-8, despite a Charlie Gallagher goal for Cavan two minutes from the end of the final. This was another match spoiled completely by grappling and dragging.

Bad as it was, it was an improvement on the first-round tie between Down and Derry. Four players were sent off and several other incidents shocked the spectators. Down were awarded 28 frees and Derry 15 in what became known as the "Battle of Ballinascreen" and became the subject of an Ulster Council investigation.

Victors over Galway in an All-Ireland semi-final of swaying fortunes, Down had to rely on a Sean O'Neill 50th-minute goal to reach the final. Cause of the problem was Galway's two goals from Jimmy Duggan and Cyril Dunne (from a penalty rebound, six minutes into the second half). At that stage Down had built up a comfortable 1-5 to 0-3 lead.

Down kept their 100 per cent record in All-Ireland finals when they beat Kerry by 2-12 to 1-13, thanks to a dramatic two-goal start.

After six minutes Sean O'Neill got the inside of his boot to a rebounding ball after Rooney hit the post. Two minutes later John Murphy got another goal, following confusion in the Kerry goal-mouth.

Kerry recovered admirably in the early stages of the second half, but their goal came too late in the 59th minute from a Brendan Lynch close-in free. Down's Brian Morgan played with a fractured jaw. Down, it appeared, could do no wrong on All-Ireland final day.

CULLOTY SAVES THE DAY

Alas for Down, the same did not hold for the Ulster final. A massive 45,000 turned out to see Down defend their Ulster title in 1969 against Cavan in Casement Park. Cavan had the game well in hand long before Gene Cusack's 22nd-minute left-footed goal secured their 37th (and, extraordinarily, their last) Ulster title. Down replied with goals from Paddy Doherty and Mickey Cole in the second half, but they were to no avail.

Offaly were big winners over Kildare in the Leinster final, 3-7 to 1-8. Kildare's defensive problems were evident after only four minutes when the goalie was bundled to the net by Mick O'Rourke, but the goal was disallowed and a free-out was awarded instead. The rules were changed to protect the goalkeeper in 1970. O'Rourke later scored the first legitimate goal after 11 minutes, Pat Keenan scored the second and Pat Monaghan first-timed to the net after the goalkeeper parried a Tony McTague shot five minutes into the second half.

Cork missed two penalties in the first quarter of the Munster final at Cork Athletic Grounds, and Kerry went on to win by nine points, 0-16 to 1-4. Denis Coughlan bounced the first penalty off the post. Donal Hunt lobbed the second at Kerry's goalkeeper.

As if a reminder was needed that these were changing times, the last 60-minute Munster final took place on the day Neil Armstrong became the first man to step on the moon.

The Connacht final went to a replay. Galway presented Mayo with a second chance, courtesy of one of the most remarkable blocks in GAA history—Liam Sammon saved Mayo when he slipped on the ball.

While trying to make sure Donnellan's shot went over the goal-line he had actually prevented a Galway goal!

In the replay, Mayo had their lead whittled back to one point with four minutes to go before they won another thrilling battle in what was becoming a great series between the two rivals. Nealon's goal sent them 1-6 to 0-4 ahead at half-time but Liam Sammon got a goal back for Galway seven minutes into the second half to make the final score 1-11 to 1-8.

The All-Ireland semi-final was drawn as well. Tony McTague scored 10 of Offaly's 12 points and McInerney the Cavan goal in an 0-12 to 1-9 draw the first day. Sean Evans, Paddy Keenan and Kilroy got goals to break the deadlock and give Offaly a 3-8 to 1-10 victory in a broken, 62-free replay.

The other All-Ireland semi-final between Kerry and Mayo was close, but extremely boring until a 50th-minute Des Griffith goal. Mayo's O'Dowd and P J Loftus both missed equalising chances as Kerry scraped through 0-14 to 1-10.

Kerry's converted goalkeeper Johnny Culloty starred with two great first-half saves and another even more spectacular stop at the start of the second half to beat Offaly by 0-10 to 0-7 in the All-Ireland final.

Meanwhile Kerry's forwards were less than impressive, turning over 0-5 to 0-2 ahead with a strong wind. But a Crowley/Prendergast half-time switch helped stabilise matters and the three-point lead was preserved when Offaly sharp-shooter Tony McTague hit the post twice. Kerry too hit the post near the end.

Offaly learned from the experience.

END OF THE PLATFORM

In the 1950s the Railway Cup, played at Croke Park every St Patrick's Day, was one of the strongest of the many GAA traditions. By the end of the 1960s it was in danger of disappearing down a siding.

The great crowds dwindled away with alarming speed. In times when the opportunity to see the great Gaelic football personalities was limited to a few big matches a year, the St Patrick's Day outing had an attraction of its own. Now thanks to television, nobody wanted to go to Croke Park on St Patrick's Day anymore.

Through the football and hurling personalities of three decades, popularity grew. The first final in 1927 was attended by an estimated 10,000 people. The attendance had climbed to 30,000 by the mid-1930s and 35,170 in 1946. It reached 40,000 by 1949 and peaked at 49,023 in 1954. The football final alone in 1955 attracted 40,280. Even semi-finals between Munster and Ulster attracted attendances of 18,527 in 1953, 20,200 in 1954, and 20,000 in 1955. By the end of the 1950s attendances had passed over the hump. In 1956 it was 46,278, in 1957 it was 43,805, in 1958 it was 36,637, and the football final on its own attracted 35,002 on St Patrick's Day 1959. Even as late as 1960, 40,473 attended.

The Railway Cup was also a forum for players from weaker counties. It brought players into the limelight like Niall Crowley of Clare, who scored three goals to give Munster victory in the 1949 football final replay. Packie McGarty of Leitrim scored the winning goal for Connacht in the 1957 Railway Cup final, where he struck up a combination with Galway's terrible twins Sean Purcell and Frankie Stockwell. Outstanding Wicklow player Georgie O'Reilly was a goal-scorer in the 1952 final. When P T Treacy of Fermanagh won the first of four medals in 1963, it now meant that a player from each of the 32 counties had won an inter-provincial medal.

By then the decline of the Railway Cups had become one of the talking-points of Gaelic games. Live television arrived in 1962.

In 1969, just four years after a crowd of 30,734 had cheered Ulster to their first three-in-a-row, the attendance at Connacht versus Munster was down to 9,166 and the competition was described as being "on its last legs."

After a promising 20,306 attendance at Ulster v Connacht in 1971 (coinciding with a major promotion of Dublin's St Patrick's Day parade) the GAA turned to contingency plans to restore some glamour to the competition. The Combined Universities entered the Railway Cups on an experimental basis in 1972. Although the footballers won the title in 1973 and beat Munster footballers in 1974, and the hurlers beat Ulster in 1972, the experiment was not renewed. Four of the Combined Universities team went on to win Railway Cup medals with their provinces: John O'Keeffe and Brendan Lynch (Kerry), Dave McCarthy (Cork) and Paddy Moriarty (Armagh).

In 1976 sideshows such as Irish dancing and athletic competitions lifted the attendance to 10,647 for one last gasp, but just two years later, 1,900 people turned up at Croke Park on St Patrick's Day, 1978.

That was the death-knell. The competition received a temporary boost when it was moved to provincial venues from 1980 on, to Ennis in 1981 and 1984, Tullamore in 1982 and Cavan in 1983. In 1987 it was moved to the autumn and the St Patrick's Day connection was finally broken.

By then Gaelic football had changed utterly. While the Railway Cup and all that it stood for was imprisoned in the 1950s, a series of unexpected changes had put a new glamour into Gaelic football that bewildered officials and *aficionados* alike.

Chapter Sixteen

Ecumenism Reigns

THE CRACK WAS EIGHTY

Unannounced and unheralded, football had changed inconceivably over a three-year period. The old leather football, which became unplayable in wet weather, was replaced with a ball that was coated in plastic. The old boots were getting lighter. Even small rural clubs were appointing team coaches. Now the playing-time of major games was to be extended by 20 minutes.

The idea was not original, but it had taken 43 years to become a reality. A motion had been passed at 1927 Congress stipulating that All-Ireland finals and semi-finals should be lengthened to 80 minutes. But under the rules of the time changes were not to be implemented for five years. This particular rule change was never implemented, apparently forgotten until another group of zealots came along with the same proposal in 1970.

While the Australians had a game that engrossed spectators for two hours, even the top-class Gaelic games were only an hour long. Compared with soccer (90 minutes) and rugby (80 minutes) Gaelic appeared to be offering spectators bad value for money.

The 1970 decision that top games would be increased from 60 to 80 minutes applied only to provincial finals, All-Ireland semi-finals and All-Ireland finals. All other matches were to remain at 60 minutes.

And if the 80-minute game needed any justification, Meath and Offaly provided it in the Leinster final. Their flowing, action-packed match never seemed to let up, before Meath eventually won by a single point, 2-22 to 5-12.

Meath went five points up before Offaly scored. Offaly hit back with four goals and led by 4-7 to 0-9 at half-time. Then two goals from Mick Fay and a point from Mick Mellett equalised. Offaly took the lead again, Meath took a three-point lead, Offaly equalised with four minutes to go, and Tony Brennan got the winning point two minutes from the end as the crowd held their breaths. Nothing like it had ever been seen before. Those that longed for a game like the Australians had shown them in 1967 licked their lips.

Meath's cavalier approach was the talk of the championship. Earlier in the year Matt Corrigan, playing centre-forward for Meath at the time, created his own bit of history by saving a penalty from Carlow full-back Pat McNally. The goalkeeper was injured at the time!

All-Ireland champions Kerry had their doubts about how to handle their first 80-minute match, when they played the Munster final in Killarney. Cork cut back Kerry's half-time lead from 14 points to six. Mick O'Dwyer improved spectacularly in the second half. Spectators wondered whether he had been holding himself in reserve! Barney O'Neill fielded magnificently for Cork, but eight points from Mick O'Dwyer and six from Mick O'Connell sent Kerry further and further ahead, for a 2-22 to 2-9 victory.

Star of Antrim's under-21 success in 1969, Aidan Hamill proved to be the find of the Ulster championship. The 20-year-old scored two goals against Monaghan to earn Antrim's place in the final. There Antrim lost to Derry by 2-13 to 1-12, and Hamill sent a late penalty rebounding off the post. Derry won their second ever title thanks to two first-half goals from Seamus Lagan and 1958 veteran Sean O'Connell. Derry's midfield lost control in the second half, but they held on to win by four elusive points.

Derry missed two penalties themselves as they went down by 13 points to Kerry in the semi-final, 0-23 to 0-10. Kerry were slow to start. While masseur Owen McCrohan tended the thigh of injured Mick O'Connell on the sideline, Derry raced into a four-point lead but things started going wrong. Sean O'Connell missed the first penalty after 21 minutes, then ignored requests to take the second when he was pulled down after 48 minutes. Instead Seamus Lagan took it and sent the ball wide.

Sligo transferred the venue of the Connacht semi-final against Galway from the decaying Markievicz Park to Charlestown "because of insurance problems." A freak goal had helped Galway beat Sligo in that semi-final, the ball bouncing awkwardly as the goalkeeper advanced to meet it.

Galway beat Roscommon by 2-15 to 1-8 in the Connacht final when they managed to eclipse Dermot Earley at midfield while Pat Donnellan had the game of his life. Then Galway's Liam Sammon hit the post twice as they went out to Meath, 0-15 to 0-11, in the All-Ireland semi-final.

The public wanted to see how Meath's panache would fare against traditional Kerry catch-and-kick in the All-Ireland final. According to the programme for the game:

> It is not so very long ago, since the very knowledgeable people were shaking their heads and dishevelling their hair over what they pronounced the corpse of Kerry football. Kerry, they said, had paid the penalty for being too rigid and tradition-bound. The game had passed them out. Failure to adapt to new ideas and new methods had found Kerry lagging behind. And while Down and Galway and others were dividing the spoils between them, the funeral of Kerry football was being well attended by those who could hardly catch and only kicked when no alternative appeared. This team is a most interesting one: plenty of traditional Kerry style, yet, plenty of the best in the modern game incorporated into a basically sound pattern. It is the integrated work of the forwards which has given Kerry a new dimension. Most of the six could easily be outmatched individually from the lists of Kerry forwards past : but when they use their talents in combination they are exciting to watch and direct in their intention. The pass and the solo are used as they were ever intended to be used—as means subordinated to an end, rather than ends in themselves. The approach of Kerry in attack suggests a new high point in football forward play: they pass or solo and drive on with an eye on the goal chance every time, but if the opening does not occur they cut their losses in time, and take a point.

It was a victory for old-time football. In what Kerry team manager Tadhgie Lyne called "Our answer to the Gormanston professors, and their blackboard tactics," Kerry defeated Meath by 2-19 to 0-18, but Kerry had to sweat out the last 12 minutes as their eight-point lead was cut back to three.

Meath pressed for an equalising goal but Mick Mellett was hopelessly wide. Then came Kerry's final rally, which was finished by a Din Joe Crowley goal just four minutes from the end. Crowley, a Garda who had failed at full-forward before striking up a great midfield combination with Mick O'Connell after switching to the position in the 1968 All-Ireland semi-final, soloed through for 40 yards before giving Meath goalkeeper Sean McCormack no chance with a spectacular shot.

Kerry led from the fourth minute to the end of the game. Four times Kerry were deprived of goals by the goalkeeper or goal-post. Crowley had a stormer and John O'Keeffe and Mick Gleeson were switched to midfield to thwart the Meath comeback. It had been a close game until 18 minutes after half-time when Mick Gleeson had a simple goal for Kerry from a left-footed ground shot which went under the goalkeeper's body.

Lyne was aware of the significance of the changes:

> Football was a very different game, even in the 1970s. The game has changed completely over the last generation, the weight of the boots and the weight of the football has changed. Gone is the day when the working man could play football at top level. Now the players are virtually professionals.

BAN WAGON

One of the extraordinary things about the GAA's ban on foreign games is how it survived on the rule-books for so long.

For three generations the GAA sounded a note of triumphalist nationalism that embarrassed even the most triumphant nationalists. The same speeches were revived each five years for the quintennial "Ban" debate. Staying with the ban was staying with "the spirit that made us strong." Appeals to make the same uncompromising stand as the stand of "Pearse, Emmett and Tone" were often emotional enough to change the minds of mandated delegates when it came to a vote. The 1930s, 1940s and 1950s are full of instances of delegates defying their voting instructions because of one impassioned speech. At one Kerry Convention in the 1960s, an anti-ban motion was greeted with such ire that even the proposer and seconder voted against it and it was defeated by 71 votes to nil!

Motions from players who wanted to play or attend rival codes were met by other motions with the opposite message, such as one from Tyrone before the 1947 Congress that the GAA should:

> Not even entertain a motion relating to foreign games until the National Flag flies over the 32 counties of a free and undivided Ireland.

Even Fianna Fáil's Sean MacEntee was to declare in 1931:

> I would like every Irishman to play the game that most appeals to him and I have no sympathy with the policy of exclusion pursued by the Gaelic Athletic Association.

The "policy of exclusion" had its origins in the 1885 ban on a rival athletic association, the IAAA, as both bodies battled for survival. With a month, the two had assumed entrenched positions, the GAA as nationalists, the IAAA as unionists, in which they would remain until 1922. In 1887 rugby and soccer were proscribed on the suggestion of former rugby and soccer player Maurice Davin, who had drawn up the rules of Gaelic football, and RIC members were debarred, because they had been shadowing GAA members and joining clubs to spy on activities. When Cork's Tom Irwin appealed against a suspension for playing rugby in 1896, however, the GAA Executive ruled that members could play any games they liked. The ban was thrown out at the 1896 Congress through the efforts of Dick Blake.

For a decade, dual players made quite an impact. The brothers Jack and Mick Ryan from Rockwell in Tipperary helped Ireland win successive triple crowns on the rugby field in 1898 and 1899. Dublin All-Ireland footballers Val Harris, Jack Ledwidge, Pat McCann and Jack Kirwan won 48 Irish soccer caps between them.

Within ten years the ban was back. First in 1901, Kerryman T F O'Sullivan called on the young men of Ireland

> not to identify themselves with rugby or Association football or any other form of imported sport which the GAA provides for self-respecting Irishmen who have no desire to ape foreign manners and customs.

In 1902 a motion was carried from one of the counties which benefited most from the relaxation of the ban, Dublin, where the rivals of clubs such as Dolphins pushed the ban through. It proposed that anyone who played rugby or Association football be automatically suspended. The ban was made optional for county committees in 1903, but restored as a compulsory ban in 1904. Police, soldiers, sailors and militiamen were also banned in 1902.

In 1922 many felt that the ban was no longer necessary, but moves to get rid of it were defeated by 21 votes to 12 in 1922, 50 votes to 12 in 1923, 54 votes to 32 in 1924, 69 votes to 23 in 1925, 80 votes to 23 in 1926, and eventually a motion allowing the ban to be debated only every third year was passed by 72 votes to 23 in 1927. According to Brendan Mac Lua, most of the ban debates were a direct reflection of the Treaty debate in the years after the Civil War: if you were anti-Treaty you were pro-ban, if you were pro-Treaty you were anti-ban.

In 1938 the GAA expelled its patron, Dr Douglas Hyde, the man who had delivered the de-Anglicising lecture of 1892, for attending an international soccer match in his capacity as president of Ireland.

In 1947 an attempt to allow GAA members to attend (but not to play) banned sports was defeated by 188 votes to 16. Even a move in 1962 to set up a commission to enquire into reasons for retaining the ban was defeated by 180 votes to 40 after a rousing speech by former GAA president Dan O'Rourke of Roscommon:

> It is that sense of allegiance to something permanent and enduring that has always been our strength. Our rules derive not only from a desire to organise health giving exercise but from a determination to defend national values, traditions and aims. That is what has given an enduring vitality to the work of the Gaelic Athletic Association. This is the force which has forged the links that bind our members. At all times we shall continue to guard our pastimes that have enriched the national life.

In 1965, before another defeat, it was suggested by Seamus Ó Riain that traditional values provided "ballast in an era of aimlessness and disillusionment." But televised soccer was now being beamed into areas where a match had never been seen. Many of these players looked decidedly un-British. One, Edson Arantes de Nascimento, rejoiced in a nickname that sounded appropriately close to the Irish for football: *Pele*. Eventually a commission was set up to report to the 1971 Congress asking what reason there was that the ban might be retained in the 1970s. The case for removal was not, as yet, clear-cut. The chairman of Congress, Pat Fanning, was in favour of the ban. He told delegates that:

> The motion [to remove the ban] is not a proposal to rescind a rule but rather a proposition to alter the fundamental structure of the Association and to open the ranks to those who never accepted us for what we are.

But when 30 of the 32 counties voted to change the rule at grass roots level, the debate came to a quiet end.

Taking down barriers reflected the spirit of the times. The ban on Catholics entering Protestant churches had just been removed, and Jack Lynch and Terence O'Neill had embraced each other at cross-border meetings.

At the 1971 Congress in Belfast, the ban was taken from the GAA rule-books without discussion. The rule prohibiting members playing "foreign" games such as hockey, rugby, cricket and soccer, (but not tennis, basketball, American football or boxing) was clearly an embarrassment—outdated, outmoded, and sectarian. Fanning now commented:

> Let there be no sounding of trumpets as the rule disappears. Nor should there be talk of defeat. If victory there be, let it be victory for the Association.

The second section of the "Ban," that on British soldiers and policemen, was also up for removal but the motion was inexplicably withdrawn. Perhaps the proponents felt that was enough revolution for one day. The issue has scarcely been discussed in the 20 years since. British soldiers and RUC men are still banned because of an 1886 police decision to shadow GAA members. Official GAA feeling is that a motion to let them in should come from the six northern counties. They say that the RUC are not interested in joining GAA clubs anyway. Only half a dozen RUC men have ever pulled on a GAA jersey where legions of soccer players defied the foreign games. Considerably more trouble is caused to progressive GAA clubs in Britain (where local policemen are also banned, although they are not a political force). In many GAA areas there is real hostility to the Royal Ulster Constabulary because of evidence of sectarian leanings in the force. GAA fields at Casement Park and Crossmaglen were both occupied by the British army. GAA players meanwhile suffer considerable harassment from both RUC and British Army, on the justification that they are anti-police. Members have been shot at army check-points, others have been killed by Unionist paramilitaries because of their sporting allegiance.

That problem was to prove even more difficult to unravel than the ban. At least soccer-playing was now legal. In Sligo, the football selectors sat up. Within two months of the ban's removal, Sligo Rovers soccer players Gerry Mitchell and David Pugh became the first soccer players to play inter-county GAA. They almost collected provincial championship medals in their first season.

OUT OF THE GARRISONS

Sligo had been in the hunt for a Connacht championship since the mid-1960s. Gaelic politics in Sligo reflected that of comparable garrison towns such as Waterford and Athlone. The country played Gaelic, soccer was the sport in the town. With a revamped team, Sligo beat Roscommon by 0-10 to 1-5 in the Connacht semi-final at Roscommon.

Sligo's Mickey Kearins, now at peak form, scored 1-8 as his side drew with Galway, 2-15 each, in the Connacht final. Pugh got Sligo's first goal that day, and former goalkeeper Peter Brennan the second. This was the closest Sligo came to a title in a decade of "almost" years.

A gift goal from a Seamus Leyden lob after five minutes of the replay gave Galway the start they wanted. But Mickey Kearins gave Sligo the lead two minutes after half-time. Galway got the lead back, only to see another goal from Sligo's soccer convert David Pugh. At the final whistle Galway were just a point ahead, 1-17 to 3-10. The fifth-minute fluke had saved them.

Kerry's three-in-a-row bid came to an abrupt halt at Cork Athletic Grounds. Having dropped Denis Coughlan for the final, at half-time Cork were 0-7 to 0-11 behind and clearly in real trouble. Their opponents were left waiting on the field at half-time as they stole an extra five minutes to plan their second-half strategy. When they re-emerged late and fired up, with Coughlan on the team, it just took six minutes for them to equalise. Coughlan scored 10 points in an historic 0-23 to 0-14 victory, a record for a substitute.

But that was as far as Cork got. Offaly had another big win over Kildare, 2-14 to 0-6 in the Leinster final, and Tony McTague scored nine points from frees as Offaly defeated Cork by 1-16 to 1-11 in a tame semi-final.

Down's old-timers beat Derry's youngsters by 4-15 to 4-11 in a refreshing Ulster final: Sean O'Neill laid on goals for John Murphy and Michael Cunningham in the first half. Michael Cunningham and Donal Davey struck twice more in the second half and then Mickey Niblock brought Derry storming back with left-and right-footed goals. It was a tremendous spectacle, played in Casement Park in the middle of Northern Ireland's most troubled year. This was to be Belfast's last final.

Galway's 3-11 to 2-7 semi-final win over Down was, however, eminently forgettable, as Down missed a penalty and had a goal disallowed in the five minutes before half-time.

For the first time in 11 years, a new name went on to the Sam Maguire Cup. Offaly lost a fierce midfield battle against Galway in the first half, trailed 0-4 to 1-6 at half-time, then switched Nicholas Clavin in to partner Willie Bryan six minutes after half-time.

A 21st-minute goal from Murt Connor gave Offaly the lead. Despite Seamus Leyden's equalising second goal for Galway, Offaly got three more points for a famous victory, 1-14 to 2-8. Colour television was there for the first time. Viewers saw the players lose control of their vertical hold, Galway shot 15 wides to Offaly's eight, 12 of these in the first half.

OFFALY'S ROVERS

For the third time in four years, Offaly inflicted a humiliating defeat on Kildare in the Leinster final. They were proving better and better prepared for the 80-minute game on each occasion. Kildare were still preparing for provincial finals on a haphazard basis. Offaly won the 1972 final by 1-18 to 2-8 with a 13th-minute lucky-for-some goal from John Cooney who forced the goalkeeper over the line with the ball.

Ulster had new champions. Donegal became the eighth county to take the Ulster title when they beat Tyrone by 2-13 to 1-11 with one of the most dramatic finishes Clones has seen. They drew level with seven minutes to go; Seamus Bonner sent a 60-yard lob to the goal; the goalkeeper let it slip through his fingers under the crossbar and they set the heather ablaze in the Rosses.

Roscommon beat Mayo by 5-8 to 3-10, despite kicking an incredible 23 wides in the final. Mick Freyne, Dermot Earley, Johnny Kelly (2) and Mick Finnegan scored the goals. Mayo stopped Sligo in extra time after a replayed semi-final. Then Roscommon stopped Galway by 1-8 to 0-7.

In the All-Ireland semi-final, Offaly beat newcomers Donegal by four points, 1-17 to 2-10, having trailed them 0-5 to 1-4 at half-time. A Dan Kavanagh goal after six minutes of the other semi-final gave Kerry a lead they never lost against Roscommon. Kerry went through by 1-22 to 1-12.

Kerry's old-timers knew 1972 was the final fling. Although John O'Keeffe, Paud Lynch and Brendan Lynch were to be there in future battles, this was Kerry's last team of short-back-and-sides, rural footballers. One of the biggest crowds since seating was installed under the Cusack Stand in 1966 turned up, 72,032. Midway through the second half of the drawn match, Noel Cooney (Offaly) and Brendan Lynch (Kerry) exchanged goals to avoid Offaly stretching their two-point lead and Mick O'Dwyer eventually equalised with five minutes to go to make it 1-13 each.

Offaly eventually broke down Kerry's resistance with a goal after 48 minutes of the replay when Pat Fenning's long speculative ball hopped over the line without a Kerry defender touching it. Kerry plunged from a two-point lead to their heaviest All-Ireland defeat ever, 1-19 to 0-13, as a result of this slip-up. McTague scored 10 points in the replay and six in the drawn match as he captained Offaly to victory.

As things started to go wrong in the second half, Kerry selector Joe Keohane looked around at the substitutes on the bench. They included 1970 minors Ger Power, Mickey O'Sullivan and John Egan. "Who have we got to send on," he snarled, "this crowd of garsúns?"

CORK HORSES

After a smell of success in 1971, Cork were yearning for something more. In 1973 they seemed to have the material. No county had enjoyed anything like the crop of under-age successes that these players had. They were used to winning. Brian Murphy had won dual All-Ireland medals at the under-18 (minor football in 1969 and hurling in 1969 and 1970), and under-21 (football in 1971, hurling 1973) levels. Jimmy

Barry Murphy, the darling of the side with a distinctive shaved head, was only 19 and had missed the 1971 under-21 success, but had dual minor and under-21 hurling medals already. The team was laden with confidence, enthusiasm and talent. Four of them, including Brian and Jimmy Barry Murphy, would add 1976 hurling medals to the football medals they won in 1973.

First they trounced Kerry. The Munster final in Cork was an extraordinary affair, as Cork flashed five past a startled Kerry in the first 25 minutes: after four minutes Declan Barron fisted in a long Denis Long free; after 11 minutes John Barrett landed a long pass in the net; after 21 minutes Billy Field scored a penalty; a minute later Jimmy Barry Murphy finished McCarthy's rebound; and after 25 minutes Barrett fisted a ball to the net when it seemed to be going wide.

Dave McCarthy gave a brilliant display. Kerry's ageing team had no answer. Nobody scored five goals against Kerry in a championship match before or since.

In the All-Ireland semi-final Tyrone, too, got mauled by Cork, 5-10 to 2-4. Ray Cummins and Declan Barron scored first, then Cork snatched 3-1 in the last 10 minutes after Tyrone's King and John Earley had goals of their own. Jimmy Barry Murphy scored two of those goals and laid on the last for substitute Seamus Coughlan.

Tyrone had won their first Ulster title in 17 years when they defeated Donegal by 0-12 to 1-7 with 14 players in the first round, Fermanagh by 1-15 to 0-11, and Down by 3-13 to 1-11. In the final they were ignited by their own defensive mistake. One of their corner-backs picked the ball up in his own square, and Down's Dan McCartan landed a goal from the resulting penalty. Tyrone responded ruthlessly: two minutes later Kevin Teague had the ball in the Down net; Brendan Donnelly sent the ball back down-field and Sean McElhatton had a second Tyrone goal a minute later and scored a third seven minutes from the end.

With Kildare having failed miserably, and going out to Offaly yet again in the Leinster semi-final by 1-15 to 2-6, Meath re-presented themselves as likely rivals to Offaly in Leinster. Offaly retained the title by 3-21 to 2-12, but their

12-point win disguised their having trailed 1-5 to 1-7 at half-time, coming back when Kevin Kilmurray fisted a 57th-minute goal over the goalie's head. Meath's full-back was booed through the second half of the Offaly match for striking Offaly star Tony McTague (scorer of 0-22 in the championship) seven minutes after half-time.

Galway got their revenge from Roscommon, 1-13 to 1-8, and beat Mayo in the Connacht final by 1-17 to 2-12 with a goal by Galway's Michael Rooney after a great passing movement shortly after half-time. They had a 1-14 to 0-9 lead 30 minutes from the end, but it crumpled as Mayo moved Sean O'Grady to centre half forward. Substitute Mick Gaffney scored a goal and Garda hero John Morley, later to die on active service during a bank raid, scored the second. In the All-Ireland semi-final Johnny Tobin scored eight of Galway's 16 points against Offaly. Second-half goals from Tony McTague and Sean Evans could not prevent the double champions going out by 0-16 to 2-8 and Galway getting revenge for 1972.

The question about the All-Ireland final was whether Galway would follow up that victory over Offaly with another championship, or whether they would come out the wrong end of another of the five-goal Cork specials. The crowd of 73,308 saw teenager Jimmy Barry Murphy score two goals and Jimmy Barrett the third in a sparkling 3-17 to 2-13 Cork win.

Barry Murphy's first, after two and a half minutes, meant Cork took the initiative and never gave it away. Barrett's 17th-minute switch to left-half-forward got the Cork attack moving. The result was a 1-10 to 0-6 half-time lead. Galway's goals came from Liam Sammon and Johnny Hughes.

Cork looked unbeatable.

Chapter Seventeen

The Swinging Seventies

HEFFO'S HEROES

Everybody got wet at the 1974 Munster final. The Kerrymen were most miserable at the end of the drenching, losers by 1-11 to 0-7 as Mick O'Dwyer ended a distinguished 17-year playing career. First as a half-back from 1957 to 1964, then as the highest scoring forward in Kerry history, the man who was humiliatingly dropped off the panel and not even togged out with the minor subs for the 1955 All-Ireland final had already left a lasting impression on football in the county. As the scenic McGillycuddy's Mist turned into wet Reeks Rain, on the sidelines in Killarney that day they were talking about him as Kerry's next trainer-selector.

Cork's match-winning goal came from Dave McCarthy after 57 minutes of struggle against vicious rain and cold. Kerry led 0-6 to 0-4 at half-time and it was nine minutes into the second half before Cork took the lead. Kerry's only point in the second half came from Mickey O'Sullivan 90 seconds from the end.

Donegal re-emerged in Ulster, drawing the provincial final 1-14 to 2-11 with Down, when Neilly Gallagher's extraordinary equaliser for Donegal 10 seconds from the end went unnoticed by Down's Cathal Rigney. He thought Down had won by a point and started celebrating!

Donegal then won the replay by 3-9 to 1-12, thanks to two controversial goals. Was Gerry McElwee outside the square when he was fouled midway through the second half? Donegal's Seamus Bonner tucked away the penalty anyway. Was Joe Winston in the square when he passed to Kevin Keeney with a minute and a half to go? Keeney punched the high ball in the net for a clinching Donegal goal.

Tyrone went out in the first round, the tragic death of 1973 Ulster final hero Brendan Dolan and loss of Frank McGuigan to America scuppered their successes.

But things were stirring in Leinster. Dublin had a new manager, Kevin Heffernan. His appointment in 1973, for a second innings as team manager, went unnoticed at first. Then came a string of victories.

The team were first dubbed the Dubs by the followers who flocked with sky-blue scarves to Hill 16. Until then it was rather draughty up there due to a shortage of Dubs supporters, a total of 60 for one Second Division League game.

One who watched the opening-round match from Hill 16 was Heffernan's club colleague Jimmy Keaveney. He was called out of retirement at the age of 29 and his sharp-shooting helped Dublin come back from 0-6 to 1-5 down to win the Leinster final by 1-14 to 1-9. "It wasn't so much a question of being asked to come out of retirement. You know he'll make you do it anyway," Keaveney was to claim.

That final started disastrously. Mick Fay had a Meath goal in less than a minute. But their five-point victory convinced the supporters to come back for a semi-final against the hitherto unstoppable Cork. In that semi-final, Dublin's 2-11 to 1-8 victory confirmed that, at last, here was a team to be taken seriously.

The match was not without its peculiarities. Cork had 16 men on the field when Martin Doherty was fouled in the square (Ned Kirby, the man he replaced, had not yet left the pitch). Jimmy Barry Murphy lashed the penalty into the net but Anton O'Toole and Brian Mullins, from another penalty, got Dublin goals back for victory.

While Dublin's wave was gathering force, Donegal's had already broken. Donegal returned to Croke Park for the second time in three years, but prolonged attacking play in the last nine minutes could not reduce Galway's winning semi-final margin by more than nine points to five, 3-13 to 1-14. Johnny Tobin's 2-6 and a Colin McDonagh goal had already done the damage.

The final was a poor game but a great breakthrough for

Gaelic football. The game was urbanised in a twinkling. Dublin canonised goalkeeper Paddy Cullen after their 0-14 to 1-6 victory. Cullen saved Liam Sammon's 52nd-minute penalty (the first goalkeeper to save a penalty in an All-Ireland final) after Sammon was fouled going through for what would have been Galway's second goal.

Sammon was a bit of a penalty specialist. He had scored a penalty in the Connacht semi-final as Galway beat Sligo in a replay, and two penalty goals as they beat Roscommon by 2-14 to 0-8 in the Connacht final. His shot, to Cullen's left, was a carbon copy of those in the Connacht final and Cullen diverted it around the post.

At the end of the game Dublin's Ashford-born captain, Sean Doherty, was presented with the Sam Maguire Cup. When the cup was presented to Billy Morgan in 1973, Doherty was a steward on Hill 16.

Galway still should have won. They led 1-4 to 0-5 at half-time through a punched goal from the edge of the parallelogram by Michael Rooney who beat off a defender to latch on to Liam Sammon's high cross. Their lead should have been larger than two points. But Galway failed to last the pace after Dublin took the lead 17 minutes into the second half. Judging by the bitter debate that followed the game, it was just as well that a Dublin penalty claim, after Anton O'Toole was fouled early in the second half, was not significant.

Why had the game in Dublin, a force between 1955 and 1965, declined? Maybe it was because televised soccer swept the city in the aftermath of the 1966 Soccer World Cup, but Dublin was a GAA wasteland by the end of the 1960s. City life had changed faster than the old-style GAA could handle. Gaelic football in Dublin had been played by immigrants to the city from the country areas where Gaelic was the only sport played. The immigrants who arrived to jobs in the Civil Service and Garda Síochána, but rarely by workers in manufacturing industry.

Interest turned to neighbouring cross-channel cities of Manchester and Liverpool for sporting inspiration. Shay Brennan played on Manchester United's team that won the

European Cup in 1968. "Match of the Day" was flashed on public-house television sets every Saturday night on the new colour televisions. Apart from selected areas almost exclusively on the Northside and most notably the St Vincent's base in Marino, Gaelic was a culchie sport.

Westmeath in 1967 (admittedly with a goal two minutes from the end), Longford in 1968 and 1970, Laois in 1971 and Louth in 1973 dumped Dublin out of the Leinster championship and kept the attendances down on Hill 16. After the 1973 defeat an incensed Kevin Heffernan announced in the dressing-room that he would get a team that was going to win. In Castlerea the following September, a group of unsmiling supporters watched Dublin dive to a 3-7 to 0-11 defeat against Roscommon and descend to the Second Division of the National Football League.

Dublin reappointed him as manager in 1974 after a brief innings between 1970 and 1972. A forward of the 1955-65 revolutionary era, Heffernan was still remembered as an innovator of the far too stagnant 1950s.

Heffernan got the job without anybody paying much notice. County secretary Jimmy Grey instigated the move to pass control of Dublin football to a three-man hard-core group of football thinkers who had a three-year target to get Dublin back into All-Ireland contention. The seconder of the motion was Eugene McGee, later a man to face Heffernan in successive Leinster finals. The Three Wise Men were to be Donal Colfer, Lorcan Redmond and Kevin Heffernan..

Heffernan came to the job with the clear idea that players needed just two things: basic skills, nothing very fancy, and the temperament for the game. He searched the county for "ability that would fit into a team. Players who would react to the rest of the team and the team would react to him. A two way system." But as opponents were to find out over the next eight years, strength, physique and physical fitness were also to rate in Heffernan's check-list.

"None of us would have even thought of doing it for anyone except Heffo," Keaveney recalled. The players became unpaid professionals, with little or no private life.

Heffernan's revival had occurred just when the great

Dublin soccer team of the 1960s, Shamrock Rovers, were at their lowest ebb. Supporters wanted a chance to imitate the Stretford End of Manchester United's Old Trafford. In despair after Dublin's GAA success, Shamrock Rovers, doyen of Dublin soccer clubs, switched their League of Ireland matches to Sunday mornings after breakfast to avoid bankruptcy. Even in wintertime the crowds were going Northside to Hill 16 instead.

The transformation would not have been possible without increased media coverage. Two evening papers generated daily stories about the young Dublin players in a town where celebrities were in short supply. The players became increasingly resentful of what they regarded as an intrusion into the lives of amateur sportsmen, and even grew suspicious of team members who co-operated with the press, such as Gay O'Driscoll. Too much coverage invariably chased too few stories. Heffernan shared the distrust. He remembered how the press made Dublin red-hot favourites for the 1955 All-Ireland final.

The Dubs approach was based on a professionalism that was alien to Gaelic ways. Heffernan was responsible for most of it. When the handpass was revived in 1975, Heffo had called upon Simon Deignan of Cavan, referee and chairman of the committee which recommended that the handpass be reintroduced, to demonstrate it and how it should be used. He recruited Tiernan McBride, later chairman of the Association of Independent Film Producers, to video the games. The videos, along with some obtained from RTE, were studied at length to find flaws in the game. Players were encouraged to criticise each other's play at the meetings.

Heffernan's crew was an unlikely bunch of champions, successors to Manchester United on the city teenagers' walls. Paddy Cullen had first played for Dublin in 1966, and stayed on as Dublin's best-known player despite an offer to play soccer with Shelbourne. He had been an All-Star replacement in 1973. He had left school at 15, worked as an electrician, a sales rep, a personnel officer; he now owns a pub in Ballsbridge.

Gay O'Driscoll had been one of St Vincent's best dual

players, and had played in an All-Ireland under-21 hurling final. He had worked in office supplies until setting up his own company after the 1974 All-Ireland final.

Much was made of the fact that team captain Sean Doherty was born in Wicklow. He played hurling for Wicklow, even after the family moved to Ballsbridge. Then in 1969 he was called up to the county team and appointed captain by Heffernan for the 1974 campaign, but was replaced by Hanahoe after the 1975 final. He had been a plumber, and went out on his own in 1972.

Robbie Kelleher was from Glasnevin and played for Scoil Uí Chonaill. He was one of the quiet boys on the team, and got off the bus in 1974 to mingle with the crowd after the All-Ireland final. After football he went on to become one of the country's top economists.

Two players who had first played in 1972, Paddy Reilly from St Margeret's and bearded Alan Larkin from Raheny, together with Leinster player George Wilson from Balbriggan, formed a half-back line that was replaced in 1975, but Larkin kept up the fight to win his place back until 1980.

Brian Mullins, like Kelleher, attended Coláiste Mhuire. A nephew of 1940s Kerry star Bill Casey, he was studying Physical Education in Thomond College at the time of the All-Ireland. After graduation he went to teach in Greendale. He played under-19 rugby for Leinster and was a good cricket-player. Most outstanding of all was his ability to recover from a terrible car accident injury which almost ended his career at the age of 25. He later became a newspaper columnist with the *Evening Herald*, and donated one of his All-Ireland medals to the Live Aid auction.

Stephen Rooney had been on the team since he was 19, seven years previously. At the start of the 1974 campaign he used to hitch from Balbriggan to training every Tuesday and Thursday night.

Bobby Doyle from Coolock, long hair flowing and sideburns sprouting, was the darling of the denim brigade. He was also the only true Dub on the team; both parents were from the city, but ironically Coolock was surrounded by farmland when he grew up. Captain in 1973, he was dropped in 1975 but back to restore his reputation as a constantly running, rampaging forward.

Tony Hanahoe had almost made it on to Dublin teams in 1964 and 1965, played between 1970 and 1972, and was recalled by old friend and colleague Kevin Heffernan in 1974. A year later Heffernan made him captain, then he became manager in 1977 when Heffernan retired.

David Hickey came from Portmarnock and had been on the Dublin team since he was 18. Yet four years later, in 1973, he was concentrating on rugby with UCD. When UCD were knocked out of the 1974 Leinster Cup Heffernan was on the phone, asking Hickey back to the team.

Hickey's close friend, John McCarthy, was the Garda on the team full of college boys and sales representatives. Recruited for the 1973 replay against Louth in the Sunnybank hotel after the drawn match, he kept his place until 1984.

Jimmy Keaveney, a veteran of the 1966 Leinster final, had been restored to the team because Kevin Heffernan's seven-year-old son had suggested it to his dad after the first-round championship match against Wexford. He was large and slow, but they say that, over 10 yards, Keaveney was one of the quickest on the panel. In the final he scored eight points and won a Texaco player of the year award and was on the threshold of a whole new career.

The 15th man was Anton O'Toole, who had failed to make the Synge Street school team. From the age of 18 he began to grow, made the Dublin team in 1972 and was still there for the 1983 All-Ireland, after a brief retirement. By then the Dubs were regarded as the second-best team in Gaelic history.

CROWD TROUBLE

No longer nobodies, Dublin went to the other extreme. They looked invincible. Every county in Leinster called for the appointment of Heffernan-style all-powerful team managers while traditionalists poured cold water on this "import from soccer." Meanwhile, the Dublin team that had claimed one representative on the Leinster team in 1974 (the about to be dropped George Wilson) destroyed all opposition. They devastated Wexford by 4-17 to 3-10, Louth by 3-14 to 4-7 and tore Kildare's defence open in the 1975 Leinster final by 3-13 to 0-8.

A set of rule changes helped them. The handpass was back, and on Simon Deignan's advice Dublin perfected the technique that had won the 1942 and 1943 Railway Cups for Ulster. They used both a wandering centre half forward and a roaming full-forward. Tony Hanahoe and Jimmy Keaveney would both stray out to the sideline and allowed Brian Mullins and Bernard Brogan to run freely along what Kildare manager Eamonn O'Donoghue described as "a dual carriageway right through the heart of Kildare's defence." Mullins popped in two goals in the 18th and 33rd minutes and Hickey found the net with a tremendous shot in the second half.

A bad-tempered clash with Wexford in Carlow was the only blemish on the Dubs' great run, and a little horseplay from the 44,182 spectators at the Leinster final. The occupants of Hill 16 demolished a fence while they were waiting for the match to start. The new urban followers were turning violent.

The ban had released a new generation of players to the game. Wicklow had future rugby international Paul McNaughton in action alongside Moses Coffey at midfield when they met Louth in the first round.

One of the cities worst hit by the ban had been Derry. Since 1970 they had been threatening to break through, with 1958 All-Ireland final veteran Sean O'Connell still on board. Derry made it after 17 years just when it appeared that Down might re-emerge. A superb third-minute goal from boxer-cum-soccer star-cum-Gaelic footballer Gerry McElhinney gave Derry a 1-16 to 2-6 victory over Down in the Ulster final.

McElhinney, who was all of 18, was set up by 1958 veteran Sean O'Connell. That sent Derry 1-5 to 1-3 ahead at half-time but when Dan McCartan missed a Down penalty, Mickey Lynch and O'Connell scored five points each, while

Down's two goals by Willie Walsh came too late to make a difference and Derry's youthful team won a surprise Ulster title.

Derry's previous appearances in Croke Park had been marred by violence. With Dublin's and Derry's followers set to come together, the GAA braced itself for the worst. There was a storm of controversy, a few fights, and a few bottles thrown. But no serious repercussions.

Derry went out in the semi-final by a surprisingly respectable 3-13 to 3-8. They seized a surprise 2-2 to 0-6 lead but crumbled. Veteran Sean O'Connell, O'Leary and Brendan Kelly, three minutes from the end, were their goal-scorers. Anton O'Toole (33rd and 63rd) and Tony Hanahoe (46th) notched Dublin's winning goals. On the other side of the fence many felt that Derry's breakthrough had come too late to achieve anything.

Just like Sligo's. Sligo won a title they had threatened to take for a decade in Connacht. But they failed so dismally in the All-Ireland semi-final that all the sideline sages agreed that 1971 was the year they should have got the breakthrough.

Luck had been on Sligo's side for a change. In the drawn Connacht final, Mayo's J P Kean had a shot miraculously scrambled clear by Sligo defenders when he hit the crossbar. Des Kearins and teenager Frank Henry scored Sligo's drawn-match goals for a 2-10 to 1-13 result. The teams went back to Castlebar, where Sligo, too old and past their best to make any impact in the All-Ireland championship, got their second Connacht title at last. Mickey Kearins, now in his 14th championship campaign, scored a vital penalty that put them back in the game after half-time when they trailed 0-7 to 0-9. Then he laid on the pass for Des Kearins 56th-minute winning goal for a historic 2-10 to 0-15 victory.

London re-entered the senior championship after 65 years, this time in the Connacht section, amid much hullabaloo, and lost 4-12 to 1-12 to Sligo in Castlebar.

The All-Ireland semi-final was a disaster. Sligo looked overweight and under-confident. The players waved to their friends in the crowd as the parade passed around the ground. Then they collapsed by 3-13 to 0-5. The new-look Kerry team were not impressive winners. They fumbled and overcarried in the face of inept opposition.

Mickey Kearins missed a Sligo penalty, and Kerry led 0-7 to 0-2 at half-time. Sligo decided to bring their full-back to midfield after 55 minutes. That was a mistake. The floodgates opened. John Egan, Pat Spillane, and Egan again harvested goals. There was a new force to challenge Dublin, but Dublin players in Croke Park that afternoon did not *really* rate their new opposition, as they lectured embarrassed Sligomen on how Kerry should have been beaten.

YOUNG KERRY

Those that had watched Kerry's 1973 under-21s beat Cork on a rainy day in Skibbereen knew that there was more to this bunch than happy-go-lucky handpassing. They had an average age of 21 and a half, the youngest Kerry team in 37 years, and had slightly sullied their reputation as a result of a poor performance in the League quarter-final against Meath. That slip-up was timed impeccably. The young team decided to answer the critics and went on to win eight All-Irelands in 12 years!

Yet it might never have happened. Kerry would not have won the 1975 Munster senior final had not nervous Cork full-back Martin O'Doherty dropped the ball into the net after just 13 minutes; Cork's quest for a first ever three-in-a-row disappeared in the panic that ensued.

Kerry won by 1-14 to 0-7 and give the first display of the "long pass, run, stop, draw the man, pass" game that was to serve them for a decade.

Kerry were more traditional in their structure than their Dublin rivals. There was a reluctance in the county to abandon the old catch-and-kick principles that had won 22 All-Irelands. They were by no means as badly off as the reports of the 1975 League quarter-final would suggest: *The Kerryman* suggested: "I don't think anybody in their right senses should say that the Kerry team as presently constituted is going to win an All-Ireland this year or in the immediate future." Any team manager in the country would gladly have accepted the produce of the 1970 minor and 1973 under-21 All-Ireland teams to build on.

Fate decreed that the man who got the opportunity was trainer-selector Mick O'Dwyer, the player who had retired less than 12 months beforehand with a pedigree that was respected all over the country, a non-smoker, a non-drinker, and a fitness fanatic.

Despite the horrendous distances the team was forced to travel to train (Dwyer himself faced a 102-mile round trip from Waterville), O'Dwyer brought his charges in to Killarney five times a week between the All-Ireland semi-final and the final. Heffernan panicked and brought Dublin into training six times a week in the run-up to the final. Kerry's firsts beat their reserves by 7-9 to 2-5 in their final trial game. Tom Woulfe commented that here at last was a match that "would be decided by the head rather than the hip."

In their separate dressing-rooms before the 1975 All-Ireland final, both were making speeches that would have got them convicted under the Race Relations Act. O'Dwyer was thumping the table with a Lucozade bottle, imploring Kerry to do it for him, for themselves, for Kerry. Heffernan was goading his players, terrifying them, asking them who would be the Judas on the team, who would betray his colleagues in the moment of truth.

Luck largely decided the day. John Egan and substitute Ger O'Driscoll got the goals. The defence slipped to let Egan in after three minutes. Egan and O'Driscoll could have had a second goal each; Ger O'Driscoll blazed wide from a great position before his goal, and Egan beat Cullen with a punched ball only to see it come back from the crossbar.

"Pouring cold water" was an appropriate expression. The Dublin team returned in to their Croke Park dressing-room to find that there was a problem with the showers. But there was a man with a hose offering "to hose down any of the players that wanted it."

Paudie O'Mahoney from Spa, near Killarney, had been on the 1970 minors and 1973 under-21s and would become part of a goalkeeping battle with Charlie Nelligan, the young goalkeeper who played in the curtain-raiser to the 1975 final.

Ger O'Keeffe was a 1975-style footballer, one of the fastest backs in the business. He started at full-back but ended up at corner-back for the championship and most of his career. He earned the nickname Gidacha after a Polish winger in the 1974 World Cup.

John O'Keeffe had been a teenage protégé, captain of St Brendan's in an All-Ireland Colleges final, a senior club midfielder at 16, a minor on the 1969 senior panel, a player in 1970. His clashes with Jimmy Keaveney caused great heartbreak. O'Keeffe was taken out of position regularly by Keaveney's wanderings until the 1978 All-Ireland final.

Jim Deenihan, honoured with the position of 23rd sub in 1972, had studied Physical Education in London and in Limerick's Thomond College. He had tamed Jimmy Barry Murphy in the Munster, by fair means and foul.

Paudie O'Shea, a 20-year-old trainee Garda from Ventry, had marked Mick O'Dwyer in a Kerry championship match. Three years a minor, he won his place in the team with a great display against Dublin in the league the previous November. He would later change his name to Páidi Ó Sé on the promptings of some Gaelgeoirí.

Tim Kennelly was the only farmer on the team of teachers and professionals, in fact a farmer's son waiting to inherit both farm and pub. He did not sleep a wink before the final.

Ger Power was the son of a Limerick All-Ireland hurler, Jackie, who was transferred to Tralee by CIE. He had saved Kerry in the 1974 drawn League final. A pasting from Anton O'Toole in the 1977 All-Ireland semi-final lost him his place on the team, then he returned as one of the country's top forwards and won an All-Star award in his new position.

Paud Lynch was one of the most skilful players on the team, a solicitor who played at midfield and at the back before his career ended prematurely. They said that under another regime he would have played until his mid-30s.

Pat McCarthy was an unexpected success in the 1975 final. Called up after the League disaster against Meath, he came from hurling territory, Churchill, and his grandfather had an 1891 All-Ireland hurling medal.

At 26, Brendan Lynch was the oldest on the team, a team member since he was 18 and played in the 1968 final. Denis "Ogie" Moran was Limerick-born, but had starred with Ballybunion teams since he was 12. Two years earlier he had won a Colleges medal with Gormanston. He was now 19, and star of the final.

Michael O'Sullivan captained the team, but did not know the result of the game until he woke up in hospital after four Dublin players sandwiched him. John Egan put down his goal to "a defensive mistake" but was to enjoy a lot of goal-making throughout the 1975 championship.

Mike Sheehy had practised free-taking at the corner of his street in Tralee, sending the ball through the narrow angle between his house and the one next door. His dead shot had let him down for the 1974 National League final, but he was to keep the touch for 10 years and turn down an offer to play professional soccer with Southampton.

Pat Spillane from Templenoe, near Kenmare, had three uncles, the Lyne brothers, with All-Ireland medals. He also had two younger brothers who would join him on the medals list. In 1975 he was the second youngest on the team, six weeks older than "Ogie" Moran and not yet 20.

Ger O'Driscoll from Valentia had been tried at midfield, and missed selection by a single vote. When he came on as substitute he replied with a goal.

ENTER KEVIN MORAN

Dublin regrouped. Things had gone badly wrong for them ever since a shock defeat in the 1975 League final, by Meath who had already ousted Kerry in the quarter-final.

In 1976 they took the League title by beating Derry, then defeated Meath in the Leinster final by 2-8 to 1-9, with a superb goal from Hanahoe after a handpassing movement, soon after Meath had taken the lead early in the second half. Meath's midfielders, Joe Cassells and Derry Rennicks, seemed to give them the facility to beat Dublin but Colm O'Rourke sent their best chance, a 53rd-minute penalty, wide.

Connacht surprise packets Leitrim faced three championship matches in successive weeks. They beat Mayo with one of the most remarkable comebacks in GAA history, making their way back from 10 points down. Michael Martin missed a penalty along the way. The following week Martin scored a dramatic last-minute equaliser from 60 yards to force a draw with Mayo. In the replay Mayo-born Eddie McHale helped Leitrim to a 2-8 to 0-10 victory, a win what was only their second championship victory in 13 years.

Galway allowed a six-point lead to be swallowed up by Roscommon for yet another drawn Connacht final, 1-8 to 1-8. To make matters worse Harry Keegan missed a Roscommon penalty, but Galway made no mistake when they ensured the margin was never less than six points in the replay. Billy Joyce dominated midfield and Pat Lindsay tipped the ball over the goalkeeper's head for the winning goal, 1-14 to 0-9.

Dublin beat Galway by 1-8 to 0-8 in a pedestrian All-Ireland semi-final, thanks to a Jimmy Keaveney goal 16 minutes into the second half. It was a poor, 67-free game on a greasy surface in which five players were booked and frequent outbursts of fisticuffs marred the play.

The grand opening of Cork's new stadium, Páirc Uí Chaoimh, also went drastically wrong. Confused spectators milled around the entrances and when they got inside stewarding was non-existent, so the event degenerated into a shambles with some of the 40,600 spectators spilling on to the field, two gates broken down, and between 5,000 and 10,000 getting in without paying.

Events on the field were almost incidental. The players found it difficult to concentrate. Dave McCarthy had another brilliant performance as Cork and Kerry drew the Munster final, 0-10 to 0-10. Mike Sheehy missed a Kerry penalty, and 63 frees spoiled the continuity of play.

A larger crowd at the replay, 45,235, saw one of the most spectacular Munster finals of all time. A more successful replay helped appease the Páirc's critics. But over the next five years it turned into a major headache for Cork's county board as the outstanding debt on the modern stadium doubled before it was paid off.

Kerry won the 1976 Munster championship by 3-20 to 2-19, and super-sub Seanie Walsh scored the turning-point goal five minutes from the end, the umpire judging that Brian Murphy caught the ball on the wrong side of the line. Cork had been leading by four points until then. Cork had a punched goal at the other end from Colman Corrigan almost immediately, but it was disallowed. Then Cork watched in disbelief as Kerry outran them in the second period of extra time.

Ulster's final was drawn too. Derry outlasted Cavan in an endurance test of a replay: Brendan Kelly, Johnny O'Leary and Mickey Lynch got the points in the closing stages of extra time after an enthralling replay that contrasted with the rugged draw between the same teams. In the semi-final, Derry, strangely enough, were leading Kerry at half-time 0-9 to 0-8. The effect of Pat Spillane being felled off the ball at a time when Derry led 0-6 to 0-2 had sealed their fate, and Derry got destroyed, 5-14 to 1-0.

An old-time crowd, of 73,588, attended the final. Dublin started explosively and won handsomely, by 3-8 to 0-10. From the throw-in Kevin Moran careered through defence, took a return pass from Bernard Brogan and sent a shot screaming narrowly wide.

John McCarthy finished a five-man move for their first goal after 15 minutes. Jimmy Keaveney sent a penalty into the top corner at the start of the second half, and Brian Mullins side-footed the third with 12 minutes to go.

Kerry had cut the gap to two points when Dublin moved Mullins to centre-forward and sprang the fresher Fran Ryder at midfield.

Dublin's transformation was easily explained. The half-back line was renewed. Dublin's selectors spent the winter of 1975-6 looking for three new half-backs and they found them.

Tommy Drumm had been a team-mate of Liam Brady's on St Aidan's school soccer teams, and had played soccer for the Irish Universities. He was just 20, when he became Dublin's first Trinity student All-Ireland medallist. Kevin Moran arrived on a motor bike at a Dublin training session in early

1976. He would last just two years before he got snapped up by Manchester United. Doctor Pat O'Neill used to tell his team-mates to hit opponents as hard as they liked, because he could look after them in hospital next week.

Bernard Brogan also restored his reputation after a poor 1975 performance in 1975. He was to kick one of the most memorable goals in Gaelic football against Kerry the following year.

THE GREATEST GAME

The All-Ireland semi-final of 1977 was the greatest football match since television and possibly the greatest ever. Tony Hanahoe conjured up two late goals from David Hickey with six minutes to go and substitute Bernard Brogan with three to go for Dublin to win.

During the second half the sides were level five times. Then came the closing stages. Kerry went two points ahead, 1-13 to 1-11. "Maybe Sam will be coming to the O'Keeffe house," captain Ger O'Keeffe recalls thinking.

Anton O'Toole's pass down-field for Dublin was going nowhere in particular, and then it dangled just that pace too far away from John O'Keeffe. O'Keeffe lunged forward, half-falling and instead of catching or breaking the ball away he turned it awkwardly slightly off-course into the hands of a surprised Tony Hanahoe.

Married three weeks beforehand, with not a whisper to his team-mates, Hanahoe was the most organised of the Dublin attack in the frenetic heat of the moment. "You could always rely on him to do the right thing," Heffernan used to say. And he did. He had Dave Hickey on his right, and found him with a short handpass. Hickey raced away alone under the blue of Hill 16, with lots of space, took just long enough to evade the defensive efforts of Jim Deenihan and Denis Moran, and he shot diagonally across the goal-mouth.

Three minutes later and nobody believed that Kerry would fail to come back at least to equalise. "Ogie" Moran floated a ball into the Dublin goal-mouth, Sean Doherty retrieved it, fell in a relieved heap, then realised his task was not yet complete and launched a 50-yard kick back down-field.

Out of chaos came the follow-up goal. The ball was juggled around among five players before a poke by Pat O'Neill helped Bobby Doyle win possession at midfield. He handpassed to David Hickey who made a long, accurate, booted pass to Hanahoe. Hanahoe turned around to look behind him, then slung the ball to Bernard Brogan, careering through at full gallop four paces ahead of Páidi Ó'Sé. Brogan took one bounce, one toe-to-hand, 12 paces in full flight, and a measured shot inside Nelligan's left-hand post.

Even the draw in the other semi-final could not compare with it. Armagh supporters had taken over Hill 16 to watch their team came back from seven points down to draw with Roscommon. Jimmy Smyth kicked the equalising point with two minutes to go for a 3-9 to 2-12 draw. Armagh weathered Roscommon's comeback from three points down to win the replay by a single point, 0-15 to 0-14.

It was an anti-climactic final, all-ticket for the first time as a result of the fear of trouble. Dublin got all the room they needed for a total annihilation of Armagh.

Jimmy Keaveney set a new individual scoring record of 2-6. His first goal came after just 90 seconds, the second two minutes into the second half, and four of the points were from frees. Bobby Doyle (13 minutes), John McCarthy (33 minutes) and Doyle again (60 minutes) were Dublin's other goal-scorers. For Armagh Paddy Moriarty scored from the first of his two penalties, seven and a half minutes into the match. Joe Kernan scored two Armagh goals (in the 46th and 51st minutes). But when Armagh needed goals badly Sean Devlin hit the post and Moriarty missed a second penalty. The 66,542 who got the scarce tickets were disappointed.

Armagh had taken back the Ulster title after 24 years when they stunned Derry with two spectacular goals in a 60-second spell before half-time. Paddy Moriarty and Noel Marley were the scorers, and Jimmy Kearins wrapped up the argument eight minutes into the second half for a 3-10 to 1-5 victory.

Two notable events occurred in Connacht. A year after beating Mayo, Leitrim were humble victims of London's first ever victory in a senior football championship match by 0-9 to 0-6. London had two Leitrim men in action against their native county. The other notable was the emergence of Roscommon, this time to stay. They had suffered three defeats to Galway in the previous eight years but got it right at last, by a single point, 1-12 to 2-8, before 18,000 spectators in Roscommon.

It was the sixth time in 16 years that a solitary point separated the teams at the end of the Connacht final—a period when four more finals had been drawn! There were only five one-point wins in the 60 years prior to that.

The 46,087 spectators who turned out to watch the Munster final in Killarney expected a closer game than Kerry's 3-15 to 0-9 victory. Cork's last score from play came after 10 minutes of the first half, and they scored only one solitary point against the wind in the second half. A gale force wind had helped Cork go 0-7 to 0-1 up after 16 minutes!

Leinster was closer. Dublin eventually beat Meath in a tense and much-criticised stop-start game by 1-9 to 0-8 with a goal from Anton O'Toole. The Dublin goal may have been thrown to the net. Meath had two shots which beat the goalkeeper but were scrambled away by defenders and also hit a hatful of wides.

Kildare had given Dublin a scare in Navan on their return from the All-Stars trip to the United States, but Bernard Brogan struck back in reply to Tommy Carew's second goal for Kildare, and won by three points. Kildare pondered that 1977 near-miss in Navan for a long time.

FIVE GOALS IN THE RAIN

Kildare's misconceptions were quickly straightened out in the 1978 Leinster final. Kildare fans in the Nally stand had bottles thrown at them from Hill 16. But that was nothing compared with the 1-17 to 1-6 defeat that was thrown at the players on the field. Kildare had Dave Hyland sent off as their hopes crumbled.

There was more trouble in the All-Ireland semi-final. Keaveney started the downfall of Down with an 18th-minute goal for Dublin. When Down's Cathal Digney was sent off a steward was cut by a flying bottle.

Ulster champions were beginning to despair of a breakthrough at Croke Park. They had a new theory: that it was only after a second successive provincial title that an Ulster team could achieve anything in an All-Ireland semi-final.

All-Ireland finalists Armagh crashed out in the first round to Cavan by 0-16 to 0-9 and Derry followed by 1-14 to 2-8 in the semi-final. That left Down and Cavan to fight out the Ulster title. Down won by 2-19 to 2-12, using their powerful new centre-field combination of 30-year-old six-foot Colm McAlarney, and 20-year-old six foot three inches Liam Austin.

Kerry's new full-forward finished scoreless as Kerry beat Cork by 3-14 to 3-7 in the Munster final. Eoin Liston, a converted midfielder from Ballybunion, earned the nickname "Bomber" on the local beach from the time the lads used to ape 1974 Soccer heroes in low-tide soccer games. He had been too heavy and unfit to make it at minor but had been spotted by O'Dwyer at an under-21 club match in Gneeveguila. For the Munster semi-final match against Waterford, Liston was selected at midfield and Seanie Walsh at full-forward, but once positions were reversed Kerry found the winning formula.

Roscommon recaptured the Connacht title by 2-7 to 0-9 but came a cropper in the All-Ireland semi-final. Kerry asserted superiority over Roscommon after 26 minutes with a Spillane goal. Ger Power and Packie O'Mahoney got the others in the second half.

O'Dwyer always held that Dublin's weakness was their inability to score long-range points, so if Kerry could stop them getting closer than 30 yards from the goal, the rest would be simple.

This time 71,503 came to watch. In 1976 and 1977 John O'Keeffe had been taken out of the full-back position by a wandering Jimmy Keaveney. In 1978 it was decided to let Keaveney go as far as he liked, where he could score points, but O'Keeffe would stay back to mind the square and keep that all-important first goal out.

The first goal had counted for so much in Dublin-Kerry matches in 1975, 1976 and 1977, as well as in League and under-21 clashes between the teams. It was one of those inexplicable superstitions that creep into football lore. Yet the O'Keeffe plan, the plan that won Kerry the 1978 All-Ireland, almost backfired. In those opening minutes Keaveney punished Kerry for the freedom he was given. Then came five Kerry goals.

John Egan struck after 24 minutes. Mickey Sheehy scored the most famous goal of all time after 32 and a half minutes, when he sent a free kick over the head of a frantic Paddy Cullen, caught off his line protesting against referee Aldridge's decision. The newly discovered six foot three full-forward Eoin Liston unveiled his fist for three second-half goals. Arguments that he was in the square for the fifth goal were overruled while nearby Hill 16 yelped at the referee. Kerry won by 17 points, 5-11 to 0-9.

Who was to blame? Earlier Ger Power late-tackled Paddy Cullen as he ran 20 yards out from the goal to clear the ball. Cullen retaliated by tripping Power as he was clearing. Aldridge was watching them when they jostled again three minutes before half-time.

Cullen complained afterwards:

—   There was no whistle. It is unusual that there would be no whistle for a free from that distance. And the referee had his back to the kicker. The ball could have been kicked from the hands. It could have been thrown into the net. It was a lot of egg on my face.

Cullen said afterwards he retaliated because Power had earlier "stuck an elbow in my face." He feels that Aldridge punished him for an earlier incident when he definitely fouled Power.

I came out in a similar situation and picked up the ball and handpassed it out. He followed through and when I was running back to the goal I tipped his ankle. He fell over. About 25,000 people saw the incident and everytime I touched the ball in the intermittent period between that and the goal, they booed me. The referee knew something had happened. As it turned out, he penalised me for the earlier incident when I had committed no foul.

When the whistle sounded Cullen automatically assumed it was a free to Dublin. He stayed off the goal-line initially because he was prepared to take the free. "It was nothing serious, but the free should have been out." Pat O'Neill, too, put the ball down assuming it was a Dublin free.

The free-in, Cullen knew, would almost certainly result in a score, and Cullen stood protesting his innocence. "This has to be a free-out," he said. Aldridge stood silently, his back to ball and kicker, facing Cullen. "There's no foul," said Cullen. "It has to be a free-out." The referee was having none of it. To the horror of watching defenders Robbie Kelleher helpfully handed the ball to Mike Sheehy with Cullen still off his line. And Mike Sheehy plopped the ball into the Dublin net.

Sportswriter Con Houlihan described the incident:

> Paddy put on a show of righteous indignation that would get him a card from Equity, throwing up his hands to heaven as the referee kept pointing to the goal. And while all of this was going on, Mike Sheehy came running up to take the kick—and suddenly Paddy dashes back like a woman who smells a cake burning. The ball won the race and it curled inside the the near post as Paddy crashed into the outside of the net and lay against it like a fireman who had returned to find his station ablaze. Sometime Noel Pearson may make a musical of this final—and as the green flag goes up for that crazy goal he will have a banshee's voice crooning: And that was the end of poor Molly Malone. So it was. A few minutes later came the tea-break. Kerry went in to a frenzy of green and gold and a tumult of acclaim. The champions looked like men who had worked hard and seen their savings plundered by bandits. The great rain robbers were out onto the field for Act Two.

Chapter Eighteen

Kerry's Finest

DUBS' DEMISE

A dollop of Dubs had threatened to retire if they won the three-in-a-row in 1978. Paddy Cullen, Sean Doherty, Tony Hanahoe, Jimmy Keaveney, Gay O'Driscoll, and Pat O'Neill would almost certainly have gone. But as Kerry players would find out half a decade later, the Dubs found it difficult to retire gracefully in defeat.

They stayed on, which was mistake, because the Dublin team was brought to a humiliating end in 1979. Kerry crushed their opponents, stylishly winning with a shattering Mike Sheehy goal after 10 minutes, another Sheehy penalty after 56 minutes, and a third from John Egan eight minutes from the end for a 3-13 to 1-6 victory.

Starting without Ger Power, losing John O'Keeffe and having Páidi Ó Sé sent off did not deter them. Jim Ronayne's controversial 46th-minute handpassed goal was Dublin's only reward for a spirited comeback attempt in the second half.

Pretenders everywhere had waited for the duopoly to crack. League champions Roscommon almost made the All-Ireland final. Roscommon beat Mayo by 3-15 to 2-10 in the Connacht final. They went out of the championship by 0-14 to 1-10 at the hands of Dublin, only because Michael Hickey scored Dublin's winning point against them four minutes from the end of a tense semi-final, minutes after a dramatic equalising goal from Roscommon's Michael Finneran. Hickey scored nine points in that semi-final, yet was taken off early in the final when he missed two 50s. The subs were not finding it easy to win a place among the Dubs.

Monaghan beat Donegal by 1-15 to 0-11 to recapture the Ulster title after 41 years, after a false start. Donegal in fact scored an opening point; but the referee suddenly realised the band was still on the field waiting to play the National Anthem. Play was stopped, the point was scratched, Amhrán na bhFiann was sounded and the ceremony of the throw-in to start the game was repeated! The second time, Monaghan took control immediately with a Kieran Finlay goal (Finlay added nine points), led 1-9 to 0-2 before Donegal got moving and never relinquished the lead.

Monaghan brought their colourful supporters to Croke Park on the crest of a drumlin. But their noisy welcome for their heroes was silenced as Ger Power slammed in two goals in the first 15 minutes for Kerry. Mikey Sheehy collected a record score of 3-5, and Liston and Spillane had goals disallowed as Kerry won by 5-14 to 0-7.

Kerry may have been at their very best in 1979. Certainly Ger Power was, scoring 2-4 as Kerry beat Cork by 2-14 to 2-4 in the Munster final. Cork missed two penalties. Clare fared worse, the wrong end of a record 9-21 to 1-9 hammering in Miltown Malbay. The Kerry 1978-9 League campaign included victories of 7-8 to 0-7 against Kildare, whose goalkeeper, Ollie Crinnigan, had just had an All-Star award announced the previous Friday, and 6-11 to nil against Laois.

One team alone was threatening to break the Dublin-Kerry axis. Dublin beat Offaly by a close-called 1-8 to 0-10 before 52,348 people in the Leinster final with the help of a controversial goal two minutes from full time. When Brian Mullins was fouled, he flung the ball at an opponent in retaliation. Instead of a Dublin free, the referee decided to throw in the ball between the two players, then threw the ball directly to Mullins. He cantered off in the direction of the Offaly goal, leaving Bernard Brogan to finish the score for Dublin's six-in-a-row. A well-worked goal by Jim Ronayne was earlier disallowed, and Jimmy Keaveney was sent off in a dramatic and often bad-tempered final. Offaly's ire was raised.

RAGGEDY ROSCOMMON

It was the genius of Matt Connor that eventually lifted Offaly out of the shadow of Dublin in 1980.

Matt Connor was third youngest of a football-mad family of eight, one of whom, Murt, won 1971 and 1972 All-Ireland medals and another, Richie, was captain of the 1982 Offaly team. Two double cousins, related on both the father's and mother's side, Liam and Tomás, were also on the 1982 team.

Matt grew up a farmyard where the kids were served by two ready-made goal-posts, the horse door on one side, the supporting walls for the diesel tank on the other. The lads would play there, commentating as they played: "A point for Laois but back down the field and a goal for Offaly."

Around the farmyard, Matt brought a football with him on his chores. Leaving a fork or a bucket down he would pick a target for himself, the small window beside the turf shed, the second rung of the ladder, even the red hen by the cowhouse door, and a ball would go flying in that direction. The pasture at the back was reserved for the "big men's ball," a much-punctured leather that Uncle John was repeatedly called upon to repair. There the local boys would gather with the Connors for impromptu games.

Matt set records at every level. He helped Walsh Island to six-in-a-row in Offaly, scored a record 5-4 for his club against Dunlavin in a Leinster Club championship game, and took over the free-taking for Offaly in 1980. He remained Ireland's top scorer for five years.

His astounding 1980 year total of 22-135 defeated Mick O'Dwyer's 10-year-old record and his match average of 11.5 in the 1980 championship may never be beaten.

In the Leinster final, as Offaly dethroned Dublin by 1-10 to 1-8 before 50,276 people, Connor scored 1-7, including the vital goal 11 minutes after half-time. He switched from corner to centre-forward, and restored Offaly morale just when they seemed to have lost all chance of winning. Dublin hit 11 wides in the first half and might have come back had any injury time been played. Kevin Moran, now in his second year with Manchester United, lined out in the semi-final for Dublin against Meath. Matt Connor scored 2-8 as Offaly weathered an early Kildare siege in the other semi-final.

The All-Ireland semi-final between Kerry and Offaly was a celebration of the handpass at its best, a year before the tactic was banned. Both sides let the game open up and Kerry snatched four goals, two from Pat Spillane, the others from Mikey Sheehy and John Egan. Kerry eventually won by 4-15 to 4-10. Matt Connor scored 2-9.

The following year's Congress banned the handpass, unimpressed by the eight-goal spectacle. This was reckoned by Kerry manager Mick O'Dwyer to be one of the best games ever played.

Clare, horrified by their drubbing in 1979, had pushed through a motion at a November 1979 Munster Council meeting that Kerry should have a bye into the following year's Munster final. Kerry were angry, and feared that lack of match-practice might damage their prospects against Cork, still one of the biggest threats to their ambitions. The fears proved unfounded as Kerry beat Cork by 3-13 to 0-12. Tim Kennelly of Kerry scored an extraordinary own point kicked over his own crossbar from 20 yards out!

Roscommon had a handpass romp of their own, winning by 9-19 to 1-10 in the Connacht championship against London, whose impressive array of warming-up exercises beforehand was the closest they came to entertaining the small crowd.

Ulster too had eight goals to celebrate, as Armagh beat Tyrone by 4-10 to 4-7 and took their sixth title with three late points, two from Peter Loughran and another from Jimmy Smyth to clinch the game after Damien O'Hagan brought Tyrone bursting back into the contest with two goals. O'Hagan had been in Long Kesh just a few years before, a remand prisoner awaiting charges of Fianna Éireann membership.

When Armagh met Roscommon in the All-Ireland semi-final Roscommon fell 0-7 to 2-6 behind at half-time. Tony McManus then wiped the lead with a 50th-minute goal, Roscommon fell behind again and Michael Finneran's goal six minutes from the end sent Roscommon through by 2-20 to 3-11.

On this showing, Roscommon were not rated a danger to Kerry's chances. But the 1980 All-Ireland was the one from Kerry's four-in-a-row that they came closest to losing.

Mick O'Dwyer was to reminisce:

> Roscommon squandered a glorious opportunity in 1980. They were strong, experienced and well-organised and made a great start but then lost faith and instead of continuing with their positive game became negative. They adopted an over-aggressive approach. It backfired completely.

Kerry fell five points behind to Roscommon in the first 12 minutes. Sean Walsh's first free was charged down by Dermot Earley, he delivered to Tony MacManus. Kerry full-back John O'Keeffe slipped. Corner-back Ger O'Keeffe came across to block McManus leaving John O'Connor unmarked and in position to take the pass and handpass to the net after 35 seconds.

A handpassed Mikey Sheehy goal brought Kerry back on level terms at half-time and eventually the Liston-less Kerry won a ragged 64-free final by three points, 1-9 to 1-6. Their lead had been only two points until the 34th minute of the second half, when Finneran late-tackled Spillane and Sheehy took a gift of a free for the insurance point.

At training on the Tuesday before the final Eoin Liston asked Mick O'Dwyer to skip press-ups because he had a sharp pain in his side. For a while he stood leaning against the fence in his togs, a doctor gave him a pain-killer, and he drove himself to Tralee to a hospital. Appendicitis was diagnosed. Liston was out from the final.

Mike Sheehy was only 75 per cent fit to play. Ger Power's leg was suspect. He was prodded with pain-killers and sent on to the field only to find, to his horror, that they wore off soon after the National Anthem sounded.

Sheehy saved Kerry in the end. He scored six frees, and all but three of the Kerry total. His best point was scored from 14 yards out, near the sideline, on the Hogan Stand side. Roscommon tried three free-takers and missed some great chances. John O'Connor and Dermot Earley scored just one free each for Roscommon! Michael Finneran missed two eminently scoreable frees in the second half.

Roscommon missed three great goal chances, too. John O'Connor misjudged a 30-yard Michael Finneran pass which bounced awkwardly, allowing Nelligan to come out to gather. O'Connor had another shot spectacularly pushed over the bar by Nelligan. And 10 minutes from the end Nelligan blocked down a Michael Finneran shot, and Páidí Ó'Sé saw Aidan Dooley about to latch on to the rebound. Páidi flung himself across the goal and miraculously saved, then held the ball off the ground to avoid conceding a penalty.

There is a theory that the short-pass game involves up to five times the amount of physical contact as the catch-and-kick game. Whatever the reason, the Kerry v Roscommon final in 1980 was the most free-ridden since the 80-minute drawn final in 1972. The ball was in play for less than 15 minutes.

The 64 frees, and the physical aspects of the game caused controversy. One Roscommon selector claimed: "You could not look at a Kerryman but there was a free." County chairman Michael O'Callaghan criticised the referee afterwards, and was deprived of an American trip with the All-Stars.

But O'Dwyer countered for Kerry: "All-Irelands are not won by physical force. Ways and means to dethrone the present Kerry side are being tried throughout the country and those who have not got the skill must resort to other tactics." The most extreme tactic of all to dethrone Kerry was the decision to change the rules of the game.

EXIT THE HANDPASS

Three separate committees had proposed several sets or rule changes in the 1970s. Those that were ignored included one made up by Kerry manager Mick O'Dwyer, Dublin manager Kevin Heffernan, Kildare manager Eamonn O'Donoghue and Roscommon All-Star Dermot Earley. The proposals were probably the only ones to have been devised completely by coaches and players:

— curtailment of the solo run
— clarification of the mess caused by the personal foul
— elimination of the fisted tackle, "because the man in possession invariably gets bruised and battered."
— clarification of the handpass rule: "either get rid of it altogether or define a throw, preferably as the one handed pitch that one sees in baseball or American football."

Defining the handpass was always a problem. The Chairman of the Referees Committee which drew up the rule that made it legal in 1975, Simon Deignan, who taught Dublin to use the technique, stated that:

> For the past twenty years players have used a fisted pass as one of the skills of the game. Today the open palm of the hand may be used in all circumstances. This is the true definition of the handpass. It is clear to us that the palmed pass may not be extended in its use beyond the boundaries of the fisted pass. A good guide line is to remember that the ball may not be allowed to rest, even momentarily, in the passing hand. In other words, there should be a clear movement in the striking of the ball off one hand by another.

That "clear movement" was a talking-point for a decade. Critics of the handpass, seen to great effect in Dublin's defeat of Armagh in 1977 and by Kerry's passing movements that yielded five goals against Dublin in 1978, seven against Kildare and six against Laois in the league, and nine against Clare in the championship, came forward from all parts. Even Kerry had passed a motion calling for the abolition of the handpass in 1980. The motion was carried by a majority of 40 votes. But it was still considerably short of the two-thirds majority required to change the rule. The handpass stayed.

Was there a clear movement when Jim Ronayne scored for Dublin against Kerry in the 1979 All-Ireland final, or when Mike Sheehy scored short-range goals against Cork and Monaghan in the same year's championship?

Throughout 1981 forces to abolish the handpass continued to muster. The next chance to get rid of it would not come until 1985. But football legislators were horrified by the events of 1980, the aggregate of 8-35 scored in a semi-final and a final that was reduced to rugged chaos. They wanted a special congress to undo the 1975 Rules and wipe 1970s-style basketball off the Gaelic rule-book.

Even where the technique was at its zenith, in Kerry, Michael Lyne complained:

> Football is becoming very much akin to basketball, or even rugby—except that forward passing is allowed. No longer do we see the high fielding, the long clearance or the long range points. The catch phrase *Backs stay back* is quickly becoming outdated. Is it not time that the GAA looked again at the contribution of the handpass to the game? It was said it would speed up play. Does handpassing back to the goalie speed up the play? Can a handpassing movement move the ball faster than a long clearance? Nowadays when possession football is the the order of the day, is there any legal way of dispossessing a player? The GAA must move now before the nauseating feature of holding possession creeps into the game.

He was backed up by other Kerry old-timers. One claimed that, as the rules of Gaelic Football rules are now framed, a team of tall basketballers from Alabama could come over and destroy the All-Ireland champions. Joe Keohane joined the charge: "I believe the game is becoming popular in convent schools and Reverend Mothers are losing their minds about it."

The hue and cry against the handpass had grown so much that a Special Congress was announced, purportedly to examine the handpass, the solo run and the personal foul. The event was to become a public execution of the handpass.

A Committee was asked to report to the Special Congress. It decided that the handpass had four advantages: it eliminated pulling and mauling from the game, it gave the player plenty of options in a tight situation, it helped the less physical player, and it speeded up the game for spectators.

The Committee listed two disadvantages of the handpass: that it changed the character of Gaelic football from a kicking game to a running game, and that it was virtually impossible to manage for referees, claiming (without much foundation) that 60 per cent of all handpasses were in fact foul passes.

It produced a slim but influential 24-page report. Future GAA president and referee, Mick Loftus chaired the Committee. It was top-heavy with officials: Jim Roche, Ciaran O'Neill, Gerry Fagan, Jim McKeever and Director General Liam Mulvihill. There were two players appointed, but Dermot Earley pulled out and Jack O'Shea was unable to attend any of the meetings.

Their decision to recommend that scores from the handpass be abolished was made on such improbable grounds that it "was a poor ending to a good movement": they claimed that it was "too simple, there is not much skill involved," it was "not in full keeping with the game of football(!)" as well as advancing more credible reasons such as "the handpass disadvantages the defence too much," and that it was "too difficult for a referee to determine the legality of a handpass where an important score was involved."

A tiny sample was asked for views on the handpass, 59 people in all. Of these, 12 were players, 15 were coaches, 14 were referees, and 18 were spectators and administrators. Only 45 replied.

The Special Congress, held at Na Fianna clubhouse, Mobhi Road, on May 9th 1981, decided it wanted to retain the handpass with scores by the hand allowed. Kerry's motion "that the handpass in play be retained" was passed on a 77/40 vote.

It was decided to define the handpass: "There must be a visible striking of the ball by the hand, and where the striking action is not visible the referee shall deem the pass as being a foul," according to a proposal from Cork and Louth. A revival of the old "If a player receives the ball by handpass, he must kick it" rule was lost. The congress then decided that scores be allowed with the fist only.

The satisfied delegates adjourned to lunch. Then some of them began to realise the mess they had created. Allowing only fisted scores would create havoc when it came to a referee having to come to a decision in a tense Junior B match surrounded by 30 footballers and the goalie's granny.

They had to reverse the morning's decision by a two-thirds majority when they returned. They decided to outlaw all scores with the hand unless the ball is already in flight. It was a vital definition that would allow Pat Spillane score a goal against Tyrone in the 1986 All-Ireland final.

The handpass had been retained in play but its new definition was, to say the least, vague. It "had to have a visible striking movement." Referees began to enforce this new "definition," whatever it meant, rigidly. The most influential managers in the country, Kevin Heffernan and Mick O'Dwyer, were both reasonably happy with the redefined handpass. They were astonished and disappointed when they saw how the new rule was interpreted by referees.

O'Dwyer maintained:

> The speedy transfer of the ball that was part and parcel of 1970s football may have helped the game. The punched pass is slower to execute, slows down play and brings about untidy play.

RETURN TO THE BOOT

Roscommon crumbled after their near miss. Their Connacht championship five-in-a-row bid came unstuck in the semi-final at Markievicz Park. They went down to Sligo by 2-9 to 1-8. Sligo's Martin McCarrick established a firm base at midfield and J Kearins scored both goals.

Meanwhile Mayo had their eye on the crown. Their championship campaign started at London Board headquarters at leafy Ruislip before 5,000 London-Irish supporters. Galway succumbed in the semi-final by 2-8 to 1-9 to a spectacular Mayo goal by Jim Bourke (17 minutes) and another by Jim Lyons (55 minutes).

In the Connacht final at Castlebar, Mayo couldn't even get

the ball into the Sligo half for the first 10 minutes of the final. When they eventually did, it hardly ever came out again. Mayo scored six points without reply as Sligo missed chance after chance, and won by 0-12 to 0-4.

Munster provided the poorest provincial final in 19 years. Kerry got the only goal in the match from Mikey Sheehy after 58 minutes and kept Cork to just a single point from play, scored by Dave Barry. Cork's tactic of switching the six backs around at intervals had no effect whatsoever on Kerry's attack. The score was a paltry two points to one at half-time. The change in the handpass rule seemed to have reduced the whole game to a shambles.

Kerry were held by Mayo for 49 minutes of the semi-final: Eddie McHale scored a splendid goal, sandwiched between two by Power and Liston, for Mayo to trail 2-7 to 1-6 at half-time. Then came utter devastation as Mayo failed to score in the second half and eventually went down to a 2-19 to 1-6 defeat. The semi-finals represented Kerry at their best, combining their preparation and skill with none of the tension of an All-Ireland final.

In Ulster Down wrapped up their 10th title in 22 years with two goals from John McCartan in the final five minutes to beat Armagh by 3-12 to 1-10. It finished an Armagh fight-back, Armagh having equalised at the three-quarter stage with a disputed Brian Hughes goal.

Teenager Greg Blayney got the game off to a tremendous start by scoring a goal with his first touch of a ball in the final. It was a time of turmoil in Ulster. A H-Block protest was held on the field at half-time.

Laois shocked Dublin by 2-9 to 0-11 in the Leinster semi-final with a great performance from John Costelloe, who shared the goals with Tom Prendergast.

Wexford too had a few moments of inspiration in beating hopefuls Meath by 2-9 to 1-11 in the quarter-final. Meathman Eddie Mahon kicked six points against his native county and John Wright landed a Wexford goal just seconds after Eamonn Barry missed a penalty for Meath. Tom Prendergast's three goals helped Laois oust Kildare. Mahon was not the only one to defy his native county: Wicklow-born John O'Leary produced a last-minute save which stopped a major Wicklow breakthrough by 0-10 to 0-8 in the quarter-final, leaving Moses Coffey and Pat Baker without a Leinster final appearance to their name.

Annual failures Kilkenny started excellently against Wexford when Paudie Lannon and Sean Fennelly scored first-half goals but two Ger Howlin fisted goals put them out by 2-11 to 2-4.

Laois did better in the final than most people expected. Offaly trailed 0-3 to 2-2 after 20 minutes, but Johnny Mooney and Tomás Connor took control of midfield, Brendan Lowry extracted two great saves from Laois goalkeeper Tom Scully and then struck the goal that started Offaly's comeback for a 1-18 to 3-9 victory. Missed chances prevented Offaly winning by more.

Offaly shook off Down in the the second half of their 56-free semi-final, Down being held scoreless for the final 16 minutes to go down 0-12 to 0-6.

The All-Ireland final was played at something less than the terrific pace of the previous year's semi-final. It was still an open game; with 31 stoppages, this was the least free-ridden final since 1966.

Kerry were missing Pat Spillane. Offaly, too, had a real injury worry. Both midfielders were badly hit. Tomás O'Connor had not trained for a week and was obviously carrying an injury throughout the match. Then Johnny Mooney fell off a turf trailer and injured his shoulder.

Although, after 61 training sessions, the team was fighting fit, Kerry's combination passing went into history with the handpass, they opted instead for the high ball into the Offaly square. It was 0-5 each at half-time and Offaly's best chance came in the second half when Gerry Carroll hit the post.

Kerry struck for four-in-a-row with three minutes to go. Seven players were involved in the move. Kerry corner-back Jim Deenihan cleared, Tim Kennelly gathered and passed to Tommy Doyle, Eoin Liston was found near the left-hand touchline; he gave a quick short-pass to John Egan, who gave another short-pass to Mike Sheehy. Offaly back Charlie Conroy advanced to take on Sheehy and left Jack O'Shea unmarked. O'Shea took the pass in full flight and crashed his shot to the net from 14 yards. The game finished 1-12 to 0-8 soon afterwards. Only 61,489 showed up, the lowest attendance at a final since 1947.

PLOTTING REVENGE

Two years after his Fiat 127 had collided with a lamp post, smashing his femur and apparently bringing a fabulous football career to an end at the age of 25, Dublin's Brian Mullins completed a remarkable comeback in 1982. He was the dominant figure in Dublin's ugly victory over Kildare that saw Kildare's John Crofton sent off.

Laois played a thrilling semi-final with Offaly, going down by 3-13 to 1-15 after they were spurred on by a goal 12 minutes into the second half, but allowed Gerry Carroll and John Guinan to run free for two goals and when Brendan Lowry got a third for Offaly it was all over.

Offaly and Dublin met again in the Leinster final but it was a disappointment. Offaly led Dublin at half-time by eight points and eventually won by nine, 1-16 to 1-7. A veteran from the 1972 All-Ireland, Seamus Darby, was recalled to the team after two years and his shrewd positional play made his comeback a success. Darby scored the winning goal in the second minute of play.

In the All-Ireland semi-final, Galway proved to be better than most people anticipated and narrowly missed doing to Offaly what Offaly did to Kerry in the final. Galway took the lead and held it until 10 minutes from the end, thanks to a Tom Naughton goal midway through the first half.

Gay McManus was soundly apportioned the blame for Galway's failure. He missed two scoring-range frees in the dying minutes of the match and Offaly stole through to the final by 1-12 to 1-11. McManus will never forget the scene as he drove past the Aisling Hotel the following day, the car window open, amid the jibes of disappointed Galway supporters. "Is he still taking frees?" a Galwayman roared.

Offaly had a new hero. Johnny Mooney was playing instead of injured Seamus Darby. He was flown home from

America for the semi-final amid an embarrassing amount of publicity for an illegal immigrant. Brendan Lowry scored their goal five minutes before half-time and also scored the winning point.

The only county waiting for an Ulster title, Fermanagh, had a rare championship run in the North. A goal from debutant Arthur Mulligan helped them beat Derry by 1-9 to 1-8 in the first round. In the second round 19-year-old Dom Corrigan scored 1-3 and towering midfielder Peter McGinnity 0-5 as they ousted Tyrone by 1-8 to 0-10.

McGinnity was one of Ulster's outstanding midfielders at the time, despite Fermanagh's lack of success. He provided one of the best moments in the All-Ireland final when he ran for about 40 yards with the ball before launching a superb left-foot 25-yard shot for the only goal of the game.

But it was a futile gesture. Armagh shot 20 wides in one of the poorest ever finals, but won their seventh title anyway as Fran McMahon and Colm McKinstry took control of midfield and ended hopes of a Fermanagh breakthrough.

Kerry were looking not too invincible at all, as they stuttered on the way to their eighth Munster title. Ger Power missed the chance of victory as Cork held them to a draw, 0-9 each, but Jack O'Shea, involved in a car crash the Friday before the drawn final, had recovered sufficiently to inspire a great replay victory by 2-18 to 0-12. Mikey Sheehy also came to the rescue with the scores: 2-4 in all.

Kerry's full-forward line, Liston, Egan and Sheehy, scored the requisite three goals to beat Armagh by 3-15 to 1-11 with another brilliant All-Ireland semi-final performance. Only 17,523 showed up.

That left Kerry and Offaly to fight out the championship. The prospect of a record five in a row All-Ireland titles came up again and again to haunt Kerry. "Five in a row/ five in a row/ It's hard to believe we've won five in a row," sang the group *Galleon* in a £5,000 single that was prepared for release the day after the game in anticipation of history. Advance copies went out to the press the week before the game. Eugene McGee recited a verse to the Offaly team before the match. He talked about smashing records, and the players all knew what he meant.

Offaly's resources were scarce, hardly comparable to the riches that Kerry enjoyed. But the team destined to stop the five-in-a-row had been built around a few players who could kick a ball 40 or 50 yards accurately with the side of the foot on the run. In the post-handpass game, that was important.

Kerry were using the handpass as the first option and then kicking as a last resort. The Offaly formula was to deny these free-flying handpassers the opportunity to catch the ball, and kick the ball themselves, leaving the hands free.

At the same time that Eugene McGee was considering Darby's recall, before the championship had even begun, Jim Deenihan knocked the ball out of John O'Keeffe's hand during a Kerry training session. Deenihan went to boot it on the ground and John Egan, Deenihan's marker, came thundering in to block down the shot. The two collided and were tossed over each other. As Egan fell on top of Deenihan there was an almighty crack. Egan's leg was broken.

In contrast to 1981, in the 1982 All-Ireland final Richie Connor overcame Tim Kennelly. Liam O'Connor kept Eoin Liston under control. Tomás Connor, missing in 1980 and 1981, was back in full flight. Padraig Dunne, a discovery of 1981, blossomed in 1982. Pat Fitzgerald, an average footballer, played out of his skin.

Offaly got everything right. The story of how they smashed the five-in-a-row dream with two minutes to go comes with at least four "what might have happened if" addendums.

Offaly had built up a lead of three points five minutes before half-time after a breathless first half. At half-time, Kerry official Seamus Mac Gearailt enthused. "If you blinked you'd have missed a score."

Rain had fallen in the morning, then cleared, then fell again at half-time. The ball and the sod were slippery. Eoin Liston fell when he was chasing a loose ball that might have ended in the Offaly net.

Substitute Seamus Darby had entered the play almost unnoticed, a replacement for John Guinan, and had yet to touch the ball. He moved to corner-forward and confused,

Guinan's marker, wing-back Tommy Doyle, followed him. Kerry's wing-back was now playing corner-back and vice versa.

Liam O'Connor delivered a pass towards Darby. Doyle got ahead, jumped early, over-committing himself, but was about to collect the ball when Darby appeared to nudge him on the back. Doyle fell forward in a bundle, Darby gathered unimpeded, ran four paces and blasted a goal past stranded goalkeeper Nelligan.

Kerry in disarray could not organise their counter-attack, so Offaly won their third title by 1-15 to 0-17. The Kerry players did not complain. They left Croke Park dazed, but not suggesting robbery.

Kerry's supporters had plenty to speculate about. What might have happened if?, they asked. If Darby's push on Doyle had resulted in a free-out? If Deenihan had been there? If corner-back Ger O'Keeffe had taken over the marking of Darby? If even the bench had seen what was going on and sent on appropriate instructions? If two doubtful frees had not been presented to Matt Connor just before the whistle, one when Paud Lynch punched the ball clear, another when Sean Lowry seemed to fall with three Kerrymen around him? If the Kerry forwards and Jack O'Shea had not flocked to defence in those closing minutes? If Tom Spillane had kept his head and passed the ball across the field in that fateful last counter-attack? Above all, if the five-in-a-row and immortality was not at issue, would Kerry players have concentrated on keeping possession and not panicked?

Martin Furlong did his part too, saving a dramatic penalty 17 minutes into the second half by advancing from his goal and charging down Mikey Sheehy's shot.

Penalties were always a problem for Kerry. The final Tuesday before the big match at a training session in Killarney's Fitzgerald stadium Sheehy took 20 penalties against Charlie Nelligan. He worked out that Furlong's weak side was to the goalie's left. Penalty after penalty was sent hurtling past Nelligan, 18 out of 20, many of them to the top corner, all to the goalkeeper's left. Nelligan was impressed.

But, when it came to the real thing, Sheehy changed his mind at the moment he was kicking the ball and decided to kick to Furlong's right side. Furlong had guessed that was where he would put it all the time.

According to Sheehy:

> Hitting it wasn't the problem. It was just that I hit it to Furlong's better side. I still think that penalty was the turning point in the game. I felt it immediately when he saved it that the five in a row was not on. All sorts of fears went through my head.

Seamus Darby was later to say that, sometimes, he regretted that goal that turned him into a celebrity. A guest at every GAA function, retelling the story and answering whether Doyle was *really* pushed or not. The man everybody bought a drink for, but who would be half-expected to repay the compliment and buy a drink back. Until the drinks to repay a compliment began to get very expensive. A celebrity of sorts except that he had a business in Edenderry and a marriage to go back to. The business declined and his life was almost ruined by the goal that prevented the five-in-a-row. Darby recovered to tell the tale.

Chapter Nineteen

Back to Catch and Kick

LAST-MINUTE MADNESS

They thought last-minute lightning would only strike Kerry once. But in 1983 Kerry lost to another tail-end goal. Kerry were two points ahead and 30 seconds away from a nine-in-a-row in Munster when Tadhgie Murphy took a high free and bustled it into the net off the post for a Cork winning goal.

A rainstorm early in the day set the scene. By the time the minor final began at 12.45 the pitch was a sheet of water. The provincial junior final was also played in spilling rain. The rain stopped before the senior final. Brave spectators began to arrive to face this torrent in the last few minutes before the senior match was due to begin. Only 17,000 showed up.

The sides were level five times before this dramatic finish. Kerry captain Jack O'Shea scored two goals and Mike Sheehy what looked like a winner in the 60th minute. But the backs rambled out of position and it all began to go wrong.

Tadhgie Murphy, the bandit-in-chief, had made his name as an opportunist when still at school. Under the experimental 13-a-side Colleges hurling rules of the early 1970s, the tiny four-foot-nothing, 15-year-old Murphy came on as a substitute and scored a last-minute winning goal for St Finbarrs, Farranferris, against St Kieran's, Kilkenny, in the 1972 All-Ireland Colleges hurling final.

This time he was dispatched to hang in around the goal-mouth, Darby-like, in the closing minutes of the 1983 Munster final.

Kerry's defence had been slightly dislocated. Regular full-back John O'Keeffe was missing, retired injured at half-time, and Paudie Lynch had moved to full-back afterwards.

Referee John Moloney was looking at his watch. Denis Allen was fouled some way from the Kerry posts and appeared to want to take the kick himself. He hesitated. John Cleary also started a run, but changed his mind. Tadhg O'Reilly took responsibility. He sent the ball soaring in over the heads of the Kerry backs and it dropped into the hands of Tadhgie Murphy. Murphy recalls how he caught and turned and shot the ball low. It ricocheted back in from the left post, behind the stranded goalkeeper:

> I think the kick into the square was longer than Dave Barry anticipated. When I realised I was inside everybody except Charlie Nelligan I only had one thought on my mind. I went up, caught it cleanly, and turned to bring the ball to my right foot as I landed. I had just two seconds to gather my thoughts and put everything into my shot. When I fell I was looking directly at Charlie Nelligan. I concentrated on putting the ball out of his reach, sending it low into the corner of the goal. That's where it went, only into the wrong corner—it hit the post and rebounded into the far corner of the net.

Time had been up for 90 seconds. Mick O'Dwyer could not remember a single stoppage during the second half. The referee had blown 35 seconds beyond the 70 minutes in 1982, when there seemed to be a lot of stoppages. Now another referee had extended time just long enough to beat Kerry.

SUNSHINE STAKES

That should have been enough drama for the year. But in Leinster two sun-soaked matches between Dublin and Meath in the quarter-final provided more thrills, for everyone except the Meath goalkeepers involved.

A goalkeeping mistake and an own goal gave Dublin a 2-8 each draw they hardly deserved the first day. Five minutes into the replay the new goalkeeper smothered the ball but allowed it to escape and trickle over his line for a goal! Dublin won by 3-9 to 0-16 in extra time with an Anton O'Toole goal after yet another mistake. Neither team looked like potential All-Ireland champions at the time.

Two well-fashioned goals in a three-minute spell before half-time did the damage against All-Ireland champions Offaly, who tamely opted out in the Leinster final before a poor 36,912 attendance, and Dublin came through by 2-13 to 1-11. Spectators spilled onto the field near the end of the game and attacked Offaly player Mick Fitzgerald after he made a wild lunge at Ciaran Duff: Fitzgerald was beaten up by Dublin supporters, then sent off by the referee.

As summer temperatures soared, the on-field drama was growing in stature, timing and grandeur. In the Dublin v Cork All-Ireland semi-final Barney Rock snatched as dramatic an equaliser as Croke Park has ever seen when he got a goal with 30 seconds to go. Brian Mullins saw Ray Hazley free to the left, and sent a well-placed pass. Hazley sent to Rock. Another split-second decision brought results:

> It was the only ball that bounced properly for me all day. Everything else went totally against me. The only place I could put the shot was low along the ground. The keeper came flying out. I just put the shot low and it went under him. If I'd kicked it a little bit higher the keeper would have got it.

That goal equalised the game 2-11 each, after Dinny Allen's two goals had given Cork a 2-6 to 1-6 half-time lead.

When the match was replayed in the bright sunshine of Páirc Uí Chaoimh, the players could not hear each other's calls because of the noise of the crowd, but fears of a riot proved without foundation.

A goal almost straight away for Dublin ensured things would not be close. Mullins (from a penalty), Ciaran Duff, Barney Rock (when a replacement for him had been asked to warm up on the sideline) and Joe McNally got four goals for Dublin's 4-15 to 2-10 win. "Hill 17," they called the Dublin supporters who descended to colourful Páirc Uí Chaoimh to a good-humoured, good-natured and memorable semi-final, probably the most atmospheric game in Gaelic football history.

Ulster had a good year. National League finalists Down

and Armagh ended up training within five miles of each other in the week before the National League final: Down in Newry and Armagh (awaiting clearance on whether Cliftonville's Mickey MacDonald would play) in Killeavy. An Ambrose Rodgers goal gave Down victory.

But neither county made it when it came to the Ulster championship itself. Instead, with new manager Brian McEniffe at the helm, Donegal won a thriller against champions Armagh by 1-10 to 0-7.

The same teams had been level eight times during the 1982 championship encounter and failed only to a late point from Mickey McDonald. Since then Donegal took six of their 1982 All-Ireland under-21 champions on board and shook champions Armagh with a third-minute Charlie Mulgrew goal.

For the Ulster final, McEniffe switched wing-backs to prevent a repeat of Derek McDonnell's runaway fourth-minute goal for Cavan. The 1974 veteran Seamus Bonner marshalled the forwards and sent a first-half penalty to the net, then bravely opted for the point from a second penalty 90 seconds from the end at a stage when Donegal still led by just two, and Donegal won by 1-14 to 1-11.

The Galway—Mayo battle was re-enacted in July when Galway won 1-13 to 1-10, largely by default, in the Connacht final at Castlebar. Galway's 12th-minute goal, shot to the net by Val Daly after a back fumbled his pick-up, proved vital when Mayo's Martin Carney struck back in the 25th minute. Mayo claimed they should have been awarded a penalty. But when they were given one in the first round against Roscommon they missed it: a great winning point by 19-year-old debutant Brian Kilkelly ousted Roscommon instead.

In the All-Ireland semi-final Kieran Keeney's 15th-minute goal gave Donegal the lead against Galway. But a miskicked free let Val Daly through for Galway's clinching goal and fortunate 1-12 to 1-11 victory five minutes from the end.

Dublin showed text-book composure throughout the game. Team manager Kevin Heffernan was tending to an injured Dublin player in the square in front of the goalkeeper. The goalkeeper miscued his kick-out, and Barney Rock fielded and sent it straight back to the unguarded net. Rock indicated after the game that Heffernan's presence contributed to the goal. "I was hardly going to check to see if my mother was looking in the stand first."

But the composure was most needed when their side was reduced to 12 players. Outbreaks of fisticuffs and a kicking incident diminished Dublin's numbers. Their remaining 12 men fell back into defence, abandoned traditional positioning, and crowded out the Galway attack by bringing both corner-forwards back to midfield.

The performance received a mixed reaction from an aghast public and officialdom. Brian Mullins, Ray Hazley and Ciaran Duff of Dublin and Tomás Tierney of Galway were all sent off, a record for an All-Ireland final, and bitterness remained for months afterwards throughout a long sequel of disciplinary hearings which never established exactly who had given Galway midfielder Brian Talty a black eye in the tunnel on the way to the dressing-room.

Joker Mickey Holden of Dublin confessed afterwards he had not realised that Dublin had a third man sent off until after the final whistle: "If I had known that I would probably have given up altogether."

CENTENARY CENTURIONS

Kerry found a new midfield partner for Jack O'Shea in 1984: Gneeveguila player and new captain Ambrose O'Donovan. "I have to live next door to these Corkmen in Gneeveguila," was his inaugural speech, before the Munster final, holding a football in his giant hands. The speech seemed to work. Kerry won their Munster title back.

Galway beat Mayo by 2-13 to 2-9 in Connacht. They were in trouble midway through the second half when two goals in four minutes from Brian Talty and Stephen Joyce swept them into the lead. Kevin McStay, the slightly-built Mayo player, basketball star and Universities soccer international, scored 1-7 and had a goal disallowed which might have given Mayo a five-point lead. Mayo resorted to a series of bewildering switches in the end. To no avail.

Ulster had a change of champions yet again. Tyrone overcame favourites Armagh by 0-15 to 1-7 to win their fourth title. The week before the Ulster final, the local paper criticised Tyrone's Frank McGuigan for scoring only three points: "That was from centre-field. *Nobody* scores points from midfield." He responded by scoring a remarkable 11 points in the Ulster final, three with his right foot, seven with his left, and one with his fist, all of them from play. "I figure if you get the couple early on it settles you down a wee bit. It's easy to get eleven points really—if you get the ball."

The 19-year-old Gerard Houlihan, a goalkeeper's son, scored Armagh's only goal of the first-round game against Donegal and the semi-final winner against Monaghan, and the second-half goal for Armagh in the final.

Others to score: the thieves who seized the semi-final takings at gunpoint from Casement Park, Belfast. Specially for the centenary the Ulster Council had decided to use Casement Park for its first major fixture in 13 years.

Meath felt they were the heirs to Dublin's crown in Leinster, but in the semi-final battling Laois gave Meath a fright, and led by three points with 15 minutes to go, 3-9 to 1-13, before Colm O'Rourke and Ben Tansey goals brought Meath through. Laois had a bigger fright in store for Meath the following year.

Offaly supplied the human interest angle of the series in the quarter-final: they trailed Longford by eight points, equalised eight minutes into the second half, and when they came back to replay their hero was the substitute goalkeeper, an under-21 player recruited from the stands called by the papers "Lazarus" (in fact Lazarene) Molloy.

Dublin v Meath was the Leinster final everybody wanted, and 56,051 showed up to watch it. Padraig Lyons missed a Meath penalty early in the game to set Dublin on course for a 2-10 to 1-9 victory on the hottest day in 1984.

Meath had felt they needed only a goalkeeper to beat Dublin. When Mickey Lyons missed the match through injury they knew they needed much more.

Ben Tansey got their goal as they struggled to come back against Dublin's 14 men (John Caffrey was sent off in controversial circumstances) on the hottest day of the finest summer this century.

Dublin's tactic of playing John Kearns as a third midfielder worked in the All-Ireland semi-final, although Dublin hit 11 wides as they kept Tyrone scoreless for the first 28 minutes of the game. Meanwhile they picked up victory goals from Barney Rock and Joe McNally.

Highlight of the pre-match build-up was a battle for the Hill 16 goal where two goalkeepers and 56 players all held their kick-around at the same end for several hilarious minutes.

Kerry easily defeated Galway in the other semi-final. Galway's four pre-match casualties were augmented by an injury to Gay MacManus during the match. Jack O'Shea had an outstanding game, and Sheehy and Egan took the goals.

Sheehy was missing from the final with an Achilles tendon injury; instead John Kennedy took the frees for Kerry—three months earlier he was not even a free-taker with his club in Ballylongford.

Kerry were in control throughout the centenary final, the second ever final to be all-ticket, and won by 0-14 to 1-6. Only two Dublin forwards scored, and Barney Rock's 43rd-minute goal for Dublin was the only goal of the match. When Dublin were inspired by that goal, so was Pat Spillane. At the end of seven minutes of frantic, post-goal play, he dispossessed Dublin's centre half back, slid the ball away from the grasp of four Dublin defenders, and Ger Power was able to place "Ogie" Moran for a Kerry point. Goalkeepers were largely redundant as both teams opted for points.

For Barney Rock it was another in an extraordinary sequence of big-match goals, against Meath, Offaly, Cork and Galway in 1983, and against Wexford, Meath, Tyrone and Kerry in 1984. For Kerry it was a relief not to be chasing a record, for a change. "Now we are going for one in a row," said Eoin Liston before the final.

AUSSIE FIRE

The dream of full international competition between Ireland and Australia, born in Adelaide in March 1970, had not been forgotten. Another team of Galahs came to Ireland in 1978, heavily beat Dublin before a 12,206 crowd in Croke Park, and lost to Kerry in Páirc Uí Chaoimh, with goalkeeper Charlie Nelligan playing the game of his life. But like its 1960s predecessors, the tour was a financial failure. An Australian tour by Kerry in 1981 was confined to two GAA teams and a poorly attended Gaelic game in Adelaide. Nobody was interested in watching international Gaelic football.

So, it was to a sense of apathy that the Australians flew in in October 1984 to revive the international contacts between the Gaelic and Australian codes. The Australian party were enjoying the doubtful privilege of being the first to represent their country at full international level. The confusing rules specially drawn up for the series involved an oval ball, goals (six points), over-the-bar points (three points), and side-post "overs" (one point). The Australians were confused by the apparent lack of any form of tackle from the Gaelic code.

When the first international got under way before a paltry 8,000 attendance in wet windy Páirc Uí Chaoimh the point of the whole series seemed lost. Until a free-for-all erupted in the third quarter. Players, substitutes and management joined in. Australia won by 70 points to 57 and their newspapers accused the Irish of being "Fancy Dans." National pride was hurt. The crowds swelled.

The second match in Croke Park drew a crowd of 18,000, (12,470 paying with 6,000 students coming in free). This time there was no bad temper, but a fast-moving dramatic game that the spectators loved. Australia levelled the score at 78 points each with two minutes to go. Chants of "Ireland, Ireland" rang around the ground as Colm O'Rourke and Clareman Noel Roche kicked the two winning points. It appeared that the international dream had at last been realised. The crowd of 32,318 the third day saw a fist-fight as well as fast dramatic football. Australia took the test series by 76 points to 71.

That was the start that the international series needed. But strangely enough, subsequent tours by Ireland to Australia in 1985 and by the Australians in 1986 did not reach the same level of interest. The Australians concentrated instead on turning the Victorian football league into a national competition, with the addition of Sydney Swans, Brisbane, and Western Australia (Perth) to their competition.

Several Irish players were signed by Australian clubs. Two made it to the big time, 1983 Kerry minor Sean Wight (a Scot who lived briefly in Ireland and whose life ambition had been to play in goal for Glasgow Celtic), and 1983 Dublin minor opponent Jimmy Stynes. Stynes was the success story of the Australian connection, a high-earning, highly regarded Melbourne Demons player. He sees a great future for Gaelic football if they market the game Australian-style, getting more women and young children to the matches.

Paul Earley of Roscommon and Liam Hayes of Meath both returned after short spells in Melbourne. In 1988 another big-name player, star Derry forward Dermot McNicholl, packed his bags. His debut for Prahran saw him score eight goals.

By 1989 broadcasting packages of weekly highlights from the Victorian Football League were being shown on Irish television. And the Australians had firmly pulled out of the international experiment.

QUICK ON THE DRAWS

Heads rolled early in the 1985 season. In the Leinster championship Laois made amends for their near-miss in 1984 by shocking Meath 2-11 to 0-7 in the 1985 Leinster semi-final at Tullamore. They did it with two goals in the 16th minute of the semi-final.

Paschal Doran scored the first, and when John Costelloe returned the kick-out with the defence hopelessly out of place, Willie Brennan scored the second. So ended Meath's All-Ireland aspirations.

Tommy Conroy and Joe McNally (in the last minute) scored Dublin's goals against an Offaly side unsettled by the absence of Matt Connor, a car crash victim the previous December. But Dublin took control of a toughly fought final in the last 20 minutes as rain lashed Croke Park in revenge for the previous year's sunshine, and won by 0-9 to 0-4.

Kerry defeated Cork by 2-11 to 0-11, as Ambrose O'Donovan was stretchered off bleeding from an off-the-ball incident that nobody saw and which went unpunished.

Early in 1985 Derry suffered a revolt by five disenchanted players and an Open Draw competition defeat against Limerick, yet came back to beat Ulster champions Tyrone with a controversial Declan McNicholl penalty goal—a decision that led to an assault on referee Greenan by Tyrone fans after the game. Derry followed this up with an impressive four-point win over Cavan to reach the Ulster final.

There the run ended. Midway through the first half of the final Eamonn McEneaney fisted the first of his two goals and Monaghan went on to beat Derry by 2-9 to 0-8. McEneaney had a good goal-scoring run in 1985, he also scored the third-minute goal in a semi-final replay to beat Armagh by 1-11 to 2-7.

A Monaghan-Armagh match in the championship had the distinction of being played with two referees: Michael Greenan (Cavan) had to take over from the limping Damien Campbell (Fermanagh) at half-time.

Both All-Ireland semi-finals were drawn. Kerry and Monaghan played an intriguing 1-12 to 2-9 draw when Eamonn McEneaney kicked a tense equaliser from a free, out at the sideline. McEneaney was haunted by people who recalled where they were when that free was taken: watching on television, listening on radio, or howling in Croke Park, a moment to mark one's career by.

Mayo came back from six points down to draw the other semi-final 1-13 each with Dublin: Billy FitzPatrick and T J Kilgallon kicked the equalising points in the last 45 seconds. A superb Padraig Brogan goal could not save Mayo in the replay, Ciaran Duff struck twice as Dublin won easily by 2-12 to 1-7 after trailing by a point at half-time.

Kerry faced a younger than ever Dublin team in the final. Joe Mcnally celebrated his 21st birthday the week before the match. Dave Synnott and Tommy Conroy were also 21, Charlie Redmond was 22, and John O'Leary, Gerry Hargan, Pat Canavan, Barney Rock and Ciaran Duff all 24. Yet it was

the older Kerry who seized the initiative with a Jack O'Shea
penalty goal after 11 minutes. They led by nine points, 1-8 to
0-2 at half-time. But when Dublin came storming back in the
second half Kerry relied on a perfectly finished Timmy
O'Dowd breakaway goal 13 minutes after half-time. That
secured victory by 2-12 to 2-8.

Dublin's comeback was spurred by two goals from Joe
McNally, a 52nd-minute shot off the crossbar that hopped
over the line and a 64th-minute goal punched under the bar.
Dublin disputed the Kerry penalty and mourned that two
claims of their own were not allowed: for a Jack O'Shea pick-
up in the square in the second half and another technical foul
by Tom Spillane.

"Dublin didn't pick the right team until half-time," one
observer commented. In the first half, Dublin had crowded
midfield and Jack O'Shea roamed free on the wings, slotting
over three points. In the second half it was Ronayne who
roamed. "Experience, nothing more, got us through that
second half," sighed Kerry chairman Frank King.

THE RED HAND WAVE

There was a shock wave across Gaelic football when a Third
Division team, Laois, won the 1986 National League.
Midfielders John Costelloe and Liam Irwin made amends for
defeat in the 1985 Leinster final by beating Monaghan by 2-6
to 2-5.

Laois's championship opponents, Wicklow, were storing
up a surprise. As they filed off the pitch after a morale-
boosting victory in a pre-season tournament, they discovered
that the referee had blown the whistle five minutes early at
the end of their O'Byrne Cup final. They held on to win
anyway.

Then Wicklow shocked League champions Laois by 2-10
to 1-9 in Aughrim in controversial circumstances. The first
argument between the teams arose over whether the venue
was suitable. Then came the sending-off spree; Wicklow
were reduced to 14 men and Laois to 13. Wicklow teenager
Kevin O'Brien, a Railway Cup star before he had made his

championship debut, scored two goals.

In the end, the 1986 Leinster championship heralded Meath's breakthrough. Meath selected Joe Cassells at corner-back and when Dublin tried the third midfielder tactic Cassells cleaned up in the centre. They beat Dublin by 0-9 to 0-7. Dublin crucially had sharp-shooter Barney Rock injured in a collision with Liam Harnan just before half-time. Joe Cassells successfully roved around on the heels of Dublin's wandering Tommy Carr, and the ghosts of 1983 and 1984 were finally banished. Meath's David Beggy had been in Croke Park just twice before—for a school tour and a U2 concert!

Kerry seemed to have more problems in 1986 as Cork's debutant full-back Denis Walsh curbed Eoin Liston. Kerry nevertheless took a six-point half-time lead and went on to win by 0-12 to 0-8. Cork twice cut the lead to three points, but could come no closer. Liston starred against Tipperary as Pat Spillane took time to sign autographs while an injured player was being tended!

Kerry struggled to beat Meath by 2-13 to 0-12 in the semi-final. A defensive mistake let Ger Power through for Kerry's first goal. Willie Maher scored the second.

Mayo were to travel on Knock Airport's inaugural flight to London for a Connacht championship tie but, as one official surmised afterwards, "We'd have been quicker walking." They flew out from Shannon instead, because of bad weather, and easily defeated London.

Galway waited until the last minute to beat Roscommon by 1-8 to 1-5 in the provincial final with a dramatic winning goal from substitute Stephen Joyce, which came at the end of a dreadfully boring and pedestrian final.

Much more spectacular than Meath's long-anticipated breakthrough was that of Tyrone in the North. They owe their 1-11 to 0-10 victory over Down in the Ulster final to a freak goal from Plunkett Donaghy, awarded when Down goalkeeper Pat Donnan stepped back over the line. Donnan denied it was over the line and one of the umpires agreed with him: "My feet were firmly on the ground, and I even felt my elbow touch the post." Donaghy had the distinction of making his senior club debut at 16—because his club, Moy, had only 14 players when it was founded, one of them his 54-year-old father.

In the All-Ireland semi-final Kevin McCabe got things right from the penalty spot: five minutes from the end of the match with Galway he tucked away the penalty that set Tyrone alight and set up a 1-12 to 1-9 victory.

Kerry won majestically by 2-15 to 0-10 in an All-Ireland final where everybody wanted Tyrone to win. They scored nine points from all angles as Tyrone tired. But by then they had suffered a fright.

Eugene McKenna was dominant as Tyrone went 0-7 to 0-4 up at half-time. Just 45 seconds into the second half Plunkett Donaghy controlled a difficult ground pass, got the ball in to Damien O'Hagan, who sent Paudge Quinn in for a goal. That left Tyrone six points clear, and a miskicked penalty from Kevin McCabe three minutes later left them seven ahead.

Two years beforehand Eugene McKenna had missed a penalty at the same goal. "Keep the ball low, or it will take off," he told McCabe before the final. McCabe put the ball in to a hollow, took seven steps in the run, but still hit the ball over the bar. "I think the ball was lighter than normal, but I was glad of the point. It would have been a big blow if we had missed it."

Man of the match, Pat Spillane, ran 50 yards for a handpassed goal (diverted to the net) in the 41st minute and Ger Power cantered through to give Mike Sheehy a second goal after 49 minutes. A brave Tyrone performance went unrewarded as they eventually failed by eight points.

Timmy O'Dowd restored a midfield dominance that Plunkett Donaghy had demolished, while unlucky Tyrone lost Eugene McKenna and John Lynch through injury within minutes of each other. Tyrone won the hearts of a nation: "We had to beat 31 and a half counties," Mick O'Dwyer said afterwards. "We didn't beat them but we had the beating of them," Tyrone manager Art McRory concluded.

There was also a theory abounding that, to beat Kerry, you had to do what Cork did in 1983, or Offaly in 1982, stick with them point for point, not allowing the pace to get too fast or the game to get too torrid, and hit them with a hammer blow in the end, like Tadhg Murphy or Seamus Darby did with a goal.

"You keep going" Pat Spillane said, "not for some mythical three-in-a-row or five-in-a-row, but basically because of the fascination to see if you can do the same again."

But Kerry could not do the same again. Kingdom Come had arrived for the greatest team in Gaelic football.

Chapter Twenty

A Second Century

APOCALYPSE CORK

Cork remember the early months of 1987 for all the wrong reasons. They remember the later months for all the right reasons.

First the bizarre. By refusing to turn out for extra time in the National League quarter-final, Cork allowed Dublin to conduct the most extraordinary ceremony in a century of competitive football. Dublin's Declan Bolger took the ball from a farcical throw-in at the start of extra time, then ran the ball to Barney Rock who kicked it into the Cork net. Cork were meanwhile packing for the train home, they protested.

Most supporters wanted to know what would have happened had Rock missed. Dublin were awarded the match anyway on the score 0-10 to 1-7, not 1-10 to 1-7 after extra time.

With newcomers such as David De Lappe and Glen O'Neill, Dublin went on to win a classic League final (now bearing a brand-name, Ford) against Kerry by 1-11 to 0-11 thanks to a first-minute goal from Ciaran Duff.

Then the unprecedented. On August 2nd 1987 Cork brought Kerry's greatest era crashing to an end. Kerry were lucky to get a second shot at the title: Mike Sheehy managed to slip through for a late goal and it was left to Larry Tompkins, Cork's Kildare migrant, who came from an 18-month stint in New York to live in Castlehaven, to score the equalising point from a free. That made the score 1-10 for Cork, 2-7 for Kerry and 49,358 gathered in Killarney the following Sunday to see Kerry's last stand.

Mick O'Dwyer gave all the impressions this was a swansong for the old 1975 boys. He called up Vincent O'Connor to rejoin the panel after four years, and sent him on for the last two minutes of the replay. The greatest team in football history went down together, 0-13 to 1-5, while one newcomer, Dermot Hanafin, scored Kerry's goal in the replay. Kerry captain Mike Sheehy missed several frees in his last big-match appearance for Kerry.

"The circus is over, it's time for a new act," Kerry full-forward Eoin Liston declared.

Larry Tompkins did not stop at that. He landed a pressure-kick point from 50 yards to earn Cork a replay with Galway, 1-11 each. Galway had shown a long-lost spirit to come back from four points down with 10 minutes to go. Right corner back John Fallon put Galway ahead with three minutes to go before Tompkins landed a point that repeated his Munster final replay-earner and earned him the nickname "Equalizer" after a popular television show.

Tompkins went on to score 11 points in the replay as Galway foundered.

The first round of the Connacht championship against Roscommon seemed to be the same sad old story for Sligo when they trailed 0-4 to 0-9 at half-time. Then a fine opportunist goal by Anthony Brennan started a revival and a goal from a penalty with two minutes to go from Mick Laffey, the only survivor of the 1975 victorious campaign, gave them a shock 2-8 to 0-12 victory. As Leitrim beat London, London's Brian Grealish, brother of soccer international Tony, fired a penalty straight at the goalkeeper.

Galway midfielder Brian Talty secured his side's victory in a poor Connacht final against Mayo, 0-8 to 0-7. Mayo failed to score for three-quarters of an hour, having led 0-6 to 0-2 at half-time.

Derry led 0-10 to 0-3 against Armagh with 20 minutes to go in the Ulster final but Armagh's 14 men (Vincent Loughran was sent off in the 17th minute) launched a comeback when subs Jim McKerr and Joe Kernan were brought in to the game, and the final score was a minimal 0-11 to 0-9. Tony Scullion roamed successfully as the loose man for Derry. In the semi-final Paul Kealey, just 18, won

Derry their final place with a last-minute goal against Cavan when he had come on as a sub in the replay after a lucky 2-7 to 1-10 draw. Derry had plummeted from First to Third Divisions of the League in successive seasons and were offered 14/1 against winning the Ulster championship the previous year!

Derry were not the only robbers in Omagh. They stole a replay from Cavan in the semi-final. The armed variety made off with the gate receipts.

But in the end it was Meath who were to make the plinth as the Sam Maguire Cup's last holders. Their ascent to the 1987 title began at hard-frosted Kells when they beat Kerry by 1-12 to 0-4 in a League match. They lost the League quarter-final at bogey venue Portlaoise. But the long evenings on the sand dunes at the beach between Mornington and Bettystown in cold and foggy April concentrated their minds. They went back to Portlaoise to beat Laois by three paltry points.

With 12 minutes to go against Laois in that quarter-final, they were in trouble. Colm Browne's long shot skidded to the net to leave the sides level, but Laois never managed to take the lead and were left instead regretting a missed goal chance in the first minute as they went down by 1-11 to 2-5.

Their 0-15 to 0-9 semi-final victory over Kildare was interrupted by an injury to referee Joe Woods, who pulled a calf muscle and had to be replaced by linesman Tomás Ó Reachtara. Meath's staying power ousted Kildare after they failed to take the lead until 12 minutes after half-time.

The Leinster final against Dublin was tough and tense. According to Colm O'Rourke: "Like boxing, whoever was able to stay up and slog it out the longest was going to win." Meath won by 1-13 to 0-12. Mattie McCabe snatched a goal after 13 minutes and Meath kept their heads after they fell behind at half-time when both sides had been reduced to 14 men.

Derry brought a sizeable number of the 40,285 spectators to Croke Park for the All-Ireland semi-final, but left their skills behind. Star forward Dermot McNicholl showed obvious signs of an injury, having aggravated a hamstring in the kickabout before the match. Meath scored two points within the first minute and the final score was 0-15 to 0-10. It took Derry 68 minutes to score their first point from play!

Meath beat Cork by 1-14 to 0-11 in an unspectacular final. Long-serving Colm O'Rourke deservedly got the winning goal 10 minutes before half-time, his halfblocked shot rolling into the net.

Seven minutes earlier Cork had their goal chance blocked by Mick Lyons when Jimmy Kerrigan seemed through for a goal: "Kerrigan did not kick the ball with conviction, and we conceded a goal that should not have happened at all," Cork manager Billy Morgan said afterwards.

The goal would have put Cork seven points ahead. Instead it was Meath who led 1-6 to 0-8 at half-time, and they went eight points ahead as Larry Tompkins, the Cork super-shooter, sent six of his eight free kicks wide in the second half. A Meath banner read: "Meath's midfield pair to leave Teddy bear." It was Meath midfielder Liam Hayes who was awarded man of the match.

MAUL OF FAME

By beating Dublin by 2-5 to 0-9, Meath completed their first ever three-in-a-row in Leinster in 1988, but only because Charlie Redmond missed a last-second penalty for Dublin. Redmond sent over the bar and fell face down on the field while Gerry McEntee slapped his back in congratulations. He had never before missed a penalty and was only appointed kicker because Mick Kennedy was injured.

This time it was Dublin's Dave Synnott who was sent off, the sending-off becoming a necessary part of every Dublin-Meath encounter. Mattie McCabe and P J Gillic scored Meath's goals in the seventh and 15th minutes of the first half. Dublin came back to equalise midway through the second half but points from Liam Hayes and Gillic, free-taking in the absence of injured Brian Stafford, put Meath back in front.

Monaghan beat Tyrone by 1-10 to 0-14 to take their 14th Ulster title when a mistake by the goalkeeper let Nudie Hughes dash in for a 27th-minute goal, the unfortunate keeper having failed to clear a long Donal Hughes ball. To add to their woes Tyrone then had a penalty claim turned down in the very last minute of play, as Noel McGinn shot wide having been bustled in front of goal.

Mayo brought 36-year-old Martin Carney, the Donegal-born schoolteacher who had first declared for them in 1979, out of retirement to score four great points in their victory by 1-12 to 0-8 against Roscommon.

Cork surprisingly struggled against rapidly improving Limerick, and trailed 0-4 to 1-3 at half-time after Eoin Sheehan set up Chris McGuinness for an 11th-minute goal. Cork eventually took the lead from a Larry Tompkins point six minutes from the end.

It was not the stuff of champions. Cork brought 35-year-old Denis Allen and soccer exile Dave Barry back for the Munster final. Allen ended up scoring the goal that beat Kerry by 1-14 to 0-16. The match erupted into a fracas near the end, and although only four players were booked by referee Pat Lane, eight were further disciplined after the game by Munster Council and both counties fined £500 each. Pat Spillane scored just one point, five minutes from the end, but 19-year-old newcomer Maurice Fitzgerald scored 10 points for Kerry, three from play.

In the All-Ireland semi-final Meath escaped a Mayo comeback when they went 10 points up, then relaxed suddenly to eventually get in by 0-16 to 2-5. Liam McHale struck for a goal in the 48th minute, Anthony Finnerty added a second and then McHale had the ball in the net again only to see it disallowed. The match yielded 52 frees and until the 21st minute the sides scored just one point each.

Cork meanwhile won a 54-free semi-final against Monaghan by 1-14 to 0-6 with a controversial goal. Brendan Murray was sandwiched in a tackle just before Barry Coffey passed to Dave Barry and he drove in a great 20-yard goal.

Cork scored the only goal of two All-Ireland final meetings with Meath after three minutes of the drawn final, when Teddy McCarthy finished a Dinny Allen-Paul McGrath move by sending to the net through the goalkeeper's legs. Meath came back to lead 0-6 to 1-2 at half-time and then

Cork failed to convert their second-half domination into scores, ending up with 15 wides as against Meath's seven.

Cork backs insisted that David Beggy took a dive when a vital 14-yard free was awarded against them 30 seconds from the end. Brian Stafford converted for the equalising point, 0-12 to 1-9 and back for a controversial replay.

Meath players were convinced that the All-Ireland final replay would be played in the wet. It rained for the week coming up to the game. The training session on Saturday night in Dalgan Park, near Navan, was reduced to a mushy, messy quagmire. Croke Park should have been the same on All-Ireland Sunday.

So the players took precautions. Bernard Flynn got studs fitted on his boots that were the maximum permitted length. Liam Hayes spent Saturday night getting long studs fitted for his boots. All the players could think of was holding their feet in the promised rain at Croke Park on All-Ireland day.

Meath started the day at the beach in Malahide: with 10 balls being kicked from player to player. Selector Pat Reynolds' sons were sent in to the waves to retrieve the bobbing balls.

But what the Meath players saw of the London-Meath curtain-raiser match alarmed them. The groundsman had kept up Con O'Leary's good work and all the rain had passed through the topsoil. The pitch was bone dry.

Brian Stafford brought two pairs of boots on to the field with him. He wore his multi-studded wet weather boots. He gave a normal pair to selector Tony Brennan. When Meath ran on to the field for a pre-match kick-around, Stafford tried a few frees: his multi-studded boots were hurting, and uncomfortable. Flynn's long studs were jarring his sole. Colm Coyle had the longest steel studs permissible. Hayes' feet were coming up in blisters soon after the second half started.

Meanwhile the photographers were objecting that Meath had not waited long enough to allow the team picture to be taken. Two officials started to move the bench, but a photographer sat on it and refused to budge. Each match this year Meath players were breaking earlier and earlier as the team picture was being taken. First Robbie O'Malley and then the rest of the back line would start racing back to the goal-mouth. After three seconds the team was broken up and some of the photographers hadn't even focused. Their protests were in vain. Meath were not going to regroup.

By the time of the parade Brian Stafford had enough of his cogs. When the parade was passing the Meath dug-out Stafford skipped in to Brennan and changed his boots. Most of the Meath players never even noticed he was gone. After four minutes of play Stafford sent a 50 sailing over the bar with his first kick of the match. The new boots worked. Stafford scored seven.

The match was tough. When Meath's Gerry McEntee was sent off for a blow on Niall Cahalane after six minutes Meath did not even have a team-talk. Automatically P J Gillic moved to McEntee's midfield spot, and the midfielders and half-forwards fell back into their own half of the field.

It worked. Meath crowded and fouled the Cork forwards, kept the score down to 0-5 to 0-6 at half-time, and eventually harried themselves into a three-point lead at the three-quarter stage.

Eleven players competed against 12 players when the ball entered the Meath half of the field. It was not a pretty sight.

When Meath went in at half-time there was no mention of the fact that this was 14 men against 15. Sean Boylan talked about the game as if it was 15 against 15.

Meath had done it before. Just months before they had won the replay of the League final against Dublin despite having a man sent off early in the first half. They had come back to beat Armagh in the League despite the fact they trailed when they had a man sent off. They had drawn with Kildare in the League three years ago despite having two men sent off and playing with 13 men against 15.

Bernard Flynn swapped his long-cog boots with substitute Liam Smith at half-time. He had never before worn Smith's boots, but the shorter studs helped him. Fourteen minutes into the second half Martin O'Connell sent a long clearance down which Flynn grasped, turned and sent over for a point that sent Meath into the lead for the first time. Two great blocks by Liam Hayes and some cool defending by Robbie O'Malley and man of the match Martin O'Connell secured the two-in-a-row.

After the victory Colm O'Rourke tossed his jersey over the fence in to the gathered Meath supporters on Hill 16. It was a gesture of thanks.

Meath had the new Sam Maguire Cup. And a hundred years after the game had been first attempted as a variation of mud-wrestling many of Gaelic football's spectators asked how far the game really had progressed.

Meath would argue that entertainment is not their business, winning is. A chorus of five generations of Gaelic footballers would heartily agree.

CRISIS

Crisis was a theme throughout the 1989 season. A crisis with rural counties denuded by emigration, a crisis with referees, a crisis with serious assaults related to games, and overall a crisis with the rules and the increasingly "hard man" tactics of top teams. "Football badly needs a good game," Mayo manager John O'Mahoney declared before the 1989 All-Ireland final.

Mayo reached the final by default. The four strongest teams, Cork, Kerry, Dublin and Meath, all ended up in the same half of the draw.

Things went predictably in both Munster and Leinster. Meath defeated Louth with a spectacular solo-run goal from Liam Hayes, then trailed Offaly by a point at half-time before crushing them 3-11 to 0-9. Dublin defeated Kildare with the help of a freak goal when Ciaran Duff's sideline ball went straight to the net, then easily dismissed Wicklow.

Meath's technique of winning matches with 14 men ran out of luck in the All-Ireland final. Colm Coyle was sent off seven minutes into the second half. Dublin led through a Ciaran Duff goal at the time, experienced a few moments of panic after a Michael McCabe goal for Meath, but came back to win with another Vinnie Murphy goal, sent in with the outside of the boot as Meath backs anticipated he would shoot to the other side.

Cork too had a moment or two of panic. An early opportunist goal when Barry Coffey sent a quick chip to John O'Driscoll helped them to lead 1-11 to 0-6 with 11 minutes to go. Kerry came storming back to lose by three points, 1-12 to 1-9, Ambrose O'Donovan's goal coming just too late.

The All-Ireland semi-final boiled over. Dublin led 1-4 to nil before referee Michael Kearins awarded two controversial penalties to Cork, both converted by John Cleary, and sent off Dublin's Keith Barr. Barr went to hospital with a broken jaw which he sustained minutes before in an off-the-ball incident. Play was stopped for 29 frees in the first half. After half-time the 60,168 spectators watched referee Michael Kearins bring both teams together in huddles to warn them to clean up the game or there would be more sendings-off. The game improved and Cork went through to the final by 2-10 to 1-9.

The warning had come too late in the year. Gaelic football had been licking the wounds to its image from the start of the season, when a Cork footballer was badly injured by what team-mates claimed was a deliberate kick by a New York player in the National League final in New York.

In Ulster an Armagh supporter struck Tyrone footballer John Lynch as he left the field at half-time in an Ulster championship match. Lynch took no further part in the action, but incensed Tyrone gave Armagh an eight-point lead then came back to win the game 1-11 to 2-7.

Four players were sent off and six booked as Tyrone beat Down in the next round. Tyrone eventually won the Ulster final with a Stephen Conway equaliser to force a second meeting with Donegal, and goals from Conway and Damien O'Hagan to win the replay.

Two were sent off and six booked as Mayo beat Galway in a replayed Connacht semi-final after Gay MacManus had brought the teams back with a last-gasp goal the first day. Mayo and Roscommon played a mercifully clean 170 minutes in the Connacht final. In extra time first Roscommon took the lead with a Tony MacManus penalty, then Anthony Finnerty and Jimmy Burke scored Mayo goals to put them into the All-Ireland semi-final. Burke did so by default, missing his kick completely, falling, and somehow propelling the ball over the line in the process.

With the 48,177 spectators at the semi-final talking of unfinished business. Tyrone's from 1986, Mayo's from 1985, it was Mayo who came through. Eugene McKenna scored a Tyrone goal at the end of the third quarter. Tyrone failed to score again while Mayo tacked on six points and went through to their first final in 38 years by 0-12 to 1-6.

Mayo flew from Knock airport on the day before the game. Four local country and western bands brought out records commemorating their achievement and armies of supporters travelled to the All-Ireland final. Their optimism seemed well-founded, while Cork worried about the prospect of losing three-in-a-row. "The population of this county will drop by 35 if we are beaten by Mayo," Cork team doctor Con Murphy said before the game.

On the field too, Cork huffed a little before winning by 0-17 to 1-11. The three-point margin was as much as they were allowed, although the knowledgeable who had been talking about Cork's inability to kill teams off commented that Cork could not succeed in getting four points ahead.

Mayo substitute Anthony Finnerty fired in the goal four minutes into the second half, and blazed another shot wide minutes later. Seven different Cork players scored. "The colour of the occasion was spectacular and matched by some of the football served up," one sportswriter commented.

There was a sigh of relief that so few frees—44 in all— were awarded. The total was in fact higher than the 1986 and 1987 finals. But it was an improvement on the battle of 1988.

NEW RULES

Sustaining that improvement was the job left to the rule-makers. The Australian series of 1984 and 1986 showed the GAA it had a pedestrian game compared with its Australian counterpart. Two-thirds of the time, the ball was out of play, being retrieved for line-balls, frees, and kick-outs. A group of football thinkers under former Dublin player Tony Hanahoe were asked to confront this problem during 1988.

The breath-takingly simple solution was borrowed straight from the Australian game. Take all kick-outs, frees and sideline balls from the hands instead of from the ground. Kicking a divit or creating any sort of elevated platform to kick the ball from was also banned.

The group decided to change the duration of the game from 35-minute halves to 20-minute quarters. The quarters were later toned down to 15 minutes. "The wind changed sides at half-time," would be written out of the football excuse-book for ever.

The handpass was brought back after its eight-year sojourn under a new definition: "Pass the ball with one or both hands provided that there is a definite striking action with the hands." Another proposal, allowing players on the run to scoop up the ball with one hand, was eventually abandoned. The tackle remains a grim issue. The committee proposed that side-to-side tackle should be delivered only by the hip or shoulder to the hip or shoulder. The Australian tackle was rejected because it is a common cause of injury in Australia and is responsible for the majority of frees in the game.

That would mean there were four legal ways to challenge the player in possession of the ball in Gaelic football: from the side with one foot on the ground, flicking the ball with the open hand when it is being bounced or toe-tapped, blocking down an intended kick or pass, and shadowing or shepherding an opponent to force him to stop, turn or move wide.

The players who first tried the new laws in October 1989 felt that overall they were an improvement on the old game. But the rules for dispossessing an opponent are as hazily defined as they have always been since the original laws were drawn up in 1885. "Play on and never mind the rules," is not dead yet as a slogan for Gaelic players.

Kingdom Come

Eoghan Corry

In *Kingdom Come*, Eoghan Corry tells the story of the great football team that dominated the Kingdom of Kerry and the whole country from 1975 to 1988 — the background, the beginnings, the personalities, the controversies and the glory of the greatest football team ever.

"Football talk is about eternal things: style, courage, speed, cunning, defeat, renewal."

Brendan Kennelly

POOLBEG